SHAMANISM AND THE PSYCHOLOGY OF C. G. JUNG

The Great Circle

Man is Born Like a Garden
ready Planted & Sown.
William Blake

SHAMANISM AND THE PSYCHOLOGY OF C. G. JUNG

The Great Circle

Robert E. Ryan, J.D., Ph.D.

To Linda, Bobby, and Bill

ISBN 1-84333-588-3

A catalogue record for this book is available
from the British Library

First published in 2002 by
Vega
64 Brewery Road
London, N7 9NT

A member of Chrysalis Books plc

Visit our website at www.chrysalisbooks.co.uk

Printed in Great Britain by
Butler & Tanner Ltd, Frome and London

Contents

Acknowledgements

For permission to reprint excerpts of their works, I wish to acknowledge gratefully the following sources: Princeton University Press for excerpts from Mircea Eliade, *Shamanism: Archaic Techniques of Ecstasy*, copyright © 1964, renewed 1992, by Princeton University Press, reprinted by permission of Princeton University Press; Princeton University Press for excerpts from C.G. Jung, *The Collected Works of C.G. Jung*, 20 vols., including figure 147 from Volume 12 of such work, copyright © 1953–1979, reprinted by permission of Princeton University Press; Routledge for excerpts from C.G. Jung, *The Collected Works of C.G. Jung*, 21 vols., 1953–1983, reprinted by permission of Routledge; Routledge for excerpts from C.G. Jung, *Modern Man in Search of a Soul*, 1933, reprinted by permission of Routledge; Harcourt Brace and Company for excerpts from C.G. Jung, *Modern Man in Search of a Soul*, 1933, reprinted by permission of Harcourt Brace and Co.; Random House for excerpts from C.G. Jung, *Memories, Dreams, Reflections*, edited by Aniela Jaffé, translated by Richard and Clara Winston, translation copyright © 1961, 1962, 1963 and renewed 1989, 1990, 1991 by Random House, Inc., used by permission of Pantheon Books, a division of Random House, Inc., and HarperCollins for excerpts from C.G. Jung, *Memories, Dreams, Reflections*, © C.G. Jung, 1967, reprinted by permission of HarperCollins Publishers, Limited. All illustrations, unless otherwise noted, are by Linda S. Ryan.

I also want to thank my wife, Linda, for all her long efforts in organizing, typing, illustrating and generally making this work possible, and my son, Bobby, for helping me explore many of the sites of shamanic culture dealt with in this book. We would also like to thank Gary and Marjorie Bergstrom for their invaluable technical assistance.

Chapter 1
"Only Connect"

> The common end of all *narrative* ... is to convert a *series* into a
> *Whole*: to make those events, which in real or imagined History move
> on in a *strait* Line, assume to our Understandings a *circular* motion —
> the snake with its Tail in its Mouth.
> **Samuel Taylor Coleridge**

"Only connect" advised E.M. Forster near the beginning of the last century. This advice may serve as a useful touchstone as we look back upon the twentieth century and attempt to find our bearings in a new millennium. For we may discover that many of the answers to what ails the modern human psyche lie ready within the depths of the human mind and that, in fact, they were previously the common property of archaic man and have been since humanity first clearly displayed those remarkable abstract and symbolic capacities which were to set us apart from all our predecessors. In fact it may be that many of our contemporary efforts in the field of psychology are, at least in part, a retracing of patterns of experience well understood in the distant past and still surviving in the world's scattered and too often ignored shamanic cultures.

In attempting to make significant connection between the ancient discipline of shamanism and modern Jungian psychology, we are comparing one of the oldest and most misunderstood psychotherapeutic and religious systems of mankind with one of its newest attempts to probe the depths of the mind — one which is often equally misunderstood. And while we are attempting to span great distances in time and differences in cultures, I am convinced that the structural and functional similarities between these two phenomena are striking and significant. The patterns of experience and transformation traced by both shamanism and depth psychology appear to be fundamental to our psychological well-being and the health of the human body. Moreover, each enlists forces and patterns of symbolism which lie at the very base of all human religious experience. In fact, the structures which we shall trace in this book may constitute the *very oldest* complex of symbols which has persisted into modern historical times within a context substantial enough to yield an intelligible and well-articulated configuration of religious experience. If we can successfully trace the parallels between these two disciplines, we shall succeed in glimpsing a long-enduring continuity of extremely important aspects of the psyche.

Shamanism — the healing and religious practices and techniques which the majority of people today most readily equate with the Native American "medicine man" — now appears to have a pedigree reaching back over 30,000 years to the Upper Paleolithic era in southern France and northern Spain. Indeed its origins may stretch even deeper still into the vast, unfathomed well of prehistory. Furthermore, it is, as we shall see, found in extremely widespread, diverse areas of the globe even into historical times. According to Mircea Eliade, a great historian of religion, it is "the most archaic and widely distributed occult tradition."[1] Such durative power and widespread appeal argue strongly that it must strike a deep accord with the human psyche and encode something fundamental to human experience. Yet the basic elements of this experience have proven to be elusive for the modern Western rational intelligence, and consequently one of our oldest, most fundamental and meaningful traditions has until recently most often been ignored or misunderstood and disparaged.

As a psychologist whose important work spanned the first two-thirds of the last century, Carl G. Jung was, to some degree, heir to this lack of insight and information, for far less was known about shamanism in the period in which he formulated his most significant theories than is known today. Yet he had some first-hand experience of shamanic communities, and references to the shaman or medicine man are scattered throughout his writings. He read Eliade's seminal book on shamanism, declared the shaman to be an early and archetypal manifestation of what he called the "mana personality," and recognized that the shaman's practices generally paralleled the process of psychological development which he termed "individuation." But perhaps because less reliable comparative material was available in his time, shamanism never received the extended attention that he devoted to alchemy, Gnosticism, certain aspects of Eastern religion or Christian symbolism. This apparent deficit, however, may ultimately be an advantage for our comparative effort. Jung himself often operated according to a method which recognized that largely unconscious, spontaneously produced parallels between various symbols and images could be more telling and important than those discovered through conscious analysis and comparison. For instance, he observed that the points of significant parallel which his own psychological findings shared with traditional Eastern religious beliefs evolved unconsciously and naturally over years of analytical practice long before he actually discovered the wisdom of the East. "Only later," he realized, "did my professional experience show me that in my technique I had been unconsciously following that secret way which for centuries had been the preoccupation of the best minds of the East."[2] In fact, Jung felt that such processes were by no means merely accidental. Western consciousness had long repressed certain age-old realities of the psyche. "For every piece of conscious life that loses its importance and value – so runs the law – there arises a compensation in the unconscious," he observed.[3] In both Jungian psychology and shamanism, the compensatory statements of the unconscious are most important guides to human endeavor, and it may be said with equal justice that in his work Jung had likewise been led unconsciously along that secret way which formed the shaman's path for centuries or, perhaps, millennia past.

This is not to imply that these points of similarity emerged entirely without mediating influences. The shaman's world survives in ancient myth and traditional lore, important sources of guidance for Jung. In his time Jung was a prime mover in attempting to awaken the modern mind to the integrating effects for the psyche of these archaic embodiments of image and symbol and to the deep wisdom of the past which they contained. He insisted that "It would be a ridiculous and unwarranted presumption on our part if we imagined that we were more energetic or more intelligent than the men of the past – our material knowledge has increased, but not our intelligence."[4] "We have merely succeeded in forgetting that an indissoluble link binds us to the men of antiquity," he asserted, a link which we can re-establish "by penetrating into the blocked subterranean passages of our own psyches."[5] Modern man stands apart from his predecessors in his reliance upon critical reason. However, from a certain standpoint, as Jung recognized, "The more critical reason dominates, the more impoverished life becomes; but the more of the unconscious, and the more of myth we are capable of making conscious, the more of life we integrate."[6]

This emphasis on integration gives our initial imperative of "only connect" a larger resonance, for it aptly describes the direction of Jung's own thought processes. With Jung the human mind once again asserts its innate ability to re-weave the fragmentation apparently characterizing our existence into an integrated and revivifying whole. What is perhaps most interesting about this eclectic Swiss psychologist, the son of a pastor pursuing a life of science, is that he lends the witness of empirical investigation to what was hitherto primarily religious speculation or philosophical theory. Jung constantly felt driven to remind both his critics and his admirers that he was first and foremost an empiricist. "Although I have often been called a philosopher, I am an empiricist and adhere to the phenomenological standpoint," he asserted.[7] "Why is it not simply stated that I am a psychiatrist whose prime concern is to record and interpret his empirical material? I try to investigate facts and make them more generally comprehensible."[8]

He steadfastly insisted that he was dealing with the results of his psychological studies and being true to the form in which he encountered them. According to him, his theory was based upon facts of observation and was not the Procrustean template by which reality was tailored to fit preconception. And while he recognized that the material discovered by psychologists may be more elusive than the more ostensibly concrete data of the other sciences, he felt that it is this material with which we must begin and which we must truly follow even though it may appear to be inconsistent or contrary to theory. Indeed, some of the most provocative results of his investigations, like those of modern physics to which he frequently compared his findings, at first seemed to resist all ordering into comprehensive systems intelligible to the rational intellect. Yet, eventually, from the apparently chaotic welter of his studies a startling uniformity and universality began to crystalize – one which would convince him of the underlying common psychological heritage of humanity.

As he was able to delve more deeply into the unconscious of his patients, he began to perceive that, "The chaotic assortment of images that at first confronted me reduced itself in the course of the work to certain well-defined themes and formal elements, which repeated themselves in identical or analogous form with the most varied individuals."[9] At the same time, during Jung's lifetime the world was blessed with a wealth of expanding data from the study of foreign and ancient cultures, bringing to light alien and archaic thought forms from around the world. A study of these materials revealed to certain theorists the striking resemblance of mythic and religious forms from highly diverse cultures over durations and distances which seemed to defy attempts to explain their universality of form strictly on the basis of cultural contacts or diffusion. Jung quickly recognized a strong resemblance between the dream and fantasy images of his patients and the materials revealed in these fields of study. He concluded that there was probably no motif in any known mythology that did not at various times appear in his patient's dreams and visionary experiences. Thus, starting with the images and symbols which he recurrently unearthed from the mental depths of his modern patients and comparing these with material from folklore, myth and the world's religions, Jung eventually felt he was able "to demonstrate the uniformity of psychic events in time and space."[10]

For him this uniformity was characteristic of a level of psychic functioning whose productions appear to be strangely significant and familiar, and yet somehow incommensurate with our rational thought. "Do we ever understand what we think?" he asks rhetorically and quickly provides an answer:

> We only understand that thinking which is a mere equation, and from which nothing comes out but what we have put in. That is the working of the intellect. But beyond that there is a thinking in primordial images – in symbols which are older than historical man; which have been ingrained in him from earliest times, and, eternally living, outlasting all generations, still make up the groundwork of the human psyche. It is only possible to live the fullest life when we are in harmony with these symbols; wisdom is a return to them. It is neither a question of belief nor of knowledge, but of the agreement of our thinking with the primordial images of the unconscious.[11]

The emphasis on "thinking in primordial images" reconnected modern man with what previously had been regarded as totally alien forms of expression from distant and long-forgotten cultures. This mode of thinking had informed humanity's mythological expression for millennia and provided it with both direction and meaning in life. At the same time, Jung emphasized how these products of symbolic thinking were present but no longer recognized in contemporary religion. Moreover, they were a recurrent source of material and inspiration in philosophy and particularly in art: "Great art till now has always derived its fruitfulness from the myth, from the unconscious process of symbolization which continues through the ages and which, as the primordial manifestation of the human spirit, will continue to be the root of all creation in the future."[12] For Jung these images, as embodied in the world's mythologies, constituted the true language by which an inner dimension of the psyche expressed itself. To fathom the modern mind we must attempt to understand the mind of the past and the highly developed systems of mythology which characterized older cultures. Such an understanding could be integral to man's psychic wholeness and to the salvation of his soul:

> For thousands of years the mind of man has worried about the sick soul, perhaps even earlier than it did about the sick body. The propitiation of gods, the perils of the soul and its salvation, these are not yesterday's problems. Religions are psychotherapeutic systems in the truest sense of the word, and on the grandest scale. They express the whole range of the psychic problem in mighty images; they are the avowal and recognition of the soul, and at the same time the revelation of the soul's nature.[13]

These "mighty images" form a universal foundation for human experience capable of supporting and unifying the fragmented human soul and reconnecting it with its source – a source toward which the revitalized soul readily tends but with which the atrophied soul of modern man has lost touch. In fact, for Jung modern man was in search of his soul. And it was Jung's great task and accomplishment to retrieve and revitalize the sick soul of modernity and reconnect it with this universal foundation, and in so doing he was simultaneously to retrieve a wisdom with a pedigree which reaches back to the horizons of historical time. For retrieving and revitalizing the sick soul is also the shaman's age-old task. Like Jung, he is the master of using primordial images to penetrate "into the blocked subterranean passages of our own psyches." Here he moves freely and effectively over the imaginal terrain of the unconscious. And, like Jung, here he finds what Albert Schweitzer termed "the doctor within." He unleashes innate structures of psychodynamic transformation which both revitalize our health and illuminate the larger mind. As we shall see he likewise integrates the conscious mind with its unconscious substratum as well as with the greater harmony with nature and cosmos latent within the deeper layers of the psyche.

For the shaman the symbol, with its universal power and significance, becomes the portal to an enduring realm beyond time and change which informs the human mind. And in the various shamanic traditions, widespread in time and space and diverse in cultural content, we shall find that the grammar of symbols employed does, indeed, display its own uncanny universality in both structure and function – a uniformity which tends to give substance to Jung's theories about the universal psychic heritage of mankind. Thus, as part of our study, we shall proceed simultaneously in two directions: one indicating the shared structural and functional similarities between various examples of shamanism diverse in time and location; the other exploring the similarities between the material which Jung elicited from modern man in the analyst's office and those age-old forms which characterize the shaman's practice. If we are convincing we shall, to a degree and on a certain level of consciousness, "demonstrate the uniformity

1. Uroboros, the snake with its tail in its mouth,
from Codex Marcianus, pictured in Jung's
Psychology and Alchemy

of psychic events in time and space." This is an endeavor which may be of significance as we hurl forward into the new millennium impelled by our faith in linear change and progress. For it may be that this onrush of progress and change is, in fact, played against an eternal backdrop of ever-recurrent form and structure within the human psyche. And in uniting the archaic with the modern on the deep level of the psyche we may have, in Coleridge's terms, made "those events, which in real or imagined History move on in a *strait* Line, assume to our Understandings a *circular* motion – the snake with its Tail in its Mouth." Here the deeper aspects of our reality assume the shape of the great circle – the snake with its tail in its mouth, or uroboros, an ancient archetype of recurrence and unity. And as we proceed to understand the manner in which these age-old structures of consciousness described in this great circle have been for millennia past and are still conducive not only to psychotherapy and health but also to the actual experience of a significant religious illumination, we may intuit that just behind them may lie our closest glimpse of Eternity.

Chapter 2

Jung's Cosmos – The Structure of the Psyche

> Consciousness is the mere surface of our mind,
> and of this, as of the globe, we do not know the
> interior but only the crust.
> **Arthur Schopenhauer**

Two Myths – Two Images of Cosmos and Psyche

Modern man, Jung asserted, is paralyzed by self-division. Our well-developed rational intellect, on the basis of which we have made such tremendous technical progress in the modern world, has come to dominate the psychic landscape and "usurps the seat where once the spirit was enthroned."[1] As such "consciousness deviates again and again from its instinctual foundation and finds itself in opposition to it."[2] So divided the conscious mind starves for the creative insight provided by the unconscious, while the unconscious is denied the light of consciousness. The universal and primordial images which, according to Jung and as will become apparent from their employment in shamanic cultures, are alone capable of working to synthesize these sundered psychic positions have been largely misunderstood and abandoned by modern culture. According to Mircea Eliade, one of the most astute modern interpreters of myth and religion, the loss of our mythic sensibility constitutes for humankind a second fall from grace and effectively divides us from an experienced truth.[3] Or, as Jung expressed the same realization, "Our myth has become mute, and gives no answers."[4]

Today, we must ask ourselves why the images which captivated and motivated so many proud and intelligent cultures of the past now mean next to nothing to us. For cultures throughout history, myth and symbol provided both existential meaning and direction and connected man with what Jung termed the objective psyche, those depths of the human mind from which our religious and creative insights and intuitions have always mysteriously been born. "They are created out of the primal stuff of revelation," Jung observes, "and reflect the ever-unique experience of divinity."[5] Such insights and intuitions provide us with a premonition of our proximity to the divine and to that slumbering image of unity and totality which, as we shall see, Jung felt lay deep within the psyche and moved it toward integration with its own depths, the world of nature from which it sprang, and a sacred cosmos.

The soul speaks of itself in primordial images. Thus, myths are psychic phenomena that reveal the nature of the soul – "symbolic expressions of the inner, unconscious drama of the psyche."[6] As products which have been shaped by passing again and again through the human mind for thousands of years, they assume the shape of the very agency which creates them. Properly understood, they become remarkably rich expressions of the spiritual condition of whole races, cultures and eras. Consequently, while they often share an uncanny archetypal universality in their main or nuclear elements, they can be bent to very different meanings and uses in different cultures reflective of the evolving conditions of those psyches which shaped them. This fact became quite apparent to me as I prepared this book and was studying a myth related to the shamanic practices of the Tamang people of Nepal.

The myth is recited in the soul retrieval ceremonies performed by the Tamang shaman and, simply stated, the basic elements are these. In primordial times, gods and men lived together in unity and harmony. So close was this relationship that they even exchanged women in marriage, as do exogamous clans to this day in Nepal. As part of the ritual involved in this marital exchange, Primordial Man was required to gather certain objects, including a deer's leg, to share with the gods. Man, angered at having to share the deer's leg with the gods, instead threw it at his newly acquired goddess wife, breaking her leg. Such human selfishness and over-reaching caused a rift between the human and the divine. The gods severed connections with man and set up barriers between heaven and earth, the immortals and our own mortal state. The Tamang ritual, as we shall examine in Chapter 3, will concentrate the full force of myth and symbol and the effective techniques which enhance their power to overcome this division between gods and men, and to resurrect that slumbering image of unity and divinity in the human soul represented by the now eclipsed paradisiacal era when men lived in harmony with the gods.

We find a startlingly similar, but partially obscured, primordial image in Greek myth at the very base of our evolving Western culture. A comparison between the two myths and the manner in which each culture envisioned them is fruitful. Nepal stands out over the centuries for a resolute religious temperament which has kept alive ancient traditions, myths and ritual practices. Greece, on the other hand, stands halfway between the mythic world and the evolving rational consciousness which would eventually give us our current empiricism and technology. It represents the evolutionary impetus which impelled us to modernity, and here we find myth in its final, twilight hours.

The myth which best captures the psychic landscape of this Greek world is, of course, that of Prometheus. However, the aspect of this myth upon which we focus initially is less well-known but fundamental to its understanding. The myth likewise describes a ritual, and only the bare details have survived. As related by Carl Kerényi, it is as follows:

When gods and men met together in Mekone, the place which is called the "Field of Poppies," *where they were to be separated one from the other,* Prometheus divided up a mighty bull. He laid it in a friendly fashion before the assembly, seeking to deceive the insight of Zeus. For himself and his people he filled the stomach of the animal with sliced meat and fat offal. For Zeus he wrapped the bones handsomely in gleaming fat. Thus the contents of neither portion could be perceived. [Emphasis added][7]

Zeus was deceived, or perhaps allowed himself to be deceived, and took the bones and fatty portion. He never forgave the treachery and, as Hesiod tells us, "from that time he was always mindful of the trick, and would not give the power of unwearying fire to the wretched race of mortal men who live on the earth."[8] Prometheus, as we know, would steal the fire of heaven for mankind and Zeus would retaliate by creating "a beautiful evil," Pandora, the first woman and a heaven-sent bride who would release sickness and death into the world. "Thus," Kerényi tells us, "was completed the separation between men and the immortal gods."[9]

Kerényi notes several paradoxical elements in this myth. Prometheus performed the deceptive ritual act, but it was humankind which suffered the consequences. Here and in the stealing of fire, he asks, why is there "the tacit identification of the cause of Prometheus with that of men?"[10] And later Prometheus, a member of the set of "the lightly living gods," will suffer injustice, torment and humiliation – "the hallmarks of human existence."[11] For these reasons, he feels, Aeschylus was able to envision Prometheus as a tragic hero, a position generally reserved for a human protagonist. On the basis of these observations and a number of complex but well-founded additional reasons, Kerényi determines that Prometheus is an "archetypal image of human existence" and that the myth as it has come down to us masks an older scenario. In this version, in the Age of Gold, when the myth takes place, gods and men lived in undivided unity and Prometheus was not a god who inexplicably champions the cause of men but Primordial Man himself in primordial times living in unity with the sacred. "The meaning of this strange sacrifice in which the gods were cheated out of the tasty morsels is simply this: that the sacrifice offered up by men is a sacrifice of foolhardy thieves, stealers of the divinity round about them – for the world of nature that surrounds them is divine – whose temerity brings immeasurable and unforeseen misfortune upon them."[12] Man's primal over-reaching sunders the sacred world, and henceforth a clear and impassable division separates gods and men in the Greek world.

The similarity between the nuclear or, in Jungian terms, archetypal elements of the Tamang and Greek myths is striking. We have 1) a golden age or paradisiacal era, 2) existing in primordial times, 3) where gods and men lived together; 4) a primordial bride sent from the heavens; 5) a ritual event between gods and men; 6) human selfishness or over-reaching in apportioning the ritual object, 7) which deprives the gods of their fair share; 8) a consequent sundering of primordial unity and a division between gods and men, 9) all of which form a unique event in the primordial era that determines the subsequent fate and existence of mankind.[13] In Nepal, where the realities of myth and ritual are still alive, they will be bent to overcoming this fate and re-establishing contact with the divine. In Greece and subsequent Western culture, where the reality of myth is in decline, the myth itself suggests a different outcome, a continued alienation and even bitter enmity between the heavens and the earth. Prometheus, as is well-known, is escorted by Zeus' henchmen, Kratos (Force) and Bia (Violence), into captivity. With the aid of the smith, Hephaistos, a wedge is driven through his breast, and he is shackled in torment to a high cliff. Zeus, with his terrifying lightning, will cast him into Tartaros, the Greek underworld. And here, according to Zeus' decree, daily a mighty eagle, red with blood, will come to banquet upon the shackled prisoner. As Prometheus is forewarned:

> All day long he will tear to rags your body,
> great rents within the flesh,
> feasting in fury on the blackened liver.[14]

Yet each night, to prolong the terrible agony, the riven liver grows again only to draw once more the ravenous bird to its anguished victim.

> When liver gnawn is swollen and grown afresh,
> Greedy he then comes back to hideous meal.
> Thus nourish I this guard of my said torture
> Which mars my living frame with endless woe.[15]

Shackled in the underworld and daily ravaged by the implacable eagle, the dread agent of remorseless Zeus, Prometheus will remain for 30,000 years.

"There are hardly any exceptions to the rule that a person must pay dearly for the divine gift of the creative fire," observed Jung, describing our modern, mechanized world which leaves so little freedom for creativity.[16] We have pointed out that, according to Jung, "myths are first and foremost psychic phenomena that reveal the nature of the soul" – "symbolic expressions of the inner, unconscious drama of the psyche."[17] And it is difficult not to see in this myth an image of the drama of the soul of Western man as he evolves into modernity. In myth it was with Prometheus that the human arts began, and he is the very image of the creative fire or energy which remains shackled in the human unconscious. For Prometheus, enchained in the underworld and daily eviscerated by the agencies of the reigning powers, is not only Primordial Man but Primordial Mind, man's collective creative legacy since time's beginning which lies deep within us. His archetypal image calls to mind Thomas Mann's description of this deep and profoundly significant level of the human psyche and its creative potential represented in the archetypal image of Primordial Times:

The association of the words "psychology" and "deeper level" has also a chronological significance: the depths of the human soul are also "Primordial Times," that deep "Well of Time" in which Myth has its home and from which the original norms and forms of life are derived. For myth is the foundation of life; it is the timeless pattern, the religious formula to which life shapes itself, in as much as its characteristics are a reproduction of the Unconscious.[18]

So envisioned Prometheus, banished to the depths of Tartaros, is the mythic creative power itself which lies deep within us all – Primordial Man who speaks in primordial images. He is the mythic and creative sensibility whose shackling sunders primordial unity and creates a cosmos and psychic landscape divided against itself. So sundered the gods become our antithesis and tormentors. As Kerényi notes, this division is indicative of the essentially limited character of the realm of Zeus. "The existing cosmos means the encompassing and the encompassed, the chaining and the chained, Zeus and Prometheus, gods and men."[19] Yet Prometheus is still what Jung called the "hidden immortal within the mortal man,"[20] that portion of the human psyche which is still most immediately related to the gods. It is only the freeing of this deep level of human potential which lies banished beneath our rational consciousness that can close the rift between heaven and earth and heal the self-division within the human psyche. It is this which the Tamang shaman, carrying forward age-old practices, is able to do. And it was precisely Jung's lifelong task likewise to release the healing and redeeming forces of this primordial, collective psyche which lies shackled beneath our isolated, imperious conscious mind – to overcome the sundered psychic landscape which characterizes modernity and free the Promethean mind from gloomy Tartaros.

Freeing the Mythic Powers of the Psyche

Jung's task was to disinter the "universal foundation" of the soul. If we can follow him in this endeavor, we shall begin to understand what shamans such as those of the Tamang have understood for centuries or even millennia – the healing and illuminative power of myth and symbol and their ability to promote human wholeness. It is only myth which can overcome that paralyzing image of the aliened and tortured human mind so graphically represented by Prometheus and unite us with the immortal part of the mortal mind. And it is Carl Jung who best can explain to the modern mind in terms it can still understand this now difficult and nearly lost but deeply human inner truth. For Jung's work shows the vital importance of these myths and symbols, and helps explain the strange similarity found among the world's primordial images such as the myth of the separation of gods and men which we just saw characterizing two radically different cultures. It helps us understand how these images originate, why they are shared by cultures widely separated by time and space, how they might open the mind to its unconscious instinctive depths and why in so doing they promote an experienced state of psychic integration which the paradisiacal eras of these myths suggest – a state which is both therapeutic and illuminative. For our contemporary time, which looks obsessively forward and outward for meaning and salvation, this process involves a radical transformation of consciousness, a "turning inside out" of our basic approaches to "the real" and a rediscovery of the riches which lie buried within the human mind.

As we begin this long journey inward, it may fortify our resolve to recall certain insights of Mircea Eliade, who was particularly sensitive to the radical confrontation with the unknown which was ushered in by the discoveries of modern psychology and particularly by C.G. Jung.

> But it is depth psychology that has revealed the most *terrae ignotae*, has caused the most dramatic confrontations. The discovery of the unconscious could be put on a level with the maritime discoveries of the Renaissance and the astronomical discoveries that followed the invention of the telescope. For each of these discoveries brought to light worlds whose existence was not even suspected.[21]

Due to these insights, he felt, "It is not impossible that our age may go down to posterity as the first to rediscover those 'diffuse religious experiences' which were destroyed by the triumph of Christianity."[22] Among these lost religious experiences, of course, he includes shamanism. Our first task in attempting this "rediscovery," therefore, will be to lay a basic foundation for understanding Jungian psychology and the natural truth which dwells in the inner man. We shall then show how this knowledge helps us understand the principles and practices of shamanism and illustrates the manner in which modern depth psychology is reclaiming an extremely meaningful aspect of our human heritage, tracing back thousands and even tens of thousands of years into our past through ever-recurrent symbolic forms.

"Jung's most important contribution to modern thought, in my opinion, lies in his recognition of the reality of mind and in his recovery of the idea of the psyche as a cosmos equal and complementary to the physical world," J.J. Clarke informs us.[23] This is a cosmos with its own form and structure, governed by its own laws and containing its own significance. Jung sets the cornerstone for our understanding of this often-ignored realm of interior reality by asserting:

> I can only gaze with wonder and awe at the depths and heights of our psychic nature. Its non-spatial universe conceals an untold abundance of images which have accumulated over millions of years of living development and become fixed in the organism. ... And these images are not pale shadows, but tremendously powerful psychic factors ... Beside this picture I would like to place the spectacle of the starry heavens at night, for the only equivalent of the universe within is the universe without; and just as I reach this world through the medium of the body, so I reach that world through the medium of the psyche.[24]

One can recognize in this comparison of the vision of the starry heavens without and the mental world within the echo of a well-known statement by the philosopher, Immanuel Kant, implying a hidden affinity between the two realms of experience. In fact, Jung was influenced since his early days by Kant, and we can trace a parallel movement in his own thought – an expansion of Kant's "Copernican revolution" moving psyche to the center of creation. For Jung, like Kant, the human mind played an important role in forming all that we experience, and mind inevitably could be detected behind the so-called "physical fact". Ultimately and undeniably, he felt, the mind has its own unconscious structuring principles which shape the world that we experience and cast it into certain defined and recurrent forms. From this vantage point the psyche becomes "the *mother*, the matrix – the form into which all experience is poured."[25]

"The idea that anything could be real or true which does *not* come from outside has hardly begun to dawn on contemporary man," Jung observes.[26] However, he notes that this "outside" physical world, which we *think* we know, and our perceptual world are two very different things. Modern science reveals that the psyche transforms or "translates" physical processes into sequences of images and, Jung informs us:

> ... it does this to such a degree that I must resort to artificial means to determine what things are like apart from myself. Then I discover that a tone is a vibration of the air of such and such a frequency, or that a colour is a wavelength of light of such and such a length. We are in all truth so enclosed by psychic images that we cannot penetrate to the essence of things external to ourselves. All our knowledge is conditioned by the psyche which, because it alone is immediate, is superlatively real.[27]

This process of "translation," of image-making, occurs behind the scenes at a level hidden from our conscious awareness and is as unconscious as the heartbeat. As such, our consciousness can fathom only a portion of its true nature, because it is the product of a preconscious psychic life which made its development possible in the first place. No matter what degree of truth we grant to the "physical fact," at its deepest levels the formal powers of the psyche act with their own autonomy and ultimately are capable of revealing structures of experience beyond those of empirical reality.

Historically, the recognition of this aspect of the unconscious was an important act of rehabilitation. Instead of being regarded, as it had been by many of Sigmund Freud's followers, as a seamy theater of repressed sexual contents, for Jung the unconscious revealed itself to be the very foundation of consciousness and creativity. In Jung's view, Freud had too narrowly interpreted the principle of order and creativity, which runs through the entire organic realm and informs the human mind, in terms of a sexuality still tainted with the moral prejudices of Freud's time. He felt that Freud's sexual theory of neurosis "makes the mistake of being one-sided and exclusive; also it commits the imprudence of trying to lay hold of unconfinable Eros with the crude terminology of sex."[28] Here, in a very significant way, Jung's interior kingdom began to deepen to reveal a relationship between man, nature and cosmos and, in a manner typical of Jung's developing insight, it was a mythical figure, Eros, who led the way. In Jung's thought, this mighty daemon of the psyche takes on the attributes of the cosmic creative force itself, mythically envisioned by the Greeks as Eros Protogonos, the first principle of all creation. Likewise, Eros in Greek myth is simultaneously the principle of unity underlying and binding together the created world, for it is also Eros who, according to Plato, makes "the Cosmos one with itself." And this dual role, at once creative and unifying, played by Eros is also shared by the human psyche. Human creativity is itself the expression of the same continuum of forces which, as we shall see, reaches back through the unconscious to the realm of instinct and ordered organic development to what Jung called the psychoid level, where human form and order originate, forming a creative continuum which unites man, nature and cosmos. And it was the psyche itself which became the oracle of this truth, for it was the symbolic images cast forth by the unconscious which initiated Jung into the depths of this interior reality.

Clinical analysis proved that the images produced by this mysterious source of form and order deep within the mind were in fact not simply random or arbitrary as they sometimes, at first, appeared to be. The psyche consists essentially of images, Jung noted. "It is a series of images in the truest sense, not an accidental juxtaposition or sequence, but a structure that is throughout full of meaning and purpose; it is a 'picturing' of vital activities."[29] This meaning and purpose had been recognized in older societies and was becoming increasingly apparent to modern psychology, which was beginning to realize that the unconscious possesses its own creative autonomy. And when this autonomy was released to express itself, Jung found that it spontaneously produced images which, in words attributed to Plato, "though to a stranger are not strange." Such images frequently reproduced portions of the world's great mythological systems even though these systems were quite unknown to the producer of these images. Yet he or she recognized such images as somehow familiar and vitally meaningful. After years of analysis, Jung was finally able to assert without reservation:

Besides the obvious personal sources, creative fantasy also draws upon the forgotten and long-buried primitive mind with its host of images, which are to be found in the mythologies of all ages and all peoples. The sum of these images constitutes the collective unconscious, a heritage which is potentially present in every individual. ... This is the reason why mythological images are able to arise spontaneously over and over again, and to agree with one another not only in all the corners of the wide earth, but at all times.[30]

It was this very universality of form revealed in these images which led Jung to postulate that myth-forming structural elements must be present in the unconscious psyche.

According to Jung there are two layers of the unconscious, a personal layer and an impersonal or transpersonal level, which he termed the collective unconscious. The personal unconscious contains such things as lost memories, painful ideas which have been repressed, subliminal perceptions which were not strong enough to reach consciousness and contents that are not yet ripe for conscious recognition. The collective unconscious, on the other hand, embodies the shared form-generating predispositions of the unconscious which, like those of the human body itself, are innate and common to all mankind and, thus, basically universal, impersonal and transpersonal. "The foundation of consciousness, the psyche *per se*, is unconscious, and its structure, like that of the body, is common to all, its individual features being only insignificant variants," Jung explains.[31] Ira Progoff points out that we must understand Jung's use of the word "collective" in "collective unconscious" more in its German than its English sense. "He meant *kollektiv*, which has the overtone not so much of the multiple experience of the group as of the inherently human."[32] In the collective unconscious, as Jung recognizes, lie "the deep-rooted, well-nigh automatic, hereditary elements that are ubiquitously present, hence the impersonal or transpersonal portions of the individual psyche."[33] Here the mind survives generations of time and change to father forth images from its depths in universal and eternal form. In a description quoted by Joseph Campbell in his book, *The Mythic Image,* and tellingly juxtaposed to the picture of a colossal statue of Shiva Maheshvara, the timeless substratum manifesting itself as the creator, preserver and destroyer of the universe, Jung poetically describes this transpersonal portion of the human psyche:

> If it were possible to personify the unconscious, we might think of it as a collective human being combining the characteristics of both sexes, transcending youth and age, birth and death, and, from having at its command a human experience of one or two million years, practically immortal. If such a being existed, it would be exalted above all temporal change; ... it would be a dreamer of age-old dreams and, owing to its immeasurable experience, an incomparable prognosticator. It would have lived countless times over again the life of the individual, the family, the tribe and the nation, and it would possess a living sense of the rhythm of growth, flowering and decay.[34]

This level of transpersonal awareness, of course, precisely embodies that "hidden immortal within the mortal man" which Jung had made it his goal to set free.

Yet despite its almost mystical implications, Jung attempted to base his theory upon firm ground consistent with his view of psychology as an emerging science based upon modern scientific principles. Due to the innate formal principles of man's mind, "the form of the world into which he is born is already inborn in him as a virtual image," he tells us.[35] This fact is simply attributable to the common structure and development of the human brain, which is inherited and which necessarily gives a certain form and direction to aspects of our experience, making it collective and universal. Jung finds the hypothesis that the structural similarity of the deep layers of the psyche is accountable for similar psychic forms among diverse individuals and cultures to be no more unusual than the well-accepted observation that the common physiological forms of the human body lead to common physiological functions. Moreover, he repeatedly tries to make a clear point of the fact that he is describing an inherited and universal unconscious psychic predisposition to organize experience in certain forms rather than "innate ideas." "There are no inborn ideas, but there are inborn possibilities of ideas ... *a priori* ideas, as it were, the existence of which cannot be ascertained except from their effects."[36] They become manifest only in the shaped material as the regulative principles which give it a particular form.

The regulative principles which shape the materials Jung calls archetypes. They are formative factors responsible for the organization of unconscious psychic processes. He refers to them as organs of the pre-rational psyche. The archetypes pre-exist in virtual form in everyone, thus accounting for the startling similarities that we encounter in the myths and symbols found in distant civilizations and in different eras. However, while today the term "archetype" is often used to describe an image or symbol recurrently found in various traditions, strictly speaking Jung draws a distinction between the archetypal representation and the archetype itself which remains forever an unconscious formative factor knowable only indirectly through its representations. "Archetypes, so far as we can observe and experience them at all, manifest themselves only through their ability to *organize* images and ideas, and this is always an unconscious process which cannot be detected until afterwards."[37] The archetype itself remains hidden but creates particular images which make visualization of it possible – that is, an approximate visualization made possible by gathering and comparing the repeated examples of such images which, through the crystalization of their common features, begin to reveal the essential nature of their deep cause that shines dimly through.

These expressions or images are often referred to by Jung as symbolic representations. Here it becomes imperative to understand just what it is that Jung means by the term, "symbol." This is of utmost importance because, as he tells us, the unconscious can only be reached by symbols, the language by which it expresses itself. A symbol is not to be confused with a sign or allegory pointing to a known factor in the "outside" world. It is, at least initially, an image of an emergent content from the unconscious which still largely transcends consciousness and is struggling to find adequate expression.

So long as a symbol is a living thing, it is an expression for something that cannot be characterized in any other or better way. ... Every psychic product, if it is the best possible expression at the moment for a fact as yet unknown or only relatively known, may be regarded as a symbol, provided that we accept the expression as standing for something that is only divined and not yet clearly conscious.[38]

Though symbols cannot be completely encapsulated in rational thought, they do not entirely escape it. Moreover, they are experienced as somehow vitally meaningful. They appear as emissaries of a certain deep formal purposiveness of the psyche, and the mind recognizes this form as intimately significant for it. Such symbols are known by their effects. They are fascinating and feeling-laden and are experienced as both spontaneous and necessary. A sense of vitality and yet inner orderedness accompanies their presence. They give hints of what lies latent and potential within the psyche; what the psyche must express if it is not to wither from the loss of its own roots and sustenance. For Jung, the archetypal symbol is a vital and necessary component in our psychic economy. "It represents or personifies certain instinctive data of the dark, primitive psyche, the real but invisible roots of consciousness."[39] The symbol mediates between this unconscious substratum of the primordial mind and the human consciousness. "It throws a bridge between the present-day consciousness, always in danger of losing its roots, and the natural, unconscious, instinctive wholeness of primeval times."[40] We shall examine the function of the symbol in more detail later in this work. For now, we shall simply point out that it is capable of leading us into the soul's depths – to that deep level "in which Myth has its home and from which the timeless pattern, the religious formula to which life shapes itself" emerges – a process which is potentially revivifying, illuminative and therapeutic.

The Depth of the Soul

At a time when man was, perhaps, more attuned to the realities of the soul, the Greek philosopher, Heraclitus, still felt called upon to remind him that, so great is this essential human attribute, you "cannot find the ends of the soul though you traveled every way, so deep is its logos." [†] This aphorism celebrating the soul's secret depths is applicable to Jung's thought on a number of levels. In the first place, as we have mentioned, he regarded the unconscious psyche as the source of human creativity and inspiration reaching back into and expressing principles of instinct, nature and finally the creation itself. Moreover, he felt that it directly linked man not only with his own wellsprings but also with the wellsprings of the primordial past; that is, to the human evolutionary past and to its older modes of expression.

In fact, the archetype does in a very real sense arise from the mists of the primordial past as well as from the organic substrate linking us to the natural world. In discussing the archetypes, Jung tells us that "they correspond to certain *collective*

[†] The Greek term here represented by "logos" has been variously defined as cause, essence, measure or ground.

(and not personal) structural elements of the human psyche in general, and, like the morphological elements of the human body, are *inherited*."[41] Jung felt that "according to phylogenetic law, the psychic structure must, like the anatomical, show traces of the earlier stages of evolution it has passed through."[42] Finally, he concluded, "The collective unconscious contains the whole spiritual heritage of mankind's evolution, born anew in the brain structure of every individual."[43] "To me it is a vast historical storehouse,"[44] he observed and added, "... every civilized human being, whatever his conscious development, is still an archaic man at the deeper levels of his psyche. Just as the human body connects us with the mammals and displays numerous relics of earlier evolutionary stages ... so the human psyche is likewise a product of evolution which, when followed up to its origins, shows countless archaic traits."[45] Thus, Jung was able to say "Together the patient and I address ourselves to the 2,000,000-year-old man who is in all of us,"[46] that representative of the legacy of ancestral life.

Here "an interior spiritual world whose existence we never suspected opens out and displays contents which seem to stand in sharpest contrast to all our former ideas."[47] We are the unknowing heirs to this interior world, and we re-echo the dim bygone in dreams and fantasies, in both their contents and their mode of representation. Dreams and fantasies represent an older mode of expression, a thinking in primordial images, or archetypal symbols, which seems to hark back to humanity's earliest mythological heritage. Jung agreed with Nietzsche that the figurative language of dreams is a survival from an archaic mode of thought. In such forms of experience, the human mind still reaches into man's deep past, both historical and biological, to a time when thinking in primordial images was apparently more prevalent. With its own autonomy and necessity, this level of consciousness is capable of spontaneously producing images which relate us back to the world of the ancestor and the 2,000,000-year-old man who is in all of us; that is, to that "dreamer of age-old dreams" who has "lived countless times over again the life of the individual, the family, the tribe and the nation."

Jung was fond of referring to this ageless transpersonal substratum of the psyche as the "rhizome level" of the mind which produces, supports and, in its timelessness, survives its various manifestations. The rhizome metaphor is apposite, for here we are approaching what Jung called the psychoid realm in which the archetype has its roots. Ira Progoff well explains Jung's conception of the psychoid level of the mind.

In Jung's scheme of thought, the psychoid level of the unconscious represents the point at which the psyche is so close to the animal world as not yet to be differentiated from it. It still is directly connected to the realm of nature in its mode of functioning, and it is thus the aspect of the human organism that can be most directly experienced as a part of nature. ... our individual contact with the psychoid level of our human nature involves an inner experience of the deep ground of the Self experienced subjectively within ourselves and also objectively as part of the whole realm of nature.[48]

Thus, for Jung the logos of the soul became deeper still, revealing our fundamental affinity with the natural world. In his clinical practice Jung noticed that certain unconscious portions of the psyche tended to assume the characteristics of a more primitive archaic and mythological level, and even to assume the qualities which are the hallmarks of instinct: automatism, non-susceptibility to influence, all-or-none reaction, and so forth. In fact, the world of instinct bore a close analogy to that of the collective unconscious, being a transpersonal, preconscious realm of autonomous, necessary and universal predispositions to organize experience, and then to respond, according to certain patterns; a realm of significant innate wisdom inherited directly from nature. Both the archetype and instinct seemed to involve the necessary production of an image with fixed properties which is capable of catalyzing a pattern of behavior. Jung notes that "... the instincts are not vague and indefinite by nature, but are specifically formed motive forces which, long before there is any consciousness ..., pursue their inherent goals. Consequently, they form very close analogies to the archetypes, so close, in fact, that there is good reason for supposing that the archetypes are the unconscious images of the instincts themselves, in other words, that they are *patterns of instinctual behaviour.*"[49]

According to Jolande Jacobi, the archetype is:

> ... an inherited mode of psychic functioning, corresponding to that inborn way according to which the chick emerges from the egg; the bird builds its nest; a certain kind of wasp stings the motor ganglion of the caterpillar; and eels find their way to the Bermudas. In other words, it is a "pattern of behaviour." This aspect of the archetype is the biological one ... But the picture changes at once when looked at from the inside, that is, from within the realm of the subjective psyche. Here the archetype presents itself as numinous, that is, it appears as an experience of fundamental importance.[50]

"Archetypes," Sherry Salman explains, "are both biologically based patterns of behavior and the symbolic images of these patterns."[51] Such images "evoke the aim and motivation of instincts through the psychoid nature of the archetype."[52] It is because the archetype operates at the deep level of instinct that it can effect energies influencing both body and mind. At the same time, the archetype as the emissary of instinct brings forward aspects of the often incomprehensible wisdom of this realm which guides the entire natural world.

For Jung, the archetypes rooted in the psychoid level of the unconscious and the instincts both have a physiological and psychological aspect and are so closely related that in the human psyche the archetype may be regarded as "*the instinct's perception of itself,* or as the self-portrait of the instinct."[53] Jung sometimes called this realm of the convergence of body and mind the "subtle body," which he felt was neither strictly mind nor matter. This deep level could be reached only by the symbol and with its natural, instinctive wisdom was an area of potential psychological and psychosomatic healing. It is here that the archetype, like the daemon Eros, begins to make "the Cosmos one with itself" and vests the form-generating power of the creation with human significance. For the image expressed in the archetype is, in a real sense, continuous with the deep formal structural patterns by which the life force expresses itself in the organism. "The archetypes, therefore, represent," as J.J. Clarke concludes, "the uniquely human means whereby instinctual, biological, energy is transformed into the meaningful symbolic life of the human psyche."[54] And, as we shall see, it is in the very depths informed by this creative power and the patterns by which it expresses itself that we discover and give form to the soul's correspondence to God.[55]

"The deeper 'layers' of the psyche lose their individual uniqueness as they retreat farther and farther into the darkness," Jung declared. Here they become increasingly collective until they are universalized, merging with the body's instinctual and biological functions and eventually with nature itself. "Hence, 'at bottom,'" he continues, "the psyche is simply 'world.' In this sense I hold [Carl] Kerényi to be absolutely right when he says that in the symbol the *world itself* is speaking."[56] "Meaning and purposefulness are not the prerogatives of the mind; they operate in the whole of living nature," Jung elsewhere explains. "There is no difference in principle between organic and psychic growth. As the plant produces its flower, so the psyche creates its symbols. Every dream is evidence of this process."[57] Just as nature, body and instinct express themselves in universal patterns with living significance, so does the human psyche, and these natural patterns are the archetypes of the collective unconscious.

The Unified World

Thus, the reach of the human soul extended farther still. Indeed, Jung once went so far as to state that "The body as a whole, so it seems to me, is a pattern of behaviour, and man as a whole is an archetype."[58] Jung, in fact, took a similar view of the cosmos itself. Properly understood, as we shall see, it was the perpetual unfolding of a continuous pattern of order, and the archetype was capable of carrying forward aspects of this patterning into the human mind. Finally, in a very real sense for Jung, as it had for archaic man, the logos of the soul deepened into the cosmic creation. Humankind, far from being orphaned in an absurd world, could experience itself as being the expression of a larger meaning and order.

These insights led Jung to an ever-expanding vision of human wholeness and relationship with the world which surrounds and supports us. For Jung, the human psyche did not develop *ex nihilo* (out of nothing), nor did it arise solely as a product of its surrounding conditions. It carries and expresses the very life forces which led to and fostered its development. "We are forced to assume that the given structure of the brain does not owe its peculiar nature merely to the influence of surrounding conditions, but also and just as much to the peculiar and autonomous quality of living matter, i.e., to a law inherent in life itself," he concluded.[59] Realizing that the archetypes do not simply repeat images received from the environment, he sensed that they somehow express the formal properties of this law inherent in life and expressed in its various forms. Yet, at the same time, mind shapes the material world we experience and, as Jung noted from the discoveries of modern physics, appears to be inextricably involved in what we perceive on several levels. In the final analysis, mind and matter, psyche and body, in both genesis and behavior, seemed to belie all dualism and to point to an intimate connection and even identity between the two. "Since psyche and matter are contained in one and the same world, and moreover are in continuous contact with one another and ultimately rest on irrepresentable, transcendental factors, it is not only possible but fairly probable, even, that psyche and matter are two different aspects of one and the same thing," he surmised.[60] "The body is merely the visibility of the soul, the psyche; and the soul is the psychological experience of the body," he elsewhere asserted.[61]

Ultimately, Jung felt that the archetype is capable of expressing an enduring order, which exists beyond our normal categories of time and space, that underlies and unites both the psyche and the material realm. In so doing, it brings forward to our awareness an intuition of the unfolding of an inherent order, harmony and meaning characteristic of the cosmos itself, for the cosmos, according to Jung, reveals and expresses "the continuous creation of a pattern that exists from all eternity ... and is not derivable from any known antecedents." This concept of a continuous pattern of creation is somewhat difficult for contemporary people accustomed to thinking strictly in terms of linear causation, although modern physics employs a quite similar model when it speaks in terms of the unfolding of an implicate order. Likewise, earlier societies often adhered to such visions of eternal and recurrent cosmic form guiding the life of man. Concepts such as the unfolding order of the Tao in the Orient, Heraclitus' logos and even Nietzsche's eternal recurrence of the same all represent man's enduring struggle to give voice to these elusive intuitions of unity. Such insights account for those rare but most revealing moments when mind and nature, relaxing their long struggle against each other, seem to embrace and reality becomes transparent to the eternal. Here, fleetingly, we are blessed and can bless, and the weary world around us reveals its unity in archetypal forms. Just such a unitive visionary moment was beautifully described by Wordsworth when, crossing the Alps, the archetypal imagination and nature coalesced and various elements of the majestic mountain scene – beautiful, sublime and terrifying – revealed themselves to be the types and symbols of Eternity.

> ... workings of one mind, the features
> Of the same face, blossoms upon one tree,
> Characters of the Great Apocalypse,
> The types and symbols of Eternity,
> Of first, and last, and midst, and without end.[62]

Such moments Jung referred to as the "rupture of time" – "numinous experiences where space, time, and casualty are abolished" – and reveal a deeper reality.[63]

In fact, similar conceptions of a continuous pattern of creation lay behind Jung's original adoption of the term "archetype" to express an *a priori* orderedness beyond time and space which the archetypal representation approximates with greater or lesser success. One such source was the work of Dionysius the pseudo-Areopagite. Here the author represents the pattern of continuous creation as the seal of God which imprints eternal form on the creation and on the human mind depending on its capacity to receive its imprint. "But someone may say that the seal is not the same and entire in all its impressions. The seal, however, is not the cause of this, for it imparts itself wholly and alike in each case, but the differences in the participants make the impression unlike, although the archetype is one, whole, and the same."[64] So envisioned, the creation reveals itself to be a continuous pattern of manifestation expressing an enduring source like the archetypal representation itself. Thus, according to Jung, "Continuous creation is to be thought of not only as a series of successive acts of creation, but also as the eternal presence of the *one* creative act."[65] By analogy we might think of Christian tradition where God always was the Father and always generated the Son, or Hindu thought where Brahman eternally bodies forth the creation. In attempting to find expression for this concept, we get the feeling that Jung was trying finally to cope with an intuition that had long lain at the heart of his thinking but was so resistant to scientific conceptualization that he hesitated to make an attempt. The theory which he termed "synchronicity" was an effort to attain empirically respectable proof of this elusive reality.

The concept of an inner orderedness capable of being experienced within the human psyche that is continuous with the unfolding of cosmic order provided Jung with the basis for this difficult theory, which recognizes a patterning across time that is not the product of material or external, deterministic causation. According to Jung, "Synchronicity ... means the simultaneous occurrence of a certain psychic state with one or more external events which appear as meaningful parallels to the momentary subjective state – and in certain cases, vice versa."[66] Yet the psychological and physical parallelisms cannot be explained strictly on the basis of causally connected events. They can be explained as mere coincidence but have an incidence of occurrence which, on the basis of his work, Jung felt was far more frequent than could be attributed to mere happenstance. The parallel events may be trivial or tragic. We may think of an old friend whom we have not seen for years and suddenly run across her at lunch or have a sudden premonition of someone's death which we discover to be true in the next day's obituaries. "The secret of the world is the tie between person and event," observed Emerson, and there have always been people with an instinct for divining this connection and riding "the tide in the affairs of men" to uncanny success.

For Jung, it is the participation in a common inner orderedness that lies beyond the normal categories of time and space by which we order reality that explains these intuitions and parallelisms. "Above all it is the fact of causeless order, or rather, of meaningful orderedness, that may throw light on psychophysical parallelism. The 'absolute knowledge' which is characteristic of synchronic phenomena, a knowledge not mediated by the sense organs, supports the hypothesis of a self-subsistent meaning, or even expresses its existence."[67] When we try to represent this knowledge literally, it is reduced to a vague intuition which seems at odds with the recognized limits of our everyday consciousness. "As soon as a psychic content crosses the threshold of consciousness, the synchronistic marginal phenomena disappear, time and space resume their accustomed sway, and consciousness is once more isolated in its subjectivity."[68] Finally, synchronicity is only a particular instance of general acausal orderedness, an inner order continuous with the pattern of cosmic creation, mediated through the autonomous functions of the collective unconscious and only dimly perceived by the conscious portions of the mind.

However, for Jung the grounding of his psychology in these images of an inherent inner order informing the creation and capable of being experienced by the archetypal imagination was not merely metaphysical speculation or abstract system-building. It had an empirical foundation wrested from his psychological probings. In his clinical work Jung found that the recovery of psychic health in his patients was often accompanied by the unfolding of similar images of formally meaningful inner order, sharing a certain universality of form, and viewed by the patient as expressive of cosmic order and harmony. The archetypes spontaneously produced at this stage bring forward into consciousness this sense of order and the patient experiences, as Ira Progoff explains, a correspondence "between the microcosm and macrocosm, for a harmony has been achieved and the individual has come into an equivalent union with the universal."[69]

> The experience of an archetypal symbol results in a sense of relationship to the interior workings of life, a sense of participation in the movements of the cosmos. The individual at such moments feels his individuality to be exalted, as though he were transported for an instant to a higher dimension of being.[70]

Progoff continues, "Its primary force comes from the fact that it has a spiritual quality and that it validates itself existentially in a person's life. The manifestation of the macrocosm in the microcosm means something of the world's divinity has been individualized."[71] This individualization of the world's divinity is experienced as an effective principle, different from the world of material causality. It is felt to be a creative force manifesting itself as an unfoldment from within, an expression of "the continuous creation" within the individual.

This experience of correspondence was often given expression by Jung's patients in the form of the mandala symbol, a circular image frequently combined with a quaternary pattern which we shall examine at length later. "Most mandalas," Jung tells us, "take the forms of a flower, cross or wheel, and show a distinct tendency toward quaternary structure."[72] They represent the experiencing of a sacred reality emanating from a central source – "Deity unfolding in the world, in nature and in man."[73] On the cosmic level, this is an image of the "continuous creation" itself, and on the personal plane precisely the experience described by Progoff that something of the world's divinity is being individualized. On the personal level, Jung and his patients sometimes experienced these images of unfolding divine power as "soul flowers" – a flower which expresses cosmic creation much like the lotus flower in Hindu and Buddhist mythology. The mandala image is often found combined with images of verticality occupying its center, for example a tree, ladder, pole, cosmic mountain, etc. Such images express the effect of such psychic integration – that is, in Progoff's terms, the experience of being transported to a higher dimension of being and source of power. For Jung, these images are symbols of a psychic integrity which imposed order on an otherwise chaotic external world and are indicative of psychic wholeness and integration. They are intimately related to symbols employing the image of a sacred "center," and they become images of the "self," the goal of psychic development, the totality of personality which attempts to unite consciousness with its deeper sources. At the same time, quite tellingly, they were experienced as god images – expressions of that slumbering image of the divinity and unity which exists potentially in each of us.

We must continually recall that these are not the abstract constructions of reason but the spontaneously produced images of the objective psyche – that level of the mind which, according to Jung, has always produced humanity's religious intuitions and the symbols that embody them. The soul expresses itself in images, and this is the sacred landscape of the soul, the immortal part of the mortal man – that dreamer of age-old dreams which outlives the generations of time and change. Finally for Jung, as for Wordsworth, the human psyche is "instinct with Godhead" and with those archetypal images which are capable of leading us back to the sacred. The rift between man and the divine recognized in Tamang and Greek myth can be bridged, and it is the experience of the archetypes which will foster this healing process.

Constellating the Transpersonal Realm

The deep level of integration implied by the psychophysical parallelisms displayed in synchronistic phenomena reinforced Jung's belief that ultimately psyche and matter are two different aspects of one and the same thing. He came to believe that they formed a single world, an *unus mundus* neither physical nor mental in the strict sense, mediated by the archetypes. As Frank McLynn notes in his biography of Jung, this convergence of the psychic and physical on an acausal level "was why the study of psychosomatic medicine, so often derided by 'scientific' scoffers, was a key aspect of any depth psychology. Since the crossover between the mental and the physical could not satisfactorily be explained in terms of conventional causality, Jung felt that the undoubted fact of psychosomatic causation was further evidence for synchronicity."[74]

"Since the collective unconscious validated archetypes, and archetypes were the key to synchronicity, it seemed highly probable that the mind-body riddle could be solved only acausally, and that psychosomatic illnesses and miracle cures were themselves aspects of synchronicity," McLynn reports. At the same time, Jung felt that the intimate relationship or even identity between psyche and matter articulated at the synchronistic level was the key to understanding the role played by the psyche in curing organic disease, and that the unconscious and the symbols which addressed it played a role in the curative process. Thus, as McLynn notes "... he was persuaded that 'constellation' of the kind of archetype that produced synchronicity could explain the 'miracle cure' even in the case of organic disease."[75] Ultimately, "The acausal principle of synchronicity, it seemed to him, so far from being mystical mumbo-jumbo, was the answer to a whole range of phenomena to which conventional science could provide no answer," McLynn concludes.[76]

Jung, as we have noted, sometimes referred to this deep realm where healing can occur as the subtle body, "a body that was at the same time spirit."[77] It is to be encountered as we press inward from personal consciousness into the transpersonal realm; it is, according to Nathan Schwartz-Salant, that aspect of the unconscious that is experienced as we descend into the body.[78] Again, this realm is neither strictly spirit nor matter, psyche nor soma, but anterior to any real division between the two. It is here that the energies of the instinctual and biological levels are transformed into the meaningful symbolic life of the human psyche. And, reciprocally, it is only the symbol which can penetrate and catalyze the forces of this deep plane in which reside the instinctive healing properties of the organism.

It is in this transpersonal realm where some of the most effective work between doctor and patient can be accomplished often on an unconscious level. Some psychologists, basing their work on Jung and particularly on his alchemical studies, have found it useful to envision this subtle body as a shared transpersonal imaginal realm that exists outside traditional notions of time, space and causality in which doctor and patient can constellate the unconscious. Within this interactive field, the goal becomes to free the psychic energies of the two or more persons – a process often referred to in terms of transference and countertransference or projection – from the personal level and enlist them on an archetypal, transpersonal plane. Techniques employing mythological symbols can often help implement this transition. Because this now becomes a field in which the archetype exercises its influence, it exerts a strongly attractive power, an impelling numinosity and transformative force. Psychological change is basic to this shared world. It is here that powerful innate forces of psychodynamic transformation can be activated and harnessed, as we shall explore in the following chapters, through mastery of the terrain of the imaginal world. According to Schwartz-Salant, "Jung says that projections from the psyche are transmitted through the medium of the subtle body and made to manifest in physical and psychic transmissions from one person to another." He continues, "I would like to amplify Jung's thought by stating that the medium of the subtle body may be projected, imaginally perceived, and experienced between two people."[79]

> If we are to engage the subtle body, the imagination must be employed; this, as Jung said, was the key to the entire alchemical opus. If one can successfully work through the subtle-body realm, there is often a chance to transform not only psychic structure but physical structure as well. Mind-body splitting can mend when the subtle-body realm is successfully encountered.[80]

Yet, at the same time, traditional ideas of "projection" and "transmission" must be tempered because the phenomena with which we are dealing are moving in transpersonal space. "These phenomena apply to another dimension of existence, a *third area* whose processes can only be perceived by the eye of the imagination. Notions of *location* are, in fact, inadequate." Consequently, Schwartz-Salant informs us, "the more deeply this field is entered, the more spatial considerations vanish. We are dealing here with an imaginal world, a *mundus imaginalis* that has its own processes." Individuals can participate in these processes. Indeed, as two parties become involved in the transformation of this shared imaginal realm, they themselves are transformed in the process.[81] "At this point," he concludes, "patient and therapist are *in the psyche* as much as it is inside of them,"[82] but the psyche thus constellated is the shared, transpersonal and archetypal psyche where "the energies and structures of the archetypes have a powerful renewing potential and ... to imaginatively energize these 'gods' and 'goddesses' opens up healing paths that would otherwise rarely become traveled."[83]

Schwartz-Salant further points out another aspect of this healing process which itself employs an archetypal pattern. He calls attention to the fact that "Jung correctly emphasizes that healing depends upon a person's ability to link to the larger world of the pleroma,"[84] – that is, the collective unconscious as it opens to the patterning forces of the continuous creation or implicate order. Because the experience of the subtle body opens to its source in the pleroma, it conforms to the age-old mythic and ritual pattern of a return to origins. "This space is a transitional area between the space-time world (where processes are characterized as an interaction of objects) and the collective unconscious – the *pleroma*."[85] Entering this transitional space can entail devastation or salvation for the conscious mind. Properly canalized, the otherwise dangerous energies from the realm of the archetype as an image of instinct can restore the connective tissue of the soul and return doctor and patient to the fullness of the unfolding power of the creation. For these energies now form, according to Schwartz-Salant, "a field that links them to the oneness of the implicate order,"[86] to the *a priori* meaning, unity and order which the archetype brings forward into human consciousness. Finally, as we shall see in subsequent chapters, at the deepest levels the archetypes are revealed to be "not pale shadows, but tremendous powerful psychic factors" with an innate form and order capable of inducing processes of transformation which are healing, revitalizing and illuminative.

Thus, as we have traced in this chapter, on the basis of Jung's clinical experience and the experiences of his patients, the boundaries of the human soul deepened to reach a world which he perceived to be the creative matrix of consciousness as well as the wellsprings of artistic and mythic creation. His logos opened inward to archaic forms of the spirit and the world of instinct, to the very formal principles of the organism, and even the patterned creation of the cosmos itself. This is "depth" psychology, indeed, penetrating and integrating interiors long closed to the Western mind. And while the modern psyche had become estranged from these roots, Jung discovered in his patients a deep need and an inherent drive which, if not thwarted by antithetical structures of consciousness, worked to restore human wholeness in the integrated personality center Jung was to call the "self," and to open these dimensions to consciousness in a process which he called "individuation." We shall examine this process in Chapters 4 and 5. However, for now let us delve into the archaic world of the shaman and, just as we endeavored to chart aspects of Jung's inner world, attempt to fathom the shaman's interior cosmos. For the shaman, as it was for Jung, the psyche is also a cosmos equal to and complementary to the physical world. Here again the world itself speaks in the symbol and the shaman employs the symbol's power to penetrate the blocked subterranean passages of our psyche to reach the transpersonal realm of the unconscious, the deep realm of the wisdom of instinct, and the harmony with nature and cosmos hidden in the psyche's depths. In a world transcending traditional distinctions between spirit and matter, mind and body, a world which opens directly to the causeless order of the pleroma, he also activates and harnesses powerful innate forces of psychodynamic transformation through his mastery of the terrain of the imaginal world.

Chapter 3

The Shaman's Cosmos

The world is deep,
And deeper than the day had thought.
Friedrich Nietzsche

"The Remarkable Similarity of the Human Psyche at All Times and in All Places"

The cosmos which Jung offers to modernity is one that runs against the grain of the thought patterns that have increasingly emerged in the West since the Enlightenment. In fact, it is contrary to the "common sense" vision we have of ourselves existing in the world. Yet many previous societies might have recognized it as truer and more significant than our construction of the world; truer, perhaps, in the sense intended by Aristotle when he implied that poetry was truer than history. Jung gauges reality against the structures of the mind which shape it, and in this anterior world he finds a realm with its own topography and laws, innate structural and functional qualities which are fascinating, illuminative, naturally therapeutic and "real because they work."[1] Here he unearths the unconscious unitary soul of mankind, for the human soul opens inward and the preconscious mind is revealed to be the germinal matrix of the form of our experience and all our creative endeavors.

Yet as we begin to fathom this inwardly determined reality, as we proceed to what we perceive as *our* first principles and *our* source, as Carl Kerényi notes, paradoxically "the world itself breaks in."[2] We discover the transpersonal world of primordial images with its archetypal configurations, for we find that the soul speaks of itself in these images which gradually begin to illuminate previous systems of expression that hitherto appeared thoroughly outdated and nonsensical. These images appeal to and enlist a different dimension of consciousness. They reach back into the past and into the deep structures of the mind to the realm of instinct and organic development, and even elicit the experience of our own continuity with the order of the cosmos now characterized by essential and enduring form and a plenitude which still invests and sustains creation. As Jung and Kerényi noted, in these symbols cast up by the deeper layers of our psyche, in a very real sense "the *world itself* is speaking," and the formal energies of creation arise to human meaning and significance. In such images, instinctual, biological energy is translated into the meaningful symbolic life of the human psyche. "As the plant produces its flowers, so the psyche creates its symbols,"

Jung noted in the previous chapter. "Every dream is evidence of this process." Elsewhere, he casts this analogy into a larger vision:[5]

> The psyche is not of today; its ancestry goes back many millions of years. Individual consciousness is only the flower and the fruit of a season, sprung from the perennial rhizome beneath the earth; and it would find itself in better accord with the truth if it took the existence of the rhizome into its calculations. For the root matter is the mother of all things.[3]

As we shall discover, the shaman likewise penetrates this root matter that is the mother of all things which lies beyond the plane of the conscious mind and tracks the soul into territories sharing many of the same features that we found in Jung's cosmos. He unearths and unleashes psychodynamic processes which alter consciousness and reveal deeper dimensions of the psyche uniting man with the world of the past, instinct and ordered organic process and, finally, with a durative realm of essential form. In the process, he provides the structure and significance capable of guiding his community and a plenitude and vital power capable of repairing health, life and the creation itself. He likewise penetrates the rhizome level of enduring and fructifying plastic power of which our senses can grasp only the outer sheath or veil and does so with similar illuminative, therapeutic and revitalizing effects. And in so doing he employs techniques and a grammar of symbols, in the expanded sense in which Jung employs the term, which in structure as well as function form striking parallels with Jung's discoveries with regard to his contemporary patients.

Jung, we noted, regarded himself first and foremost as an empiricist recording "individual facts" gleaned from patients without conscious preconception as to any overall conceptual framework into which these isolated observations might fit. Yet these observations began to crystalize into larger structures characterized by recurrent well-defined themes, symbols and formal elements which repeated themselves in identical or analogous forms in the most varied individuals. As these configurations of the unconscious revealed themselves, he was able to recognize their similarity to mythic and religious forms from diverse and remote cultures, and he began to discern what he regarded as the underlying psychic unity of mankind. "We can find psychic forms in the individual which occur not only at the antipodes but also in other epochs with which archaeology provides the only link,"[4] he asserted, and concluded that "the archetypal structure of the unconscious will produce, over and over again and irrespective of tradition, those figures which reappear in the history of all epochs and all peoples, and will endow them with the same significance and numinosity that have been theirs from the beginning."[5]

For Jung, as we have noted, these figures embodied the representations of basic formal predispositions innate but unconscious in the human psyche which guided their formation. Jung came to recognize that he was guided to many of the principles of his theory by a similar sort of predisposition, a dim foreknowledge emanating from the unconscious and guiding him in the direction of deeper understanding. As we observed in the first chapter, he noted specifically with regard to his encounter with Eastern thought, of which he had been entirely ignorant when he first formulated these principles, that in his clinical work he "had been unconsciously led along that secret way which has been the preoccupation of the best minds of the East for centuries," and thus discovered principles which bore an uncanny similarity to certain aspects of these systems of thought and practice.

It is interesting to begin our examination of the relationship between Jung's thought and shamanism from this perspective and to ask to what extent Jung was "unconsciously led along the secret way" which had guided the shaman for what may be many millennia past. And in conjunction we shall proceed in two related directions regarding Jung's hypothesis as to the underlying psychic unity of mankind. First and most basic to our study, we shall examine the manner and extent to which shamanism bears similarities to Jung's own findings gleaned from years of in-depth analysis of his patients. If these parallels are convincing, they will serve to exemplify this psychic unity which in this instance would bind significant and meaningful contemporary mental processes back to those of humans of a very distant past. And at the same time, noting the durability and universality of the shamanic phenomenon itself in diverse and remote areas of the globe and over incredible reaches of time, we shall inquire to what extent these various shamanic traditions in their structural and functional similarities point to a similar identity of "psychic forms in the individual which occur not only at the antipodes but also in other epochs with which archaeology provides the only link" and, therefore, also stand as proof of this underlying psychic unity of our race.

Indeed, shamanism has left its traces and sometimes still persists into the present in many diverse and widely separated cultures around the globe and throughout history. Shamanic ideologies and techniques are documented among the primitive peoples of Australia, the !Kung Bushmen of Africa, certain peoples of Siberia and Central Asia, the Malay Archipelago, in diverse areas of the Americas as well as other regions around the world. In the Americas, shamanism strangely bears witness to the truth of the statement which we just quoted from Jung, for we find traces of shamanic culture tucked away at each antipode, the Arctic north of the Inuit and the Antarctic south of the Ona of Tierra del Fuego. And similarly we are also discovering its existence in civilizations "with which archaeology provides the only link," for recent archaeological discoveries have shown strong shamanic influences among Olmec and Classic Maya cultures. Likewise, shamanism has left its trace in Shang Dynasty China, in Norse mythology and in ancient Greek myth and religion. In fact, it seems to have a most ancient pedigree dating back to and perhaps even beyond the moment of the transition from the Lower to the Upper Paleolithic. As we noted in Chapter 1, the cave art of southern France and northern Spain appears to testify to the shamanic presence over a period of time which, with the most recent startling discoveries at Chauvet and elsewhere, now appears to extend back at least 30,000 years into our human past.

Thus, shamanism takes on the characteristics of a most durable and widespread expression of the human mind. Indeed, Eliade has noted that, because it entails the condition of ecstasy, aspects of the shamanic experience may be "co-existent with the human condition."[6] Yet what is most fascinating about this rich and complex phenomenon is that it bears strikingly precise structural and functional similarities in areas of the world where possible cultural exchange appears either extremely unlikely or extraordinarily remote in time. As we proceed, we shall witness many of these similarities which have also arrested the attention of some of the field's best scholars. For instance, Eliade notes the "disconcerting" similarity between the Siberian and Central Asian pattern of shamanic initiation and that which "is found again, almost to the letter, in Australia."[7] Johannes Wilbert, based upon his study of shamanism among the remote Warao of Venezuela, likewise notes a close resemblance between Warao initiation rites and those of the Australian Aborigines half a world and a wide ocean apart "not only in general content but in specific detail." He notes, "It will have been immediately apparent to anyone familiar with the literature on shamanism that the Warao experience contains much that is near-universal, or at the very least circum-Pacific."[8] Peter T. Furst, commenting on Wilbert's observations, further notes that certain very specific symbolisms in Wilbert's description of Warao initiation practices also quite precisely parallel certain initiatory experiences in Siberian shamanism, and he goes on to observe:

> One cannot help but wonder whether such common experiences by shamans in widely separated regions of the circum-Pacific area are to be explained in terms of real historical relationships, survivals perhaps of some ancient shamanic substratum predating the settling of the Americas from Asia, or in terms of the unconscious and the language of symbols by which it communicates (e.g., Jung's "archetypes"). Perhaps there is something of both here; in any event, the correspondences between Asian and American shamanism are far too close and too numerous to be explained away as mere coincidence.[9]

And, in fact, these "correspondences" range more widely still and seem to be more difficult to explain, for we can find very similar experiences described in the remote bush of the African !Kung Bushman, among the Aborigines of Australia and, I believe, outlined on the ancient cave walls of the Upper Paleolithic.

The debate between diffusion and independent origination with regard to such correspondences especially between Asia and the New World is, like that between determinism and free will, old, knotty and possibly incapable of resolution. Perhaps Furst is correct that there is "something of both" involved in these similarities. Stuart

Fiedel in *Prehistory of the Americas*, considering the ultimate source of certain "strangely similar traits," including shamanism, between Asian and New World cultural development, concludes that "we must entertain the possibility that these convergences arose either because the human mind is 'prewired' so that it works in only so many ways ... or because certain deep-seated psychological themes were established in the Upper Paleolithic cultures of Asia and continued to find expression periodically in descendant cultural traditions in Asia and America."[10] He notes that diffusionist theories seem to be losing ground today generally to those founded on independent origination and further observes that, even where diffusion is a tenable explanation, "It must be shown why the imported innovations were acceptable to an existing culture."[11] In other words, there must be a need or predisposition on the part of a people to accept such an influence, and, consequently, we must conclude that if the phenomenon, like shamanism, is very widely distributed, it must be a widespread and nearly universal predisposition. In a similar vein, Roger Walsh has argued that, even if some remote migratory or diffusionist theory would succeed in accounting for these diverse manifestations of shamanism, "It is difficult to explain why shamanic practices would remain so stable for so long in so many cultures while language and social practices changed so drastically."[12] When we take into consideration the propensity of these human expressions to differentiate, we bring into focus how truly remarkable it is that the basic structure and function of the symbols that form the heart of shamanism have remained essentially unchanged. Thus, whether the world's shamanic traditions are largely the independent expression of similar deep mental structures over long periods of history or are the remote result of ancient migration or diffusion, their far-flung acceptance, similarity in precise detail and exceedingly long maintenance by diverse cultures argue strongly that they appeal to and express underlying psychic predispositions and structures shared by all mankind.

Jung, of course, had his own explanation for the existence of such similarities in human symbolic expression over times and distances which seemed to defy explanation by theories employing cultural diffusion or migration as an answer.

> Comparative religion and mythology are rich mines of archetypes, and so is the psychology of dreams and psychoses. The astonishing parallelism between these images and the ideas they serve to express has frequently given rise to the wildest migration theories, although it would have been far more natural to think of the remarkable similarity of the human psyche at all times and in all places. Archetypal fantasy-forms are, in fact, reproduced spontaneously any time and anywhere, without there being any conceivable trace of direct transmission.

He goes on to comment upon the genesis of these archetypal images.

> The original structural components of the psyche are of no less surprising a

uniformity than are those of the visible body. The archetypes are, so to speak, organs of the pre-rational psyche. They are eternally inherited forms and ideas which have at first no specific content. Their specific content only appears in the course of the individual's life, when personal experience is taken up in precisely these forms.[13]

Thus, the specific content of the archetype may have a personal or local aspect which fleshes out or clothes its appearance. However, to the gifted or trained eye, the basic form of the primordial image or archetype is discernible operating beneath the surface and providing the formal structure of the expression. Both Joseph Campbell and Mircea Eliade make similar observations with regard to the recurrent structural patterns found in shamanism.

Discussing the widely shared symbols and patterns in shamanism and the universality of an imagery which remains basically the same despite its local expressions in a specific culture, Joseph Campbell notes:

> The phenomenology of shamanism is locally conditioned only in a secondary
> sense ... And since it has been precisely the shamans that have taken the lead
> in the formation of mythology and rites throughout the primitive world, the
> primary problem of our subject would seem to be not historical or
> ethnological, but psychological, even biological; that is to say, precedent to the
> phenomenology of the culture styles.[14]

For Campbell, as for Jung, "there is a formative force spontaneously working, like a magnetic field, to precipitate and organize the ethnic structures from behind, or within, so that they cannot finally be interpreted economically, sociologically, politically or historically. Psychology lurks beneath and within the entire historical composition, as an invisible controller."[15] Speaking specifically of the recurrent structural similarities found in the world's shamanic traditions, he notes that this force "moves within, and is helped, or hindered, by historical circumstance, but is to such a degree constant for mankind that we may jump from Hudson Bay to Australia, Tierra del Fuego to Lake Baikal, and find ourselves well at home."[16]

Thus, from this perspective, the shamanic experience is cast against and reflects the inner template of the human mind, and this template or "formative force" working from within provides it with a universal form. Eliade expresses a similar thought from a different vantage point. He notes that the local expressions of myth and tradition, despite their ostensible diversity, speak to and galvanize such universal forms within the shaman's mind which he is everywhere able to employ to guide his ecstatic journeys. Consequently, these journeys share a basic common form though found in diverse cultures. "In order to bring out the universal character of the ideology implied in shamanism," Eliade informs us that while the shamans may inherit the local traditions and mythologies of their tribe or culture, it is their particular gift, enhanced by traditional and ecstatic training, to be able to fathom their true archetypal structure and function and to appropriate this pattern of experience to an inner, psychological cosmos. "They only interiorized it, 'experienced' it and used it as the itinerary for their ecstatic journeys," he tells us.[17] The symbols that for other members of the community merely carried forward an accepted traditional truth for the shaman awakened an experienced "inner" reality which assumed much the same form in shamanic traditions throughout the world. Eliade explains this important point in detail.

> In the archaic cultures communication between sky and earth is ordinarily
> used to send offerings to the celestial gods and not for a concrete and
> personal ascent; the latter remains the prerogative of shamans; ... only they
> transform a cosmo-theological concept into a *concrete mystical experience*. ...
> In other words, what for the rest of the community remains a cosmological
> ideogram, for the shamans (and the heroes, etc.) becomes a mystical
> itinerary.[18]

This "concrete mystical experience" is possible because for the shaman, as it was for Jung, the psyche, or the imaginal world, is a cosmos equal to and complementary to the physical world. It has its own features, its own terrain and laws, which can be learned and mastered with effort and ability. Again, the characteristics of this world are real and "they are real because they work." And its features are, as we shall see, quite similar to those of Jung's cosmos, for it follows the soul inward from personal consciousness back to the ancestral forms represented in the collective unconscious, and farther to the world of instinct where mind and body begin to converge and, finally, to the very formal principles of the organism and the cosmos itself. It is here in the soul's interior where man interfaces with the powers of the pleroma that the shaman is endowed with a power that he can employ to cure and revitalize. The journey is both initiatory and transformative and is based upon his own "concrete mystical experience," his ability to find beneath the outward forms of myth and traditional lore an effective mystical itinerary to an experienced reality. Thus, as Campbell observes, shamanism is the earliest example of "the serious use of myth hermetically, as *mārga*, as a way to psychological metamorphosis."[19] And, as it did in Jung's cosmos, it is the mythic symbol which reveals the structure of the shaman's cosmos and fosters the transformation of consciousness which it both reflects and effects.

In the previous chapter we examined the myth of the separation of gods and men shared by the Greek and Tamang people, and we may recall that in the Western world represented by Greek tradition in which myth has lost its potency the story perceptively envisages Primordial Mind shackled in the underworld awaiting release in a far distant future. As we noted, in contrast, in Nepal, where myth and symbol are living realities, they are employed to overcome this mythic image of man's self-division and alienation from the Divine. Here shamanic ritual creates a transpersonal space, which reaches into that deep realm Jung termed the "subtle body" in which the symbol can operate to transform both body and mind. As we shall see in this chapter, in such rituals the shaman recites the culture's primordial myths, uses techniques such as dancing and drumming known to enhance the mind's receptivity to the archetypal symbol and adroitly manipulates the dominant cultural symbols of the Tamang people to work an effective cure for his patient in ways long misunderstood and scoffed at by Western intelligence. Yet, armed with our knowledge of Jung and working toward an understanding of how shamanic cultures themselves view the mythic symbol, we shall begin to open to the Western mind these age-old practices which, though now nearly lost to us, have for millennia been an important and highly effective part of our human heritage.

"In the Symbol the *World Itself* is Speaking"

The shaman everywhere is the great master of "thinking in primordial images." Like the artistic genius in our world or the prophet of earlier times, the shaman, in Jung's terms, seems to have a direct line to the unconscious. He is able to galvanize the deep plastic powers of the archetypal imagination, Campbell's common formative force working like a magnet from behind or within, to open individual experience to its transpersonal base. In fact, for the initiated shaman, as for Jung, "in the symbol the *world itself* is speaking."

It is thus that nearly everywhere it is the shaman who keeps and passes from generation to generation the tribe's mythology and traditional lore. It is also the shaman who has the insight to explain the deeper levels of significance to be found in such material and in the dreams and visionary experiences of the members of his community. The Oglala Sioux *yuwipi* man, or shaman, refers to himself as *iyeska*, "interpreter" or "medium," because one of his chief functions is to interpret the meaning of the visions of others.[20] He is able to do so effectively because he is a "*wakan* person" – he is a medium for the primordial force, *wakan*, informing the Sioux sacred world.[21] In his interpretations and visions it is, in fact, this world force which is speaking.

The Tukano shaman of the Vaupés region of Colombia is likewise called upon to interpret and elucidate the underlying significance of the visionary experiences of his tribe which are often enhanced by hallucinogens. The mythology surrounding this function is highly informative and, like the interpretive gift itself, helps to bind together the levels of the Tukano mythic universe. For the shaman is said to partake of a "supernatural luminescence" which allows him "to interpret mythical passages, genealogical recitals, incantatory formulas, dreams or any signs and portents a person has observed. The *payé's* [shaman's] interpretations thus 'shed light' upon these matters, in the strictest sense of the expression,"[22] Gerardo Reichel-Dolmatoff informs us based on his field work with the Tukano people. In the person of the Tukano shaman the normally merely reflective mirror of the mind becomes a lamp relying upon its archetypal imaginative powers to illuminate the inner form and significance of traditional lore, myth, dream and vision. But this lamp is, in fact, a conduit or channel of illumination. The shaman's soul "illuminates" precisely because it participates in the creative power of the Sun Father, the creator and sustainer of mankind. It is directly from this cosmic formative force that the shaman receives his luminescence and interpretive ability and from which the symbolic world of myth and visionary experience receive their shape and significance.[23] Again, for the Tukano *payé*, in the symbols of myth, dream and vision "the *world itself* is speaking." It is because the shaman's soul is endowed with this cosmic formal power expressed in the archetypal symbol that he can in dream and vision travel back to its source, to the very time of the creation itself which remains an atemporal force available in vision and trance. Here he experiences an enduring realm of both essence and power which invests our world with its recurrent form, a vision quite similar to Jung's view of the "continuous creation" and its perpetual expression through the archetype. The experience of an encounter with the creationtime source reaffirms the validity of the archetypes which support communal belief and is a source of "seminal" power revitalizing the creation.

As we shall see in more detail later, the Australian Aboriginal shaman likewise travels back to the creationtime in dream and vision. The creationtime is recognized as an enduring source which provides the archetypal patterns and symbols that govern his existence. At the same time, this primordial source is a realm which is currently accessible to the shaman. It is a world which speaks in the symbols of dream, vision and myth, and, as such, it is commonly known also as "the dreamtime." The intimate relationship between this creative, archetypal substratum of the Aboriginal's existence and his myth and lore is emphasized by the fact that in the languages of the various tribes the same term generally applies equally to both realities, the dreamtime and the tribe's body of myth and traditional lore.

Indeed, we shall witness this experience of visionary access to what Jung called the pleroma – the creative source and its archetypes, recognized by him as healing, empowering and illuminative – both explicitly or by implication repeatedly in the world's shamanic traditions. It follows the same general pattern of a revitalizing "return to origins" that we traced in "Jung's Cosmos" which, as Eliade has convincingly shown, also informs much mythology. For example, the Navaho shaman symbolically returns to the Place of Emergence during his curative ceremonies. Here he is able to perceive the "inner form" of the creation, for the inner forms of all things were given to them at the time of creation and constitute their essential, paradigmatic reality. The perception of this ideal or inner form transmutes our ordinary reality into a mythic, archetypal world with its own reality. This transformation has a regenerating effect which the Navaho expresses in the phrase *sa'ah naaghái bik'eh hozhóón*, best translated as according-to-the-ideal may-restoration-be-achieved.

The Navaho shaman is a master at the effective manipulation of the mythic symbols, both verbal and visual, which were revealed at the time of the creation. Thus, the power and significance of the symbol again emanate from the world-creative source itself, and they are capable of leading back to it. To emphasize this realization, the Navaho preface their most important symbolic rites, particularly their curing ceremonies and the shaman's initiation, with a repetition of their creation myths, and the archetypal symbols employed in turn are meant to return human consciousness to its source – which is the very source of cosmic life itself. As Eliade observes:

> The ceremony also includes executing complex sand paintings, which symbolize the various stages of Creation and the mythical history of the gods, the ancestors and mankind. These drawings (which strangely resemble the Indo-Tibetan *mandala*) successively re-enact the events which took place in mythical times. As he hears the cosmogonic myth and then the origin myths recited and contemplates the sand paintings, the patient is projected out of profane time into the fullness of Primordial Time; he is carried "back" to the origin of the World and is thus present at the cosmogony.[24]

This rearticulation of personal consciousness with the creation itself, the pleroma, again envisioned as a continuous and accessible reality, is effected through the transformative power of the archetypal symbol, and it is through such symbols that health and harmony with the cosmos are to be attained.

We can see here emerging, though only tenuously at this point, structural and functional similarities in these widely separated shamanic traditions which do, in fact, begin to suggest an underlying psychic unity of mankind supportive of Jung's hypothesis. But what is perhaps more imperative at this time is to take notice of the manner in which each of these cultures portrays its own experience. And, just as Jung declared that his process of psychological transformation *must be experienced* to be effective, it is important to remember that this is a reality which is actually experienced by the shaman and is not simply credal belief, inherited tradition or dogma. It is numinous, revitalizing, illuminative experience with a felt intensity which is the oracle of its own truth. First, we may note that in each tradition it is, at least in part, the shaman's ability to "think in primordial images" which marks him for his calling and opens the inner world. Through these images the shaman masters and expresses an inner reality which these societies recognize and experience as being paradigmatic and transpersonal. It is, thus, not simply that these shamanic traditions bear striking, even at times uncanny, archetypal correspondences with one another over time and distance which lends witness to Jung's claims with regard to the underlying psychic unity of mankind. What is, perhaps, more impressive is that they recognize, revere and base their techniques and practices on the mind's innate archetypal capacity itself – its ability to participate in a durative, paradigmatic realm such as the Australian dreamtime or the time of creation among the Navaho and the Tukano. Symbols and images penetrate and express something much akin to the collective unconscious as a shared, transpersonal level of reality expressing the continuous cosmic creative process, the changeless formal principles underlying creation and informing the human mind. And it is the archetypal symbol which carries cosmic form and order into human experience.

In the shaman's cosmos, just as they do in Jung's, the archetypes bring forward to our awareness an *a priori* inner-orderedness which expresses the pattern of creation itself, "the continuous creation of a pattern that exists from all eternity," in Jung's terms. Again, creation exists as an accessible atemporal source of form and order, and to experience the archetype in its fullness is to be projected back to the creationtime itself in a now familiar configuration of experience. Here, in the dreamtime, the mind becomes one with the source of paradigmatic form; it becomes Jung's dreamer of age-old dreams which "exalted above all temporal change ... would have lived countless times over the life of the individual, the family, the tribe and the nation ..."

At this point, we might again quote Ira Progoff who, in the previous chapter, informed us that through the effect of the archetype the mind experiences a correspondence "between the microcosm and the macrocosm, for a harmony has been achieved and the individual has come into an equivalent union with the universal." In such an experience, he notes, one feels that "something of the world's divinity is being individualized." "The experience of an archetypal symbol results in a sense of relationship to the interior workings of life, a sense of participation in the movements of the cosmos. The individual at such moments feels his individuality to be exalted, as though he were transported for an instant to a higher dimension of being."

As we have mentioned, Jung learned from his clinical studies that the mind tends spontaneously to represent this experience of being transported to a higher dimension of being by symbols of verticality such as the tree, pole, ladder, mountain, etc. Quite revealingly, we also shall see precisely these same symbols recurrently in our study as characterizing the shaman's mystical experiences from all over the world. Jung found that the representations of Hermetic philosophy and alchemy epitomized this process of natural association by recurrently regarding the tree as the image of the stages of human spiritual transformation.[25] This tree, the philosopher's tree, grows by cultivating the eyes of the mind, the alchemists tell us[26] – the same "inner eye" which the shaman cultivates in his initiation. Likewise, as we briefly mentioned in the previous chapter, the psyche tends to express the experience of micro-macrocosmic harmony and correspondence in the form of the mandala symbol, an image of paramount importance in Jung's work. As we may recall, mandalas most often assume the form of a flower, cross or wheel, and display a distinct tendency toward a quaternary structure. They represent the experience of a sacred reality emanating from a central source and portray "Deity unfolding in the world, in nature and in man." On the personal level, this is precisely the experience described by Progoff that "something of the world's divinity is being individualized." As we noted, on the microcosmic level, Jung and his patients sometimes experienced and identified these images of unfolding divine power as "soul flowers."[27] Jung found that among his patients these two archetypal symbolisms, symbols of verticality and the mandala form, were intimately related and sometimes combined to suggest the unified world itself, the perception of reality's paradigmatic unfolding from a divine source as well as the correlative experience of being transported to a higher dimension of being and source of power.

In our study of shamanism we shall see repeatedly these same symbolisms imaging the same inner experiences of the shaman. The pole, ladder, mountain and particularly the tree, most often with cosmic associations – i.e., the World Tree – with an incredible frequency reaching back, I believe, to the Upper Paleolithic era, mark the shaman's ascent "to a higher dimension of being," his return to the creationtime source. Just as Jung emphasized that for the alchemist the symbolic tree grows by cultivating the eyes of the mind, so also for the shaman does it represent his increasing spiritual illumination. As one Siberian shaman informs us, "According to our belief, the soul of the shaman climbs up this tree to God when he shamanizes. For the tree grows during the rite and invisibly reaches the summit of heaven."[28] In certain traditions, such as the Buryat of Siberia or the Mapuche of Chile, the shaman will actually climb a tree or ladder to symbolize his ecstatic ascent. Eliade sees this archetypal configuration in numerous cultures as being related to a very early belief that at the beginning of time such a vertical structure connected the world of gods and men in a pre-lapsarian state of harmony which somehow became violently severed, leading to a separation of the gods and men. "From that moment on, only a few privileged personages – heroes, shamans, medicine men – have been able to ascend to heaven," he notes.[29] And, as exemplified in the above-mentioned mandala-like sand paintings of the Navaho, which quite literally represent "Deity unfolding in the world, in nature and in man," the mandala form is also recurrently encountered in shamanism (see Chapter 9). In many shamanic traditions various expressions of these two symbolisms frequently combine. In these images a mandala-like structure combines with a central tree, pole, ladder or mountain to mark the shaman's sacred cosmos, a cosmos which unites in pre-existent order and harmony individual life with the cosmic life which surrounds and informs it.

An illustrative example is the visionary worldview of the Maya. In the Maya cosmos, the true form of the creation (much akin to the Navaho ideal or "inner form") is envisioned to be in the configuration of a mandala, a quaternary structure with the World Tree standing at its center. In ritual this Tree symbolizes a return to the creationtime, for First Father created the world by raising the World Tree at its very center separating the sky from the earth. Thus, the center again represents the source from which a sacred reality unfolds into the creation. Similar trees occupy the four cardinal directions which are each marked by a deity identified with its quarter. In fact, each cardinal point is characterized by its own tree, color, god, bird and rituals, as was the tree at the center, indicating that all reality emanates in four directions from the central source. This archetypal configuration of reality, according to Linda Schele and David Freidel, "provided the fundamental grid for the Maya community and for the surface of the world."[30] It was an image of the sacred, of "Deity unfolding in the world, in nature and in man."

The Maya king, who clearly employed the symbols and techniques of the shaman, became ritually identified with this central axis of creative power and essential form in ceremonies employing techniques of ecstasy.[†] The Tree was simultaneously the vehicle of his ecstatic ascent to a higher dimension of being and a conduit of divine cosmic power which the Maya express by the term *itz*. *Itz* is the "cosmic sap of the World Tree"[31] and on the tree bloom "white flowers,"[32] a Classic Maya term which stands for the concept of the soul – a configuration of images quite reminiscent of those spontaneously experienced by Jung's patients as "soul flowers." The flower is a traditional form of the mandala symbol, and these blossoms on the branches of the World Tree represent the unfolding of the creationtime realm of power and essential form in human existence, in the microcosm. In such instances, these combined symbols of the mandala and the central axis coalesce to suggest, as they did for Jung's patients, the mind's access to a higher transpersonal realm as well as cosmic life unfolding from a divine source to inform both the world and the human mind, particularly through the vehicle of its production of the archetypal symbol.

The Huichol Indians of the Sierra Madre region of Mexico, who set out with their shaman on the peyote hunt to "find our life," – that is, cosmic life – beautifully capture in a kindred image the sense of harmony implicit in this centering of the soul in its source. The soul of the shaman among the Huichol ascends in ecstasy by virtue of a different vehicle of ascent, the peyote. The ritual song of the shaman and the initiates who have followed his soul's journey well expresses the intensely experienced reality of divine meaning and power unfolding in the world, in nature and in man. For we are all, they tell us, the children of

A brilliantly colored flower,
A flaming flower.
And there is no one,
There is no one,
Who regrets what we are.[33]

It is this flower, the peyote flower, which naturally becomes the image for the pilgrims' experience of the cosmic life informing and giving transpersonal meaning to the creation. As the plant produces its flower, so the psyche creates its symbols from this very source. And again in such symbols "the *world itself* is speaking" and the mind becomes an expression of cosmic life and meaning.

[†] In Maya iconography, the king is recurrently depicted in the form of the World Tree itself. In an interesting archetypal parallel, Mercurius, as the principle of transformation and spiritual growth in alchemy, is frequently envisioned as the philosopher's tree (see *Psychology and Alchemy*, Figs. 214, 231, 252).

The Science of the Soul

It was Jung's challenge to retrieve and revitalize the sick souls of his contemporary patients and to reconnect them with their universal foundation, and in his efforts to do so he gradually unearthed the lineaments of an ancient wisdom reaching back far into history and, simultaneously, deep into the psychophysiological continuum from which consciousness evolves. According to him, neurosis was self-division and the severing of the psyche's essential contact with its own deep structures. "From this universal foundation no human soul is cut off; only the individual consciousness that has lost its connection with the psychic totality remains caught in the illusion that the soul is a small circumscribed area, a fit subject for 'scientific' theorizing," he informed us. "The loss of this great relationship is the prime evil of neurosis."[34] Psychotherapy's proper task was to deal with "the perils of the soul and its salvation," and he frequently spoke of contemporary mental illness as a "loss of soul" which only the arduous process of psychic integration could repair. "For thousands of years the mind of man has worried about the sick soul, perhaps even earlier than it did about the sick body," he observed.[35]

For Jung, psychology was still the science of the soul, and the very same can be said for the art of the shaman. "This small mystical elite," Eliade emphasizes, "not only directs the community's religious life but, as it were, guards its 'soul.' The shaman is the great specialist in the human soul; he alone 'sees' it, for he knows its 'form' and its destiny."[36] The shaman is a master of ecstasy, and during his trance experiences his own soul is released from his body to find its way into the underworld or to ascend to the heavens. In so doing, it traverses an inwardly revealed but at the same time very real transpersonal realm with its own features, perils and laws which the shaman is able to master. This is *terra incognita* and yet, at the same time, the strangely familiar world revealed in dream and vision, and it is the shaman's gift, reinforced by training and discipline, that he can chart this territory and bring back its riches to his community, integrating them with its conscious life as expressed in myth and traditional lore. "Shamans and medicine men are men who remember their ecstatic experiences," Eliade observes, an ability which results in the deepening of all the psychomental faculties. "The shaman stands out by the fact that he has succeeded in integrating into consciousness a considerable number of experiences that, for the profane world, are reserved for dreams, madness or post-mortem states."[37] Yet these experiences can be retrieved because, as Jung also came to realize, the journey is not, strictly speaking, one of discovery but of rediscovery. It is an "unforgetting," a recovery or anamnesis, of structures innate to the human psyche, connecting it with what Jung described as the unconscious unitary soul of mankind which silently structures the most significant levels of human reality and stamps our deepest personal experience with the forms of the transpersonal.

In many shamanic traditions throughout the world, one of the most common, and frequently the most common, diagnosis of illness is a loss of the soul. "The principal function of the shaman in Central and North Asia is magical healing," Eliade notes with regard to an area of the world with a strong and relatively well-studied shamanism. "Several conceptions of the cause of illness are found in the area, but that of the 'rape of the soul' is by far the most widespread. Disease is attributed to the soul's having strayed away or been stolen, and treatment is in principle reduced to finding it, capturing it and obliging it to resume its place in the patient's body."[38] It is only the shaman who can find the alienated soul and restore it to its rightful place.

The shaman both "guards" the soul of the community and retrieves it when it becomes lost to man in this world. As we have seen, the shaman guards the soul and helps prevent its alienation by being the keeper of the myths, symbols, rituals and objects of art of his people which secure the soul by connecting it with its deeper sources. And he can retrieve the lost soul because, as Eliade notes, "through his own preinitiatory and initiatory experiences he knows the drama of the human soul, its instability, its precariousness ..."[39] As we shall trace as we proceed, these experiences lead the shaman through an initiatory crisis of psychic disintegration, a return to origin, both within the psyche and the cosmos, and a renewal with enhanced power. The shaman's initiatory experience is a process of both psychic and cosmic integration which very clearly parallels the structural and functional stages of Jung's individuation process. It involves the very same encounter with the collective unconscious, the realm of instinct and ordered organic process and, ultimately, with nature and cosmos which we explored in the previous chapter. Thus, the flight of the soul has both a psychic and cosmic aspect for the shaman because in his visionary world the two are inseparable and psyche is experienced as opening into cosmos.

As it was for Plato, the soul is the "linchpin" of the cosmos for the shaman. It connects the psyche with its own vital roots in the greater source of power which creates and sustains it. It was this relationship which engendered the soul's "luminescence" in the Tukano shaman that he derived directly from the Sun Father. The shaman's initiatory experiences and the ceremonies of soul retrieval that he performs for his patient operate to effect a transformation of consciousness meant to recover the universal foundation of the soul by opening it through the vehicle of the symbol to the creative source itself. As Jung recognized, it is the archetypal symbol which brings the energy and therapeutic effect of this revitalizing reality forward into human consciousness. In myth and ritual, as we have seen, this is experienced and expressed as a return to the very fountainhead of perfection and plenitude, the creationtime itself. As Eliade notes with regard to the healing ceremonies of the shaman and his patient, "Made symbolically contemporary with the Creation of the World, the patient is immersed in the primordial fullness of life; he is penetrated by the gigantic forces that ... made the Creation possible."[40] Indeed, in such traditions, for any creative effort to be effective, it must be an extension of the creative act par excellence, the cosmogony itself. Therefore, according to him, the very ritual or chant to be employed in any effort to cure the patient must itself be traced to its own origin as an integral part of the cosmogonic myth.[41] It is only in this manner that the medical ritual is invested with power, a power capable of re-creating life.

> Now, all the medical rituals we have been examining aim at a return to origins. We get the impression that for archaic societies life cannot be *repaired*, it can only be *re-created* by a return to sources. And the "source of sources" is the prodigious outpouring of energy, life, and fecundity that occurred at the Creation of the World.[42]

We can tie together many of the observations which we have made in this chapter and chart our way forward by returning to and closely examining the ritual performance, symbolism and techniques employed by the Tamang shamans of Nepal in their soul retrieval ceremonies.[43] Larry G. Peters informs us that during his work with the Tamang he had the opportunity to observe numerous shamanic healing *puja* (rituals), performed by Bhirendra, his key informant, and his disciples. Here they would play the drum, sing the sacred stories and enter into ecstasy, dispatching their souls from their bodies. In a particular ritual, the *karga puja*, which he examines in detail, the woman who sought to be cured was diagnosed as suffering from a theft of the soul and spirit possession, which Peters associates with a state of psychological dissociation that manifested itself during the ritual.[44]

The initial phases of the ceremony begin with Bhirendra and his disciples drumming and singing some of the most important of the *sherab*. These are songs that relate the cosmogony, anthropogeny and the now familiar myth of the separation of men and gods. Importantly, the story which relates the separation of men and gods gives a structure that sets forth the rules for the successful performance of the *karga puja*.[45] As we recall, the story relates how in primordial times gods and men lived together like men do today who exchange women with members of exogamous clans. Having given Primordial Man a goddess to wed, the gods assigned him the task of gathering together certain ritual objects, including a deer's leg. However, the man, angered at having to share the deer's leg with the gods, threw it at his goddess-wife, breaking her leg. The gods took back their daughter, broke off relations with men and set up curtain-like gates of various materials, which even today act as barriers between heaven and earth.

In the next two stages of the ritual, offerings are made and *mantras* repeated to the planet gods and to the *nag* or serpent spirits. However, these are not mere supplications to heaven and earth but "acts of manipulation." "Once the *mantra* is said, the spirits are under control."[46] Next, Bhirendra's most advanced pupil begins to play his drum loudly and rapidly in a manner quite different, Peters notes, from that earlier employed during the *sherab* recitations of the sacred songs. Now shaking rapidly and staring into space, he eventually falls into a state in which he is possessed by his tutelary deity, his spirit guide. The spirit guide is able to inform the disciple that the patient's soul has been stolen by a sprite. The disciple recommences his drumming and begins to shake again. Suddenly Kumari, the patient, also begins to shake violently and lets out a blood-chilling scream. This is a manifestation of her possession or dissociation, and speaking in a voice not her own she challenges the shaman, profanes the sacred ritual area and attempts to destroy the images of the gods.[47] Once the possessing spirit has manifested and identified itself, Bhirendra and his disciple are able to exorcize it from Kumari's body and to set about the most important task, the retrieval of her own soul, on one level indicative of the psychic integration which will subsume the state of dissociation and possession.

In the soul retrieval portion of the ceremony the symbolism becomes quite interesting, and it continues and completes the themes announced at the ritual's inception. Bhirendra draws a sacrificial effigy (luey) on the ground and "a tall (perhaps five-foot [1.5 m]) banana tree was nailed into the mud floor at the luey's head." He begins to dance and beat the drum. While dancing, Bhirendra calls upon his helping spirits to protect him. Then he "opened the gates" and sent his soul from his body to rescue the patient from Yama Lok (World of Death). Peters calls our attention to the fact that these gates are the same barriers the gods used to separate themselves from man. "The breach in relations between men and gods is bridged during the 'magical flight' of the shaman's soul," he notes.[48]

Bhirendra calls for the assistance of his spirit guide, increases the tempo of drum and dance and lapses into a state of possession and trance, falling to the ground and lying there immobile. During this period, his soul departs from his body and ascends the banana tree to retrieve the patient's lost soul. Bhirendra rescues the lost soul from Yama Lok, substitutes the effigy for it to appease the spirits of the World of Death and returns the soul to the ailing patient. "The returning of the soul is symbolized by placing a white flower (narling mendo), also known as bhla mendo, or soul flower, upon the patient's head as blessing (tika)."[49] The soul is now retrieved and the patient's health ostensibly restored.

All this, indeed, seems strange judged by the canons of modern medicine. Yet based on what we have explored so far, we can begin to fathom this age-old ritual addressed to the soul. For, as we know, the soul speaks of itself in primordial images, and here we again find that ancient symbolic language in which the psyche speaks and in so doing restores the integrity of both body and mind. We recall that Jung informed us that the unconscious can only be reached by symbols which are images cast up by the psyche of a content that largely transcends consciousness. They represent an attempt to elucidate something that still lies hidden or something that has yet to be. As we said earlier, such symbols are auguries of what the psyche *must* express or experience and provide the directive signs we need in order to carry on our lives in harmony with ourselves. As such, as Jung has told us, "the archetype is an element of our psychic structure and thus a vital and necessary component in our psychic economy." It casts a bridge between the conscious mind and the transpersonal psyche — the natural, unconscious instinctive wholeness deep within each of us. The symbol, thus, leads us into the soul's depths.

We also recall that, as we have examined in the previous chapter, for Jung this process of recovering the soul's integrity, the rapprochement between human consciousness and the revitalizing preconscious levels which create and animate it, was experienced as a return to origin, to the plane of the continuous creation, on both a microcosmic and macrocosmic level. We noticed that this was likewise mirrored in the shaman's cosmos, and we traced this symbolism among the Tukano of South America, the North American Navaho, the Australian Aborigines and other shamanic societies. The practices of these cultures elucidated and verified Eliade's general observation that medical rituals in shamanic cultures "aim at a return to origins, ... [for] life cannot be *repaired*, it can only be *re-created* by a return to sources. And the 'source of sources' is the prodigious outpouring of energy, life, and fecundity that occurred at the Creation of the World." For any reality to be effective, including the curative ritual itself, it must continue the paramount creative act, i.e., the cosmogony.

Now we have re-established touchstones sufficient to help us understand the Tamang ritual, for it began with the cosmogony and continued tracing the creative process through the anthropogeny and the sacred history of the people. This included the story of the separation of gods and men which outlines the rules for the performance of the *karga puja*; i.e., the curing ritual that we have been describing. At this point several archetypes become apparent. Not only is the primal world-creative act the necessary foundation of all creation, including the ritual itself, but also the myth recalls the paradisiacal era of unified existence which Eliade sees lying behind much shamanic ideology, where mankind was once united with the gods. Here, through an act of foolish self-assertion, humanity ruptured its relationship with the plenitude of the original creation resulting in the fragmentation symbolized in this context by the erecting of curtain-like gates of various materials which acted as a barrier between Heaven and Earth, between the Source and the creation. Humankind consequently suffers a cosmic dissociation on a macrocosmic plane which mirrors the patient's own dissociation on the microcosmic level. Yet the ritual is cosmically sanctified to heal the rift and, in Jung's terms, "for those who have the symbol the passage is easy."[50] As we shall see, the psychic cosmos which the shaman traverses is not random and chaotic but one with its own laws – laws which, at least in part, are expected to respond to the symbols and techniques manipulated by the shaman. It is thus that in the early parts of the ceremony he does not supplicate but commands the spirits.

The use of drum, dance and other enticements to summon the tutelary spirit is important in Tamang shamanism for, as Peters has well-illustrated elsewhere, the Tamang shaman's initiation is one which evolves from an uncontrolled possession by the spirits to one in which he is gradually able to gain control of and to possess the powers which initially possessed him.[51] The shaman, who traditionally mediates between this world and the next, can gain such control because these spiritual entities, like those of the middle or daemonic world elsewhere, are denizens of a transpersonal world which at the same time and without contradiction constitutes, as it does in Jung's work, the deep levels of the individual mind that connect it back to cosmos. We shall examine this experience in more detail in the next two chapters, but what is important here is that it is the shaman's ability to possess the powers of possession which allows the disciple in this ritual to exorcize the possessing spirit and to overcome the state of psychic dissociation suffered by the patient. For the patient's state of dissociation reflects the dissociation between men and gods, earth and heaven, the conscious mind and the preconscious psyche, and the shaman is the great mediator transcending dissociations on each of these levels.

With regard to this patient, this process of integration is one which will become familiar. It involves the ritual lowering of the threshold of consciousness through drum beat and other techniques. This provokes an unleashing of the repressed or blocked forces of the unconscious such as occurred when Kumari spoke in another voice and lost her conscious control, precipitating a crisis state. Yet, as Jung knew and Peters notes, crisis as a psychological experience has its own value, and in shamanism crisis frequently is the preamble to cure in patterns we shall experience repeatedly. Peters sees this process partly as a salutary catharsis of repressed unconscious contents and, perhaps more importantly, as a restructuring or resynthesis of the patient's personality which the crisis experience is known to help effect. He further notes that at this stage the mind is particularly susceptible to suggestion. "Things learned in this state are believed with such conviction that they are analogous to conversion experiences."[52] It is in this state of increased susceptibility that the most important cultural symbols are marshaled and adeptly employed to restore the patient's soul and to heal the rift between the conscious mind and the preconscious, between fallen humanity and the gods. For the crisis of the alienated patient and the crisis of fallen humanity will be overcome by a familiar pattern of symbolism. In fact, the symbols are precisely those which Jung found in his contemporary patients fostering and reflecting the healing state of deep psychic integration and wholeness. One aspect of this pattern of symbolism is that of the vertical axis which once united heaven and earth and which, as we know, symbolizes access to a higher dimension of being. As we have mentioned, we shall find this same axis worldwide in the symbol of the tree, ladder, ritual pole or cosmic mountain. In the ecstasy of magical flight, Bhirendra ascends this axis in the form of the ritual banana tree which he has constructed. This is a symbolism which, as Peters recognizes, repeats the well-known archetype.

> The banana tree conforms to the symbolism of the *axis mundi* described by Eliade. He mentions that, in cultures the world over where shamanism is practiced, there is the concept of a central axis (sometimes conceived to be a pole, ladder, bridge, and often a tree) that connects the various levels of the universe, and that traversing of these levels is made possible because they are linked together by this axis.[53]

Moreover, the symbolism follows the larger pattern of a return to origin symbolic of healing and renewal as well as that of a return to the pre-lapsarian condition of unity with the source. The shaman's soul ascends through the very gates which were the barriers the gods used to separate themselves from men. As Peters noted, "the breach in relations between men and gods is bridged during the 'magical flight' of the shaman's soul." And in a now familiar symbolism, which Jung discovered in the spontaneous images of his patients and which we saw half a world away from Nepal disinterred with the long-lost knowledge of the Classic Maya, the unified soul, successfully returned to the patient, is symbolized by a white "soul flower." The flower itself is an archetypal form of the mandala symbol – of the power of the divine unfolding in the world, in nature and in man. Correspondingly, the white soul flower in Tamang thought is associated with a level of consciousness informed by *shakti*.[54] *Shakti* is the "power" which the shaman harnesses. It is the power which animates the cosmos, and it is capable of revitalizing the ailing patient. True to its archetypal form, the mandala symbol heralds the patient's psychic integration – the recovery of her connection with the deep layers of the psyche and the creative sources which inform them.

Peters continues his discussion of the Tamang ritual by examining the techniques used by the shaman and aptly comparing them with Western psychotherapy in order to account for their effectiveness. In so doing, he enlists some perceptive observations by Lévi-Strauss. He notes that, according to Lévi-Strauss, shamans, like psychotherapists, provide a language by which the inexpressible can find expression and further the healing process. Emphasizing the psychotherapeutic effectiveness of symbolic communication, especially when dominant cultural symbols are manipulated during the collapse phase in which the psyche of the patient is particularly impressionable, he calls attention to Lévi-Strauss' contention that symbols and symbolic gestures have the capacity to reach to the patient's complexes in cases where the spoken word would be intercepted by the patient's defenses, a position which is quite similar to Jung's.[55] He notes the many cultural associations which have become attached to a symbol such as the white soul flower and its ritual employment, and concludes that, because of the cultural importance attributed to such symbols and the complex web of associations they entail, their employment can be extremely effective. They are capable of simultaneously representing under a single form the norms and values of a culture. Victor Turner, he notes, calls such symbols "dominant symbols." Their function is to transform "the obligatory into the desirable." "Because dominant symbols are cultural symbols, the people are," according to Turner, "preconscious of them, that is, they are available to consciousness although the individual is only marginally aware of them."[56]

This analysis is very incisive and is representative of a high level of awareness with regard to the therapeutic value of the symbol particularly when embedded in a ritual matrix. It is analogous to Jung's observations concerning the numinosity of the symbol, its capacity to transform psychic energy, its ability to bypass the rational consciousness and reach and express the unconscious and its overall psychotherapeutic effect. And, as we shall see, as part of this psychotherapeutic effect Jung also recognized and himself experienced the crucial role of crisis in leading to cure. However, keeping Jung's work in mind, we might attempt to penetrate a step deeper and ask why is it that these particular symbols have become dominant cultural symbols? What impelled these specific configurations to their culturally important roles? And remembering the ground which we have previously covered in this chapter, we might ask why so many of these dominant cultural symbols in remote Nepal are the same as those which exist in so many other shamanic traditions. For the central characteristics of this ritual are familiar and resonate with distinct similarities to diverse aspects of shamanism which we have examined or shall soon review. We can briefly list many of these elements: the symbolic framing of the entire procedure in creationtime power and plenitude; the tracing of the form and origin of the healing ritual itself back to the cosmogony and anthropogeny; the recollection of the pre-lapsarian unity of gods and men which the shaman at least temporarily accesses and restores; the breach of this unity by a human transgression at time's beginning; the concepts of soul flight and spirit possession; the manifestation of the spirit guide; the overall configuration of Kumari's experience as a descent into the chaos of her mental crisis and her subsequent rebirth on a consecrated level; the ritual effigy associated with the tree; the world of the dead or ancestors to which the soul retreats; the vertical *axis mundi* of ascent to a higher dimension of being represented by a tree; the visionary climbing of this tree by the shaman to reconnect the fallen world with the original pleroma; the symbol of the "gates" the shaman must penetrate on his journey; the overall configuration of a return to origin; the access to cosmic power or *shaki*; and the white soul flower or mandala form representing the all-suffusing immanence of this power to which the ritual opens human experience – these are all now or will soon become familiar symbols and archetypes found almost everywhere in shamanism. And we may note that they are not only structurally the same in the various cultures, but also that they are used to elicit functionally similar therapeutic effects. Certainly they are dominant cultural symbols fostered in the minds of the Tamang since birth to the point that they have a deeply ingrained or, in Turner's terms, preconscious availability. But given their structural and functional similarities across time and distance, we must ask whether they do not have a deeper preconscious availability as virtual images in which the human mind is predisposed to organize its most significant psychic experience. This is, of course, precisely Jung's argument based upon his finding the very same symbols and archetypal configurations performing similar structural and functional roles in his contemporary patients.

The Power of the Symbol

"The psyche consists essentially of images," Jung has told us. "It is a series of images in the truest sense, not an accidental juxtaposition or sequence, but a structure that is throughout full of meaning and purpose; it is a picturing of vital activities." The symbols and patterns of symbolism composing this level of the psyche's activity, Jung recognized, express an inner dimension of the psyche, durative, paradigmatic and transpersonal. When the shaman in dream, vision or ritual ecstasy purports to travel to this realm, this is not merely figurative or metaphorical. He actually experiences this archetypal world and its effectiveness; he traverses it, masters its perils and powers and returns a man of power. And the features of this imaginal realm are experienced to be much the same everywhere. They can be reproduced in ritual or they can "materialize" spontaneously in dream, vision and ecstasy – an involuntary statement of the human mind reflective of its inner template of formal powers. Eliade refers to this realm as a "mythical" or "mystical geography,"[57] Johannes Wilbert as a "cosmic landscape" which appears in trance[58] and Jean Houston as a "geopsychic realm perceived in a state of altered consciousness." Houston describes it as a *mundus imaginalis*, an intermediate realm that is experienced to be "as ontologically real as the sensory empirical world" and compares it with Jung's similar visionary world.

> ... this world can be experienced only by those who, like the shamans, exercise their psychospiritual senses, and through this special form of imaginal knowing gain access to a visionary world that is not unlike the *mundus archetypus* of Carl Jung. There, shamans, dreamers and visionaries return again and again, ... a place where the self moves freely amid archetypes and universals, listening to the pulse and dynamic transforming patterns of the Universal Dance.[59]

It was a similar recognition which provoked Jung to exclaim, "I can only gaze with wonder and awe at the depths and heights of our psychic nature. Its non-spatial universe conceals an untold abundance of images which have accumulated over millions of years of living development and become fixed in the organism." And, importantly, he goes on to note, "these images are not pale shadows, but tremendously powerful psychic factors."

As "a structure that is throughout full of meaning and purpose," the psyche has its own innate creative autonomy; an autonomy anterior to our conscious purposes. This autonomous activity, often operating in a manner compensatory to conscious attitudes, is capable of integrating various levels of the psyche. It manifests itself as a natural psychodynamic pattern of transformation capable of revealing the true depth of the human soul which, as we saw in the previous chapter, reaches far into the human past and enlists the images of the collective unconscious. These images carry a natural capacity to penetrate the deep roots of the psyche and even to reach into the world of instinct, the psychoid realm where psyche once again touches and awakens the natural wisdom of the body and of nature, and finally the revitalizing experience of the pleroma or continuous creation itself. This is a world experienced as a source of power on the one hand and of patterns of recurrent and essential form immune to time and change on the other.

As "a picturing of vital activities" the psyche seems to catch a glimpse of itself in transformation and bodies forth this process in a series of images which, with time, practice and a knowledge of traditional imagery, we can begin to understand and manipulate. Because these images frequently picture the very process of transformation taking place in the psyche which produced them, they are sometimes referred to as autosymbolic. They mark the stages of the psychodynamic process and reflect its inner laws, its recurrent purpose and direction. And, as Donald Sandner notes:

> Yet symbols do more than that. They may not only provide a vocabulary and
> an explanation, but also change the psyche by converting energy into a
> different form, a form that can heal. As Jung said: "The symbols act as
> transformers, their function being to convert libido from a 'lower' into a 'higher'
> form. This function is so important that feeling accords it the highest value."[60]

The symbols, thus, potentially both reflect and effect a healing transformation of consciousness. They express the unconscious, and they in turn can effect further transformation on the conscious level for the psyche which produced them and for other minds to which they are exposed.

Now we may, perhaps, gain further insight into the shaman's ritual manipulation of archetypal symbols in the *karga puja*. In Chapter 2 we saw how the psychotherapist and his patient can mutually constellate aspects of the unconscious in a shared imaginal space. The doctor works to free psychic energies from the personal level and to enlist them on an archetypal, transpersonal plane to create an interactive field projected, imaginally perceived, and experienced between two or more people. The transition to this shared transpersonal plane of experience is often effected through the use of mythological, archetypal symbols. In the process, the parties experience that deepening of consciousness and rapprochement with the natural wisdom of the instincts and the somatic system we discussed as constituting Jung's integrated psychic cosmos. This is the realm of the "subtle body," prior to any division between mind and matter, a body that is at the same time spirit. It is that aspect of the unconscious which is experienced as we lower the threshold of consciousness and "descend into the body." And, according to Jung, this is also the realm where the symbol best operates, for "the place or the medium of realization is neither mind nor matter, but that intermediate realm of subtle reality which can only be adequately expressed by the symbol. The symbol is neither abstract nor concrete, neither rational nor irrational, neither real nor unreal. It is always both ..."[61] It is here, where mind and body are very closely allied or perhaps merge on the acausal, synchronistic level, that healing can occur.

On this plane, doctor and patient move in a shared transpersonal realm which exists outside traditional notions of time, space and causality. "Patient and therapist are *in the* psyche as much as it is inside of them," Schwartz-Salant explained. This is a field in which the archetype now moves, and it carries a strongly attractive power, an impelling fascination and transformative force. It is at this deep level that innate and powerful forces of psychodynamic change can be unleashed and guided through archetypal symbols of transformation for, as he told us, "the energies and structures of the archetypes have a powerful renewing potential and ... to imaginatively energize these 'gods' and 'goddesses' opens up healing paths that would rarely become traveled."

Schwartz-Salant also pointed out that "healing depends on a person's ability to link to the larger world of the pleroma," the collective unconscious as its archetypes open to their source in the unfolding reality of the continuous creation. Following a pattern which is now familiar, it is the lowering of the threshold of consciousness and the descent into the unconscious which opens the mind to what it experiences as the healing power of the Source itself. "The descent into the depths always seems to precede the ascent,"[62] Jung informs us in recognition of an important archetypal pattern, and it is the engaging of this deep level of the psyche that paradoxically opens us to the pleroma, the plenitude of the Source as it informs and sustains creation. The archetype, thus, canalizes psychic energy to integrate the conscious mind, the unconscious and the cosmic life which informs them. This is a form of soul retrieval, for the dissociation of these levels is an enervating loss of soul, and it is this integrative field which reawakens the connective faculty Jung recognized to be the human soul.

Returning to the karga puja, we are now able to recognize a ritual symbolic world which everywhere potentially opens through the archetype to the healing plenitude of the cosmic creation. Its initial stages set the scene by reciting the cosmogony and anthropogeny, thus grounding the ritual itself in this creative force. Dance, drum, chant, the ritual surroundings and the adroit manipulation of archetypal symbols lower the threshold of consciousness and move psychic energies from a personal to a shared, transpersonal plane. It is at this level that the symbol can do its work reaching into the "subtle body" where healing can occur. Here, shaman, patient and other participants move in a ritual matrix, a world which constellates the unconscious into an interactive field that facilitates and guides the projection and imaginal perception unleashed during this process. At this stage we might again say that the shaman and patient "are in the psyche as much as it is inside of them." As ritual space, this world exists beyond traditional notions of time, space and causality. It is one governed by archetypal patterns of transpersonal experience which open to their timeless acausal source. And in archaic societies the archetype moves in this ritual space with an effectiveness, impelling force and transformative power which may be lost to the modern mind. For traditional peoples, the innate archetypal patterns which are activated in this ritual space are cultivated since birth and psychic energy trained in their directions. As such, this interactive field is highly charged and potentially more effective in canalizing psychic energy than that constellated between psychotherapist and patient today. An entire tradition forms its background and support. Moreover, the ritual atmosphere of drum, chant, costume and other traditional aids and symbols everywhere reinforces this reality and its effect. Each of these factors combines to form a synergy, adding impetus to the reintegrating psychic function natural to the archetypal level of experience and working to overcome Kumari's dissociation and the dissociation between gods and men described in the anthropogeny.

The descent into the unconscious, archetypal level, which culminates in the shaman's deep trance state, again symbolically opens through archetypal symbols into the pleroma. "The descent into the depths always seems to precede the ascent," and it is in the depths of trance that the shaman ascends the now familiar tree symbolic of the *axis mundi* which, as we shall see, is traditionally envisioned as uniting the three worlds, the lower, the middle and the higher. As Peters noted, based on Eliade, "traversing of these levels is made possible because they are linked together by this axis." In one aspect of its meaning, this connecting axis marks the link between the conscious mind (the middle, everyday world), the unconscious (the lower) and the pleroma (the higher world), for the shaman descends from consciousness into the unconscious in trance, and then, in the trance state, he ascends to the source, the world of the gods, re-establishing the pre-lapsarian unity which served initially as the background for the entire ritual.

We can now recall Eliade's observation that "... all the medical rituals we have been examining aim at a return to origins. We get the impression that for archaic societies life cannot be *repaired*, it can only be *re-created* by a return to sources. And the 'source of sources' is the prodigious outpouring of energy, life and fecundity that occurred at the Creation of the World." Or, returning to the world of the psychotherapist, we may likewise recall Schwartz-Salant's assertion that "Jung correctly emphasizes that healing depends on a person's ability to link to the larger world of the pleroma." For this is precisely what occurs symbolically in this ritual by virtue of the archetype which both unites the conscious mind with its roots and, simultaneously, brings forward the experience of the healing plenitude of the Source into human consciousness. The healing of the dissociation between these levels of consciousness symbolized in the connecting link of the *axis mundi* is equivalent to restoring the connective faculty of the human soul. It is, as the ritual recognizes, a soul recovery. The soul, now linked through the archetypal symbol to the plenitude of the unfolding reality of the pleroma, is now aptly symbolized by the soul flower which archetypally grows on the World Tree. The flower image, as we have said, is a traditional form of the mandala, of the manifestation of the macrocosm in the microcosm, with its attendant experience that "a harmony has been achieved and the individual has come into an equivalent union with the universal." Together, the central tree and the flower image again suggest the mind's access to a higher dimension of being and power as well as power's unfolding from a divine source to inform both world and mind. These symbols carry forward the healing force of psychic integration with sacred cosmic life, induced by the ceremony and the symbols and techniques it employs to unleash innate psychodynamic forces which again have the potential to awaken us to the archetypal realization that we are all the children of

A brilliantly colored flower,
A flaming flower.
And there is no one,
There is no one,
Who regrets what we are.

Chapter 4

The Psyche's "Strange Symbolic Wanderings" –

Jung's Individuation Process

The conscious mind will enjoy no peace until it can rejoice in a fuller understanding of its own unconscious sources.
Lancelot Law Whyte

Two Types of Thinking

Plato recognized that the "tendance of the soul" was philosophy's primordial calling. This process involved leading the soul back to its vitalizing creative sources from which it too easily became estranged in a world whose chief concerns made men more like cattle that, head lowered and vision trained to the ground, were largely content "to feed, fatten and fornicate." Jung found a similar concern with the soul to be psychology's chief calling, a recovery of the soul's universal foundation and the expansion of human consciousness which this implied. His psychic cosmos reconnected man with modes of symbolic expression and psychological transformation employed by men in the past and in many non-Western cultures. It re-established the vital relationship between the conscious mind and its instinctual roots and reached back farther to the natural principles of form and order which govern and coordinate organic growth and also guide the development of man, both in body and mind. Whereas Freud had asked "What is the origin and nature of psychic conflict?," Jung tried to pierce beyond this level to discern a deeper source of psychic, organic and even cosmic coordination, harmony and universality to which the soul was naturally heir.[1] And he found that the vehicle which both expressed and led us back to this sacred source was the archetypal symbol. In such symbols "the *world itself* is speaking" – the human past, nature and cosmos rise to meaningful form in these universal images cast up from the mind's depths. It is by virtue of such timeless images that man, if he is capable of claiming his inheritance, is not simply empirical man – time-ridden and transient – but transcendental man as well, sharing in the universal, transpersonal and eternal.

The tendency to produce symbols or, as Jung also referred to this process, to think in primordial images is rooted deeply in the human past and for thousands of years revealed to humankind its relationship with a sacred cosmos. It still survives, often in a severely diminished form, in contemporary art and religion, and reasserts itself each time our head hits the pillow or even as we drift into revery in moments of relaxed concentration. However, though thinking in such images is innate and apparently to some degree will always be with us, Jung recognized contrary structures of consciousness which tended to repress or exclude the recognition and acceptance of this early mode of human expression. These structures centered around a very different orientation to "the real" which he found characterized by, and to a surprisingly large extent actually created by, what he referred to as "directed thinking." Whereas thinking in primordial images enlists the resources of the preconscious mind, directed thinking seems to be more closely allied to the ego and to concentrated, intentional thought. At least the ego tends to regard such thinking as its ally or instrument, though often deeper motive forces are, in fact, at work. According to Jung, the unconscious is indifferent to the purpose and direction which characterize the ego. It shares in the impersonal objectivity of nature. On the other hand, the ego is generally concerned with our personal adjustment to the environment. Directed thinking, therefore, has been a key to man's evolutionary adaptation and development. "The process of adaptation requires a directed conscious function characterized by inner consistency and logical coherence," Jung informs us. "Because it is directed, everything unsuitable must be excluded in order to maintain the integrity of direction. The unsuitable elements are subjected to inhibition and thereby escape attention."[2]

Many sources of potential input and distraction, both "inner" and "outer," are excluded from this concentrated focus to maintain its steady direction. However, for our purposes, the most important victims of such exclusion have been the productions of the unconscious mind. To a degree this was a necessary sacrifice to the success of the human endeavor, as Jung readily recognizes. "The resistance of the conscious mind to the unconscious and the depreciation of the latter were historical necessities in the development of the human psyche, for otherwise the conscious mind would never have been able to differentiate itself at all."[3] Directed thinking has been a tremendously effective instrument of culture which "has produced a readjustment of the human mind to which we owe our modern empiricism and technics."[4] "But," Jung adds, "modern man's consciousness has strayed rather too far from the fact of the unconscious."[5] We might say that, as the conscious mind seized more and more of the light, the unconscious grew correspondingly darker and the seeds of a dangerous division in the mind of man were sown at the expense of its connecting faculty, the human soul.

Directed thinking has certain typical characteristics, according to Jung. It expresses itself more or less in verbal form. It is generally directed outwards, toward the outside world, and thus becomes a thinking that is adapted to external reality. It tends to imitate the successiveness of events taking place in the objective world so that the images produced inside our minds repeat the same strictly causal sequence appearing in the events taking place externally. And finally, it has the tendency to cause mental fatigue.[6] The effort involved in directed thinking has yielded very substantial benefits to mankind, and no one should be foolish enough to discard it as an instrument of continued success. Yet, like anything substantial, directed thinking brings a darkness in its wake. What begins as a tool of thought becomes its template; that which we directed subtly begins to direct us. Man becomes immersed in a structure of consciousness which progressively draws him away from the central moorings of the soul in a process that Jung found repeatedly in his clinical observations. The strictly outward orientation assumed by this mode of thought, he realized, naively overlooks the fundamental difficulty that "the real vehicle and begetter of all knowledge is the *psyche*."[7]

As thinking becomes adapted to external "reality," we tend to forget that the mind inevitably plays a central formative role in all that we experience. As such, thinking now assumes exclusively dualistic and causal patterns of representation. When our thought strictly imitates the world presented to us by the senses, the forms of experience which for ages unlocked the world of the spirit are forgotten. In a world characterized by objects, we have the tendency, as the poet Blake noted, to become what we behold; that is, to regard ourselves as just another object in a world of objects. And, forgetting that "All deities reside in the human breast," the same dualistic thinking projects God into the distant heavens. Moreover, from the standpoint of psychology, viewing mind in imitation of the movements of matter distorts our interpretation of psychic processes in a causalistic and often reductionist fashion. While through our intense concentration on this realm of objects we gain the ability to manipulate the fixed and inert counters of a material reality, the mind loses the essential understanding that it is instrumental in creating structures of consciousness capable of a more creative and fulfilling relationship with the world. The soul with its innate formal powers is by nature self-determining and active in the formation of our reality. Its passive receptivity and reactive role in a purely material world of colliding objects is moral lethargy and an abdication of its role as creator.

The structure of consciousness which Jung associated with directed thinking tends to operate upon the principle of divide and conquer. In addition, the divisions upon which it trains its concentration tend to be those that most disturb the harmonious soul. As Lancelot Law Whyte points out, modern human consciousness tends to neglect or take for granted what he refers to as "perfectly ordered processes" and stresses the disorders, conflicts, disharmonies and inadequacies with which we all must cope.[8] Yet history has left us ample evidence that great civilizations, which were less in the control of directed thinking than is ours, employed and revered as central points of cultural reference concepts denoting a universal ordered process uniting man, nature and cosmos. Such terms as *rta, dharma, tao, me, maat* and many others guided the thought and behavior of Indian, Chinese, Sumerian, Egyptian and other civilizations, and served to anchor our human existence in a larger order. We shall see somewhat similar concepts fundamental to societies with a strong shamanic tradition expressed in such terms as *itz, wakan, orenda, shakti, n/um* and others. In fact, the term "cosmos" itself originally meant for the Greek mind order, beauty and the sacred – a meaning which meekly survives almost as a parody of its predecessor in our term "cosmetic."

Having lost a sense of the greater whole, humankind becomes immersed in particularity, fragmentation and alienation. "Western man is held in thrall by the 'ten thousand things'; he sees only particulars, he is ego-bound and thing-bound and unaware of the deep root of all being," Jung laments.[9] "Swamped by the knowledge of external objects, the subject of all knowledge has been temporarily eclipsed to the point of seeming non-existence," he concludes.[10] Gradually individuals are drawn to the ultimate act of bad faith against themselves. They see themselves as the sum total of their external relationships as sanctified by the reigning attitudes of the collectivity. Jung calls this structure of conscious "the persona." It is the identity individuals assume under the weight of social pressure and the need to conform.[11] We become identified with our profession, position in society and the patterns of thought and behavior which are characteristic of the community in which we find ourselves. Such people ultimately become merely the products of compromise, imposed by social order and expectation, at the price of their essential identity.

One of the chief casualties in the process by which the human spirit shrivels into the hollow facade of the persona is the sensibility which was once open to symbolic expression. This process of becoming divided from our myth-producing faculty has tended to occur both in the individual person's life as he grows to maturity and in the historical evolution of human consciousness in general, at least in the West. Children, according to Jung, have a greater receptivity to primordial images which are similar to those that we find in primitive cultures and which still survive in our dreams. Previous societies employed these images regularly and effectively to temper the over-reaching tendencies of directed thinking and to reveal the source of the ideal world in the human soul. Today, crushed under the heavy hand of directed, logical thought – what Jung has called a "monotheism of the conscious" – this level of the real is misunderstood and distorted.

> In actual fact, however, the ideal has been turned by superficial and formalistically-minded believers into an external object of worship, and it is precisely this veneration for the object that prevents it from reaching down into the depths of the soul and transforming it into a wholeness in keeping with the ideal. Accordingly, the divine mediator stands outside as an image, while man remains fragmentary and untouched in the deepest part of him.[12]

"God must be brought to birth in the soul again and again," Meister Eckhart admonishes us. Yet he also notes that most people expect to find Him as an external object, like the cow in their neighbor's field. Jung points out in dismay and frustration that today even intelligent people are no longer able to understand the meaning and purpose of symbolical truth. As a consequence, "Symbolical truth is exposed undefended to the attacks of scientific thought, which can never do justice to such a subject, and in the face of this competition has been unable to hold its ground."[13] The once vital symbol, now misconstrued, has hardened into dogma. All the bridges connecting traditional belief with the inner experience of the individual have broken down and only the assertions of blind faith now support it. Orphaned in the world of the rational consciousness, symbolic images are misunderstood and repudiated by a sensibility to which they have become unintelligible. Literal and rational interpretations yield absurdities, and when the bastions of dogma begin to yield to the forces of criticism, these absurdities are easily repudiated. The demise of that symbolic sensibility which once guided previous civilizations makes the empty world of the persona even more hollow and absurd. Thinking loses its vital connection with its psychic depths, the very connection which constitutes the reality of the soul with its formal and mythic powers. Man is stretched between the *sacrificium intellectus* necessary to impel the famous leap of faith made in fear and trembling and a more resolute but ultimately barren skepticism.

We should not misunderstand, however. Jung is not primarily interested in social criticism. He is not telling us to forsake society to become forest ascetics or to take up the banner of various reform movements which he saw as paradoxically only involving people more deeply in the collectivity with its creeds and endless cascade of "isms." He is detailing the anatomy of modern despair and meaninglessness which he had encountered in his patients. Somewhat like the Buddha, he determines that there is suffering, that suffering has a cause and that the cause can be overcome. And like many schools of Eastern or more ancient thought, he finds that this cause is itself a structure of consciousness. It is, to again quote William Blake, the very "mind-forg'd manacles" by which we shackle ourselves to a world view which exalts the conscious mind, externality and an identification with the collectivity at the expense of the inner resources which have for thousands of years enriched man's existence. And, perhaps most importantly, he finds that among these neglected inner resources are compensatory factors which have an innate, natural tendency to transform consciousness if we can open ourselves to its sources.

The Call of the Inner Self

Though modern consciousness had become estranged from its roots, Jung discovered in his patients a deep need and an inherent compensatory drive which, if not frustrated by the contrary mental tendencies we have been discussing, worked to restore human wholeness and to open hidden dimensions of the psyche. He called this process "individuation." This drive was so basic, so innate to the human mind, that Jung found that his cases spontaneously demonstrated an unconscious "knowledge" of the individuation process and its historical symbolism quite naturally as though these were latent structures struggling to emerge. He recognized this to be an expression of those primordial images which called man back to his origins – a deeply rooted universal disposition within the psyche which was itself a naturally occurring pattern of behavior and, therefore, together with the symbols in which it spontaneously expressed itself, archetypal.

We can trace a general pattern of experience frequently followed by this process of transformation which often occurs spontaneously, whether we will it or not. At times, in the initial phases of this process, our excessive reliance on the structures of consciousness associated with directed thinking and its obsessions leads to a dissociation between the conscious mind and the unconscious. The more a person attempts to assert his or her will over the surrounding world, the more real becomes the threat of getting lost in one-sidedness and becoming alienated from the true foundations of one's existence. "A negative attitude to the unconscious, or its splitting off, is detrimental in so far as the dynamics of the unconscious are identical with instinctual energy," Jung informs us. "Disalliance with the unconscious is synonymous with loss of instinct and rootlessness."[14] Yet the energies of the unconscious, if not productively appropriated, will nevertheless have their say. Generally, the unconscious processes stand in a compensatory relationship to the conscious mind and ideally the two psychic factors complement one another to form a totality, which Jung calls the "self." However, when the compensatory offerings of the unconscious are rebuffed, the energy charge of the repressed content increases. If this process continues, soon repressed compensation becomes rebellion. As Jung points out:

> ... a consciousness heightened by an inevitable one-sidedness gets so far out of touch with the primordial images that a breakdown ensues. Long before the actual catastrophe, the signs of error announce themselves in atrophy of instinct, nervousness, disorientation, entanglement in impossible situations and problems. Medical investigation then discovers an unconscious that is in full revolt against the conscious values, and that therefore cannot possibly be assimilated to consciousness, while the reverse is altogether out of the question.[15]

Thus begins a process of dissociation which can lead to the "splitting off" of unconscious contents and eventually to forms of neurosis and even to schizophrenia.

Very importantly, a similar phenomenon may occur when the unconscious strives to convey an emergent new creative content – often a deeply needed mode of self-expression or a spiritual calling for which the conscious mind is not yet prepared.

> Just as a mother awaits her child with longing and yet brings it into the world only with effort and pain, so a new, creative content, despite the willingness of the conscious mind, can remain for a long time in the unconscious without being "repressed." Though it has a high energic value it still does not become conscious. Cases of this sort are not too difficult to explain. Because the content is new and therefore strange to consciousness, there are no existing associations and

connecting bridges to the conscious contents. All these connections must first be laid down with considerable effort, for without them no consciousness is possible.[16]

When such highly charged emergent contents are isolated in the unconscious, the normal flow of psychic energy between the unconscious and conscious mind becomes disturbed. This can take the form of a damming up of the libido, or psychic energy, and, again, marks the beginning of a dissociation between the conscious and unconscious mind. "The longer the stoppage lasts, the more the value of the opposed positions increases; they become enriched with more and more associations and attach to themselves an ever-widening range of psychic material."[17] As the gap between the conscious and unconscious grows wider, the fatal splitting of the personality which can lead to neurosis or to schizophrenia grows nearer and nearer. Jung equates this process with "those well-known 'perils of the soul' – a splitting of the personality ('loss of soul') and reduction of consciousness," both of which naturally result in an increase in the power of the unconscious. "The consequences of this are a serious danger not only for primitives;" he warns, "in civilized man, too, they may give rise to psychic disturbances, states of possession, and psychic epidemics."[18]

Denied the possibility of expression and acceptance by the conscious mind, these split-off portions of the psyche tend to assume a life of their own. In certain situations they become both autonomous and purposive, sometimes subtly and sometimes "with iron grip," leading the psyche in the directions in which *they* need to follow. Jung notes that in these cases there arise more complex states within the unconscious which tend to evolve into fragmentary psychic systems.

> The more complicated they are, the more they have the character of personalities. As constituents of the psychic personality, they necessarily have the character of "persons." Such fragmentary systems are to be found especially in mental diseases, in cases of psychogenic splitting of the personality (double personality), and of course in mediumistic phenomena. They are also encountered in the phenomenology of religion. Many of the earlier gods developed from "persons" into personified ideas, and finally into abstract ideas.[19]

According to Jung, "Insanity is possession by an unconscious content that, as such, is not assimilated to consciousness, nor can it be assimilated, since the very existence of such contents is denied."[20] "Now it is an axiom of psychology," he tells us elsewhere, "that when a part of the psyche is split off from consciousness it is only *apparently* inactivated; in actual fact it brings about a possession of the personality, with the result that the individual's aims are falsified in the interests of the split-off part."[21] Yet this is a falsification only within the realm of the assessments of consciousness, because beneath the surface the full psyche works with its own intentionality. In a manner reminiscent of Blake's "Bible of Hell" and his belief that if Satan had written the Good Book we would have a quite different history related, what appears on the surface to be rebellion is from the standpoint of the unconscious only an assertion of due rights, rights with a primordial claim to self-expression.

In the excerpts quoted above, it must have become obvious to the reader the extent to which Jung deems it appropriate and even necessary to employ the terms of archaic belief systems to describe these psychological processes. Employing the language of another time, these are the "perils of the soul." The dissociation which alienates man from the depths of his psyche is a "loss of soul," and the influence of the split-off complexes can result in a "possession." Such complexes have their own apparent autonomy and intentionality. They begin to approximate separate personalities and, in strictly psychological terms, they can assume the character of gods, daemons and other sometimes malevolent and sometimes beneficent guiding forces. In fact, Jung goes so far as to state that "If tendencies towards dissociation were not inherent in the human psyche, fragmentary psychic systems would never have been split off; in other words, neither spirits nor gods would ever have come into existence."[22]

With regard to the "reality" of these entities, Jung's position is difficult to harmonize with our Western ways of thinking. He notes that it is not within the competence of the psychologist to establish the metaphysical truth or untruth of these phenomena; he must be content to determine, so far as possible, their psychic effect. Western science has tended to regard them as "wholly illusory."

> But there is no scientific justification for such an assumption; the substantiality of these things is not a scientific problem, since it lies beyond the range of human perception and judgment and thus beyond any possibility of proof. The psychologist is concerned not with the substantiality of these complexes but with psychic experience. Without a doubt they are psychic contents that can be experienced, and their autonomy is equally indubitable. They are fragmentary psychic systems that either appear spontaneously in ecstatic states and evoke powerful impressions and effects, or else, in mental disturbances, become fixed in the form of delusions and hallucinations and consequently destroy the unity of the personality.[23]

"The products of the splitting tendencies are actual psychic personalities of relative reality," he tells us.[24] To the extent consciousness can recognize them as the carriers of a deeper significance, they are not only real but effective on a psychic level. Until this is accomplished, however, they have a fragmenting and threatening effect on human consciousness.

Here we must return to one of the touchstones of our study. Jung is describing these processes and resultant split-off complexes from the standpoint of the psychologist as is his calling and duty. Yet we must constantly recall that "psychological" does not mean "merely psychological," as he has forcefully reminded us. The realm of the psyche has its own claim to reality equal to that of the "outside" world revealed by the senses. These entities are forms of the mind's own self-revelation. They often express the call of man's innermost self and represent psychic realities that are "real because they *work*." They have their own dynamic and potentially integrative function which, if properly channeled, can become an attempt at self-healing on the part of nature.

For many previous civilizations whose intellectual credentials we can only admire, this daemonic inner realm had its own reality which was readily heeded and honored. In the form of the daemon or genius it was recognized as the emissary of man's deepest inspirations. Studying this concept in its Greek and Roman expressions, Ernst Cassirer concludes:

> It is not what outwardly befalls a man but what he fundamentally is that
> constitutes his demon. It is given to him from birth, to accompany him
> through life and to guide his desires and his actions. In the sharper form
> which this basic intuition assumes in the Italic concept of genius it becomes,
> as the name itself indicates, the actual creator of the man, and not only his
> physical but also his spiritual creator, the origin and expression of his personal
> particularity. Thus, everything that possesses a true spiritual form has a genius
> of this sort.[25]

As man's spiritual creator, it was also conceived as his point of interface with the world beyond. As Paul Friedländer recognizes, describing Plato's use of the concept, "It is the idea or view of 'the demonic' as a realm 'intermediate' between the human level and the divine, a realm that, because of its intermediate position, 'unites the cosmos with itself.'"[26] As man's spiritual creator, this emergent creative content, this daemon, must have its due. Jung recognized in his own life that "There was a daimon in me, and in the end its presence proved decisive. It overpowered me, and if I was at times ruthless, it was because I was in the grip of the daimon."[27]

In fact, the libido, which Jung recognized in its mythic guise to be the ancient daemon Eros, was best envisioned according to him as an expression of psychic energy continuous with the cosmos, thus connecting man with his source in the beyond. As we have noted, Jung was fond of quoting the wise Diotima from Plato's *Symposium* to the effect that Eros is "...'a mighty daemon, ... for everything daemonic is the intermediator between God and man.'" It is this indwelling Eros who impels our inspired creativity and simultaneously connects us back to the realm from which all creation proceeds. "To have a genius is to live in the universal ... " Coleridge once observed, and for Jung this mediating power is effective precisely because of the peculiar quality of the archetype which, as we learned in the previous chapters, carries forward this universal reality. Indeed, with regard to the entire archetypal realm of the collective unconscious as an emergent informing spiritual source, Jung noted that he could just as well describe the same reality in terms of "God" or a "daemon" if he sought to express himself in mythic language.[28]

We must envision Jung's understanding of these psychic entities in this manner. Properly understood, they potentially represent the primordial wisdom of the innermost self which reaches beyond our individual consciousness. Here they enlist the wisdom of the collective unconscious, the realm of instinct, the healing powers of the "subtle body," and even, as archetypes, penetrate to the synchronistic level and mediate our relation with the plenitude of the "continuous creation" or pleroma. They, thus, rearticulate into unity the fragmented depths of Jung's psychic cosmos which we explored in Chapter 2. As such, they do indeed unite the cosmos with itself.

In this sense, Jung notes that it is the transpersonal archetype which speaks through the individual, helping him overcome psychological dissociation and beckoning him toward an expansion of consciousness. The archetype has a strongly attractive and numinous quality which can even assume the form of a spirit in dream or vision. "Often it drives with unexampled passion and remorseless logic towards its goal and draws the subject under its spell, from which despite the most desperate resistance he is unable, and finally no longer even willing, to break free, because the experience brings with it a depth and fulness of meaning that was unthinkable before."[29] For Jung, " ... the archetype represents the authentic element of spirit, but a spirit which is not identified with the human intellect, since it is the latter's *spiritus rector*."[30] As the authentic element of spirit, it is this which summons man to his destiny in the sense implied by Heraclitus when he observed that man's character or daemon is his fate. "Anyone who is conscious of his guiding principle knows with what indisputable authority it rules his life," Jung affirms on the basis of personal experience.[31] Such a man must separate himself from the anonymity of the collectivity. "He *must* obey his own law, as if it were a daimon whispering to him of new and wonderful paths. Anyone with a vocation hears the voice of the inner man: he is *called*."[32]

The unconscious is innately driven to express the inner man, both to give form to his integrated psychic wholeness and the spiritual principle which animates it. Jung refers to the impetus for this drive to self-expression and psychic integration as "the entelechy of the self,"[33] which urges us to express our essential identity and the demands of the spirit despite the contrary dictates of ego-consciousness and the concessions of the persona. Jung believed that humankind's spiritual capacity is itself akin to an instinct which expresses itself with urgency in the human soul. "The spiritual appears in the psyche also as an instinct, indeed as a real passion, a 'consuming fire,' as Nietzsche once expressed it. It is not derived from any other instinct, as the psychologists of instinct would have us believe, but is a principle *sui generis*, a specific and necessary form of instinctual power."[34] For Jung, the natural predisposition of the human soul is to express itself in religious and mythic forms, to give birth to the world of the spirit.

For those who refuse or cannot heed this call, the consequences can be dire. If the promptings of the soul are turned away, the dissociation between the conscious mind and the unconscious widens. The products of the unconscious now assail the conscious mind in forms which threaten its unity, effectiveness and even sanity if it is not prepared for their contents. However, "In this dilemma we can at least comfort ourselves with the idea that the unconscious is a necessary evil which must be reckoned with, and that it would therefore be wiser to accompany it on some of its strange symbolic wanderings, even though their meaning be exceedingly questionable. It might perhaps be conducive to good health to relearn Nietzsche's 'lesson of earlier humanity.'"[35] Jung, himself, had learned this lesson, and been forced to recognize, as Nietzsche had before him, that such a state of disorientation is indeed an illness. However, just as Nietzsche compared his own periods of illness to a pregnancy, it contains the potential of things to come which can be nursed to a vital existence. Here in this theory of "creative illness" lay one of Jung's most significant contributions to modern psychology, though in fact it was a truth resuscitated from the forgotten past. These disturbances are not mere irritations to be drugged into a numbed quiescence but are often a call to the larger life which the psyche carries hidden within itself if they are guided in the proper direction. Properly understood, they are signposts and not impediments; they are attempts at a new synthesis of life. As Jung explains in *Modern Man in Search of a Soul*, "A psycho-neurosis must be understood as the suffering of a human being who has not discovered what life means for him. But all creativeness in the realm of the spirit as well as every psychic advance of man arises from a state of mental suffering, and it is spiritual stagnation, psychic sterility, which causes this state."[36] Yet man's extremity is God's opportunity or, as Jung was fond of quoting from the poet Hölderlin:

Danger itself
Fosters the rescuing power.

"I myself have known more than one person who owed his entire usefulness and reason for existence to a neurosis, which prevented all the critical follies in his life and *forced* him to a mode of living that developed his valuable potentialities," Jung observes. "These might have been stifled had not the neurosis, with iron grip, led him to the place where he belonged."[37]

The Descent into the Domain of the Symbol

The iron grip applied by the inner self — whether the result of the dissociation between the conscious and the unconscious caused by repression of unconscious contents or that created by one's inability to assimilate emergent realities emanating from one's own depths — can enlist a person, whether he wills it or not, to accompany the psyche on "its strange symbolic wanderings." And it is the innate symbolizing capacities of the mind which will become the "rescuing power." For beneath the troubled surface of the conscious mind, the unconscious works with its own purposes in a process which we might call "mythological deepening" – a descent into the depths which can potentially free the wellsprings of the dammed libido, overcoming dissociation and opening consciousness to the plenitude of the apparently dark and chaotic background which informs it. Frequently, Jung found that this process was imaged spontaneously as a descent into the unconscious envisioned as the mythic land of the dead, the land of the ancestors. Yet, properly understood, the ancestors are the source of a person's life, and their realm represents a reality which is "ancestral" to, or antecedent to, our own. It is essential for man to realize, Jung insists, that "his beginnings are not by any means mere pasts; they live with him as the constant substratum of his existence, and his consciousness is as much molded by them as by the physical world around him."[38] It is, therefore, not surprising that one of the initial phases of the process of psychodynamic transformation is to uncover this buried mythological substratum.

We have spoken of the process of psychological dissociation as a damming of the flow of libido and the formation of an opposition between the conscious mind and the unconscious. Jung notes that this condition would persist in a stalemate if that which he refers to as a process of regression, the backward movement of the libido, did not begin to take place in this situation. "By activating an unconscious factor, regression confronts consciousness with the problem of the psyche as opposed to the problem of outward adaptation," he tells us.[39] It is natural that the conscious mind should fight against accepting the regressive contents, yet it is finally compelled by the impossibility of further progress to submit to the regressive values. Such regress leads to an increase in the value of those psychic processes which are not primarily directed toward our adjusting ourselves to the world around us. As such, the subliminal elements of the unconscious begin to gain increased influence over the conscious mind.

While this influx of unconscious contents initially can be highly disconcerting to the ordered realm of consciousness, it can also contain the germs of a new dimension of consciousness and vital possibilities for the future.

> I have called this "potential" psyche the collective unconscious. If this layer is activated by the regressive libido, there is a possibility of life being renewed, and also of its being destroyed. Regression carried to its logical conclusion means a linking back with the world of natural instincts, which in its formal or ideal aspect is a kind of *prima materia*. If this *prima materia* can be assimilated by the conscious mind, it will bring about a reactivation and reorganization of its contents. But if the conscious mind proves incapable of assimilating the new contents pouring in from the unconscious, then a dangerous situation arises in which they keep their original, chaotic and archaic form and consequently disrupt the unity of consciousness.[40]

The return to this archaic world with its chaotic wealth of images is most dangerous; it is a journey into that long-buried aspect of the psyche which can easily overwhelm the conscious mind, for here we encounter the same psychic material which is found in psychosis and in the insane. "This is the fund of unconscious images which fatally confuse the mental patient," Jung observes. "But it is also the matrix of a mythopoeic imagination which has vanished from our rational age."[41]

We recall that, in the process of dissociation, the repressed or denied elements are capable of forming split-off complexes with their own autonomy and purposiveness. The deeper the dissociation, the more these complexes take on the character of actual personalities with mythological associations. "In the end, such complexes – presumably in proportion to their distance from consciousness – assume, by self-amplification, an archaic and mythological character and hence a certain numinosity, as is perfectly clear in schizophrenic dissociations."[42] This is an integral part of the process of regression, for "when psychic energy regresses, going even beyond the period of early infancy, and breaks into the legacy of ancestral life, then mythological images are awakened: these are the archetypes."[43] In this manner, regression or, as Jung sometimes referred to the process, introversion, introduces us to our "legacy of ancestral life," the transpersonal psyche which potentially exists within each of us. This is the world of the "2,000,000-year-old man who is in all of us," and Jung found that frequently this level of consciousness was appropriately associated with the image of the wise old man or cultural ancestor. Indeed, Jung discovered in analysis that the autonomous split-off complexes which became manifest at this stage often clothed themselves in these very forms – strangely attractive archetypal images with an archaic and mythological character which was symbolic of their "anterior" reality. Properly assimilated into consciousness, such figures had the capacity to assume the role of spiritual guide and lead the psyche through the apparent disorder of the inner world. In fact, Jung himself, as we shall see, was guided by such a figure in the form of an ancient citizen of the Egypto-Hellenistic world who appeared to him as a strange character named Philemon and led him from psychic chaos to fulfillment and illumination.

With regard to this initial stage of the psyche's strange symbolic wanderings, he tells us that the soul establishes our relationship to the unconsious:

> In a certain sense, this is also a relationship to the collectivity of the dead;
> for the unconscious corresponds to the mythic land of the dead, the land of
> the ancestors. If, therefore, one has a fantasy of the soul vanishing, this means
> that it has withdrawn into the unconscious or into the land of the dead. There
> it produces a mysterious animation and gives visible form to the ancestral
> traces, the collective contents.[44]

Jung compares this process to the primitive concept of soul loss. Ultimately, however, the encounter with the world of the ancestor can be a rediscovery of that hidden wealth of inherited forms and images, those "'pathways' gradually traced out through the cumulative experience of our ancestors." Jung held that "to deny the inheritance of these pathways would be tantamount to denying the inheritance of the brain."[45] On the other hand, the recovery of this reality is potentially equivalent to the experience of a renewal which taps the deep roots of the psyche and its primordial myth-making creativity.

This same revitalizing experience was celebrated by archaic man in rites of renewal that from time immemorial employed the symbolism of a return to the ancestral realm of the dead which, paradoxically, becomes the source of life and renewal.

> The symbolism of the rites of renewal, if taken seriously, points far beyond the merely archaic and infantile to man's innate psychic disposition, which is the result and deposit of all ancestral life right down to the animal level – hence the ancestor and animal symbolism. The rites are attempts to abolish the separation between the conscious mind and the unconscious, the real source of life, and to bring about a reunion of the individual with the native soil of his inherited, instinctive make-up. Had these rites of renewal not yielded definite results, they would not only have died out in prehistoric times, they would never have arisen in the first place.[46]

The descent into the land of the ancestors leads to the realm of those archetypal first principles "to which," in the words of Carl Kerényi, "everything individual and particular goes back and out of which it is made, while they remain ageless, inexhaustible, invincible in timeless primordiality, in a past that proves imperishable because of its eternally repeated rebirths."[47] It is here that we return to the eternal ancestor, to "that dreamer of age-old dreams," who "having at its command a human experience of one or two million years, practically immortal, [has] lived countless times over the life of the individual, the family, the tribe and the nation."

The reader may have noted that in describing the psychological process encoded in rites of renewal Jung speaks of the collective unconscious as retaining the "deposit of all ancestral life right down to the animal level." We recall from the previous chapters that complete psychological integration involves our regaining contact with the often buried world of instinct. Jung found that the psyche expressed this compensatory drive in another important symbolism which accompanies and supplements that of the ancestor as the guide of the spirit. He found in analysis that when the demands for psychodynamic adjustment came from within as the call of the "essential man," it seemed indeed to point to that portion of the psyche connecting us back to our deepest origins in the realm of instinct. The penetration of this level of the psyche which expresses the "hitherto hidden 'real' personality," Jung held, is the "aim and end of every regression."[48] This "aim and end" is marked in myth, vision, dream and fantasy by particular images which display their origin. Such images are activated by an energy which derives from the sphere of instinct and, as such, expresses itself as instinctuality. "This dynamism is represented in dreams by theriomorphic symbols," Jung tells us. "All the lions, bulls, dogs and snakes that populate our dreams represent an undifferentiated and as yet untamed libido, which at the same time forms part of the human personality and can therefore fittingly be described as the *anthropoid psyche*."[49] Likewise, it is from this source that there also arise as an important variation of this same symbolism those "images of 'divine' beings, part animal, part human," which are so characteristic of mythology.[50] Such theriomorphic (having the form of animals) and therianthropic (both human and animal) creatures produced in images spontaneously arising from the unconscious represent man in his potential "wholeness," which is, according to Jung, "both God and animal — not merely the empirical man, but the totality of his being, which is rooted in his animal nature and reaches out beyond the merely human towards the divine."[51] It is here that we reach that deep level of convergence of body and mind which for millennia naturally healed both before consciousness evolved to its present position of pre-eminence. And it is also at this level that we experience the foundation of the psyche's mysterious ability to produce symbols which we experience as having religious significance, whose numinosity and power can either overwhelm us or represent our salvation. Thus, Jung further notes with regard to these images which the psyche produces in the process of its regression and rapprochement with its instinctual roots that "The guise in which these figures appear depends on the attitude of the conscious mind."[52] If it is negative towards the unconscious, these creatures assume a threatening form; if positive, they become spiritual guides for the psyche's difficult journey of transformation.

In his work with his patients, Jung continually encountered such symbol formations, the purpose of which was to transform libido. It is essential to a proper understanding of Jungian psychology to realize that activating such collective images or archetypes potentially has a compensatory and curative effect such as has always pertained to myth. This is an integral part of the psychodynamic process of individuation for, as we shall see in the next section, the symbols produced can actually act as guides, leading the libido in the proper compensatory direction. It is these symbols, and the techniques that increase their effective power, which will establish the "connecting bridges" capable of rescuing the psyche from dissociation and the threat of insanity — freeing and then canalizing the wellsprings of psychic energy to reconnect the psyche with its vital source.

Chapter 5

The Symbol as a Bridge Reaching Out for an Unknown Shore

My rhymes more than their rhyming tell
Of the dim wisdoms old and deep,
That God gives unto man in sleep.
William Butler Yeats

The poet Novalis once perceptively observed, "We don't know the depths of our mind. The secret path leads inward. Inside, or nowhere, are the realms of Eternity, the past and the future." Jung's clinical work revealed that it was the symbolic image which fathomed this inward path back to the womb of the past that paradoxically proves to be the germinal source of all our creative futures and, finally, of the ever-incarnated forms of the realms of Eternity. In so doing, it leads man from the isolation of personal consciousness to a larger inner orderedness and transpersonal meaning. It rescues him from the crushing impersonalization of a world of purely material reality and introduces him to the source of an unfolding creative vitality which he expresses and of which he is, simultaneously, the expression.

Although the initial stages of this journey inward are confusing and apparently senseless, indeed often threatening to the uninitiated consciousness, with continued pursuit direction and meaning can begin to crystalize into what Jung came to recognize as a dynamic pattern which is potentially present in each of us. This pattern, the existence of which is frequently awakened by the very process of regression or introversion that we examined in the previous section, is itself instinctual and archetypal. As such, patients in analysis, according to Jung, demonstrated an unconscious "knowledge" of what he termed the individuation process and of its symbolism which expressed an innate capacity for psychic transformation.[1]

The goal of the individuation process is nothing less than a transformation of consciousness. The process leads to a shift of the center of one's personality from the ego to the integrated psychic structure which Jung called "the self." As such it is initiated by loosening our too exclusive dependence on those structures of consciousness already discussed associated with the ego, perhaps best characterized as an immersion in directed thinking obsessed with externality and perpetually drawing the ego into objecthood. As we remember, the personality structure which takes its form and identity from sheer externality and dispersion is the "persona." "The aim of individuation is nothing less than to divest the self of the false wrappings of the persona," according to Jung,[2] while at the same time overcoming the equal but opposite dissociation of unconscious contents. It can thus be characterized as a sort of initiatory purification and rebirth. The dissolution of these structures of consciousness helps to reconnect man with his symbolic faculty. When not obstructed by opposing structures of consciousness, the psyche has a remarkable capacity for compensatory change, for the psyche is transformed by the relationship of the ego to the contents of the unconscious. The assimilation of unconscious contents into the conscious mind is a process which naturally has far-reaching effects on the conscious attitude. "This means that the psychic human being becomes a whole, and becoming whole has remarkable effects on ego-consciousness which are extremely difficult to describe," Jung informs us.[3]

Yet, though difficult to describe, these effects can be experienced. Indeed, it is one of the hallmarks of Jung's thought that they *must* be experienced. Theoretical familiarity with the process is inadequate for mere knowledge and actual realization are incommensurate. No body of knowledge, revealed truth, inculcated belief or the wager of blind faith can substitute for the experience in which the soul reaches back to and is revitalized from its sources. "The needful thing is not to *know* the truth but to *experience* it," Jung tells us. "Not to have an intellectual conception of things, but to find our way to the inner, and perhaps wordless, irrational experience – that is the great problem."[4]

This realization points to a second hallmark of this process. It is indeed a "way" to a distant goal, a "venture" or journey of the soul along pathways with their own guideposts marking the stages of a transition which manifests both its own inner laws as well as a thoroughgoing purposiveness in the integrity of its direction. And employing the *image* of the path in our thinking to represent the transformative process is appropriate, for it brings into focus the archetypal configuration of this journey which, itself, enlists an older form of "thinking," thinking in primordial images, and initiates the rearticulation of Jung's inner cosmos by reuniting us with the collective unconscious and its ancient mythopoeic powers. For Jung, "the archetypes are the forms or riverbeds along which the current of psychic life has always flowed" – pathways engraved in the mind of humanity.[5] The unconscious can only be reached along such pathways, i.e., by archetypal symbols. The symbol is the key to the unconscious because the unconscious expresses itself in these forms; it is a "creative force which wraps itself in images,"[6] a fact modern man tends to forget or ignore. Yet it is essential that we recognize, as David Ray Griffin observes, that "the soul is essentially an imagining, symbolizing process, and that we function much more basically in terms of symbolic images than we do in terms of (allegedly) literal concepts."[7] Traditional cultures had long recognized this fact. In early societies, dream interpretation, myth, art and religion effectively employed symbolic images to ground man in this creative source.

The dream was also an important source of psychic information for Jung. With regard to dreams he notes that, "It is only in modern times that the dream, this fleeting and insignificant-looking product of the psyche, has met with such profound contempt. Formerly it was esteemed as a harbinger of fate, a portent and comforter, a messenger of the gods."[8] Modern psychology has succeeded in restoring some of the dream's lost prestige. "Now we see it as the emissary of the unconscious, whose task it is to reveal the secrets that are hidden from the conscious mind, and this it does with astounding completeness."[9] As such, dreams are an attempt to translate through symbols the inner secrets which are natural to mankind into a language which is potentially open to consciousness. They tend to be compensatory to the state of the conscious mind and bring forward our unconscious needs, fostering the process of individuation. Contrary to Freud's view that the dream is essentially a wish-fulfillment, Jung held that potentially "the dream is a spontaneous self-portrayal, in symbolic form, of the actual situation in the unconscious."[10] Such dreams produce symbols of an archetypal nature which are capable of depicting the stages of individuation; they are "self-portraits of the psychic life-process."[11] Yet, at the same time, the content of the dream often seems to come from levels beyond our personal experience. "We do not feel as if we were producing the dreams, it is rather as if the dreams came to us. They are not subject to our control but obey their own laws," Jung observes.[12] He points out that older societies felt that in dreams a god or daemon spoke to the sleeper in symbolic language. The society's dream-interpreter had the appointed task of fathoming the dream's cryptic message. In fact, he felt that the ancient idea that the dream is an emissary of a divine source contains its own truth. Dreams express the deep needs of the soul, and the logos of the soul reaches back into that which man has traditionally experienced as the Divine. "As the eye to the sun, so the soul corresponds to God," Jung tells us, and concludes that " ... the believer should not boggle at the fact that there are *somnia a Deo missa* (dreams sent by God) and illuminations of the soul which cannot be traced back to any external causes."[13]

The symbol functions in much the same manner in myths, which is not surprising for it has often been recognized that, in a sense, mythology is the collective dream of humankind. Yet, just as modernity is not attuned to the revelations of the dream, so likewise we have lost our faculty for understanding the mythic sensibility. Again, it is directed thinking manifesting itself as critical reason which alienates man from myth's revitalizing powers, for when critical reason dominates, myth is misunderstood and becomes distorted and empty. Critical reason perpetually attempts to impose all kinds of literal, rational explanations on mythic experience which have been totally inadequate in their attempts to clarify what myth is trying to express. "So far mythologists have always helped themselves out with solar, lunar, meteorological, vegetal, and other ideas of the kind," Jung observes. "The fact that myths are first and foremost psychic phenomena which reveal the nature of the soul is something they have absolutely refused to see until now."[14] For Jung, the primordial language of myth is the most natural expression of these psychic processes which myth is able to present with an unparalleled richness and wealth of suggestion.

> The primitive mentality does not invent myths, it experiences them. Myths are original revelations of the preconscious psyche, involuntary statements about unconscious psychic happenings, and anything but allegories of physical processes. .... A tribe's mythology is its living religion, whose loss is always and everywhere, even among the civilized, a moral catastrophe. But religion is a vital link with psychic processes independent of and beyond consciousness, in the dark hinterland of the psyche.[15]

Carrying these observations a step further, Jung asks, "What is the use of a religion without a mythos, since religion means, if anything at all, precisely that function which links us back to the eternal myth?"[16] It is the mythic symbol in the world's religions which links us back to the "eternal myth" – that is, to the recurrent and universal productions of the collective unconscious and its archetypal expressions which are the common heritage of mankind spontaneously arising in the human psyche. And these recurrent and universal productions are highly significant because, as we shall see, they lead the mind to experience a deeply meaningful and sacred reality. "For," as Jung tells us, "it is not that 'God' is a myth, but that myth is the revelation of a divine life in man. It is not we who invent myth, rather it speaks to us as a Word of God."[17]

Other forms of human expression serve kindred ends. Jung notes that traditionally artists have always relied upon the symbol and its ability to enlist and express the deep sources of human creativity. The artist, he observes, seems to have a direct line to the unconscious and its rich treasury of transpersonal images. He plumbs the mind's depths and in so doing reshapes the psychic life of humankind. According to Jung, such an artist raises human experience to a higher level: "Whoever speaks in primordial images speaks with a thousand voices; he enthrals and overpowers, while at the same time he lifts the idea he is seeking to express out of the occasional and the transitory into the realm of the ever-enduring."[18]

One is reminded of an observation made by Thomas Mann:

> There is no doubt about it, the moment when the story-teller acquires the mythical way of looking at things, the gift of seeing the typical features of characteristics and events, that moment marks a beginning of his life. It means a peculiar intensification of his artistic mood, a new serenity in his powers of

perception and creation. This is usually reserved for the later years of life; for whereas in the life of mankind the mythical represents an early and primitive stage, in the life of the individual it represents a late and mature one.[19]

Jung's own observations on the impact of myth and archetype in the realm of art are similar: "The creative process, so far as we are able to follow it at all, consists in the unconscious activation of an archetypal image, and in elaborating and shaping this image into the finished work. By giving it shape, the artist translates it into the language of the present, and so makes it possible for us to find our way back to the deepest springs of life."[20]

The observation that the archetype enables us "to find our way back to the deepest springs of life" is not simply a colorful but idle manner of expression. The archetypes expressed in dream, myth and art function in a thoroughly dynamic way and provide the directive signals for a transformation of consciousness. As Jolande Jacobi observes, "Whenever it [the archetype] clothes itself with adequate symbols, which is not always the case, it takes hold of the individual in a startling way, creating a condition of 'being deeply moved.'"[21] Jung, as we know, refers to this attractive force of the archetype as numinosity and notes that it has the effect of gripping us as though we were moved by an instinct. It is in the "iron grip" of this attractive force that the overall configuration of the individuation process begins to crystalize for the subject.

The psyche is capable of the spontaneous production of archetypal symbols which, during the process of dissociation and the "mythological deepening" characteristic of regression or introversion, act in a manner compensatory to consciousness. Such archetypes are numinous centers of attraction and directive force which are capable of canalizing libido in certain directions, and they work with their own autonomy, authority and purposiveness. That there exist such spontaneously operating psychic factors beyond the human will is at first disconcerting; yet, remembering the autonomy of the entire autonomic system which similarly sustains us and fosters our well-being, it ought not to be surprising. At any rate, for Jung it is a reality.

> They are to be regarded not only as objects but as subjects with laws of their own. From the point of view of consciousness, we can, of course, describe them as objects, and even explain them up to a point, in the same measure as we can describe and explain a living human being. But then we have to disregard their autonomy. If that is considered, we are compelled to treat them as subjects; in other words, we have to admit that they possess spontaneity and purposiveness, or a kind of consciousness and free will. We observe their behaviour and consider their statements.[22]

The fact that these autonomous contents manifest a certain lawfulness in the statements they make helps us understand them. They always represent the psyche speaking of itself in the form of images which depict the living processes of the psyche itself. In such archetypes, psychic processes are transformed into images in introspective intuitions which somehow capture the state of the unconscious. Such images have been referred to as autosymbolic, for they reflect the stages of the very psychic process of transformation which produced them. They are self-perceptions of the libido in the form of images presented to the conscious mind. In its "expression" of the deep sources of the psyche, the archetype also works by "impression" to draw consciousness into an awareness of the inner order it represents. As Jung notes, in so doing, such structures not only express order, but they also assist in creating it. Thus, they help effect the transformation of consciousness which reintroduces man to the reality of the formal powers deep within the psyche. In this manner, the symbol reacts upon its maker and, as such, in the archetypal process man is both the redeemer and the redeemed.

This rapprochement with the shaping power of the soul has the further effect of resuscitating the lost mythic or archetypal sensibility. The conscious mind opened to its creative powers now becomes attuned to the deep statements of the psyche – to the language of primordial images by which humankind expressed its most significant intuitions and insights over aeons. The experience of a deep-seated accord between the archetypal symbol and the *a priori* structuring faculties of the collective unconscious creates a feeling not of cognition but recognition, of the symbol as somehow previously known, something fascinating, inexplicably significant and even fateful in its encounter. We are reminded of an expression of Plotinus: it is "something which the Soul names as from an ancient knowledge and, recognizing, welcomes it, enters into unison with it." The awakening of this center with its symbolic sensibility and receptivity transforms consciousness. It now acts like a magnet, Jung observes. "Like a magnet, the new centre attracts to itself that which is proper to it"[23] – and thus a world awakens which is experienced as just as real, just as effective and psychologically true, as the world of outward reality.

In fact, Jung refurbishes the metaphor of the magnet used by Plato in the *Ion* and uses it to image this expanding area of sensibility. In Plato, the magnet or stone of Heraclea, as a symbol of man's participation in divine creative inspiration, not only attracts what comes into its proximity but also vests it with a power like its own, enabling it to set up a similar network of attraction. Even so, according to Jung, do the powerful symbols emanating from this imaging faculty of the soul mysteriously attract all with whom they come into contact and, awakening them to the heritage of the collective unconscious, allow them to experience and express symbols with a similar numinous power of attraction. This magnetic process revolutionizes the ego-oriented psyche by setting up, in contradistinction to the ego, another goal or center, one which functions symbolically, an organ of the soul.

Understanding the symbol and the laws of the psychic cosmos in which it operates opens several doors to the psychologist. During the process of dissociation and the lowering of the threshold of consciousness associated with regression, the conscious mind is subjected to an onrush of images of a symbolic and increasingly mythological character which threaten to overwhelm it. Jung has described the tension caused by this influx from the unconscious in terms of William James' "bursting point," and the failure of the conscious mind to cope with this onslaught orchestrated by a repressed unconscious which is now in revolt can lead to schizophrenia and other forms of mental illness. However, Jung discovered that the same lowering of the threshold of consciousness could be induced gradually and deliberately by specific disciplines and techniques in a manner less threatening to ego-consciousness, thus facilitating the synthesis of conscious and unconscious contents. He found that by employing and analyzing the images of dream, myth and the patient's artistic endeavors – i.e., the same psychologically integrating forces we examined previously – as well as the similar visionary productions of a process he at one point termed "trancing" but later called "active imagination," he had the tools to prepare the way for this process of rapprochement.

Active imagination is a method for bringing forward gradually those contents of the unconscious that lie below the threshold of consciousness which otherwise threaten a spontaneous and often anarchic eruption into consciousness. It first relies on systematic exercises to eliminate critical attention and lower the threshold of consciousness, inducing a suspension of our typical reliance on directed thinking and our outward orientation. These techniques help to make space for the primordial image and to reawaken the imagination. As a "lowering" of the threshold of consciousness and a part of the process of introversion, Jung himself often experienced the initial phase of this process in terms of images reflecting a literal descent. Joan Chodorow relates, " ... sometimes he imagined climbing down a steep descent; other times he imagined digging a hole, one shovelful of dirt at a time. With each descent, he explored the landscape and got better acquainted with the inner figures."[24] As Jung experimented with the process, he struggled to define it. "Sometimes the process was referred to as 'trancing,' 'visioning,' 'exercises,' 'dialectical method,' 'technique of differentiation,' 'technique of introversion,' 'introspection' and 'technique of the descent.'" Finally, he settled upon the term "active imagination."[25] The object of the process is to fathom and release that fund of images which is the common inheritance of the transpersonal psyche and, following a now familiar pattern, the descent is a perilous journey. Such subliminal contents possess a high energy charge which, when released by active imagination, may overpower the conscious mind, taking possession of the personality. "This gives rise to a condition which – temporarily, at least – cannot easily be distinguished from schizophrenia, and may even lead to a genuine 'psychotic interval,'" Jung warns.[26] Yet his analytic method was based upon his firm conviction that the imagination held natural healing powers, and the second phase of the process of active imagination was an intense psychological and spiritual confrontation with these emissaries from the background of consciousness. "Through her active participation, the patient merges herself in the unconscious processes," Jung observed, "and she gains possession of them by allowing them to possess her."[27] Properly managed, this descent was capable of effecting both the integration of these highly charged contents with the larger human psyche and, simultaneously, a further deepening of symbolic experience.

The ultimate goal of psychic integration could be further assisted by a process of synthesis which Jung termed "amplification." Jung became convinced that the mere analysis of dream and imaginative material was ultimately reductive and kept the analysand within the confines of his own neurosis. Analysis, he felt, must be followed by synthesis because "... certain kinds of psychic material mean next to nothing if simply broken down, but display a wealth of meaning if, instead of being broken down, that meaning is reinforced and extended by all the conscious means at our disposal – by the so-called method of amplification ... Just as analysis breaks down the symbolical fantasy-material into its components, so the synthetic procedure integrates it into a universal and intelligible statement."[28] By this procedure, the disturbances emanating from the unconscious can be, at least in part, successfully interpreted, understood and accepted into consciousness. Because the psyche clothes its statements in images which are to be found in mythologies from all over the world, placing these statements within a mythological context is the most effective method of fathoming their significance, of integrating them into "a universal and intelligible statement." "It is absolutely necessary to supply these fantastic images which rise up so strange and threatening before the mind's eye with a sort of context so as to make them intelligible. Experience has shown that the best way to do this is by means of comparative mythological material," Jung concluded.[29] Mythological motifs form the "Ariadne's thread" leading us to the inner meaning of these images.

In describing this process of amplification, however, Jung notes that in many instances the procedure can be long and difficult. The streams of fantasy sometimes give no hint of their origin or hidden purpose. Often there is a high degree of "conscious cramp" which hinders expression and must be broken down by a continuous and long-sustained effort to elaborate upon the imagined materials.[30] He found that this elaboration could be accomplished in numerous ways: dramatic, dialectic, visual, acoustic or in the form of dancing, painting, drawing or modeling. In *Modern Man in Search of a Soul*, Jung remarks, concerning his use of painting in the practice of amplification, that the patient can give form to his own inner experience by painting it. "For what he paints are active fantasies – it is that which activates him. And that which is active within is himself, but not in the sense of his previous error when he mistook his personal ego for the self; it is himself in a new sense, for his ego now appears as an object actuated by the life-forces within."[31] In this way, individuals learn to experience their own deeply creative depths, and the characteristics of the works produced reveal the nature of the forces which created them. Such creative experience becomes something more than mere fantasy; it participates in the mythopoeic power of the archetypal imagination and becomes both transpersonal and possessive of a life and logic of its own, capable of initiating affirmative transformation in the human psyche.

As usual, Jung found traditional analogues from non-Western and earlier cultures which utilized similar techniques to lower the threshold of consciousness and assist the process of introversion or regression, thus helping to disinter the inner man and the forces latent in his soul. These processes functioned by activating the symbolic capacities of the imagination in a manner analogous to active imagination. He recognized that these techniques had been employed for centuries in the meditative activities of the Buddhists or in the largely unconscious symbolizations of the alchemists. According to Jolande Jacobi, "The *opus* which the alchemist brings forth and the *imaginatio*, which is the psychic instrument whereby the Eastern mystic 'produced' Buddha, are based on the *active imagination* that leads Jung's patients to the same experience of symbols and through them to the knowledge of their own 'centre', the self." She notes that according to Jung, "*Imaginatio* is the active evocation of (inner) images ... an authentic feat of thought or ideation, which does not spin aimless and groundless fantasies 'into the blue' ... but tries to grasp the inner facts and portray them in images true to their nature." Jacobi concludes that this process is "an activation of the profoundest depths of the soul, intended to promote the emergence of salutary symbols."[32]

Jung noted that to aid this process and to foster the lowering of the threshold of consciousness different societies had traditionally employed a number of techniques. Meditation and contemplation are common examples. In *Symbols of Transformation*, he notes that solitude and fasting have long been well-known means of opening the mind to its unconscious sources. Trance states, ecstasy and hypnotism also effectively open the flow of unconscious contents. Moreover, ritual can function in a similar manner. "In abstract form, symbols are religious ideas;" Jung notes, "in the form of action, they are rites or ceremonies."[33]

Jung was particularly impressed by the manner in which the practice of alchemy had, largely unconsciously, effected this process of transformation, fostering introversion and utilizing various techniques, as well as the traditional lore embodied in myth, Hermetic philosophy and Christian tradition, to open the unconscious and at the same time to mediate its contexts with the conscious mind. Alchemy, of course, was the long-pursued and ill-fated attempt to change base metals into gold. However, according to Jung, alchemy was not simply concerned with chemical experimentation. In their myriad repetitions, its processes assumed the shape of the psyche itself, becoming a theater for the projection of unconscious psychic contents as the alchemist labored long into the night tracing unknown chemical transformations. "In order to explain the mystery of matter, he projected yet another mystery – namely his own psychic background – into what was to be explained," Jung tells us. "This procedure was not, of course, intentional; it was an involuntary occurrence."[34] In this way, the alchemical retort became a mirror reflecting the processes of the human unconscious. Jung felt that alchemy was thus a valuable but neglected chapter in the evolution of the Western psyche, for the increasing differentiation of ritual and dogma in the Christian Church tended to alienate consciousness from its roots, while alchemy, on the other hand, steadfastly though unconsciously preserved the bridge to the unconscious.

Much as occurs in dream, vision or the implementation of the process of active imagination, for the alchemist "when contemplating the chemical changes that took place during the opus, his mind became suffused with archetypal, mythological parallels and interpretations."[35] In their attempts to delve into the secrets of matter, Jung noted, the alchemists had unexpectedly uncovered the unconscious and its processes, particularly the symbolism of the individuation process. In a revealing appropriation of the mythic heritage embodied in the Hermetic tradition, the psychopomp Hermes-Mercurius leads the process of transformation eventually meant to produce the enduring reality of the *lapis*, the philosopher stone. Tellingly, Mercurius is both the substance transformed and the agent of transformation, just as man is both the redeemed and the redeemer in the individuation process. The *nigredo* or blackness is the initial state in the process of transformation. Here, "when the search lies heavy upon the searcher," the alchemist's perilous journey begins into the darkness of the human mind. This stage represents the lowering of the threshold of consciousness and the confrontation with the *prima materia* or *massa confusa*, the welter of chaotic and threatening material emerging from the unconscious as originally encountered in introversion or regression prior to efforts to synthesize these contents with the conscious mind. The alchemists employed two important techniques to assist the process of introversion and aid the synthesis of unconscious contents. These were mediation and imagination or, as found in the medieval texts, *meditatio* and *imaginatio*.

The first implies more than we initially may associate with meditation. Quoting Ruland's *Lexicon alchemiae*, Jung points out: "The word *meditatio* is used when a man has an inner dialogue with someone unseen. It may be with God, when He is invoked, or with himself or with his good angel."[36] This follows the same pattern of the encounter with the daemon or spirit guide found within which we have experienced before.

> The psychologist is familiar with this "inner dialogue;" it is an essential part of the technique for coming to terms with the unconscious. Ruland's definition proves beyond all doubt that when the alchemists speak of *meditari* they do not mean mere cogitation, but explicitly an inner dialogue and hence a living relationship to the answering voice of the "other" in ourselves, i.e., of the unconscious, ... a creative dialogue, by means of which things pass from an unconscious potential state to a manifest one.[37]

Yet, for the alchemist, the unconscious potential state addressed in this creative dialogue reaches farther into the depths of man's being and the forces which innately inform it. *Meditatio* has the ultimate goal of opening the eye of the soul to its informing powers – to "that inner light which God has lit in nature and in our hearts from the beginning."[38] Man must "see with his spiritual eyes,"[39] and so seeing "'learns' the *lumen naturae* through dreams, among other things."[40] "'As the light of nature cannot speak, it buildeth shapes in sleep from the power of the word' (of God)."[41]

It is because the inner man is naturally endowed with this informing power represented by the *lumen naturae* that *meditatio* can combine effectively with *imaginatio*. *Meditatio* puts the mind in contact with the plastic powers of the soul, the imagination, and the imagination gives form to the deepest parts of our psyche reaching into the transpersonal unconscious. Here the formal power of the soul expresses the same power which informs the creation itself; it functions as vice-regent of God, it is God's lieutenant or viceroy, the analogue of the *Deus Creator*.[42] Therefore, as in Jung's theory of synchronicity, at a deep level the creative force animating mind and matter is one. For the alchemist, an all-pervasive creative power shared with nature and the divine informs the mind in the process of *imaginatio*, and delving deeply into the creative powers of imagination was a key to unlocking the inner-working of God's cosmos.

For Jung, *meditatio* and *imaginatio* were the twin pillars supporting the processes of introversion and amplification in alchemy which opened the mind to its revitalizing unconscious contents. The enigmatic and shifting chemical transformations taking place in the alchemical laboratory were something like a dynamic Rorschach test driving the alchemist's mind back to its creative depths and eliciting the plastic powers of *imaginatio*. We noted earlier that these archetypal expressions of the imagination were often spontaneously contextualized and amplified in a Hermetic or Christian framework, or one which combined elements of both, and projected upon the blank screen of the unknown chemical transformations being observed. As "introspective intuitions that somehow capture the state of the unconscious," they reflected naturally a process which images *imaginatio*'s experience of its own participation in the creative source of mind and cosmos. I want to offer by way of illustration an interesting example which Jung presents in *Psychology and Alchemy* so that the reader can get a sense of how the process worked upon the mind of the investigator. In this procedure, the experimenter is advised to gather "common rainwater in a good quantity" and to mediate upon the vessel in which it is placed.

> When this has been done, take a drop of the consecrated red wine and let it fall into the water, and you will instantly perceive a fog and thick darkness on top of the water, such as also was at the first creation. Then put in two drops, and you will see the light coming forth from the darkness; whereupon little by little put in every half of each quarter hour first three, then four, then five, then six drops, and then no more, and you will see with your own eyes one thing after another appearing by and by on top of the water, how God created all things in six days, and how it all came to pass, and such secrets as are not to be spoken aloud and I also have not power to reveal. Fall on your knees before you undertake this operation. Let your eyes judge of it; for thus was the world created. Let all stand as it is, and in half an hour after it began it will disappear.

Finally, the visionary alchemist concludes, "By this you will see clearly the secrets of God, that are at present hidden from you as from a child. You will understand what Moses has written concerning the creation; you will see what manner of body Adam and Eve had before and after the Fall, what the serpent was, what the tree and what manner of fruits they ate: where and what Paradise is, and in what bodies the righteous shall be resurrected;..."[43]

Here in the depths of introversion the powers of *imaginatio*, the formative principles of the unconscious, are elicited in full force. Its plastic powers are contextualized in terms of Christian mythic archetypes. Yet the overall configuration of experience it describes is a universal one. The choice of context illustrates an important symbolism. The creative power of *imaginatio*, vice-regent of *Deus Creator*, expresses itself in terms of the cosmic creation itself, the very process of which, at this stage of its transformation, it experiences itself as an expression. "Fall on your knees before you undertake this operation. Let your eyes judge of it; for thus was the world created." These are "the secrets of God" – His primal act of creation revealed from the source of the spiritual eye, the archetypal imagination within the inner man. It reflects the rediscovery of the deep source of our own creative power symbolically expressed which Jung recognized transformed and expanded human consciousness, and it carries a corresponding sense of illumination and sacredness. Man's imagination is led back to its source which is simultaneously envisioned as the source of a plenitude that creates and informs reality.

Traditional disciplines such as alchemy or the meditative practices of the Buddhists confirmed Jung's findings with regard to the salutary effects of the processes employed in active imagination and amplification. Utilizing the images of dream, vision, myth and art, supplemented by practices such as dance, dramatic enactment, etc., he found that he could assist introversion and free the symbolic wellsprings of the mythopoeic imagination, releasing its revivifying symbols. Understanding the symbol and the manner in which it functions enabled him to use deliberately these images to release and guide the transformative psychodynamic processes innate in the unconscious in a more controlled manner. In so doing, he was able to induce a gradual rapprochement between the conscious mind and the unconscious forces which threatened to overwhelm it, while at the same time opening consciousness to the significant spiritual creative contents existing within the archetypal psyche. Such processes provided the material for constructing the "connecting bridges" which deepened and integrated consciousness, opening human awareness to the spiritual significance of a transpersonal world with its own significant form and order. This world constituted a *mundus archetypus* which, itself, as we shall see in Chapter 8, reflected in primordial symbols the very process of transformation of consciousness which he recognized as the individuation process. And these apparently new and creative techniques were also "connecting bridges" in another sense, for in following the psyche's "strange symbolic wanderings," Jung had, in fact, been unconsciously led along that secret way which had guided the shaman for thousands of years – a path which leads to some of the psyche's oldest, deepest and most meaningful secrets.

Chapter 6

The Shaman's Call, Crisis and Cure

Danger itself
Fosters the rescuing power.
Hölderlin

The Call and the Crisis

"The World split into shallow surface and deadly darkness, and lost its delicate life in the Soul."[1] So Catherine Keller describes the result of the dissociative tendencies inherent in the human mind both as it strives to cope with the problems of day-to-day living in the modern world and in the long evolutionary struggle which has led to the progressive differentiation of our rational consciousness – the "readjustment of the human mind to which we owe our modern empiricism and technics," in Jung's terms. As Jung observed, the resistance of the conscious mind to the unconscious and the depreciation of our preconscious resources were historical necessities for the development of the contemporary human mind and the precision of its conscious thought. But, as he further noted, "modern man's consciousness has strayed rather too far from the fact of the unconscious."

Under the reigning "monotheism of the conscious," our human consciousness, as Lancelot Law Whyte so well described the process, becomes dispersed, and in attending to contrasts, stresses disorders, conflicts and inadequacies while neglecting the harmonies. The sense of reality as ordered process tends to become lost to man in a world characterized by particularity and fragmentation. The domination of the rational intellect and directed thinking causes the mythic offerings of the preconscious mind to be refused or misunderstood and distorted in the manner described in Chapter 4. Our modern tendency to naive realism steadfastly chooses to ignore the basic fact that "the real vehicle and begetter of all knowledge is the psyche." Subject to these pressures, the soul, the linchpin of our psychic cosmos, splinters and becomes lost to us, and man, alienated from the vitalizing formal powers of his existence, is cast adrift. It was thus that Jung envisioned the self-division characterizing modern man.

In a world where a vision of ordered process holds some sway, opposites tend to be seen as balancing one another and the ancient law of enantiodromia prevails. Action proceeding too long in any one direction eventually calls for compensation in the other. Our society's reverence for "progress" tends to blind us to this reality. However, progress does, in fact, entail loss. For example, the development of the art of writing was an unparalleled boon to mankind. Yet this method of recording data and thought has led to the progressive weakening of the human memory which in certain societies with an oral tradition could flawlessly recite lore that presently takes volumes to retain. Today, the television takes much of the work of our imagination from us and the computer provides the thinking which we previously had to perform to synthesize information. Man's mind is becoming merely accessory to his instruments, and as such his faculties wither. We might be inclined to agree with William Blake that our over-reliance on such devices tends to "turn that which is Soul & Life into a Mill or Machine." And in a vein more immediately relevant to this work, he who was once both empirical and transcendental man, under the forces of dissociation described by Jung, has shriveled to become merely empirical, technological man – modern man in search of a soul.

One aspect of shamanism can be viewed fruitfully as an age-old, perhaps partially instinctive, compensatory reaction to this splintering of the soul. It represents the innate wisdom which warned humanity against straying too far from the fact of the preconscious and the harmonious relationship with the larger world it holds. Shamanism developed over long periods of time and was careful to preserve its roots in its historical and psychological sources. For the shaman, the world of the past with its wealth of symbols – that is, the world of the ancestors which continually repeated itself in time – and the hinterlands of the mind, the dreamtime source, remained one and the same. We can see this from the very horizons of our knowledge of modern Homo sapiens. The prominent French scholar, André Leroi-Gourhan, describing the religious symbolism of the well-known cave art of the Upper Paleolithic period (38,000–11,800 B.P.) in northern Spain and southwestern France, notes the tremendous religious ·conservatism which he recognizes as paradoxically characterizing this long era of otherwise startling human development. It is this period in man's history which John Pfeiffer has called "the creative explosion." [2] Yet early man's spiritual life apparently retained its form and substance over thousands and even tens of thousands of years. Leroi-Gourhan finds a religious symbolism "absolutely continuous in development from the earliest artistic manifestations down to the end of the Magdalenian period," an astounding duration of approximately 25,000 years. [3] Moreover, according to him, this continuity implies its own substantial prehistory. "If one point is solidly established, it is this:" he tells us, "when the first cave sanctuaries made their appearance, the figurative system and the underlying ideology it presupposes had existed for several millennia." [4]

It is probably during this early long-enduring period of religious symbolism that we find the first substantial concrete evidence of shamanism still manifest on exquisitely decorated cave walls, displaying an aesthetic sensibility rivaling anything we produce today. Over millennia, the same grammar of symbols was tenaciously preserved. And into historical times the shaman is still the guardian of these very same symbols which he keeps for his tribe or culture. It is through these age-old symbols and the techniques which accompany them that the shaman continually protects the unity of the human soul, integrating the conscious mind with its preconscious levels, its instinctual roots, and the natural principles of form and order which relate our being back to nature and cosmos.

It is in this way that the shaman maintains our heritage as both empirical and transcendental man. As numerous authors have recognized, he is the great "mediator of worlds." The shaman "exists in two worlds," Åke Hultkrantz notes, "and acknowledges the validity of both, his mastery deriving from his ability not to confuse the two."[5] It is well-known that people in primitive cultures have an acute awareness of the world around them. Survival in a hunting society demands the keenest perception of minute details of the physical world, both its dangers and opportunities. Traditionally, the shaman functions well in this empirical world. Yet, at the same time, he is heir to a deeper world. As Michael Harner points out, the shaman recognizes structures of consciousness which are as "real" as, or even more real than, our empirical reality.[6] As mediator of realities, the shaman brings both realms into fruitful contact with one another, and it is, in one aspect, this revitalizing integration of these diverse worlds that the central axis uniting the shaman's cosmos symbolizes. And just as in Chapters 2 and 3 we were able to discern a striking parallel between Jung's psychic cosmos and the inner cosmos traversed by the shaman, here we shall see that the methods of achieving the deepening and integration of consciousness which Jung described in his individuation process very much resemble the processes and techniques the shaman has experienced and employed over the ages to effect a similar transformation of consciousness.

We can specify a few important points of resemblance initially. Both the individuation process in depth psychology and the process by which the shaman receives his vocation in the world's shamanic traditions recognize that the human psyche contains innate patterns of transformation. As Jung has noted, "the unconscious is a process and ... the psyche is transformed or developed by the relationship of the ego to the contents of the unconscious." In each discipline, the removal of structures of consciousness which hinder transformation and the lowering of the threshold of the conscious mind potentially release dynamic forces with their own form, order and significance. Each is a process of transformation, the hallmark of which is actual experience – intense personal experience which is the oracle of its own truth as opposed to the credal principles or structures of faith which we in the modern West often regard as the primary supports of our own belief systems. In shamanism and in depth psychology, mere knowledge or the acceptance of revelation are far less important than actual realization.

As psychodynamic processes, Jungian individuation and the shaman's transformation can each be envisioned as a "way" – a journey which is often perilous, along the razor's edge, as Jung as was fond of saying. As such, myth and symbol, in the expanded sense employed by Jung denoting an emergent unconscious content striving to find expression, act as guides, marking the way to transformation. As Jung repeatedly points out, this age-old process of transformation repeated again and again over the aeons has left its deposit in the world's symbols and the manner in which they function. In shamanism, as well as in depth psychology, the revitalizing of the symbolic, mythopoeic sensibility allows the symbol to open our awareness to a transpersonal reality – to the universal foundation of the human soul and the wisdom it contains.

Moreover, in each the symbol shares certain features which contribute to this functional aspect. In shamanism, as in depth psychology, the symbols, though often the products of isolated experience, are also simultaneously recognized as having a universal significance and application. And, just as Jung himself discovered in his contemporary patients, in shamanic tradition the symbol also frequently is capable of portraying the transformative process itself. It is as if the psyche is somehow able to glimpse and capture in an image the stages of the psychological transformation which it is undergoing and, in so doing, help integrate them into consciousness. Seen within the context of the grammar of symbols which surrounds it, the symbol reveals the direction in which it would lead the overall psyche. As Jung noted, this "directedness" of the symbol can be envisioned as a pathway graven into the mind or the riverbed, along which our deepest experiences flow, leading us back to their sources. Seen from a larger perspective, such symbols potentially both *effect* and *reflect* the process of transformation and the ultimate experience to which it points. As such, they reveal that man can transform himself by means of his own inner resources; he is potentially both redeemed and redeemer in one person in both the world of the depth psychologist and that of the shaman.

Like the process of individuation itself, the experience of call, crisis and cure by which the shaman typically receives his vocation has an overall structure and significance we now classify as initiatory. The future shaman frequently experiences a deep psychological crisis sometimes leading to complete disintegration of the personality and to madness. The process may be envisioned as a descent into psychic chaos involving a dissolution of the profane structures of consciousness and a preparation for rebirth on a higher level of awareness.[7] This dissolution of the profane man and lowering of the threshold of consciousness track the initial stages of regression or introversion recognized by Jung in which man must divest himself of the "false wrappings of the persona," which bind him to the everyday world, and must confront the chaos of the unconscious. Yet, in each system of experience, in Jung's terms, "valuable seeds lie in the chaos," and the successful initiate will tame the chaos and return a man of power and transpersonal experience.

As we remember, one of the characteristics of the individuation process which so fascinated Jung was that it often occurred spontaneously. Moreover, his patients frequently exhibited what he regarded as an unconscious or latent awareness of both the process and its universal symbols. It was as if these were innate structures awakened within the psyche which were pressing to express themselves. He saw this as a predisposition to follow a psychodynamic pattern of behavior which was, itself, in the repeated similarities of its expression, an archetype.

The shaman's initiation into his profession also expresses an archetypal pattern. It carries a similar structure and expresses itself in the same historical symbols, which manifest themselves in other shamanic initiations, in cultures greatly separated by time and distance. And, as we shall see, these same symbolisms share a structure and function very similar to those which Jung found in his contemporary patients marking the process of individuation. Finally, and most interestingly, while these symbols are often employed in intentionally orchestrated initiation ceremonies, they can also spontaneously initiate the candidate in his dreams, visions and ecstasies, or during periods of unconsciousness, initiatory illness or apparent madness. Eliade has made this clear in his *Rites and Symbols of Initiation*. Speaking specifically of the experience of the shaman, he notes that, "Sometimes initiation is public and includes a rich and varied ritual; this is the case, for example, among some Siberian peoples. But the lack of a ritual of this sort in no way implies the lack of an initiation; it is perfectly possible for the initiation to be performed in the candidate's dreams or ecstatic experiences."[8] The shaman encounters the same symbols of transformation which are utilized in public ritual spontaneously in his dreams and visions, and he experiences them as effective forces of initiation. In other words, they naturally effect the same pattern of transformation we shall find in the shaman's initiatory experiences in general.

The shaman frequently receives a call to his profession from what he experiences as emergent forces of the spirit world. They reveal themselves in dreams, ecstasies and even periods which many commentators and novitiate shamans themselves equate with madness. Stanley Krippner tells us, "In Okinawa spirits notify the elect through visions and dreams: most of the recipients who are 'called' attempt to ignore the spirits, but eventually surrender." "Among the Inuit Eskimos," he informs us, "one is 'called' by dreaming about spirits. The dreamer is then possessed by an animal spirit that compels him to withdraw from society and wander naked. Eventually the initiate gains control over the spirit and celebrates his victory by making a drum."[9] According to Jay Miller, among the Yuki of northern California, the shaman-to-be received his call in an unsought vision that could not be refused. In the process, "'The prospective doctor fell into or remained in a trance, bled at the mouth, kicked and jerked. His symptoms were recognized by older doctors, who took him under their care and performed the ... doctor dance in a brush shelter.'"[10] The ritual of the doctor dance then aids him in overcoming his temporary affliction and in assimilating what was revealed to him in vision. These are the first steps toward his vocation.

Åke Hultkrantz similarly notes with regard to South American shamanic cultures that throughout the whole continent "the potential medicine man is suddenly struck by a call from the spirits; in many places they handle him roughly and among the Araucanians he is forced to accept the office against his will."[11] On the other side of our globe, in distant Nepal, Bhirendra, the Tamang shaman with whom we are familiar from Chapter 3, notes the sudden onset of his call. "When I was 13," he informs us, "I became possessed. I later learned that the spirit was my dead grandfather, but at the time I did not know what was happening. I began to shake violently and was unable to sit still even for a minute, even when I was not trembling."[12] Under the influence of such possession, Bhirendra is driven to seek solitude in the forest and cemetery. And a Siberian shaman, Semyonov Semyon, relates his experience as follows:

> "When I shamanize, the spirit of my deceased brother Ilya comes and speaks through my mouth. My [deceased] shaman forefathers, too, have forced me to walk the path of shamanism. Before I commenced to shamanize, I lay sick for a whole year: I became a shaman at the age of fifteen. The sickness that forced me to this path showed itself in a swelling of my body and frequent spells of fainting. When I began to sing, however, the sickness usually disappeared."[13]

This experience illustrates another feature of the shaman's call which we have seen in some of the preceding examples. Quite typically this summons to a spiritual vocation cannot be refused. "Most shamanic traditions take the position that refusal to follow the spirit notification will result in sickness, insanity or even death," Krippner observes.[14] Eliade affirms that this is true of Siberian and Central Asian shamanism and of other traditions as well. He likewise calls our attention to Park's observation on North American shamanism that "Usually a person is reluctant to become a shaman, and assumes his powers and follows the spirits' bidding only when he is told by other shamans that otherwise death will result."[15] As simply expressed by the Native American medicine man Rolling Thunder, referring to his own spiritual calling, "It is a power which comes to you, which you have to honor, respect and use; otherwise it can make you sick."[16] As was the case with Semyonov Semyon, at times it is just such a sickness which forces one to the shaman's path and only shamanizing will alleviate it. Repeatedly the shaman experiences the fact that, whether he wills it or not, he is compelled to become a voice for the sacred.

Shamans, we have noted, are those members of the human community who experience the sacred more intensely than others. They are, according to Eliade, "...persons who stand out in their respective societies by virtue of characteristics that, in the societies of modern Europe, represent the signs of a vocation or at least of a religious crisis. They are separated from the rest of the community by the intensity of their own religious experience."[17] The signs of such a vocation or impending crisis are often manifested in certain preliminary conditions which mark the novitiate as one to be called. Eliade notes that, "The candidate becomes meditative, seeks solitude, sleeps a great deal, seems absent-minded, has prophetic dreams and sometimes seizures. All these symptoms are only the prelude to the new life that awaits the unwitting candidate."[18] Elsewhere he notes this same withdrawal of interest from the everyday world. With regard to the Buryat of southern Siberia, he relates that in the case of hereditary shamanism, "the souls of the ancestor-shamans choose a young man of the family; he becomes absentminded and dreamy, is seized by a need for solitude, has prophetic visions and undergoes fits which leave him unconscious."[19] Borgoras notes that among the Chukchee of northeastern Russia the candidates manifest a similarly characteristic behavior.

> Half unconsciously and half against his own will, his whole soul undergoes a strange and painful transformation. This period may last months, and sometimes even years. The young novice, the "new inspired" (tur-ene'nitvillin) loses all interest in the ordinary affairs of life. He ceases to work, eats but little and without relishing the food, ceases to talk to people and does not even answer their questions.[20]

Linton summarizes the common features found at this stage in the making of a shaman as follows:

> As one reads accounts of the "making of shamans," one finds that there take place certain uniform, or almost uniform, experiences. For example, the shaman as a child usually shows marked introvert tendencies. When these inclinations become manifest, they are encouraged by society. The budding shaman often wanders off and spends a long time by himself. He is rather antisocial in his attitudes and is very frequently seized by mysterious illnesses of one sort or another.[21]

In a similar manner, we may recall that Bhirendra, during the initial phase of the call to his vocation, likewise felt compelled to seek withdrawal and isolation in the forest and cemetery.

Bhirendra ultimately learns that the force behind his call is the spirit of his dead Grandfather. As we have seen, the onset of the shaman's crisis is often announced by and his initiation conducted by creatures from the spirit world. These creatures most often appear in the form of ancestral shamans, the tribal ancestors, or in theriomorphic (animal) or therianthropic (mixed human and animal) forms. As we have witnessed with regard to the summoned novice, in many places these spirit beings "handle him roughly," as Hultkrantz observed. In fact, as applied to many shamanic traditions, this is a gross understatement. The novice frequently experiences his own death, disembowelment, piercing with arrows or lances or complete dismemberment until only a skeletal presence remains, all inflicted by these spirit beings. Sometimes, as we shall see, creatures in animal form assume a terrifying aspect and devour the candidate. These are not isolated experiences but uncannily occur spontaneously over wide ranges of time and in isolated portions of the globe. They announce the beginning stage of initiation, the dissolution of ordinary consciousness and the descent into the unconscious mind which represents the initial phase of an overall psychological process with its own archetypal and purposeful configuration.

We can obtain some understanding of this meaningful and effective pattern of experience if we examine portions of an initiatory dream of a Samoyed shaman from Siberia recorded by A.A. Popov. The dream is an interesting exercise in the reading of archetypal shamanic symbols and an apt illustration of Jung's contention that the dream is "nothing less than a self-portrait of psychic life-processes." As we found in the case of the Siberian shaman, Semyonov Semyon, crisis frequently precipitates illness, and illness often leads to visionary experience. In this case, the candidate's ecstatic initiation occurred when, sick with smallpox, he lay unconscious for three days and appeared so nearly dead that he barely escaped burial. Yet, during this period of relaxed consciousness, his soul is called inward into a realm of symbols which will become increasingly familiar to us as we continue our study. From the crisis of his sicknesses itself, which becomes articulate in his extremity, he learns that "From the Lords of the Water you will receive the gift of shamanizing. Your name as a shaman will be Huottaire (Diver)," an appropriate term for one who will fathom the depths. First suckled at the breast of the Lady of the Water, "Diver" receives from her husband, the Lord of the Underworld, the indispensable companions of the soul's journey, two theriomorphic spirit guides, an ermine and a mouse, who will lead him into the Underworld. Here he encounters "the Lord of Madness and the Lords of all the nervous disorders." Still preceded by his guides, he comes to the realm of the ancestral shamanesses from whom he gains strength in his throat and his voice. Here in the depths, we are told, "He was then carried to the shores of the Nine Seas. In the middle of one of them was an island, and in the middle of the island a young birch tree rose to the sky. It was the Tree of the Lord of the Earth." The birch is the initiatory World Tree of the Siberian shaman, and it is from this tree which rises to the sky that the shaman is said to make the drum, which, Eliade tells us, traditionally projects him to the center of the world, the place of the shaman's ecstasy. And from a branch of this tree our novitiate is instructed to make his drum, the instrument of his curative profession.

His guides now lead him into a cave, but one which paradoxically proves to be a "bright cave, covered with mirrors, in the middle of which there is something like a fire." Ultimately, he discovers that it seems to open upward to a source of light. In the cave he encounters two figures who incarnate versions of the Mother of Reindeer, who give birth to and dispense from the cave supernatural reindeer. The inner world symbolized by this cave becomes a source of power, and we are told of the initiate "When he shamanizes, he mentally turns toward this cave." Let us examine the remainder of this transformative experience.

Then the candidate came to a desert and saw a distant mountain. After three days' travel he reached it, entered an opening and came upon a naked man working a bellows. On the fire was a cauldron 'as big as half the earth.' The naked man saw him and caught him with a huge pair of tongs. The novice had time to think, 'I am dead!' The man cut off his head, chopped his body into bits and put everything in the cauldron. There he boiled his body for three years. There were also three anvils, and the naked man forged the candidate's head on the third, which was the one on which the best shamans were forged. Then he threw the head into one of three pots that stood there, the one in which the water was the coldest...

The blacksmith then fished the candidate's bones out of a river, in which they were floating, put them together and covered them with flesh again. ... He forged his head and taught him how to read the letters that are inside it. He changed his eyes; and that is why, when he shamanizes, he does not see with his bodily eyes but with these mystical eyes.

From this experience the formerly ailing candidate now awakens, still in his hut, but mystically endowed with the power of a shaman.[22]

The dream seems strange indeed. Yet it describes the pattern of an experience with its own form and significance. Here we shall simply outline certain significant characteristics which will become more familiar as we proceed. We have the equation of illness, dreams or unconsciousness, and spontaneous initiatory experience. The transformation is envisioned as a perilous journey – a descent into the chaos of the watery depths or the Underworld of the unconscious mind. We also may note the appearance of the theriomorphic spirit guides; the return to the realm of the ancestors and, quite pertinent to this section of our study, the encounter with the Lord of Madness and the Lords of all nervous disorders. Then, passing beyond the Lord of Madness and the realm of the ancestors within this Underworld, we discover the chief symbol of the shaman's power and ecstasy, of his transcendence and connection with the revitalizing powers of the cosmos, the central tree from which he receives his vocation symbolized by his drum. As we saw among the Tamang in Chapter 3, accompanied by the drum beat, in ecstasy the shaman ascends such a tree to the source of life and the creation itself. Appropriately the spirit guides now lead the shaman-to-be to what we shall recognize to be an archetypal representation of the return to the creative source in many of the world's shamanic traditions – the realm of essences which are to be incarnated in the world of time represented in the animal forms produced within the cave. The paradox that the descent into the darkness of the unconscious will lead to the illuminative experience of the revitalizing source is symbolized in the cave, typically dark, which is somehow bright and opens upward to a source of light above. This, of course, repeats the pattern of finding the central World Tree reaching the heavens in the depths of the Underworld. We shall find quite similar archetypes in other shamanic traditions where they also become the source of the shaman's power and illumination. And, finally, we have most graphically represented the symbols which summarize the entire pattern of experiences: the utter dissolution of consciousness and its resynthesis on a consecrated plane. Here the novice's experiences lead him actually to believe "I am dead." He is decapitated, and his body is chopped into bits and boiled in a cauldron for three years at the hands of this spirit smith of the soul. We can hardly imagine more extreme images of the dissolution of the old self. Yet he is then forged a new head on the anvil "on which the best shamans were forged," his bones are rearticulated and vested with flesh again and, perhaps most tellingly, in the fierce intensity of this inward crisis, the spirit smith "forged his head and taught him to read the letters that are inside it. He changed his eyes; and that is why, when he shamanizes, he does not see with his bodily eyes but with these mystical eyes." From this deep and harrowing experience he now awakens, an initiated man of power.

Here we see epitomized the archetypal pattern of the dissolution of the old self, the descent into the realm of the Lord of Madness and the Lords of all the nervous disorders, a return to the source and a rebirth on a consecrated level of existence. For the present, let us concentrate on the crisis of initiatory illness or madness, both of which appear in this dream as somehow being a necessary preliminary to illumination. Eliade asserts, " ... the shamanic vocation often implies a crisis so deep that it sometimes borders on madness. And since the youth cannot become a shaman until he has resolved this crisis, it is clear that it plays the role of a *mystical initiation*."[23] We might also remember that the Tamang shaman Bhirendra informed us that "when I was thirteen, I became possessed," an uncontrolled possession called "crazy possession" which frequently marks the inception of the Tamang shaman's career.[24] Among the Tungus Eliade notes, "It seems that there is always a hysterical or hysteroid crisis, followed by a period of instruction during which the postulant is initiated by an accredited shaman."[25] A.A. Popov corroborates this for the Siberian shaman in general.

> Explorers who assiduously studied Siberian shamanism on the spot revealed a long time ago that, prior to becoming shamans, the selected persons suffered from physical and psychic diseases for years.
>
> In every case, these diseases were accompanied by peculiar hallucinations and visions of great importance. It was said that during the illness both the constitution and the mental frame of the selected persons underwent a thorough change, while special assistant spirits escorted them on their way to the different deities and spirits, and made them acquainted with each other.[26]

We noted above the fit-like symptoms of the Yuki shaman and the initiatory illness of Semyonov Semyon which manifested itself in psychosomatic symptoms and fainting spells before he began to shamanize. In fact, Eliade refers to the shaman as a madman who has been cured and, often, as one who has cured himself. "To obtain the gift of shamanizing presupposes precisely the solution of the psychic crisis brought on by the first symptoms of election or call," he concludes.[27] Or, as another Siberian shaman was informed by his spirit guide in his initiatory dream, "If you find the spirit of madness, you will begin to shamanize, initiating (new) shamans."[28]

Larry G. Peters observes that "In fact there seems to be general agreement that the shaman, during the critical calling, suffers some form of psychopathology, although there are various opinions as to what this illness is."[29] Julian Silverman, he notes, compares such experiences to acute schizophrenia. Indeed, according to Silverman, certain acute schizophrenic behaviors in our contemporary culture share core psychological features with the shaman's initial crisis at least as it manifests itself in many instances.[30] He notes that each endures an initial condition of fear, impotence and failure where the subject experiences himself as not conforming to the dictates of ordinary society. This condition leads to a period of intense preoccupation, isolation and estrangement, and then a narrowing of the field of attention amounting to a self-initiated period of sensory deprivation. In the next stage of this process:

> The already unstable and weakened "psychological self" is disorganized by this drastically altered environment and is inundated by lower order referential processes such as occur in dreams or reverie. Owing to the depths of the emotional stirring that triggered the whole process, the world comes to be experienced as filled with superpowerful forces and profound but unimaginable meanings.[31]

In this phase there is a fragmentation of one's self-concept as it has been culturally determined and an "eruption into the field of attention and a flood of archaic imagery". Finally, the last stage involves a "cognitive reorganization," and it is here that essential differences between the shaman and the contemporary schizophrenic arise.

While these core factors parallel one another in type and in sequence, the attitudes of each society (i.e., shamanic and contemporary) toward the manifest symptoms differ widely and, correspondingly, so does their resolution.

> In primitive cultures in which such a unique life crisis resolution is tolerated, the abnormal experience (shamanism) is typically beneficial to the individual, cognitively and affectively; he is regarded as one with expanded consciousness. In a culture that does not provide referential guides for comprehending this kind of crisis experience, the individual (schizophrenic) typically undergoes an intensification of his suffering over and above his original anxieties.[32]

In the modern West, the individual frequently succumbs to this chaos of images flooding the mind. In such cases, "the inner chaos is not, so to speak, worked through *or* is not capable of being worked through." On the other hand, in the shaman's society the illness is somehow guided to a favorable outcome according to patterns long recognized and implemented by a sympathetic cultural tradition, a process which our contemporary society seems seldom capable of understanding or implementing.[33]

Other observers point to hysterical symptoms, dissociation, brief reactive psychosis, atypical psychosis and other such explanations as possible diagnoses of the shaman's initiatory crisis. Roger N. Walsh, while recognizing that such diagnostic categories may be helpful, simultaneously cautions against the "trap of reductionism." "Once a diagnostic label and mechanism such as dissociation are suggested, there is a grave risk of reducing the entire process ... to nothing but dissociation. Thus a rich, complex and culturally valued process, when slotted into a Western diagnostic category, can easily be diagnosed and dismissed as nothing but a curious cultural variation of a common defense mechanism."[34]

Walsh likewise points out that many shamans receive their call without suffering any such psychotic episode. This is true, but it does not reduce the importance of the configuration of experience we are here examining. As we shall see, the basic pattern of breaking down the socially constructed self and a lowering of the threshold of consciousness, accompanied by a descent into chaos preliminary to a transforming resynthesis, is "imitated" in patterns of public initiation and initiatory quests for vision. It is also frequently found spontaneously manifesting itself in initiatory dreams as we have mentioned previously. As Eliade points out, the sufferings brought on by this crisis experience correspond to initiatory tortures, the psychic isolation experienced by the elected is reproduced in the ritual isolation and the solitude experienced in initiation ceremonies, and the dissolution and disorientation of consciousness, the descent into chaos experienced by the sick man, is symbolized in the dismemberment and related experiences typical of ceremonies of initiation.[35] This, Eliade tells us, is in fact a "traditional schema" and it is somehow finally capable of turning crisis to cure. In this regard, Peters notes:

> ... seen from a relativistic point of view, shamanism is not a pathological delusion, but is comparable to what Spiro calls a "culturally constituted defense." The shaman's training is a set of psychotherapeutic techniques designed to channel and guide the chaotic feelings created during the calling into a culturally constituted pattern.[36]

Yet, while on one level it is a culturally constituted pattern, on another it shares a cross-cultural universality which transcends time, space and the inflections of local or historical expression. As Campbell notes:

> In the various provinces the visions differ, likewise the techniques of ecstasy and magic traditionally taught; for the cultural patterns through which the shamanistic crisis moves and is realized have local histories and are locally conditioned. Yet the morphology of the crisis ... remains the same wherever the shamanistic vocation has been experienced and cultivated.[37]

And, speaking of the shamans who undergo this crisis, he observes that, as we have previously noted, its basic features are psychological and deeply spontaneous and that it is "to such a degree constant for mankind that we may jump from Hudson Bay to Australia, Tierra del Fuego to Lake Baikal, and find ourselves well at home."[38]

Moreover, the deeply psychological and transpersonal element of these experiences is not only shown in the cross-cultural patterns they share but also in the functional similarity of these images of dream, vision and ecstasy everywhere. For these patterns, and the historical images in which they express themselves, indeed, have a functional aspect. In fact, Jung's observation on the healing properties of such a pattern of symbols applies equally well in this context: "it is evidently an attempt at self-healing on the part of nature." The pattern of experience is, itself, potentially curative. Thus, according to Eliade, " ... the shaman is not only a sick man; he is, above all, a sick man who has been cured, who has succeeded in curing himself. Often when the shaman's or medicine man's vocation is revealed through an illness or an epileptoid attack, the initiation of the candidate is equivalent to a cure."[39] As Eliade elsewhere notes, in these situations "The initiation was tantamount to a healing; among other things, it brought about a new psychic integration."[40] The shaman cures himself of his initiatory illness and afterwards can cure others precisely because he experiences it, understands its psychodynamic aspects and integrates them into consciousness. "Whether they still are or are not subject to real attacks of epilepsy or hysteria, shamans, sorcerers and medicine men in general cannot be regarded as merely sick; their psychopathic experience has a theoretical content. For if they have cured themselves and are able to cure others, it is, among other things, because they know the mechanism, or rather, the *theory* of illness."[41]

Whereas modern Western man tends to topple into the chaos of psychosis, the shaman's culture employs "a set of psychotherapeutic techniques designed to channel and guide the chaotic feelings created during the calling into a culturally constituted pattern," which rescues him from the brink of disaster and ultimately is conducive to his empowerment. This pattern of experience, or "traditional schema" in Eliade's terms, also appears to be cross-cultural and potentially spontaneous or innate, and it not only turns crisis to cure for the shaman and others, but also potentially transforms and expands consciousness. Can we achieve some understanding of this process, or is it forever lost to the "monotheism of the conscious" characterizing modern man?

From Crisis to Cure

If we return to Jung we find that his psychological observations clarify many aspects of this shared pattern of experience which expresses itself in a universal symbolism to guide the psyche's passage through the stages of call, crisis and cure. For we remember that the process of individuation is also a process of transformation of consciousness. Moreover, it demonstrates an unconscious predisposition to produce symbols and a pattern of behavior which is itself archetypal. And like the call of the shaman, this urge to transformation arises spontaneously from the depths of the psyche. The unconscious, Jung recognized, harbors a distinct spiritual drive and a closely related urge to human psychic integration. "The spiritual and religious need," we learned, "is innate in the psyche," and "the spiritual appears in the psyche also as an instinct, indeed a real passion." This emergent urge to spiritual expression becomes man's secret "*spiritus rector*," asserting itself against the everyday world of the persona with incredible strength. As they do during the shaman's call, these unconscious creative contents press forward in dreams, visions and sometimes in more urgent and desperate attempts at self-expression verging on schizophrenia.

Yet the inertia of the everyday world does not readily give up the field to what Jung terms a "spiritual calling" for reasons which Jung found easy to recognize. Though the content of the spiritual calling has a high energy value, it does not become conscious because the content is new and therefore strange to consciousness. There are no existing associations and connecting bridges to the conscious contents. All these connections must first be established with considerable effort, for without them no consciousness is possible. As Sherry Salman notes, "Jung argued that the archetypal symbols which emerge from the unconscious are part of the psyche's *objective* [i.e., universal and transpersonal] religious 'meaning-making' instinct."[42] Yet she also notes that these emerging symbols must be realized subjectively within each individual, and it is this process of realization, what Jung refers to as a laying of connecting bridges, which is essential to the success of spiritual transformation.

The shaman, Eliade told us, is one who experiences the sacred more intensely than the other members of his community. Or, as Campbell sensitively recognizes, his call and crisis are precipitated when he is struck from the depths within by the "absorbing force of what for lack of a better term we may call a hierophantic realization."[43] This dawning spiritual realization gathering force in the unconscious, as we have seen, announces itself in the form of premonitory dreams, visions, ecstasies and even periods of possession or madness. It will eventually become the shaman's "*spiritus rector*" and the guide to his transformation. However, again natural conditions tend to resist the impetus to transformation, and the shaman often initially attempts to reject or cannot assimilate his calling, the force of which, like Jung's emergent creative contents, then becomes repressed. Such repression frequently expresses itself in illness, and the shaman will be exposed to long periods of ecstatic and traditional training in the culture's myth and lore before these contents can be subjectively assimilated – he too must lay the "connecting bridges" of which Jung spoke.

Before this task can be accomplished, however, his condition expresses familiar symptoms. The inability of the conscious mind to cope with this emergent reality and the resistance offered by the world of the persona lead to the feeling of intense preoccupation and estrangement recognized by Silverman as characterizing the initial stage of the shaman's call. In such a situation, as we learned from Jung, we can expect the libido to withdraw from the "outside world" and a process of introversion and isolation to begin.

As Jung noted, at this stage one experiences a listlessness, moroseness and depression. "One no longer has any wish or courage to face the tasks of the day ... one no longer has any disposable energy." "The listlessness and paralysis can go so far the whole personality falls apart, so to speak, and consciousness loses its unity ... ," a condition which Jung recognizes "corresponds to the primitive's loss of soul."[44] This process of withdrawal and isolation, of course, parallels Silverman's second stage of psychological behavior following the shaman's call and precisely reminds us of the observations of Borgoras and Linton concerning the novitiate's introversion. It also recalls Eliade's description of the initially called shaman: "The candidate becomes meditative, seeks solitude, sleeps a great deal, seems absent-minded, has prophetic dreams and sometimes seizures. All these symptoms are only a prelude to the new life that awaits him."

Prelude they may be, but a prelude full of strident disharmonies which warn us of the difficult journey to follow. We have noted that according to Jung, although this emergent realization has a high enough energy value to burst into full consciousness, the conscious mind is not yet prepared for such content. As such, this unexpressed force remains suspended in the domain of the unconscious, and if its energy content is strong enough it tends to evolve into a fragmentary psychic system or split-off complex. Jung observed several very interesting features pertaining to these complexes, many of which we have difficulty understanding because they offend against the exclusive integrity of an ego which would prefer to turn a deaf ear to them. Of course, this is often what caused much of the problem in the first place. However, to summarize what was said earlier, these split-off complexes, if not integrated with consciousness, actually assume a character of their own. "As constituents of the psychic personality, they necessarily have the character of persons," Jung previously informed us. Moreover, they manifest and assert their own autonomy. They possess, as we have noted, their own goals and with "iron grip" attempt to impose them upon the overall psyche. As products of the transpersonal or archetypal psyche, they frequently carry forward its "religious 'meaning-making' instinct." Thus, they are capable of assuming distinct spiritual qualities. The longer the stoppage of energy associated with their urgent content persists, the stronger becomes the force they potentially carry – "they become enriched with more and more associations and attach themselves to an ever-widening range of psychic material." These additions vest them with an almost irresistible attractive appeal, increasing the tension between their power and the natural resistance of consciousness. This tension leads to conflict and soon these contents are pitted in their efforts against and threaten the exclusive integrity of the conscious mind. Failure to assimilate their urgent contents can lead to neurosis, states of possession or schizophrenia. The associations with which they are charged become increasingly archaic and mythological in content, and a welter of anarchic images assails the unprepared consciousness. Finally, and perhaps most tellingly, Jung found that these split-off complexes very frequently presented themselves in two important forms: the wise-old-man or the cultural ancestor – i.e., that 2,000,000-year-old man who is in all of us and carries the legacy of our unconscious psychic heritage – and creatures with theriomorphic or therianthropic characteristics, indicative of our potential relationship to the deepest layers of the psyche, the "essential" man whose call is innate in each of us.

Let us now return to our description of the shaman's call, crisis and cure. In doing so, however, we must suspend our own prejudices and keep in mind one of the most important touchstones of Jung's thought and the shaman's experience – events experienced by the mind in what we would call the "psychic or inner world" have their own claim to a reality equal to that which the same mind imposes on the unknowable world presented by the senses. Each is a realm of experience in which we seek durable laws with their own universality which allow us to track and predict change or transformation in that realm. We must suspend our reductive tendency to regard as "merely psychological" an inwardly encountered pattern of experience capable of producing powerful transformations in a process which has enlisted the depths of the human mind for perhaps tens of thousands of years, thus holding a pedigree enduring far longer than any of the discoveries of our Western scientific materialism.

In the shaman's world, symptoms of withdrawal and isolation, we noted, often accompany the call and portend the process of introversion which is to follow. At this juncture, as Jung also found true of the process of individuation, the world of the psyche and not that of outward circumstance forces itself into prominence. Here, as long as we do not assume that it exhausts the reality of these experiences, it is illuminating to apply Jung's observations concerning the qualities manifested by the split-off complexes of his contemporary analysands with the shaman's experiences, for the points of parallel are quite striking.[†] In accordance with Jungian thought, we might say that these emerging spiritual realities emanating from the unconscious begin to dissociate from a conscious mind not yet prepared for their revelation. In accordance with the spiritual nature of the unconscious and its symbols, they are experienced as emissaries from the spirit world. And, as Jung so often found, they begin to manifest their own autonomy and become a force capable of guiding the psyche in their own direction. We remember that the shaman often initially resists their call. However, ultimately such resistance proves either futile or fatal. Refusal of their call traditionally means sickness or insanity, as we have noted, for failure to integrate their contents will lead to neurosis, other illnesses or the full-blown split of the psyche we recognize as schizophrenia. The longer the psyche resists the compelling force of these subliminal subjects, the higher the charge of their contents grows. They become enriched with more and more associations of an archaic and mythological nature until at last, as

---

[†] In speaking of split-off complexes, we are temporarily assuming the risk of, as Walsh notes, "imposing Western cultural diagnostic perspectives, thereby reducing and pathologizing these rich phenomena to mere diagnostic categories." Yet we must remember that Jung viewed and actually experienced these spiritual entities as having a greater reality. For him, the unconscious opens inward; it is our connection with the formal powers of nature and the cosmos, and in such expressions of the spirit, as we remember, "the *world itself* is speaking."

Silverman notes, "the psychological self is disorganized." The shaman becomes overwhelmed by a flow of archaic and mythological imagery from the depths of the unconscious psyche and, frequently, a form of possession or initiatory illness follows. This is the moment of crisis, for this welter of archaic material may create a chaos from which there is no return. On the other hand, it may offer the very material which can serve to build the connecting bridges that will reintegrate and empower the psyche and enable this emergent reality to assume the form of *spiritus rector*, the guide to the deeper reality of the spirit.

In the examples of the shaman's call which we examined at the inception of this chapter, the spiritual entities who announced the call to transformation were most generally the deceased ancestors of the tribe or culture or creatures assuming an animal or mixed animal and human form. This is a phenomenon found throughout the world with an uncanny consistency. And, as we have noted, this is precisely what Jung found in his work. The emerging reality of the *spiritus rector* had a distinct tendency to assume these very forms and, in fact, as the final chapter shows, it did so within the depths of Jung's own psyche at a time of deep and desperate crisis and led the way from crisis to cure. In the shaman's world, it is these same creatures who will lead him to enlightenment, for they emanate from the world of the primordial symbol and are masters of the inner or imaginal world through which he must journey if he is to gain integration and power. They represent the potential for mythological deepening – the laying of bridges by virtue of the ecstatic and traditional training which will reconnect the shaman with his own depths and powers.

As we have stated, for Jung symbols are the best possible expression of an as yet unknown creative content within the unconscious, something that has yet to be and seeks subjective realization. When he speaks of symbols, he is speaking of emergent realities in the form of primordial images or archetypes pressing forward from the unconscious and often acting in a manner which seeks to provide compensation for something lacking in the conscious mind. And if we speak of the ancestors or animal spirit guides as bearing certain symbolic associations, this is not to imply they "stand for" or are an allegory of something else. Jung found that often the split-off complexes of his patients actually presented themselves in these very forms and had an effective reality of their own. Yet, at the same time, the forms of the ancestor and the theriomorph carried telling characteristics which portrayed the deepening process that would provide the material for the mind's salvation. For instance, the image of the ancestor seemed to emerge at that moment when psychic energy regresses, going beyond the period of early infancy, and breaks into the legacy of ancestral life. When we have tapped into this legacy, mythological images are awakened. These are the archetypes of the collective unconscious. As we noted, Jung found in analysis that his patients specifically equated the world of the ancestors with the confrontation with the collective unconscious. According to his findings, "the unconscious corresponds to the mythic land of the dead, the land of the ancestors," and, as such, man's "beginnings are not by any means mere pasts; they live with him as the constant substratum of his existence." It is this wealth of archetypes which, for both the shaman and for Jung's patients, will serve as the vehicle of transformation and rearticulate the vital connections between the conscious, the unconscious and the mind's deeper sources in instinct and cosmic life.

Similar observations apply to the image of the theriomorph. These psychic figures, Jung felt, emanate from and represent that portion of our psychic life connecting back to our origins in instinct, somatically based patterns of behavior and response and eventually to nature itself. As Ira Progoff noted, this "level of the unconscious represents the point at which the psyche is so close to the animal world as not yet to be differentiated from it. It still is directly connected to the realm of nature in its mode of functioning, and it is thus the aspect of the human organism that can be most directly experienced as a part of nature." "The archetype as an image of instinct is a spiritual goal toward which the whole nature of man strives: it is the sea to which all rivers wend their way," Jung proclaimed.[45] Activating such collective images potentially has a compensatory and curative effect. Such images, properly entertained, canalize the libido and act as a guide for our psychic energy, redirecting it in the compensatory direction demanded by the needs of the psyche as a whole.

In the shaman's world, almost everywhere it is most often the ancestors or spiritual entities with a theriomorphic form who announce the call and lead the shaman's initiation into the psyche's depths. Indeed, throughout human history the roles of the ancestors and the theriomorphs often converged in the totem animal ancestors of so many archaic and shamanic cultures, thus representing in a single symbol these two deep layers of psychological reality. In these guiding spirits, the experience of a transpersonal archetypal reality speaking through the individual, on one level of expression, combines with the effective power of the symbol as a transformer of libido, on another plane of reference, to indicate the age-old experience of the manner in which these figures can become the guide to the larger world of the spirit.

We may take a few brief examples. In Australian Aboriginal shamanic tradition, it is frequently the ancestors who announce the call, often in dream, escorting the novitiate on an initiatory celestial flight. They or their representatives initiate the shaman either in spontaneous ecstatic experience or in traditional ceremony and training. They indeed represent the "legacy of ancestral life." For the Aborigines, Jung's observation that "man's beginnings are not by any means mere pasts, they live with him as the constant substratum of his existence" is a guiding reality. The ancestors at the beginning of time established an enduring, paradigmatic reality which guides and informs all human action, as we have previously observed. According to Eliade, "Indeed, the events that took place in the mythological times, the 'Dream Time,' are religious in the sense that they constitute a paradigmatic history which man has to follow and repeat in order to assure the continuity of the world, of life and society."[46] Yet this primordial reality does not exist only in the historical past. It is presently accessible to humans and particularly to the shaman. Moreover, it is accessible precisely because the archetypal reality of myth and initiatory ritual opens the mind to the dreamtime realm of the ancestors. Consequently, in the language of most of the tribes, myth, ritual and sacred traditional lore are referred to by the very same term that denotes the ancestral dreamtime.

In fact, this paradigmatic realm, this "constant substratum of his existence," is for the Aborigine an immanent though often initially preconscious reality which can be recovered through the processes inherent in initiation or spontaneous ecstatic experience. A portion of the soul is actually believed to be descended from a Wondjina, a mythical ancestor. This is "a particle of the ancestor's 'life'" which is immanent in each human being, and it is ultimately the embodiment of the dreamtime. In essence, each man is potentially the mythical ancestor or dreamtime hero, and his soul innately carries the characteristics of an archetypal reality associated with the ancestral realm. "His most secret self is a part of that sacred world ... ," Eliade points out. "But he does not know his own real identity: this must be revealed to him through initiation rites. Thus, one may say that the initiation reinstates the young Australian in his original spiritual mode of being."[47] In initiation, the ancestors through myth and ritual progressively thin the distance between life and an understanding of the creationtime paradigms which inform it. This process, as Eliade recognizes, is again a rediscovery of preconscious origins, a recollection of an archetypal reality which is innately known. Here his acts are not only the same acts as those of the original ancestor at time's beginning but also he actually is the ancestor and shares his "glorious pre-existence."[48] In Jung's terms he, indeed, incarnates "the 2,000,000-year-old man in all of us."[†] Thus, the dreamtime is the informing reality of both the microcosm and the macrocosm, an archetypal world carried forward in the objective psyche which announces itself to the Australian shaman, as it did to Jung's patients, in the form of the wisdom-bearing ancestor as guide to the recovery of our legacy of primordial, transpersonal wisdom.

In Australia, another important source of the shaman's call and initiation is the mythical rainbow snake, Unggud, a feathered serpent frequently regarded as having anthropomorphic characteristics. This therianthropic creature appears in dreams and visions and leads or even carries the candidate on his back in celestial flight to his initiation. In certain instances, the initial episodes involving this serpent or kindred creatures are terrifying and lead to the shaman's dismemberment or disembowelment, or his being engorged and excreted by the mythical serpent – sometimes, in a rebirth symbolism, in the form of a child. Unggud is a denizen of the paradigmatic ancestral realm, a totem ancestor, and in some tribal mythologies is an important source of the cosmic creation itself, i.e., the source of cosmic life.

[†] Jung makes a very similar comment in "Concerning Rebirth." "So, too, primitives try to change themselves back to their ancestors by means of certain rites. I would mention especially the Australian conception of the Alcheringamijina [Dreamtime heroes], ancestral souls, half man and half animal, whose reactivation through religious rites is of the greatest functional significance for the life of the tribe." (C.W., Vol. 9, 1, para. 224.)

In fact, theriomorphic symbols, as we have noted, almost universally accompany the shaman's transformation of consciousness. The shaman's ritual costume frequently reflects this association with a headdress bearing animal horns and a robe consisting of various animal skins, pendant paws or tails, bird feathers, etc., all with specific symbolic reference to transformation. Indeed, in many cultures the shaman ritually or in ecstasy transforms into the mythical animal. The South American Tukano shaman in a drug-enhanced ecstasy actually experiences his transformation into the animal companion jaguar form. It is in these states of altered consciousness that the Tukano shaman can travel back to experience the source of cosmic life, the creation itself. In Central America, artifacts from the ancient Olmec culture reflect similar shamanic transformations graphically revealing various stages of the shaman's change into an animal-like form. Recent progress in the translation of the Maya system of writing has revealed a similar symbolism with an interesting set of connotations. The glyph, which was first recognized as bearing this symbolism, is composed of a king or ruler's face half-covered with an animal pelt. It has been translated *way*, which means to transform, but also to dream as well as animal spirit guide and sorcerer or shaman.[49] It also appears to be related to the later term *naual* or *nagual* which Dennis Tedlock tells us in some contexts refers to the "spiritual essence or character" of a person or animal.[50] Now if we recall that Jung found that frequently 1) *the therianthropic spirit guide,* 2) announced the call to *transformation,* 3) in *dream* and 4) tended to appear in this form when the demand for psychodynamic adjustment came from deep within as the call, in Jung's terms, of the "essential man," i.e., his *spiritual essence or character* – which represents the anthropoid psyche connecting us back to the world of instinct and back farther into cosmos – we have a remarkably congruent set of symbols and ideas on both a structural and functional level. As Jung has told us, such therianthropic images represent human psychic integration, a "wholeness which is both God and animal – not merely the empirical man, but the totality of his being – which is rooted in his animal nature and reaches out beyond the merely human into the divine." It is fitting, then, that in the Maya world the *way* also leads not only to the animal realm but also back to the divine cosmic source itself. We learn that transforming into the *way*, the shaman and others in ritual traveled back to the enduring source of creation, a sacred parallel world of essence revealed in trance which is believed to be anterior to and informing our physical reality.[51] Thus, like many of their shamanic counterparts, in therianthropic transformation the Maya entered this essential source of archetypal form and creative power.

Mircea Eliade well captures this widespread symbolism. Speaking of the meaning implicit in the ancient Chinese shaman's symbolic metamorphosis into the animal spirit, often identified with the ancestors or the source of cosmic life itself, he explains:

By becoming this mythical animal, man became something far greater and stronger than himself. We are justified in supposing that this projection into a mythical being, the center at once of the existence and renewal of the universe, induced the euphoric experience that, before ending in ecstasy, showed the shaman his power and brought him into communion with cosmic life.[52]

Thus, these figures symbolize and their emergence actually leads to the deepening of consciousness through which the shaman experiences a sacred unity with cosmic life in the manner which we have described. Properly assimilated to consciousness, they do, in fact, represent the primordial wisdom of the innermost self, enlisting the collective unconscious, the realm of instinct and the natural wisdom of the body. In so doing, such archetypes bring forward the experience of the source of cosmic life as a reality accessible to man. As *spiritus rector* they incarnate a law we must obey if we are to fathom successfully the psyche's "strange symbolic wanderings."

Yet the assimilation of these unconscious contents into consciousness is by no means easy, as we know from our study of Jung. They at first assail the conscious mind in forms which threaten its unity, its direction and even its sanity if it is not prepared to accept their reality. Their initially threatening and fragmenting effect is represented in the visions of shamans worldwide. We recall the observation of Hultkrantz that often "the potential medicine man is suddenly struck by a call from the spirits; in many places they handle him roughly ... " We may also recall the initiatory dream of the shaman Huottaire (Diver) in the spirit world where he envisions his head to be severed, his body chopped to bits and everything placed into a cauldron and boiled for three years. Or we may note the continuation of the ecstatic experience of Semyonov Semyon, called to the profession by his deceased shaman forefathers, which we offered in the first section of this chapter. His story continues describing the visionary experience of his personal transformation:

> After that, my ancestors began to shamanize with me. They stood me up like a block of wood and shot at me with their bows until I lost consciousness. They cut up my flesh, separated my bones, counted them and ate my flesh raw. When they counted the bones they found one too many; had there been too few, I could not have become a shaman.

He continues, "the same things happens to every Tungus shaman. Only after his shaman ancestors have cut up his body in this way and separated his bones can he begin to practice."[53]

Eliade notes that these fragmenting visions of dismemberment, piercing or disembowelment at the hands of the spirit beings issuing the call are found in various forms worldwide.[54] Professor A.P. Elkin describes this configuration of visionary experience with regard to the Australian shaman where "two totemic spirits or heroes 'kill' the postulant, cut him open from his neck to his groin, take out all his insides and insert magical substances [quartz crystals]."[55] Eliade points out that the Inuit shaman experiences his own dismemberment in vision during his initiation.[56] Among the Plains

Indians of North America, actual practices of dismemberment and piercing have survived into historical times in association with the shaman's quest for vision. And the iconography of the Classic Maya reveals similar practices in which the vision-seeker is pierced through the genitals or through the tongue, running a finger-thick rope through the aperture and allowing the blood from this self-piercing to soak into papers which composed burned offerings employed to summon the ancestors to attend these ceremonies of "autosacrifice."

Such images of decapitation, dismemberment, disembowelment and piercing graphically portray the fragmenting effect initially created by the urgent unconscious contents cast up by the objective psyche and their effect on the natural resistance of the conscious mind. If the psyche cannot progress beyond this stage of transformation, as we know from our study of Jung, these forms and their contents can become fixed and consequently can destroy the unity of the personality. This process, of course, spurs the illness or madness which attends the refusal of the call in the shaman's world. "The wider the gap between conscious and unconscious, the nearer creeps the fatal splitting of the personality which in neurotically disposed individuals leads to neurosis and, in those with a psychotic constitution, to schizophrenia and fragmentation of personality," Jung informed us. "The danger lies in those well-known 'perils of the soul' — a splitting of the personality ('loss of a soul') and a reduction of consciousness, both of which automatically increase the power of the unconscious. The consequences of this are a serious danger not only for primitives; in civilized man, too, they may give rise to psychic disturbances, states of possession and psychic epidemics."

In a manner consistent with these observations, in the world's shamanic traditions this stage of psychic experience is likewise frequently equated with a soul loss, a splitting of the personality and, as we have noted, with the experience of possession. We may recall from Chapter 3 the case of Kumari among the Tamang of Nepal, her dissociation, possession and loss of soul, and Bhirendra's initial state of possession when he is called to his profession by his deceased shaman Grandfather. In fact, Larry G. Peters and Douglass Price-Williams in their study of shamanism in forty-two different cultures found evidences of the experience of spirit possession in a majority of them.[57] Frequently such possession is spontaneous, an initiatory possession often interpreted as an illness. As we shall see, it is precisely when the novitiate gains mastery over the spirits who possess him that he becomes a full-fledged shaman. And, as Peters informs us in the case of Bhirendra's possession, it is only through extended traditional and ecstatic training that such possession can be overcome.[58] Initially such states of possession imply a reduction of consciousness and an increase in the power of the unconscious in a manner parallel to Jung's observations. As such, they present themselves as a threat to the conscious mind.

Frequently, at this stage, the shaman's visionary experience aptly portrays the state of being overcome by unconscious contents as one of being engorged by a therianthropic or theriomorphic creature. These forms, of course, express our connection and confrontation with the deep levels of the unconscious as we have examined. Thus, in his visionary experience the Australian shaman is frequently portrayed as initially being swallowed by the therianthropic serpent, Unggud, or some similar beast. Among the Inuit, a bear plays an analogous role, at times in conjunction with a dismemberment symbolism, and among the Classic Maya this part was sometimes performed by a jaguar or serpent. Each symbolism graphically portrays the lowering of the traditional defenses of the conscious mind as well as the automatic increase in the power of the unconscious and the threat of an overwhelming possession by these contents – the same contents which Jung found frequently heralded the process of psychological transformation, the descent into chaos which threatened insanity but could also hold salvation.

As we have noted, for Jung, this stage of psychological experience received one of its most telling expressions, or perhaps projections, in the alchemist's experience of the *nigredo*, the mind's immersion in the chaotic blackness of the *prima materia*. Yet, as Jung informed us, valuable seeds lie in the chaos, and the alchemical visionary experience gave this realization archetypal expression. For the *lapis* itself, the adamantine reality of the philosopher's stone and the enlightenment it holds, traditionally lies buried within the welter of the *prima materia*. The *nigredo* is specifically envisioned as a womb and the source of rebirth and renewal. The ego death of the shaman, so graphically depicted in images of dismemberment, disembowelment, bloodletting, etc., seems to embody the same pattern of experience throughout diverse areas of the world, and the ultimate goal of the initiatory experience is expressed in an important and recurrent form of symbolism which bears a striking similarity to the alchemical vision of the imperishable reality of the *lapis* buried within the *prima materia* experienced upon the dissolution of ego-consciousness.

We can see this significance and underlying purpose begin to emerge with regard to the symbols which we have been describing. Eliade tells us that " ... in the spiritual horizon of hunters and herdsmen bone represents the very source of life, both human and animal. To reduce oneself to the skeleton condition is equivalent to re-entering the womb of this primordial life, that is, to a complete renewal, a mystical rebirth."[59]

> We are here in the presence of a very ancient religious idea, which belongs to the hunter culture. Bone symbolizes the final root of animal life, the mold from which the flesh continually arises. It is from the bone that men and animals are reborn; for a time, they maintain themselves in an existence of the flesh; then they die, and their "life" is reduced to the essence concentrated in the skeleton, from which they will be born again. Reduced to skeletons, the future shamans undergo the mystical death that enables them to return to the inexhaustible fount of cosmic life.[60]

From a larger perspective, the symbolism of dismemberment and reduction to bone implies a return of life to its ultimate and indestructible essence, the same ultimate and indestructible essence represented by the *lapis*.

And while there may be different local expressions by which the overall symbolism is represented, the underlying pattern remains much the same. For the Siberian and Eskimo shamans, this essential reality, expressed in the dismemberment symbolism, is imaged in the reduction to bone. Likewise, the Australian shaman, during his initiatory dismemberment, becomes the literal embodiment of the world of "indestructible essence," for this is what the newly implanted quartz crystals, which we described above, represent. Just as was the case in Siberia, the same symbolism has a cosmic value. The durative reality symbolized in the quartz, the new essence of the shaman, represents the imperishable and paradigmatic reality which underlies and supports our transient creation. In returning to his "source," the Australian shaman returns to "The Source" where each individual life experiences its origin in cosmic life. We might also recall the Maya shaman and the blood of his autosacrifice. In the Maya world, blood is itself symbolic of essence – the world was created by a blood sacrifice, and sacrificial blood is the source of the generation and regeneration of the cosmos, the very stuff of the "inexhaustible fount of cosmic life." Thus, the ritual letting of blood is a return to essence on an individual and a cosmic level. Moreover, among the Maya, reduction to bone likewise symbolized a return to essence and a potential rebirth, for "bone" and "seed" or "essence" are homophones among the Maya and the Maya frequently employed homophones to suggest symbolic relationships. In each case, among widely separated cultures, the dismemberment symbolism has naturally appropriated an element which expresses an underlying goal and a return to the source of cosmic life. In each case, symbols implying initiatory death yield to a larger pattern promising illumination and rebirth upon a consecrated level.

Perhaps we can gain an understanding of the intuition which naturally informs and directs this configuration of symbolism by recalling a statement Jung made in the prologue to his autobiography:

> Life has always seemed to me like a plant that lives on its rhizome. Its true life is invisible, hidden in the rhizome. ... I have never lost a sense of something that lives and endures underneath the eternal flux. What we see is the blossom, which passes. The rhizome remains.

> In the end the only events in my life worth telling are those when the imperishable world irrupted into this transitory one. That is why I speak chiefly of inner experiences, amongst which I include my dreams and visions.[61]

It is this "something that lives and endures underneath the eternal flux" that, as we shall see in the next chapter, the shaman's natural capacities and training enable him to experience in vision. In his vision training, "the imperishable world [which irrupts] into this transitory one" becomes a guiding reality and the vehicle of his transformation. For it is the archetypal patterns at the root level of existence which become a bridge between the world of imperishable form and that of time and change.

In Jungian terms, the shaman experiences that "He is of the same essence as the universe and that his own mid-point is its center."[62] He has, in Eliade's terms, been shown his power and brought into communion with cosmic life. The shaman experiences himself as, in some sense, continuous with the creative plenitude and inner wisdom of nature and the cosmos. And in this regard Jung's observations again are revealing, for partaking of this wisdom of nature and cosmic life causes a transformation of the theriomorphic images which have expressed this reality. As we noted earlier, Jung found that "The guise in which these figures appear depends on the attitude of the conscious mind: if it is negative towards the unconscious, the animals will be frightening; if positive, they appear as the 'helpful' animals of fairytale and legend."[63] Thus, in this process of transformation, with increased insight forms which at first assailed the shaman are ultimately to become the sources of this inner wisdom, and the very forces of the unconscious that previously threatened to engorge the shaman now become his guides. They reveal themselves to be attempts at self-healing on the part of nature through the symbols of transformation natural to the unconscious. Consequently, in a telling symbolism, the very bear which devoured and dismembered our Inuit shaman becomes his totem guide, the jaguar and the serpent become the spirit guides of the South and Central American shaman and the serpent which engorged the Australian shaman becomes the vehicle of his ascent to the dreamtime. It is these figures which so frequently appear during the shaman's ordeal of initiation, and it is they who lead him to his power. Under their guidance, cosmic life and purpose become articulate, and we can truly say that in these symbols "the *world itself* is speaking."

And the archetypal pattern in which the world speaks is a now familiar one – one which Jung recognized to be typical of the process of regression or introversion which naturally occurs to break the stalemate between the resistance of the conscious mind and the urgings of the unconscious *spiritus rector*. In a configuration of experience which recalls Jung's vision of creative illness, beneath the surface of the troubled consciousness the psyche has, indeed, been working in a manner which confirms the intuition of purposive direction expressed in the symbolisms we examined above. Everything psychic contains its opposite, as Jung has noted, and just as the symbolism of dismemberment ultimately presages rebirth and the forms which troubled consciousness become its guides, so the processes of dissolution of consciousness which threaten the novitiate silently work toward ultimate enlightenment. Seen from a larger perspective, the dismemberment symbolism implies an ego death, the divestiture of the false wrappings of the persona which bind the mind to the everyday world. It symbolizes the same lowering of the threshold of consciousness which marks the first stages of the inward journey and the shift in attention from the world of outward circumstances to the inner world of the psyche and to the universal forms that lie in the dark depths of the psyche's interior. It is here that the conscious mind is potentially irrigated by the flow of primordial images from the collective unconscious. This is the same revelation at the end of the same journey recurrently described by Jung, the treasure from the depths, the seeds of the mythopoeic imagination which lie in the chaos awakened through introversion that he repeatedly found in his patients. The reward is great, but the risk is real.

> Though such imagination is present everywhere, it is both tabooed and dreaded so that it even appears to be a risky experiment or a questionable adventure to entrust oneself to the uncertain path that leads into the depths of the unconscious. It is considered the path of error, of equivocation and misunderstanding. I am reminded of Goethe's words: "now let me dare to open wide the gate / Past which men's steps have ever flinchingly trod."[64]

It was the shaman, with the assistance and understanding of his culture and tradition, and especially those archetypal symbols of the native tradition which are capable of guiding and transforming psychic experience, who did first "dare to open wide the gate / Past which men's steps have ever flinchingly trod." It was he who dared to follow the strange symbolic wanderings of the psyche into the chaos of the unconscious and to bring its contents back to the surface in a meaningful way. For it is not the illness but the cure, which the depth of crisis reveals, that lies at the heart of shamanism. As Eliade told us, "their psychopathic experience has a theoretical content. For if they have cured themselves and are able to cure others, it is, among other things, because they know the mechanism, or rather, the *theory* of illness." The shaman, based on his own experience, is able to harness the "attempt at self-healing on the part of Nature" which Jung saw expressed in archetypal symbols. Employing the mind's innate healing capacity, he moves from crisis to cure in his own visionary experience and in other rites and ceremonies and is able to communicate this experience to others.

The shaman chooses to exercise rather than exorcise the overtures of the spirit. And at times his journey leads him to the brink of madness, for here, as Jung notes, lies the matrix of a mythopoeic imagination capable of overwhelming and holding captive the conscious mind or of revealing the deep world of symbolic contents which give ultimate form and power to human experience. "If you find the spirit of madness, you will begin to shamanize," we have been told by a Siberian shaman whose journey, as we shall see, will lead him to the source of his power. Or, as Plato informs us at the beginning of Western civilization, the greatest blessings come by way of madness, or mania, and of its forms the greatest is erotic mania. And, as we know from Jung, it is the daemon Eros who awakens the mind to the powers of the cosmos which "in-form" it. Ultimately, it is these formal powers through which the world itself is speaking in primordial images that are capable of rearticulating the inner template of the soul and creating an imaginal world with its own structure and function in the manner and form which we shall proceed to examine in the following chapters.

Chapter 7

Connecting Bridges

We must unite conscious man with primitive man.

C. G. Jung

The Shaman's Traditional and Ecstatic Training

Operating under our initial imperative of "only connect" with which we began this book, in the previous section we attempted to illustrate the telling correspondences between certain spontaneous initiatory experiences of the shaman and the initial stages of the process of individuation which Jung found in his contemporary patients. And, in fact, each of these processes gave a larger meaning to this imperative, for each revealed an overall process of psychological transformation, the stages of which are innate in the mind of man. When reawakened, they, indeed, served to "connect" the mind naturally back to its own formal vitalizing sources, its archetypal and universal creative and spiritual foundation from which it becomes alienated only to its peril and diminution.

We noted that, much in accordance with the configuration of the initial stages of Jung's process of individuation, the shaman receives a spiritual calling, i.e., in Jungian terms is exposed to a new creative content emanating from that deep layer of the unconscious which seems to produce overtures we experience as spiritual, the depths of which are not easily assimilated by the conscious mind. This experience creates first a period of withdrawal of interest from the world at large, absent-mindedness, a tendency toward meditative silence and solitude and sometimes prophetic dreams and even seizures. These characteristics herald a process of introversion which modern psychology associates with dissociation and regression, but behind which Jung recognized what shamanic cultures had perceived long before him – that this process harbored an overall compensatory and eventually salutary direction and purpose. What appears as regression has the potential effect of a relocation of the focal point of the real inward, of making man come to grips with the dark background and source of his own consciousness. In the process, it frees the wellsprings of the mythopoeic imagination and lets loose those archaic images which have guided man over the aeons but which have been largely lost or "literalized" by the modern West. Frequently, these images become manifest in the form of actual personalities with a significance and directive power of their own. Confronted with these images cast up from the hinterlands of the psyche, the mind's stability hangs most precariously in the balance between possible mental illness and the expansion of consciousness and illumination which are the shaman's goals. At this stage, the inner world can either remain a chaos and overwhelm the conscious mind, or it can constellate a middle world capable of rearticulating the vital connection between consciousness and its archetypal instinctual roots reaching back to what Jung termed, and the shaman experiences as, "the deep root of being."

For both Jung's patients and for the shaman, exposure to this fund of imagery could occur naturally in dream, vision, trance or states of possession involving an often sudden lowering of the threshold of consciousness and an abrupt encounter with the powers of the our inner realm. In archaic cultures with a well inculcated mythological heritage, society's dominant images fostered the mind's natural tendencies toward a spontaneous resolution of the psychological crisis. Over the hundreds of centuries of human experience, archaic cultures became adept at recognizing and guiding these unleashed powers in an affirmative direction. Myth and the ritual activities which framed and supported the culture of these societies reinforced the archetypal pathways of the mind inherently capable of taming the chaos into innate order and significance. In the modern demythologized West, however, such spontaneous resolution is far less probable. Yet Jung discovered another approach to the problem. As we remember, he found that instead of a precipitous lowering of the threshold of consciousness which suddenly confronted the conscious mind with the often overwhelming task of assimilating the contents that have burst in upon it, he could effect this lowering of the threshold of consciousness and the process of assimilation intentionally and gradually in a more methodical and controlled manner.

This process, which we examined in Chapter 5, generally can be seen as involving three stages. Implicit in each is a recognition of the role that the mind plays in structuring reality and a corresponding recognition of the innate structures of transformation in the human psyche which can be intentionally activated and guided. For Jung, the first stage generally dealt with releasing the transformative capacities of the mind by eliminating those structures of consciousness which impeded these capacities. It was initially necessary to temper our exclusive reliance on the conscious mind and our submission to its obsessive habits of externalization and directed thinking. This process had the ultimate objective of creating space for a greater receptivity for the primordial image.

Jung, we remember, associated this stage of lowering the threshold of consciousness with techniques of descent as well as visionary and trance experience. He recognized this stage as being analogous to the stage of the *nigredo* in alchemy and used it to prepare the way for the second stage of this process which, as we know, involved application of various techniques to elicit the primordial image and then to amplify its significance and attempt to assimilate its contexts. Finally, in the third stage, after a long arduous process of working with these figures – of psychological and spiritual confrontation with and realization of their contents – these images began to present a world with its own transpersonal form and significance, consisting of archetypal patterns with revitalizing power and an apparent wisdom of their own.

While these techniques are regarded as the modern and innovative tools of the depth psychologist, they do, in fact, have a long history. We find a very similar set of procedures existing for perhaps millennia and employed over the long ages in the shaman's world. The process of the shaman's initiation very often involves long periods of intentionally induced transformation, of what Eliade refers to as traditional and ecstatic training. It is this training which will construct the "connecting bridges" which can deepen and integrate the candidate's psyche. This training process frequently employs techniques which bear many affinities with those utilized by Jung in his attempt to effect psychic integration in his patients. We can trace the same general stages in the shaman's initiation and training, for it likewise involves an intentional removal of certain structures of consciousness and the lowering of its threshold to promote regression or introversion. Moreover, it likewise entails the activation of innate processes of transformation through the eliciting, enhancing and assimilation of the primordial images unleashed from the unconscious. And finally, it guides and canalizes these unleashed energies and forces into a world of transformative symbols, a transpersonal *mundus imaginalis* very much the same in both structure and function as that which Jung was able to discover utilizing similar processes with his contemporary patients. In short, the shaman anticipated by centuries many of what we currently regard as the modern techniques of depth psychology and, as we shall see, may have perfected them to a greater degree than we have done to date.

"When the surface has been cleared, things can grow out of the depths,"[1] Jung asserted with regard to the preliminary stages of individuation, and the initial stages of shamanic initiation and training well exemplify this maxim. These first stages both symbolically express and help effect what Eliade has called "a break with the universe of daily life."[2] According to him, the ultimate objective of this process is "to make the novice die to the human condition and to resuscitate him to a new, transhuman existence."[3] The disciplines employed work together to further spiritual progress by deconstructing both the thought processes which bind the candidate to the everyday world and the empirical self. On the one hand, the shaman is intentionally exposed to liminal, or borderline, situations which challenge traditional social forms and conventional wisdom as to what constitutes reality. As Mary Schmidt emphasizes, the result is that the traditional ways in which we organize our experience are broken down and no longer fit the situation.[4] In Jung's terms, we might say the well-ingrained habits associated with directed thinking and its obsession with externality are intentionally undermined as a first step toward freeing the mind for thinking in primordial images. For directed thinking and the language it employs creates a picture of the world which we unwitting and through habit blindly accept; a picture which, to paraphrase Wittgenstein, holds us captive and which we cannot get outside of; it lies in our language and our language seems to repeat it to us inexorably. Freeing the mind for the primordial image potentially opens a new perspective. As a consequence of these disciplines, the social, cultural and epistemological categories traditionally accepted as reality lose their hold on the individual, and he must seek reality and definition elsewhere. This occurrence, of course, reminds us of Jung's observation that one must divest oneself of the "false wrappings of the persona" – that acquired identity by which we define ourselves in terms of societally accepted categories of reality and identity – to begin the process of individuation which has as its goal the creation of a psychic center beyond the ego.

Therefore, the shaman's initiation works simultaneously to deconstruct not only the traditionally accepted assumptions about the reality of the empirical world but also the empirical self, or ego, as well. In Eliade's terms, in the initiatory process "the profane man is being dissolved" and the source of his reality is being relocated on a deeper plane of psychic existence. This stage of the discipline mirrors those spontaneous initiatory experiences we examined earlier which image the radical dissolution of ordinary consciousness in terms of violent dismemberment, piercing, sacrifice, madness or even death. Symbolically, this is an "ego death." However, the procedures utilized to induce this experience are sometimes so severe and extreme that they do, in fact, result in the death of some novitiates. Long periods of isolation, sometimes in extreme temperature conditions, sleep deprivation, fasting, pain stimulation, hypoglycemia and dehydration, forced hypermotility, restricted mobility and the ingestion of hallucinogens all work to lower the threshold of consciousness and alter its structure by inducing introversion.

We can begin to sense the extremes to which these procedures frequently resorted in the following story recorded in the North American arctic wilderness. A Caribou Eskimo shaman, Igjugarjuk, informed Knud Rasmussen about his painful transformation. "All true wisdom is only to be learned far from the dwelling of men, out in the great solitudes, and is only attained through suffering," he related to the Danish ethnologist. "Privation and suffering are the only things that can open the mind of man to those things that are hidden from others." For his initiation, this Inuit candidate was placed on a small sledge and carried far away from his home to the other side of Hikoligjuaq, "the great water with ice that never melts." Here he was led into a remote hut, isolated in the vast frozen emptiness of Arctic desolation.

No food or drink was given him; he was exhorted to think only of the Great Spirit and of the helping spirit that should presently appear, and so he was left to himself and his meditations.

After five days had elapsed, the instructor brought him a drink of lukewarm water, and with similar exhortations, left him as before. He fasted now for fifteen days, when he was give another drink of water and a very small piece of meat, which had to last him for a further ten days. At the end of this period, his instructor came for him and fetched him home. Igjugarjuk declared that the strain of those thirty days of cold and fasting was so severe that he "sometimes died a little." During all that time he thought only of the Great Spirit, and endeavoured to keep his mind free from all memory of human beings and everyday things. Towards the end of the thirty days there came to him a helping spirit in the shape of a woman. She came while he was asleep, and seemed to hover in the air above him. After that he dreamed no more of her, but she became his helping spirit.[5]

Other societies likewise use starvation and the sweat bath, bloodletting, long periods of exhaustive dance and the mesmerizing monotony of chant and drum beat to "open the mind of man to those things that are hidden from others." Richard Noll points out that these and other techniques have the effect of increasing the mind's receptivity to vision. He quotes Fechner to the effect that in the process "the attention feels as if drawn backward toward the brain."[6] This phrase reminds us of Jung's observation that the various introspective techniques he employed focus the attention on the "background of consciousness." Jung, in his "Commentary on *The Secret of the Golden Flower*," had spoken of such processes as being able to "heat the roots of consciousness and life," what elsewhere in the work was referred to as the "germinal vessicle" of consciousness, the very point where it emanates from the unconscious life processes themselves and ultimately from the all-sustaining cosmic force.[7]

Perhaps we can provide these groping attempts to give expression to such experiences with a more scientific underpinning. In an effort to establish a psychophysiological model of trance experience, Michael Winkelman interestingly indicates that such states do in a sense draw us backward toward or even into the brain and focus attention on the background of consciousness, for they relate to the "deeper" or older parts of our brain. He finds that the various techniques used in shamanic practice induce responses which rely upon the hippocampal-septal region of the mind, "part of the phylogenetically older part of the brain," which "includes terminal projections from the somatic and autonomic nervous systems." These activities stimulate patterns of response that can lead to "erasure of previously conditioned responses, changes of beliefs, loss of memory and increased suggestibility."[8] Thus, they help accomplish the "break with the universe of daily life" and the initiatory dissolution of the profane self. In addition, these same processes, he noted, tend to produce a state of "openness" or "impressionability," making possible a resynthesis of personality comparable to that which the Tamang patient, Kumari, experienced in the *karga puja* ritual described in Chapter 3.

Yet, as Jung experienced, simply clearing the surface is most often not enough; the depths must be plumbed and awakened and their contents assimilated with the larger psyche. The world composed by the thought habits dominated by directed thinking must make way for the emergent reality of the symbol, for the symbol is potentially both the guiding force which opens the portal to the archetypal realm and, simultaneously, the vehicle which mediates this deep level with consciousness. We recall that Jung saw this process at work in the dual techniques impelling the psychological transformation experienced by the alchemist. *Meditatio* was capable of fathoming the depths and awakening the *lumen naturae* which "buildeth shapes in sleep from the power of the word," the plastic formal power anterior to consciousness which shapes human experience. It was this process which reawakened the mythopoeic faculty, the true imagination, capable of organizing experience in accordance with archetypal patterns of reality. This newly awakened sensibility, Jung noted, acts like a magnet; like Plato's stone of Heraclea, it not only attracts all that is proper to it into its orbit but invests what it attracts with a similar power of transformation. Much akin to Joseph Campbell's common formative force operating across cultures and eras, it works from behind or within to cast experience against the archetypal template of the human mind and invests it with transpersonal significance. This awakened sensibility, which Jung recognized as *imaginatio,* is now able to harness this symbolic capacity in the service of psychodynamic transformation. Jung saw this synergy between *meditatio* and *imaginatio* as a precursor of his own process of active imagination. Active imagination, as we remember, utilized such psychic expressions as dream, vision or imaginative states, sometimes approaching trance, as well as the guiding force of the mythic symbol, and dance, rhythm and art to induce the gradual and intentional lowering of the threshold of consciousness and promote an introversion intended to shepherd the mind back to its form-generating sources. These procedures then became the vehicles for the often long and difficult spiritual discipline of integrating the contents emanating from this level with the larger psyche.

The traditional and ecstatic initiatory training techniques used over the centuries by the world's shamanic traditions trace very much the same archetypal pattern of experience and employ kindred techniques to guide it. But, just as we experienced examining the measures first used to remove profane structures of consciousness, the means employed strike the modern sensibility as much more extreme and yet, at the same time, perhaps potentially more effective than their modern analogues. Training in the interpretation and amplification of the products of the imaginal realm revealed in dream and vision, often utilizing the tribe's mythic lore as a key to this realm, is complemented and deepened by prolonged practice in trance experience. These disciplines are coupled with ritual, dance, song and chant, and often supplemented by the use of various hallucinogens. The cumulative effect of these processes is heightened by a ritual and sacred world where the culture's art everywhere bodies forth the middle world of the archetypal imagination. Such procedures have for hundreds of years successfully canalized the initiate's psychic energy to transform and expand consciousness.

Jung characterized dream interpretation as "the stone which the builders rejected"[9] in constructing our modern approaches to reality, at least until he, Freud and a few others attempted to re-establish its revelatory credentials. However, it was not so rejected in archaic cultures, and in the world's shamanic traditions it has always been a key to opening the inner life, an important emissary from the background of consciousness. Dream interpretation plays an important role in the shaman's initiatory training. The dream and the symbols in which it clothes its meaning are understood to be forms of the mind's own self-revelation and, at the same time, to reach back to and express the powers of Creation. Just as it is among the Australians, the dreamtime is the creationtime, a return to original realities in mind and cosmos. Eliade makes this clear:

> ... the shaman's instruction often takes place in dreams. It is in dreams that the pure sacred life is entered and direct relations with the gods, spirits and ancestral souls are re-established. It is always in dreams that historical time is abolished and the mythical time regained – which allows the future shaman to witness the beginnings of the world and hence to become contemporary not only with the cosmogony but also with the primordial mythical revelations.[10]

"Among the Mohave and the Yuma power comes from the mythical beings who transmitted it to shamans at the beginning of the world," he notes. "Transmission takes place in dreams and includes an initiatory scenario. In his dreams the Yuma shaman witnesses the beginnings of the world and lives in mythical times."[11] According to Jay Miller, among the Lushootseed Salish, dream, the immortals and the creative power expressed in song and dance were directly equated. "Among the Lushootseed, the immortals were known as sqëlalitut (derived from the verb qëlalitut, 'to dream, envision'), who provided access to the facet of power called syud, a partnership with an immortal conferring pigwëd, 'song and dance attuned to power.'"[12] To this way of thinking, dream, power and ritual song and dance formed a continuum expressing the immortal forces informing creation.

We have already noted that it is frequently through the emergent spiritual reality emanating from the preconscious and announced in dreams that the shaman is called to his vocation and initiation. We have likewise seen examples illustrating Eliade's assertion that "it is perfectly possible for the initiation to be performed in the candidate's dreams or ecstatic experiences." The power of the dream symbol to canalize and transform psychic energy was well recognized in shamanic cultures and is aptly expressed in the Classic Maya's vision of the spirit guide, the way. This term, as we have noted, means both "to dream" and "to transform," and in the form of the spirit guide very well captures the power of the dream symbol to guide and transform consciousness.

For Jung also, as we know from Chapter 5, the dream transformed consciousness. The entire individuation process could be embodied in or effected by a sequence of dreams or sometimes by a "big dream," a single experience. He held that the dream is a spontaneous self-portrayal, in symbolic form, of the actual situation of our unconscious. Yet, at the same time, it reaches back to a more significant level. The dream is "a communication or message from the unconscious unitary soul of humanity,"[13] i.e., the transpersonal collective unconscious. As such it expresses the reality of the ancestors and of the 2,000,000-year-old man who is in all of us. "And where do we make contact with this old man in us?" he asks rhetorically. "In our dreams," we are informed.[14]

> The dream is a little hidden door in the innermost and most secret recesses of the soul, opening into that cosmic night which was psyche long before there was any ego-consciousness, and which will remain psyche no matter how far our ego-consciousness extends. ... All consciousness separates; but in dreams we put on the likeness of that more universal, truer, more eternal man dwelling in the darkness of primordial night. There he is still whole and the whole is within him ... [15]

As we have learned from Jung, in its full reach the dream expresses the *lumen naturae*, the formal power shared by man and nature and, ultimately, the soul's correspondence with God's creative plenitude. Thus, finally for Jung as it does for the shaman, the dream connects us with cosmos and the power which creates and sustains reality. In more modern terms, we might say that with its archetypal revelations the dream brings forward the enduring synchronistic source, the "continuous creation."

These qualities make the dream symbol a frequent point of entry into the unconscious for both the shaman and the depth psychologist. However, Jung discovered that a sometimes more predictable and tractable way to "follow the psyche on its strange symbolic wanderings" was the intentional inducement of visionary experience – a sort of active daydreaming, especially when the involvement is so deep as to produce a virtual trance state. This technique, as we know, he eventually called active imagination. The process is actually closely related to dream interpretation, for frequently the point of departure for such a visionary excursion is, in fact, a particular dream image. Because such images are often compensatory and point the way to individuation, they are an effective means to unleash the innate process of transformation potential within the psyche. And this process, we remember, could be most effectively spurred forward by contextualizing these images within those patterns of experience produced in the world's mythologies, further aiding the ends of transformation.

The shaman likewise does not wait for visionary experience to come to him and uses similar intentional techniques to lower the threshold of consciousness and provoke such experience. As Serge King notes, "Where the shaman is concerned, the verb 'to dream' is to be taken in a very active sense. In other words, what for most people is a passive experience is, for the shaman, an intentionally creative act."[16] Jean Houston refers to this process as "one of the most critical aspects of shamanic training – activation of the capacity for inner imageries and visions. In altered states, the neophyte shaman practices mental and physical imagery so vivid that it blocks out the awareness of normal perception and bodily feeling ... . So developed can the shamanic imaginal or secondary body be that it seems he or she is actually having a full physical experience of another place or dimension."[17] As she points out, it is frequently by utilizing such techniques that the shaman finds his spirit guide, his answering voice within, and first experiences the reality of the imaginal dimension which Jung was to call the *mundus archetypus*.

These processes, like the dream interpretation procedures examined previously, parallel Jung's understanding of *meditatio*. Here one also fathoms the depths of the inner world where one enters a dialogue with "the answering voice of the 'other' in ourselves." And here one releases the wellsprings of the mythopoeic imaginative faculty. In Jung's experience, this prepared the way for *imaginatio*, the process of producing, working with and mastering this imagery in the service of an expansion of consciousness and the building of the "connecting bridges" critical to psychic integration. The shaman's training is similar, as we can see from Houston's description of the second phase of the shamanic visionary training. "Once the novice can experience such lifelike imagery," she asserts, "the second phase of training begins, aimed at teaching him to orchestrate and control inner imagery and visionary content."[18] Richard Noll emphasizes this aspect of the shaman's training. "Shamanism is an ecstatic healing tradition which at its core is concerned with the techniques for inducing, maintaining and interpreting the experience of enhanced mental imagery," he maintains. Shamanic training in this process of vision cultivation is a two-phase process. "First, the neophyte shaman is trained to increase the *vividness* of his visual imagery through various psychological and physiological techniques." Once the novice gains access to such vivid imagery, there begins a second phase of shamanic mental imagery training which is aimed at increasing control over internal imagery and "actively engaging and manipulating the visionary phenomena."[19] Again, we experience a two-step approach, one intended to free the wellsprings of the imaginal world, and the other a disciplined confrontation with the contents elicited and meant to canalize their power and reveal their significance.

Lee Irwin in his work, *The Dream Seekers*, illustrates in detail the quest for visionary experience among the native peoples of North America and the manner in which it informs an entire "visionary episteme" for their tribes.[20] Elements of this quest for vision can be found in most of the world's shamanic traditions. We have discussed the often extreme measures taken with the purpose of lowering the threshold of consciousness and inducing vision, and have offered the isolation, sensory deprivation, fasting and exposure of the Inuit shaman, Igjugarjuk, as a graphic example of these procedures. Another well-known example comes from the Sioux Indians who intentionally induce visionary experience in a similar manner. The Sioux characterize their fervent desire for such experience as "crying for a vision." An example of such a quest is given by the Sioux Indian known as Leonard Crow Dog or, more appropriately, by his Indian name, Defends His Medicine. In this account, the candidate for vision undertakes his quest on a lonely hill fasting in a vision pit – an L-shaped hole with a short horizontal passage deep under the roots of the trees. As we shall see in Chapter 9, this archetypal combination of an underground passage and the roots of a tree associated with vision and enlightenment is a recurrent image in shamanic cultures. It is through fasting, isolation, the exposure to the sweat bath and the stimulation of tobacco that these seekers deliberately induce the deepening of consciousness which in the right mind will trigger vision.

It is here in the vision pit that Defends His Medicine sat, alone, wrapped in a quilt, waiting:

> Now I was all by myself, left on the hilltop for four days and nights without food or water ... If Wakan Tanka, the Great Spirit, would give me the vision and the power, I would become a medicine man and perform many ceremonies wrapped in that quilt ...
>
> Suddenly, before me stretched a coal-black cloud with lightning coming out of it. The cloud spread and spread; it grew wings; it became an eagle. The eagle talked to me: "I give you a power not to use for yourself, but for your people."[21]

Here, "asleep, yet wide awake" in vivid trance in his "earth hole," his vision pit beneath the tree, after the rigors of the sweat bath, long isolation and fasting, this shamanic postulant is granted the vision which confirms his vocation as a *yuwipi* and invests him with power to use not for himself but for his people.

Among the Oglala Sioux, the *yuwipi* men are considered "*wakan* people," people invested with the same visionary power acquired by Defends His Medicine on his vision quest. As such, "The *wakan* people were also instructors, interpreters of the sacred myths and directors of the great ceremonies," according to William K. Powers.[22] "Visions manifested themselves as uninduced revelations, or they might be sought in the vision quest (*hanblečeya* 'to cry for a vision, dream'). *Wakan* things were difficult to understand for the common man, and so certain persons were invested with the power of interpreting the multitudinous wonders of *Wakantanka*."[23] In fact, as we have mentioned, according to Powers, the *yuwipi* man may call himself *iyeska*, "interpreter" or "medium," because one of his functions is to interpret the meanings of visions. It is due to his visionary power received directly from the Great Spirit and his training in the tribe's myth, lore and rituals that he is able to unlock the meaning contained in the visions received by others on their vision quests and to contextualize such visions within the tribe's myth and lore to elucidate their significance within a larger context, thus furthering the novitiate's initiatory training.

Jung, we recall, employed the mythic symbol in much the same way in dream and vision interpretation and to guide active imagination. He, like the shaman, found that the way to achieve that level of integration where man "is still whole and the whole is within him" was not through endless analysis of the dream or visionary image which only dissects, separates and lessens its import and effect, but through the synthetic process of amplification which "integrates it into a universal and intelligible statement." "The figurative language of dreams is a survival of an archaic mode of thought,"[24] he tells us, i.e., of thinking in primordial images, the understanding of which is the Rosetta Stone of dream interpretation. Such dream images must be understood symbolically. As we noted in Chapter 5, "It is absolutely necessary to supply these fantastic images which rise up so strange and threatening before the mind's eye, with a sort of context so as to make them intelligible. Experience has shown that the best way to do this is by means of comparative mythological material." Because the psyche in dream and vision frequently expresses itself in such symbols, contextualizing these images "which are to be found in the mythologies of all ages and all peoples" within the framework proper to them, i.e., the world's mythologies, helps us fathom their meaning and gives them an expanded significance. "If it is a dream of this kind, it will as a rule contain mythological motifs, combinations of ideas or images which can be found in the myths of one's own folk or in those of other races. The dream will then have a collective meaning, a meaning which is the common property of mankind," Jung informs us.[25] Myths represent the condensed wisdom of the ancestors, the original revelations of the preconscious portions of the mind distilled generation upon generation until they express the very form and significance of the preconscious psyche itself. It is thus that relating the visionary symbol to myth vests it with "a meaning which is the common property of mankind" and links us back to "the eternal myth," for myth at this level is the most perfect expression of man's participation in the form generating powers of cosmos.

A similar practice can be found in many shamanic cultures, as we noted in the case of the *yuwipi* man. The shaman, as we know, is the repository for his culture's mythic traditions. He stands out in his community as one who has an almost uncanny understanding of and the ability to "experience" the significance of myth, to "interiorize it," in Eliade's terms. He is one who can transform traditional lore into concrete mystical experience with meaning and direction. His traditional initiation and training rely heavily on procedures in which he is immersed in tribal mythic lore, and his ecstatic exercises are meant to reawaken and heighten the mythopoeic faculty which is capable of illuminating mythic structures. It is this training and natural ability which allow him to interpret the visions of the members of his culture by providing them with a mythic context. At the same time, contextualizing his own dreams and visions within the tribe's mythic heritage helps give them form and significance for himself and his people. As Mary Schmidt observes, "The shaman must render his visions themselves into culturally utilizable form, partaking, as Drury holds, 'of the cosmic dream of his own mythical heritage.'"[26]

Among the Inuit, "the *angakoqs* [shamans] played the important role to preserve and interpret the ancient traditions. Their name derives from the word *anga*, which means 'maternal uncle' or, more generally, 'one who commands respect.'"[27] When he is narrating tribal myths, the ancestors are said to speak through the shaman, and because he carries this condensed wisdom of the ages, the wisdom of myth, he is able to interpret the dreams and visions of his people. The power which allows him to do so is *Sila*, the power of nature, the world and the universe, and "a powerful shaman was *silatuujuk*, well-endowed with spirit or life force."[28] Among the Tukano, as we shall examine later, the people seek visionary experience in a trance induced in part by the hallucinogen, *yajé*. "The individual hallucinations do not constitute a private world ... they are freely discussed, and anyone will ask questions and solicit answers," according to Reichel-Dolmatoff.[29] It is the *payé*, or shaman, who can best provide their meaning, and this he does by contextualizing the vision within the local mythology. In so doing, he "integrates it into a universal and intelligible statement," in Jung's terms. He will inform the vision-seeker that what he experienced represents the Master of Game Animals or some other figure within the tribe's mythology and thus vest the vision with a larger collective significance. The *payé's* power of interpretation, as we discussed, is a product of his luminescence, his illumination which he receives directly from the force of the Creation itself, the Sun Father. "This supernatural luminescence of the *payé* is said to manifest itself when he speaks or sings, or when he explains his or others' hallucinatory experiences." Reichel-Dolmatoff informs us that, "Closely related to this concept [the shaman's luminescence] is the ability of the *payé* to interpret mythical passages, genealogical recitals, incantatory formulas, dreams or any signs and portents a person may have observed. The *payé's* interpretations thus 'shed light' upon these matters, in the strict sense of the expression."[30]

Among the Tamang shamans of Nepal, Larry G. Peters informs us, "Training is both ecstatic and didactic [traditional]. It involves mastering a trance state which at first overwhelms the individual; and there are numerous *mantra* and myths to be memorized."[31] In the process, through continued practice in trance accompanied by the disciples who "sing the myths with the guru," the novice submits to a state he experiences as spirit possession. The training moves from an initially uncontrolled state called *lha khoiba mayba*, crazy possession, in which he is utterly controlled by the powers of possession, to a final state characterized by his control of these powers.[32] Here we are rather precisely reminded of Jung's description of the effect of active imagination. "Through her active participation the patient merges herself in the unconscious processes, and she gains possession of them by allowing them to possess her. In this way she joins the conscious to the unconscious." Peters relates that:

After the calling, all Tamang shamans must find a guru in order to be initiated, a process involving the learning of a body of myths and mastery of ritual methods and techniques, including trance states. ... I observed that the guru functions as a psychotherapist in that he explains to his trainees the meaning of their dreams, hallucinations and paroxysms and places them within the context of an initiatory system. The shaking becomes identified as the possession of an ancestor, and the visions and dreams are related to mythology and other aspects of the belief system.[33]

Peters analogizes this adroit use of myth and lore with the practice of the psychiatrist, and the comparison is apt. Just as it was for Jung, it is myth and traditional lore which elucidate and amplify the meaning of the dreams, hallucinations and uncontrolled trance visions of the novice and contextualize them into an initiatory schema capable of inducing resolution and control over an imaginal psychic content which initially overwhelms the candidate. Finally, as we remember from Chapter 3, the successful candidate becomes invested with *shakti*, psychic power continuous with that which forms the creation, a power which he encounters at the heart of the imaginal world.

Thus, for Jung and the shaman, understanding, amplifying and contextualizing the symbols which emerge in dream and vision reveals their larger provenance and sacred source. They are revealed to be the archetypal products of the continuous creation itself; that is, of the luminescence of the Sun Father or of the source of life and the universe represented by *Sila*; they are forms of cosmic *shakti*, or the expression of *Wakantanka*, the Great Spirit. In Eliade's terms, like all truly creative acts, "true" being vested with the sense and prestige of ontological truth, they are an extension of the cosmogony. Ultimately, dream and vision constellate the same experience of a harmonious convergence between the microcosm and the informing reality of the macrocosm toward which the process of individuation itself was directed. We can see an example of this cosmogonic background which frames and informs the vision quest if we examine the symbolism inherent in the ceremony of the sweat bath which helped induce the experience of Defends His Medicine which we discussed earlier.

Hultkrantz has noted that certain Indian tribes "regard the sauna as a microcosm; its construction and the simultaneous lighting of the new fire symbolize the cosmogony."[34] The Sioux ritual suggests a similar symbolism anchoring vision in first principles. The sweat bath, which initiates the vision quest by prolonged exposure to heat, lowering the threshold of consciousness and inducing a loss of self, is purposely constructed as a miniature representation of the cosmic creation. The fire pit, a round hole, is dug in the exact center of the little hut which is to house the sweat bath. "That's the universe, the whole universe contained within this tiny *oinikaga tipi*," his father explains to Defends His Medicine.[35] His uncle arranges the fire pit inside the hut. "He placed one rock first in the center of the pit, then four rocks around it, then one more rock on top of the middle one. These represented the earth, the four directions of the universe and the sky."[36] Once the sweat bath is functioning, Defends His Medicine is told, "This steam is the holy breath of the universe. Hokshila, boy, you are in your mother's womb again. You are going to be reborn."[37] The lowering of the threshold of consciousness induced by the sweat bath thus is envisioned as a process of, in Jungian terms, "heating the roots of consciousness and life," i.e., cosmic life, almost in a literal sense. This is a return to origin in now familiar terms, and here individual vision and cosmic creation coincide. It is from this creative center shared by man and the universe that all true vision and illumination symbolically derive.

The Tukano likewise frame their intentional quest for vision against a similar cosmogonic background. The hallucinogen, *yajé*, not only helps guide the mind to vision but also has its own mythic pedigree which relates it back to the Creation and the Sun Father. It is not surprising then that the *yajé* ritual involves a return to primordiality, to the time of creation itself. *Yajé* is mixed in a pot with its own peculiar symbolism.

> The *yajé* pot (*gahpí soró*) should be made by an old woman who smooths and polishes the inner and outer surfaces with a hard, smooth yellow stone. The Tukano view this stone as "a phallus which shapes" the vessel, which in turn is considered to be a uterine receptacle.[38]

"As a matter of fact the *yajé* pot represents the uterus, the maternal womb, and hence is a cosmic model of transformation and gestation," we are told.[39] "First the individual enters the vessel's vagina as a phallus and then he assumes an embryonic state which, eventually, leads to his rebirth."[40] But this entry is also a transformation of consciousness and a regenerative return to the source of cosmic creative power. The symbolism of the *yajé* pot repeats the symbolism of the cosmogonic creation where the phallus of the Sun Father entered the center of creation, the cosmic womb itself or "manifestation house" where creation receives a visible form. As in the Sioux ritual, microcosmic and macrocosmic creation coincide in the symbol of the center and, in visionary experience, the seeker returns to the source and is reborn in vision. Just as the Sioux quester is told, "Hokshila, boy, you are in your mother's womb again. You are going to be reborn," so within the womb of the *yajé* pot the Tukano visionary "assumes an embryonic state which, eventually, leads to his rebirth." And this is regarded as a rebirth from the cosmogonic source as well, for we are told, "Once inside the receptacle he becomes one with the mythic world of the Creation."[41]

Thus following the psyche on its strange symbolic wanderings again describes, as it did in the individuation process, an age-old archetypal pattern. The *yajé* ceremony and the visions it yields ultimately become the connecting bridge to the source, the cosmogony and its primordial mythical revelations. We can see this clearly in the Tukano visionary experience itself. Here, inspired by *yajé* and the mythic background which frames the experience, the seeker at first perceives what Reichel-Dolmatoff identified as phosphenes which often mark the inceptional phases of trance experience.[42] Phosphenes are momentary perceptions that appear in our field of vision as a chaotic array of dots, specks, star-like or irregular patterns. They result from a self-illuminating power of the visual sense apart from any external light source and are frequently induced by hallucinogenic drugs. As the trance experience continues, these subjective images begin to give way to more complex forms appearing like people, animals or other creatures. Those who, like the shaman, know how to interpret these visions see in them familiar mythological elements. As Reichel-Dolmatoff points out, the vision is, at least in part, the product of the projection of local cultural contents on the hallucinatory subject matter. However, when we examine the vision, we can see that there is a deeper, transpersonal factor at work, for the ultimate vision shares a certain universality with the traditions we have been examining. Again, behind the local cultural inflections we see the magnetic power of Joseph Campbell's common formative force at work, drawing the individual elements into conformity with the archetypal forms of the human mind. The ritual participant, sharing the luminescence of the Sun Father, now becomes in vision continuous with this cosmic creative process. He "becomes one with the mythic world of creation" and gives representation to the depths of this archetypal experience by projecting it onto the chaos of the phosphenes which now assume the form of the mythical creation itself, "for in all chaos there is a cosmos," Jung tells us, "in all disorder a secret order."[43] The trance experience tends to assume the shape of

> ... a visit to the place of Creation, the *fons et origo* of everything that exists, and the viewer thus becomes an eyewitness and a participant in the Creation story and the moral concepts it contains.[44]

Here the entranced Tukano Indian perceives the creation of the cultural paradigms that inform his life, the world of ancestors, "the origin of the ornaments used in dances, the feather crowns, necklaces, armlets and musical instruments, all are seen." He witnesses the division into phratries and the origins of the laws of exogamy. But most important he sees the Cosmic Fount itself, the continuing source of creation as a reality accessible in trance.

> The Milky Way appears and the distant fertilizing reflection of the sun. The first woman surges forth from the waters of the river, and the first pair of ancestors is formed. The supernatural Master of the Animals of the jungle and waters is perceived, as are the gigantic prototypes of the game animals, the origins of plants — indeed, the origins of life itself.[45]

Again, such vision is experienced as leading back to and participating in the source of all creation. Here, in dream and vision, as Eliade observes generally, " ... historical time is abolished and mythical time regained — which allows the future shaman to witness the beginning of the world and hence to become contemporary not only with the cosmogony but also with the primordial mythical revelations."

And lest we begin to doubt the archetypal nature of this experience, let us recall

Jung's description of the alchemist in Chapter 5 who, experiencing a lowering of the threshold of the consciousness after long hours in the laboratory, the work hard upon him, has a very similar visionary experience. Here, concentrating upon the chaos of the randomly shifting transformations taking place with the alchemical retort, as we recall, the plastic powers of the imagination spontaneously project a vision in which, historical time being abolished and mythical time regained, he also becomes contemporary with the creation and its primordial mythic revelations. He becomes witness to "how God created all things in six days, how it all came to pass, and such secrets as are not to be spoken aloud and I also have not power to reveal."

> By this you will see clearly the secrets of god, that are at present hidden from you as from a child. You will understand what Moses has written concerning the creation; you will see what manner of body Adam and Eve had before and after the Fall, what the serpent was, what the tree and what manner of fruits they ate: where and what Paradise is, and in what bodies the righteous shall be resurrected; ...

Though clothed in an Hermetic and Christian framework, we have the same archetypal involuntary statement of the psyche expressing its creative source, an introspective glimpse of the actual experience of the psyche in the depths of vision where it becomes one with and projects the cosmogony and its mythical revelations. The alchemist, like the Tukano visionary, returns to the time of the creation, "the *fons et origo* of everything that exists, and the viewer thus becomes an eyewitness and participant in the Creation story and the moral concepts it contains." Through the natural visionary capacities of the mind again "historical time is abolished," as Eliade has told us, and the visionary becomes "contemporary not only with the cosmogony but also with the primordial mythical revelations." Here, in deep visionary experience, the archetype again depicts itself as carrying forward into human consciousness the paradigmatic creative powers of the creation itself, and in such primordial symbols once again we may say that the world itself, its plenitude and creative power, is speaking.

Further Connecting Bridges: Ritual, Dance, Trance and Art

The unconscious is "a creative force which wraps itself in images" as we have seen throughout this work. Its creations are often spontaneous and involuntary. They enter the field of inner perception as finished products, as in dreams. Yet, at the same time, they can be "self-portraits of the psychic life process" and, as such, these images are not random or lawless but properly experienced and understood have a form and significance capable of guiding psychic experience and becoming, in Joseph Campbell's terms, "a way to psychological metamorphosis." They are capable of turning crisis to cure, chaos to illumination, by uniting the mind with its own creative source in the unconscious, symbolically expressed as a recovery of or return to origin as we have seen in this chapter. The mind archetypally experiences this source as "The Source," for the symbol awakens our sense of the bond between human life and the beyond expressed in the archetypal patterns of man's larger transpersonal background which give this bond its force and reality. For the initiated mind, the symbols become emissaries of this inner order. They provide directive signs to an emergent order of reality and ultimately open the portal to a realm of enduring significance. At the same time, they revive the natural symbolic capacities of the mind, its innate "luminescence." This process fosters a rebirth of our symbolic sensibility, the creation of new symbols and, ultimately, the emergence of a different level of "the real" which Jung termed the *mundus archetypus*. And just as Jung attempted to activate this process by the techniques of active imagination, so over the generations have shamans used techniques of dream interpretation and vision training, amplified and guided by the wisdom contained in myth and symbol, to lead the mind back to its source and awaken its natural capacity for transformation.

But the similarity between the shaman's visionary techniques and Jung's process of active imagination is broader still. Jung found that he could rely on a number of other vehicles to help awaken, bring forward and give form to the imaginal world. These included dance and rhythm, song, the creation of ritual and dramatic enactments, sandplay and various art forms. He found that dance, which was often combined with ritual and dramatic elements, was particularly effective because symbolic enactment with the body is more efficient than ordinary active imagination.[46] Such expression, he felt, seemed to enlist the "motor imagination" suggesting a deep level of coordination between mind and body expressing itself in patterned movement. This interpretation fits very well with his understanding of ritual behavior in general, which borders closely on the body's deep realm of instinct. "In abstract form, symbols are religious ideas;" Jung has told us, "in the form of action, they are rites and ceremonies." Instinct and the archetypal symbol, we recall from Chapter 2, meet in the concept of patterned behavior, and the patterned behavior of ritual seems to express a deep connection between each.

Moreover, ritual actions function like symbols in general. Ritual actions assist introversion and enlist the archetypal level of the psyche to aid the conscious mind in times of distress or crisis. Speaking of such ritual events, Jung observes:

> When therefore a distressing situation arises, the corresponding archetype
> will be constellated in the unconscious. Since this archetype is numinous, i.e.,
> possesses a specific energy, it will attract to itself the contents of
> consciousness — conscious ideas that render it perceptible and hence capable
> of conscious realization. Its passing over into consciousness is felt as an
> illumination, a revelation or a "saving idea." Repeated experience of this
> process has had the general result that, whenever a critical situation arises,
> the mechanism of introversion is made to function artificially by means of
> ritual actions which bring about a spiritual preparation, e.g., magical

ceremonies, sacrifices, invocations, prayers and suchlike. The aim of these ritual actions is to direct the libido towards the unconscious and compel it to introvert.[47]

In his "Commentary on The Secret of the Golden Flower," Jung noted, "Through the ritual action, attention and interest are led back to the inner, sacred precinct, which is the source and goal of the psyche and contains the unity of life [i.e., cosmic life] and consciousness. This unity once possessed has been lost, and must now be found again."[48] Ritual actions focus on the "background of consciousness;" they "heat the roots of consciousness and life" to create a unity with cosmic life which makes the adept a conduit and exponent for that power. Through this introversion we form a bridge between the conscious mind, the unconscious and the realm of instinct and nature, a relationship which is revivfying for the psyche, i.e., "felt as an illumination, a revelation or a 'saving idea.'" In this manner, ritual helps create a psyche anchored in its own deep sources.

For the shaman, as we have seen in Chapter 3, ritual is an important tool of transformation. We might recall the *karga puja* and the manner in which it fostered introversion and enlisted the archetypal level of the psyche to aid the conscious mind in the time of Kumari's distress and crisis. In symbolically reopening the gates separating gods and men, it did, indeed, create a unity with cosmic life. Moreover, in shamanic practice, ritual is often combined with dance to achieve similar effects. Dance is a frequent ritual preparation for the shaman's ecstatic journey to the deep sources of the psyche. Andreas Lommel notes that in Siberia "some shamans dance so wildly that in the end they sink down as though dead; others get into such a violent ecstasy that they have to be held fast and bound, and this can be done only by several men exerting all their strength."[49] The !Kung Bushman shamans also dance until exhausted to enter trance, and similar practices are to be found in the Americas and elsewhere. In fact, in some cultures the shaman's dance traces the stages of his perilous trance journey to the other world. Here the dance represents the journey itself. The symbolic equivalence of the dance and the journey is appropriate for, from another standpoint, dance is one of the traditional paths leading to trance experience. The exhausting movement required by dance can assist in the lowering of the threshold of consciousness and the triggering of those processes which, as we have discussed, science has determined can lead to visionary experience. Thus the symbol of the trance journey and the vehicle inducing it become one in an experience which has always inhered in dance where movement is subsumed in pattern and the continued repetition of the pattern evokes the experience of an identity with the eternal patterns of the cosmic life which informs it.

A striking example is the Sioux sun dance. In this ritual dance, in the center of the camp circle a hole is dug where a sacred pole made from a cottonwood tree will be erected. The finding, cutting, transportation and ceremony surrounding the pole are all marked by a repeated ritual emphasis of the number four or the four directions. These combined symbols provide an overall ritual setting of circle, center and quaternity. The central pole has cherry branches attached to it near its top which are regarded as the nest of the Thunderbird. Once the pole is in place, the warrior societies dress in their finest clothes and prepare for the ground flattening dance. Here they dance away from and back to the sacred pole – first to the west, then in the remaining cardinal directions. "At the end of the dance, a flattened area in the form of a cross has been stamped into the earth,"[50] William K. Powers informs us – again, a quaternary pattern with the symbolic bird-topped pole at its center. Here, indeed, dance movement is subsumed in pattern, and the continual repetition of this pattern evokes the experience of our identity with the eternal form of the sacred life which informs it, tellingly expressed in the archetypal mandala form. Again, that image of unity and totality slumbering in the unconscious of each of us gradually emerges to reveal the Divinity informing man, nature and the world. In ritual and in dance, a sacred imaginal world is constructed, a *mundus imaginalis* which naturally expresses itself in the form of a quartered circle with a central pole, a now familiar configuration of primordial symbols suggesting the breaking of the plane to a higher dimension of consciousness. It is on and around this mandala-like structure that the sacred dance occurs where young braves "sacrifice themselves" to gain the knowledge and power of *Wakantanka*.

Powers describes the heart of the ritual in which the braves pledge to dance in one of four ways: gazing at the sun, pierced, suspended or dragging buffalo skulls. In the first type of dancing, the dancer gazes straight into the sun for the entire day. In the second and third, the dancer's breast or the flesh over his scapulae is pierced, wooden skewers are inserted and he is suspended above the ground either from the sacred pole or from specially constructed posts. In the fourth type, the flesh over the dancer's scapulae is again pierced, and thongs are attached to one or more buffalo skulls which he must drag around in the dance area. "In the last three forms, the dancers must sacrifice themselves until the flesh has torn through,[51]" Powers informs us.

Here, in ceremonies orchestrated by the shaman, sacrificing everyday vision to gaze at the sun or sacrificing the everyday self in now familiar symbolisms of piercing and dismemberment, the novices in dance traverse the imaginal world symbolized in the mandala image, driving themselves to exhaustion to gain access to the power and cosmic life its unfolding form represents. Finally, they succeed in becoming conduits of this sacred force.

> After all the dancers have been freed from their ordeal, the sun dance is over. The men, however, are imbued with sacred power as a result of their ordeal and communication with *Wakantanka*, and they may invest some of their power in the sick by placing their hands on them.[52]

This dance ending in the acquisition of sacred power recalls Jay Miller's observation concerning the Lushootseed Salish Indians who through ritual entered into a partnership with the immortals who blessed them with "song and dance attuned to power." Indeed, among many shamanic cultures, song as well as dance was also considered an access to cosmic life and power and, according to Miller, among some tribes, "Songs controlled the world and all in it."[53] "Song, emphasized by percussion, was and is the basic idiom for life and potency in Native America, both in belief and in practice, because its rhythm, measured pace and beauty duplicate the potent flow believed to be animating the universe."[54] In certain tribes, again spontaneously appropriating a variation of the mandala image, this conception was symbolically portrayed as a pulsating spider's web. The web's center was regarded as the spot of the origin of creation, Miller informs us. "In tribal rituals recreating the origin of the world, this image was evoked by the text and rhythm of a sacred song. Of all acts, song best represented this universal kinesis of ebb and flow, rhythm and harmony, diffusion and concentration, rings and radials around a central intersection."[55] Here song and rhythm are recognized as the most appropriate expressions of the sacred power of creation itself – again of Divinity informing man, nature and the world as Jung described the primordial mandala form. And it was song which made this power accessible to humankind. In fact, according to Miller, the Huron and Iroquian term for power (orenda) is derived from a root meaning song. "Having a tune, melody, rhythm and flow, it was only appropriate that the bond between an immortal and a human be represented by the song passed between them. Thereafter, it marshals power when needed to help self or others."[56]

The shaman's access to cosmic life and power is frequently, as we have seen above, symbolized by the image of the sacred center and often by the central tree or pole which unites the cosmos with itself. This same larger pattern recurrently is associated with certain shamanic instruments which induce ecstasy and galvanize power. For instance, the drum, the rhythm of which fosters the shaman's ecstasy, is frequently said to be made from the central World Tree, it depicts the "mystical itinerary" of the shaman's journey on its sides and often the Cosmic Tree itself as *axis mundi*. As Eliade notes, "By the fact that the shell of his drum is derived from the actual wood of the Cosmic Tree, the shaman, through his drumming, is magically projected into the vicinity of the Tree; he is projected to the 'Center of the World,' and thus can ascend to the sky."[57] Thus the drum becomes both the symbol of and vehicle impelling the shaman's ecstasy. A drum of the Siberian Evenk recently forming part of a display from the Russian Museum of Ethnology depicts a similar symbolism. Behind the skin of the circular drum is suspended a metal cross forming an encircled quaternity whose intersection represents the mid-point of the world. Here, at its center, it has an opening which "symbolizes the entrance into the mythical shamanic worlds."[58] This entry into the shamanic worlds is, of course, the very experience the drum is meant to induce. Eliade succinctly summarizes the symbolism of the drum. "We will only note that the drum depicts a microcosm with its three zones – sky, earth, underworld – at the same time that it indicates the means by which the shaman accomplishes the break-through from plane to plane and establishes communication with the world above and the world below."[59]

A similar symbolism sometimes is found in the shaman's rattle. The rattle, the rhythm of which helps induce the shaman's trance, is like the drum both a symbol and vehicle of ecstasy, and this role is sometimes made explicit. Throughout South America, the shaman's rattle is often feathered at the top suggesting magical flight and trance experience. Among the Tukano we can discern a larger pattern which may be implicit in many shamanic traditions. The Tukano shaman's rattle is topped with the feathers of the oropendola bird, symbolic of the Sun Father. In ritual, the rattle is closely associated with the *axis mundi* symbolism, the world center where the shaman ascends to the Creator, the Sun Father. Thus again, like dance, song and drum, it both symbolizes and induces the experience of shamanic ecstasy and breaking the plane to cosmic life.

Another example is the Tlingit Raven rattle as a symbol of ascent. This rattle repeatedly employs the same basic shamanic motifs. It is carved in the shape of the raven. The raven carries a shaman on its back on his ecstatic journey, and on their way they are accompanied by the kingfisher, the shaman's spirit guide, who provides him with sustenance, i.e., power, on the magical flight. The Raven in Tlingit mythology is said to have founded shamanism, and here he is appropriately the instrument of the soul's flight to its inner source, the breaking of the plane to a different dimension of consciousness. As such, the Raven rattle, like the World Tree, incorporates the symbolism of uniting the three realms, for the kingfisher dives beneath the surface of the sea, lives on the land and soars above it, a symbolism which Peter and Jill Furst recognize is traditionally borne by such birds in this part of the world.[60]

Thus, ritual, song, dance, drum, rattle and the techniques which accompany them all function "to heat the roots of consciousness and life" and to elicit and release the creative plenitude which we share with the cosmos. As we have seen, they are recurrently associated with the symbol of the center, the mandala image and the vertical *axis mundi*. In each case they tend to be both symbols and vehicles of transformation. They are adroitly employed to help form a bridge between the conscious mind, the unconscious and the cosmos, a relationship which is revivifying for the psyche, as Jung observed based upon his employment of similar techniques in active imagination.

The shaman's training and the ritual procedures which surround and enhance his trance experience employ all these techniques and interwoven symbolisms. In addition, song, dance, rhythm, drum beat and the shaking of rattles frequently accompany dramatic enactments which are also adroitly employed to deepen the shaman's experience. Thus, while the shaman's trance sometimes may involve an almost comatose state which leaves his body immobile while his spirit journeys to distant realms, in a surprising number of instances, either preliminary to his journey or throughout its entirety, there is a close ritual rapport and even communication between the shaman and his audience. Larry G. Peters and Douglass Price-Williams have called attention to the peculiar nature of the shaman's community-oriented trance. Surveying the properties of trance experience in some forty-two different shamanic societies they note: "in 34 of the 42 societies surveyed, there was communication between the shaman and the audience during trance."[61] Here a mutual relationship is formed between the shaman and his audience using the techniques which we have described in this chapter to inspire one another to deeper and deeper levels of experience. Often the shaman "transports" the participants by describing the rigors and triumphs of his journey, and the audience chants, sings and drums him on his way.

Jay Miller describes the dramatic soul retrieval ceremony among the Lushootseed Salish in a manner which brings out the role of song, drum and rhythm in the shaman's trance journey.

> Approaching a plank house while a ceremony is going on, the senses are overwhelmed by rhythmic pounding from drums, batons and voices ... Such would have been the arena of the [Soul] Recovery rite. People came together and beat time to each others songs. Here, however, there was a single predominant focus: the shamans traveling to and from the land of the dead, with everyone helping them in thought, deed and song. The audience took its place as witness and amplifier, singing and pounding backup for the doctors.[62]

So impelled, the shamans begin their inward journey to the land of the ancestors.

Peter and Jill Furst note similar features in Inuit ritual among the Iglulik. When a cure is needed or hunting has been unsuccessful, the people gather in a particular house. Here the shaman will begin his descent and the people will assist him on his journey.

> He calls for his spirit helpers, all the while intoning, "The way is made ready for me; the way opens before me." The people answer, "Let it be so." When his spirit helpers arrive, the earth opens and closes again behind his spirit, for he is now in deep trance and his spirit has left his body. He struggles with hidden forces and at last shouts "Now the way is open!" The people hear his moans as if coming from farther and farther away, and they know that he has begun his journey. Their eyes still closed, they sing songs of encouragement.[63]

Thus encouraged, he makes his perilous journey into the depths – to Sedna, the Ever-Copulating One, mother of sea animals and source of fecundity.

Yet the effect is reciprocal and the shaman through his trace state and its attendant ritual activities is able to acquire and bring back to his community the riches of the imaginal realm. Thus, according to Andreas Lommel, in a description which reminds us rather precisely of the role played by active imagination, "Shamanizing consists essentially in rendering the mythological images of the group tradition lively and productive, in employing them to strengthen the collective soul by depicting them and making them conscious. Thus the shaman's activity is to an important extent an artistic one: miming, acting, singing, dancing and painting."[64] He further notes that these acts are often done in a trance-like state which is artificially induced. In such a state in which the control of the conscious mind is relaxed in favor of the productions of the unconscious, the images of the tribe's mythological tradition are experienced by the shaman with particular intensity – an intensity which he can communicate.[65] Lommel concludes:

> Thus shamanism is above all a method, a psychic technique, with which, in a particular cultural situation, especially in a certain "dreamlike atmosphere" still achieved today in Australia, psychic images and energies, that is to say traditional ideas or myths of a particular group, can be re-experienced, ordered, intensified, given artistic shape and communicated by means of the trance of an individual specially prepared for this activity. The result of this activity is a strengthening of the collective psyche.[66]

Through the disciplines and techniques which we have discussed, the shaman overcomes those structures of consciousness which impede vision and fosters those which come to its aid. "For," as Jung tells us, "it is the function of consciousness not only to recognize and assimilate the external world through the gateway of the senses, but to translate into visible reality the world within us."[67] The shaman, we recall, has an exceptional ability to integrate into his awareness a considerable number of experiences that, for ordinary consciousness, are reserved for dreams, madness or post-mortem states. Through practice in vision and trance he gives increasingly defined shape to his inner images. And, as Andreas Lommel recognizes, this process is experienced by the shaman as a communication with the spirit world, and the transcending of ordinary states of consciousness is perceived as a journey into the Otherworld.

> It is evidently a very ancient technique which is not yet accessible to modern psychology, but which represents a means of curing certain depressive states, based on thousands of years of experience. The essence of this process of self-healing consists in imposing order and form upon these confused and chaotic images, which threaten to overwhelm the individual.[68]

In Jungian terms, this process involves an alteration in which ordinary consciousness gives way to deeper sources of experience. "The change is apparently brought about by the emergence of the historical part of the psyche," Jung tells us, i.e., the transpersonal, archetypal plane of awareness, the hidden foundation of psychic life. "From the fact that the change heightens the feeling for life and maintains the flow of life, we must conclude that it is animated by a peculiar purposefulness," he asserts.[69] For in depth psychology as in shamanism, this change is marked by the experience of an access to creative energy, the power of cosmic life itself. The experience of an archetypal reality brings forward an awareness of the revitalizing source and its powers, as we have learned. In Progoff's terms, the individual feels as if "something of the world's divinity is being individualized." Here, as in alchemy, in vision, dream, ritual and trance the mind, indeed, becomes vice-regent to *Deus Creator* and is able to reproduce from the unconscious the enduring patterns of a world of eternal form.

The results of this deepening of consciousness are nowhere better reflected than in the art forms of the shaman and his society. "The work of art," the German philosopher Friedrich Schelling long ago observed, "reflects for us the identity of the conscious and the unconscious activities." Yet, recognizing the true depths of the human soul, he also envisioned the work of art as the "expression of the infinite in and through the finite," a reflection of the "ideal in the realm of the real." As such, art naturally forms an effective "connecting bridge" between the unconscious and the conscious mind, as well as between the ideal and the real, thus displaying the infinite in and through the finite which, incidently, was also Schelling's definition of the beautiful. For in the shaman's world, art constantly reinforces the "connecting bridges" laboriously constructed in the shamans' traditional and ecstatic training in a world view which, quite contrary to our own, everywhere endeavors to reawaken the mind to the creative force which sustains and informs it.

"The shaman is not merely a medicine man, a doctor or a man with priestly functions; he is above all an artistically productive man, in the truest sense of the word creative – in fact, he is probably the first artistically active man known to us," claims Lommel.[70] From the horizons of history, visual art has played an important role in the shaman's world, and it is through such art that the soul ministers to itself and reclaims its place as linchpin in the psyche's cosmos. Here again, art has a functional aspect. It acts as a spiritual force reconnecting the soul with its universal foundations. Gerardo Reichel-Dolmatoff notes that among the Tukano the phosphenic forms, which heralded the world of vision, have become favored art forms to adorn the various practical artifacts and even the dwellings of Tukano society.[71] As such, everywhere the common world opens into the visionary, to the womb of the creation and, eventually, to the cosmic fount itself overcoming dissociation and grounding the mind in its healing source.

This curative function of art is made explicit by the Navaho. Here, through art, the patient is projected into a visionary, archetypal world; a world which the Navaho explicitly recognize as bringing the ideal into the real. "For the Navaho," according to Donald Sandner, "healing is not directed toward specific symptoms or bodily organs, but toward bringing the psyche into harmony with the whole gamut of natural and supernatural forces around it."[72] The Navaho employ the art of the sand painting to create this rejuvenating experience. These paintings are usually made with colored sand by the medicine man and his assistants on the floor of a ceremonial hogan. They reflect patterns brought back from the gods by the Navaho chant heroes and, like other healing rituals which we have examined, are thus an extension of the cosmogonic creation itself. They frequently have the general form of a mandala which, as we know, can be seen as the infusion of the mind, nature and cosmos by Divine formal power. As such, as Sandner notes, "In several paintings the Place of Emergence is shown as a large circle at the center, with the sacred mountains, sacred plants, clouds, animals and birds arranged around it. The patient is placed in the midst of this world, surrounded by symbols of growth, fertility and immense creative power."[73] The central Place of Emergence is the origin of man and of the world as we know it. Here the first human couple, male and female, made their appearance. Typical of the mandala form, the ancillary figures surrounding the Place of Emergence generally carry a quaternary symbolism or structure. For instance, they may be arranged in the four cardinal directions, or portrayed in four different colors, or they may bear a relationship to the four sacred mountains which delineate the Navaho landscape, both its physical reality and its "inner form."

The Navaho believe that all natural things possess an "inner form." This inner form, given to reality at the time of creation, gives life to all things. The sand painting functions as a middle world, the connecting bridge between the ideal world of inner form and the "real," everyday world of our experience. It, thus, can reawaken the patient and the participants in the ceremony to the inner forces which animate and are the true source of the creation and of the patient himself. As such, as Sandner notes, the mandala image specifically functions on two levels, the macrocosmic and the individual or microcosmic plane.[74] On the macrocosmic level, the physical landscape of the Navaho territory is, through the symbolism of the sand painting, analogized to and assimilated with the ideal world, making it transparent to its source. On the microcosmic plane, the mandala allows the shaman to conduct the patient back to his own origins, the hidden foundations of his being, to renew his energy for the healing process. The outcome is analogous to a soul recovery and vests the patient with his true inner form.

Opening into the plenitude of cosmic creative power, the mandala becomes a potent field of energy. "Every sand painting is a pattern of psychic energy," Sandner tells us. "The painting focuses power, and the medicine man transfers it to the patient through the physical medium of the sand. The patient not only makes use of the power of the figures in the painting, he becomes that power."[75] The sand painting thus becomes the repository for symbols of transformation, channeling psychic energy according to archetypal patterns. This process is aided by now familiar techniques. The effect of the ceremony is enhanced by songs, prayer, masked dancers and chants which lower the threshold of consciousness and allow the symbols to operate with an enhanced effect. In this way, the ceremonies reinforce the symbols and the psychic transformations implicit in the sand paintings. One of the most famous chants describes how the Navaho Heroes, Monster Slayer and Child of the Waters, at the behest of the medicine man, meet at the center of the Navaho country and descend into the Place of Emergence to revive the sick soul of the patient. In a manner which parallels and reinforces the symbolism of the sand painting, as they venture to the place of beginnings the physical landscape is gradually transformed into an archetypal configuration, and the patient, in whose words the experience is expressed, is projected into the primordial mythic world – the very same world of the archetype which, in Chapter 2, Nathan Schwartz-Salant employed to effect powerful transformations in his contemporary patients.

In such ceremonies the medicine man symbolically becomes the supernatural power. "The medicine man is exalted into a powerful being, what Jung called the mana personality,"[76] Sandner observes. Through the sand art form of the mandala he becomes the focal point of cosmic power, a conduit bringing creationtime plenitude into the present world and connecting the patient with the rejuvenating world of archetypal realities. Here we may recall Eliade's observation, quoted in Chapter 3, about these Navaho ceremonies.

> As he hears the cosmogonic myth and then the origin myths recited and contemplates the sand paintings, the patient is projected out of profane time into the fullness of primordial time; he is carried "back" to the origin of the World and is thus present at the cosmogony.

This process, according to Sandner, allows "the patient to identify with those symbolic forces which once created the world, and by entering into them re-create himself in a state of health and wholeness."[77]

The paintings are allowed to remain intact only an hour or so while the ceremony takes place, and then their materials are returned to the natural world from which they came. Yet in this hour they work powerful transformations through their projection of the patient into an archetypal world translucent to its inner form and source. We might paraphrase William Blake to capture their effect, for through them the patient sees "a World in a pattern of Sand / and Eternity in an hour." Like all true art, assisted by the various techniques which lower the threshold of consciousness and bring forward the transpersonal psyche, the paintings join consciousness to the creative powers of the unconscious mind and rearticulate the relationship between the ideal and the real. As we have noted, the Navaho have a phrase which captures this process, sa'ah naaghái bik'eh hozhóón, a nearly untranslatable pair of concepts central to Navaho religion whose meaning is closely guarded by the Navaho chanters. Gladys Reichard has translated this phrase as "according-to-the-ideal may-restoration-be-achieved," a rendition which rather precisely captures the transformative power of art in the shaman's world.[78] For the sand painting technique forms the connecting bridge between the ideal and the real, the unconscious transpersonal psyche which strives for expression and the conscious mind which simultaneously strives for substance and rejuvenating content. And the shaman himself becomes the archetype of the mana personality, the connecting bridge itself, which brings transpersonal content and the power which accompanies it into our mortal existence.

Chapter 8

The Journey Through Jung's *Mundus Archetypus*

This is not a journey for the feet; the feet bring us only from land to land; nor need you think of coach or ship to carry you away; all this order of things you must set aside and refuse to see: you must close the eyes and call instead upon another vision which is to be waked within you, a vision, the birth-right of all, which few turn to use.
Plotinus

In the Navaho ceremony, which we examined in the last chapter, the reawakening of the transpersonal plane of experience through the symbol and the techniques that increase its power and effect crystalizes into an imaginal realm with its own reality and effectiveness, a configuration which can "translate into visible reality the world within us." Jung found a very similar experience galvanized during the progression of his individuation process reflecting and effecting the psyche's transformation as he tracked it through its strange symbolic wanderings. Because the unconscious is a creative force which wraps itself in images, the inner drama of the psyche as an acting and suffering subject in search of its own deepest wellsprings announces itself at the various stages of its evolution in certain symbols. These symbols, in the manner we have endeavored to explain, often embody introspective glimpses of the psyche which capture the stages of its transformation. They portray the drama of self-redemption which Jung recognized reflects the individuation process. And because these images are cast up from a common psychic substratum of a supra-personal nature which is present in everyone, they express a certain universality of form and pattern that was shared by Jung's contemporary analysands and by mythic and artistic creations from the remotest of times. Such images express an emergent and compensating reality seeking rapprochement with the conscious mind, but a rapprochement which simultaneously transforms consciousness. As such, they express an autonomy and purposiveness which, as we have learned, "is evidently an *attempt at self-healing* on the part of Nature." They function in a thoroughly dynamic manner to guide psychic energy in salutary directions and in so doing exert a fascinating and possessive influence on the conscious mind. As the eye of the imagination is awakened to their form and message, they assume the shape of a realm of their own, a *mundus archetypus* with its own terrain – a world with characteristics which are "real because they work."

It is impossible to exhaust all the particular forms in which this archetypal pattern of psychodynamic transformation that we have been describing in the previous chapters is expressed. However, we can attempt to summarize much of the process with which we have dealt previously and move forward to a conclusion by examining certain typical images by which this emergent pattern of experience announces itself. As a process involving transition and progress toward a pre-existent goal, the experience often portrays itself in the form of a journey. The journey symbolism naturally expresses the role of the archetypal symbol as *mārga* , as a "way" to psychological transformation. Frequently, it is a perilous journey, "a hard road," "the longest road," the journey "along the razor's edge." It is characterized by impediments which the persona, or everyday consciousness, cannot pass, i.e., the narrow door, the tight passage, the clashing opposites. These obstacles block the journey's progress, at least until this form of consciousness becomes transformed. The structure of the journey often shares much in common with various rites of initiation and hero myths, particularly the hero's "night sea journey."

In a manner consistent with what we have learned, the call to transformation is conveyed from the daemonic realm by figures expressing its emergent inner compensatory reality. The assimilation of this urgent "call" from the inner world frequently has a fragmenting effect on the everyday conscious. However, secretly " ... consciousness, continually in danger of being led astray by its own light and of becoming a rootless will o' the wisp, longs for the healing power of nature, for the deep wells of being and for unconscious communion with life in all its countless forms," Jung tells us.[1] "For this reason there have always been people who, not satisfied with the dominants of conscious life, set forth – under cover and by devious routes, to their destruction or salvation – to seek direct experience of the eternal roots, and, following the lure of the restless unconscious psyche, find themselves in the wilderness ... ," that is, the wilderness of the collective unconsciousness and the numinosity and fascination of its archetypes.[2] Images of an alienating departure from the light world of the conscious mind mark this stage of the journey and portray its fragmenting effect on consciousness in symbols of death, sacrifice and more particularly of self-sacrifice, mental dissolution, piercing or violent dismemberment of the body. "In the fact of sacrifice the consciousness gives up its power and possessions in the interests of the unconscious," Jung tells us.[3] Such sacrifice is a renunciation of egohood.[4] This parallels the "voluntary death" in rites of initiation and the dissolution of consciousness which leads to the *nigredo*, the chaotic blackness, in alchemy.

Yet from chaos springs creation and "the sacrifice of the libido that strives back to the past necessarily results in the creation of the world."[5] In other words, Jung sees an underlying purpose hidden in the symbolism of those who undergo such a death, sacrifice or dismemberment. "Clearly, they have been overpowered by the unconscious and are helplessly abandoned, which means they have volunteered to die in order to beget a new and fruitful life in that region of the psyche which has hitherto lain fallow in darkest unconsciousness and under the shadow of death."[6] Ultimately, the act of sacrifice is a return to the source and rebirth. Examining the archaic symbolism of self-piercing with one's own arrow, Jung notes that the arrow is a libido-symbol and that the meaning of this "piercing" is two-fold; it is an act of union with oneself, a self-fertilization and, at the same time, also a self-violation, a self-murder. "Being wounded by one's own arrow signifies, therefore, a state of introversion."[7] Here the psyche sinks back into its own depths, back to its source. "When the libido leaves the bright upper world, whether from choice, or from inertia, or from fate, it sinks back into its own depths, into the source from which it originally flowed, and returns to the point of cleavage, the navel, where it first entered the body."[8]

Jung found that the process of introversion was recurrently imaged by the unconscious in a series of motifs employing the idea of a descent. The ritual *descensus ad inferos* was one such archetypal representation of a descent into the dark world of the unconscious. The *nekyia* from the eleventh book of the Odyssey in which Odysseus goes down into the world of the dead to conjure up the departed from Hades was another archetypal example, as was the ancient myth of Gilgamesh who descended to the world of the primal ancestor and dived into the sea to find the source of immortality represented by a magical herb only to have it stolen by a serpent as he tried to return to the world of men. Likewise, Jung found this experience represented in the "numberless myths" which Leo Frobenius had categorized under the description of "the night sea journey" in which the solar hero is devoured by a water monster in the west and descends on a perilous journey carried within the belly of the beast in an eastward direction. Discussing Jung's view of the "mythologem of the sun-hero who dies, journies through the underworld and is eventually resurrected," Sherry Salman notes that "the mythologem expresses several fundamental themes which hold true: death-rebirth, as a psychological process, the healing power of creative introversion, the struggle with regressively charged libido, and the descent through the personal psyche into the wellsprings of psychic energy, the objective psyche."[9] "The purpose of the descent as universally exemplified in the myth of the hero is to show that 'only in the region of danger ... can one find the treasure hard to attain,'" Jung tells us.[10]

In his work with his patients, Jung found repeatedly that the descent into the unconscious was represented by images of entry into the earth, a cave or a tunnel or by water – especially large bodies of water – or immersion in water or in a well. He himself experienced such symbolisms for the process of introversion, we remember, in the early stages of active imagination where he actually visualized each stage as a digging deeper and deeper into the earth, and he likewise found such images of descent associated with the process of *meditatio* in alchemical symbolism. As we remember, he saw in the process of the withdrawal of libido from the external world a "soul loss" in which the soul descends into the mythic land of the dead, the land of the ancestors, i.e., the collective unconscious. There it gives visible form to the ancestral traces, that is, the forms of the collective unconscious. These images bodied forth the psyche's introspective intuition of the very processes it was undergoing and which it needed to undergo. They were indeed the self-perceptions of the libido which both lived and simultaneously directed the drama of individuation beginning with the call from the depths, the fragmentation of the persona and the lowering of the threshold of consciousness where the conscious psyche, descending into the unexplored regions of the mind, confronts the ancient powers of the unconscious. It is here in each of us that the soul braves the heart of its fated ordeals.

And the ordeals are, indeed, experienced as fated or preordained, for the dark realm of the unknown psyche holds a fascinating and irresistible attraction which becomes more and more overpowering the farther we penetrate into it. Here the inner world of psyche and not environment becomes paramount. "The discharge of energy into the environment is therefore considerably impeded, the result being a surplus of energy on the side of the unconscious: hence the abnormal increase in the autonomy of the unconscious figures, culminating in aggression and real terror."[11] It is here that the psychological danger of disintegration becomes real, and the mind is exposed to a welter of archaic and mythological images emanating from the unconscious and sometimes crystalizing in the "personalities," often in the form of an ancestral figure or theriomorph, assumed by the split-off complexes. At this stage, there exists the very real risk of an inundation by such unconscious contents which may take the form of a psychosis if the conscious mind is unable to come to terms with them.

At this level, the psyche experiences the threat of possession by these apparently daemonic forces, and the connective faculty of the soul with its mediating function is lost. The soul descends into the depths, mythically into the world of the ancestors, the anterior world of the collective unconscious. As introversion progresses further, it approaches the deep level of instinct, again imaged by the psyche's own self-perceptions. It is here that there frequently arise those recurrent images of animal-like forms or of beings which are part human, part animal. Such "theriomorphic symbols always refer to unconscious manifestations of the libido," Jung notes.[12]

A common instance of this theriomorphic symbolism assumes the form of the snake, dragon, reptile or a monstrous fish from the ocean's depths. Here, as in the night sea journey, the theriomorph actually swallows the hero just as the unconscious engorges the introverting psyche. Reptilian and kindred forms are fit images for the deepest layers of the human mind which biologically still retain vestiges of this stage of development, and the confrontation in dream and vision with these forms images a deep level encounter with the unconscious. Speaking of the serpentine form, Jung notes that "among the Gnostics it was regarded as an emblem of the brain-stem and spinal cord, as is consistent with its predominantly reflex psyche. It is an excellent symbol for the unconscious, perfectly expressing the latter's sudden and unexpected manifestations, its painful and dangerous intervention in our affairs, and its frightening effects."[13] As one approaches closer and closer to this world of instinct, the urge to avoid confrontation and to flee back to the realm of the ego and its well-structured reality grows in intensity. Yet Jung came to realize that there are no purposeless psychic occurrences and that the psyche is at all times secretly working toward its goal. As we trace the path of the psyche's regression, we may hold as a touchstone Jung's observation that "Psychologically, however, the archetype as an image of instinct is a spiritual goal toward which the whole nature of man strives; it is the sea to which all rivers wend their way, the prize which the hero wrests from the fight with the dragon."[14]

Regression potentially promises progression, and the psyche likewise bodies forth this deep intuition in myth and dream. Jung felt that the relationship between the principles of regression and progression was well portrayed in the myth of the whale-dragon studied by Frobenius. Here the journey of the hero symbolizes the movement of libido. The swallowing of the hero by the whale-dragon is emblematic of the inward movement of regression, and the journey to the east, known as the night sea journey, images the effort to adapt to the conditions of the inner world of the psyche. Entry into the innards of the animal represents the complete withdrawal of interest from the outer world, and the overcoming of the monster from within marks the successful assimilation of the contents of the unconscious. Unknown to the engorged consciousness, the journey has been steadily eastward, toward sunrise. The hero's emergence from the monster's belly, which occurs at sunrise, signals the recommencement of progression.[15] It is within the belly of the beast in the depths of introversion, where the psyche confronts its symbolic powers, that it is able to overcome the monster from within by adapting to the conditions of the inner world and bringing them back to the surface in a meaningful way. "There, through its introversion and regression, contents are constellated which till now were latent. These are the primordial images, the archetypes, which have been so enriched with individual memories through the introversion of libido as to become perceptible to the conscious mind .... "[16] This process of confrontation and retrieval marks the critical point in the subject's introversion.

... his libido streams back to the fountainhead – and that is the dangerous moment when the issue hangs between annihilation and new life. For if the libido gets stuck in the wonderland of this inner world, then for the upper world man is nothing but a shadow, he is already moribund or at least seriously ill. But if the libido manages to tear itself loose and force its way up again, something like a miracle happens: the journey to the underworld was a plunge into the fountain of youth, and the libido, apparently dead, wakes to renewed fruitfulness.[17]

Beneath the surface in the process of introversion, the psyche works with its own purposiveness to awaken this renewed fruitfulness. In the scenario of typical images that we have examined, as the libido streams back to the fountainhead it has cast up images, introspective glimpses in the form of symbols, portraying the course of its potential integration. We have traced the psyche's regression in typical images of introversion – entry into a tunnel, cave, the earth, immersion in the sea or other body of water, etc. These were accompanied by images of alienation, departure, sacrifice and dismemberment which evidence the threat to the ego inherent in penetrating the deeper levels. The hazards of the perilous journey, the clash of opposites and the hero's adventure beneath the sea each image the challenge to consciousness represented by the unconscious and its archetypes, and the descent into Hades, the realm of the ancestors, and deeper descent into the realm of the bestial images all portray processes which threaten a disintegration of consciousness. Yet it is one of the tenets of Jung's psychology that "every psychological extreme secretly contains its own opposite or stands in some intimate and essential relation to it."[18] At the nadir of its descent, the mind has the innate potential to undergo a process which Jung termed "enantiodromia," an illuminating conversion to an opposite form which casts experience in a different light. Again, "The descent into the depths always seems to precede the ascent," as Jung has informed us.

Returning to Chapter 2, we recognize that viewed from a different perspective these images portray the rearticulation of the levels of psychic integration which we examined in that chapter; that is, the penetration beyond the plane of personal consciousness, the potentially fructifying immersion in the transpersonal collective unconscious, the rapprochement with the deepest levels where the archetype is an image of instinct and, finally, a return to the fountainhead where the world itself speaks in the form of the symbol. Ultimately, it is through introversion that one is regenerated and reborn. The *descensus ad inferos* is harrowing. "But the source is underground and therefore the way leads underneath; only down below can we find the fiery source of life," Jung reminds us. "These depths constitute the natural history of man, his causal link with the world of instinct. Unless this link be rediscovered no *lapis* and no self can come into being."[19] It is only by experiencing, confronting and eventually fathoming the significance of these transpersonal images formed over the millennia that consciousness becomes grounded in its revivifying roots. This is the ultimate, though unconscious, goal of regression. The symbols serve as a means of expression, as bridges and pointers, mediating unconscious contents with the conscious mind and thus function as uniting symbols. They open personal consciousness to the numinosity of the transpersonal, the plenitude of "the Fountainhead."

The confrontation with the symbolic life on this level reawakens the mythopoeic faculties, the formal shaping powers of the soul. This occurrence transforms the ego-oriented psyche, as we noted, by setting up in contradistinction to the ego another goal or center, one which functions symbolically, an organ of the soul. This transformation is represented by the appearance of primordial images such as the recovery of the light (the *lumen naturae*); the return to the Fountainhead (the source of creation itself); or the discovery of the *lapis* (the enduring reality of the philosopher's stone, which is everywhere but always difficult to disinter). Like the magnet this sensibility unites and transforms all that is brought into its orbit. Symbolically, it becomes a center which unites the opposites, for, as we know, "every psychological extreme secretly contains its own opposite." It helps effect the process of enantiodromia, or conversion to an opposite form, in which the very forces which threatened consciousness with annihilation ultimately are seen as marking the way to its empowerment.

Jung found this process of transformation frequently inherent in the images by which the psyche speaks of itself. Thus, the engorging sea monster, unknown to the hero, travels eastward to sunrise and rebirth. The path of the harrowing journey, therefore, naturally leads to illumination. "Often the monster is killed by the hero lighting a fire inside him – that is to say, in the very womb of death he secretly creates life, the rising sun."[20] "When Jonah was swallowed by the whale, he was not simply imprisoned in the belly of the monster, but, as Paracelsus tells us, he saw 'mighty mysteries' there," Jung relates.[21] Mastering these mighty mysteries in the darkness of the unconscious will lead to the illumination which frees him. The engorging and the night sea journey are preludes in the archetypal portrayal of the psyche's eternal drama. That this fated encounter is ultimately salutary is revealed in myth and dream by the ambiguity of the serpentine and related forms that threaten to engulf the conscious mind – they often hold a hidden relationship with the dreamer and the hero. "Clear traces of the original identity of hero and snake are to be found in the myth of Cecrops. Cecrops was half snake," he observes.[22] In myth, Indra and the dragon Vritra are, in fact, brothers, and in killing Vritra, Indra is guilty of Brahminicide. A similar identity lurks behind the hero and dragon or serpent opposition in other myths. "The idea of transformation and renewal by means of a serpent is a well-substantiated archetype," Jung notes.[23] The serpent can be a healing symbol, as is apparent from the caduceus or the symbolism of Kundalini yoga. Certain Christian sects identified Christ and the serpent.[24] Christ compares himself with the Moses-serpent, Jung points out,[25] and in alchemy the dragon, as an image of the *prima materia* which harbors the *lapis*, becomes winged and a symbol of ascent. As such, it becomes a variant of Mercurius, the divine and winged Hermes.[26]

Other images of the unconscious undergo similar symbolic transformations in the fire of imaginative illumination. The earth into which consciousness descends becomes an image of the mother and of rebirth. The cave shares a similar symbolism – it contains a hidden treasure or within its depths it becomes bright, illuminated by fire or by a flaming tree. Ritually, it becomes an archetypal locus of initiation. "The cave is the place of rebirth, that secret cavity in which one is shut up in order to be incubated and renewed," Jung tells us.[27] It is, itself, the symbol of the unconscious process of transformation. Water as a symbol of immersion in the unconscious ultimately becomes the symbol of the freeing of the libido, the waters of life. And, perhaps, the most important transfiguration occurs with regard to the figures of the daemonic realm crystalized by the unconscious, i.e., the ancestral and particularly the theriomorphic forms which present themselves to consciousness. As we have learned, "The guise in which these figures appear depends on the attitude of the conscious mind: if it is negative towards the unconscious, the animals will be frightening; if positive, they appear as the 'helpful animals' of fairytale and legend." The initiated soul is able to see these figures from its depths as guiding forces, forms of revelation from the transpersonal realm. Such an archetype of the spirit symbolizes what Jung recognized to be the pre-existent meaning hidden in the chaos of the unconscious, the ancestral inheritance of archetypal wisdom stored in the "vast historical storehouse" of the collective unconscious and the deep wisdom carried by the theriomorph as an image of instinct. "This atavistic identification with human and animal ancestors can be interpreted psychologically as an integration of the unconscious, a veritable bath of renewal in the life-source," he concluded.[28]

Such symbolisms are attempts to overcome the dissociation between the conscious mind and the genuine source of life, the unconscious. This integration is the treasure hard to attain, the formation of the *lapis* within the *prima materia* of the unconscious psyche. Here regression reveals its purpose and can be seen as a process of transforming psychic energy through the primordial symbols of the objective psyche. Regression ultimately becomes progression. The process is well-summarized by Sherry Salman:

> Regression is a powerful event: it contains both the illness and its potential cure. Libido needs to flow backwards, passing through the phase of parent/child relationships in order to reach deeper wellsprings of psychic energy. ... Jung considered regression and introversion not only potentially adaptive, but the *sine qua non* of healing, if successful. As libido regresses and turns inwards during illness, symbols emerge from the unconscious ... Symbols are like living things, pregnant with meaning, and capable of acting like *transformers of psychic energy*.[29]

Because archetypal symbols function as images of instinct, they "evoke the aim and motivation of instincts through the psychoid nature of the archetype."[30] They enlist and employ the deep instinctive wisdom of nature which healed body and mind for millennia before consciousness and the ego seized the reins. This healing effect is reflected in the symbols which now emerge from the psyche, as Salman again points out.

> But what eventually happens to the libido during regression? Jung observed the *spontaneous reversal of libido*, which he called *enantiodromia*. This

occurrence of a "return to the opposite" characterizes the nature of the libido's flow, and has been depicted in literature and mythology as the sun's return from the belly of the night, the journey back from the center of the earth, or the poet's ascent from Dante's *Inferno*.[31]

Symbols of unity and harmony, power and essence, illumination and ascent now lead the psyche in a new direction which simultaneously unites the archetypal realm with the conscious mind and opens our wisdom to the transpersonal foundation of life – the enduring reality the alchemist symbolized in the philosopher's stone.

The crystalization of such symbols as the *lapis* reflecting the intuition of the emergent reality of a central part of the psyche reaching back beyond our transient world to an enduring source confirmed the direction which Jung began to see take form in his patients. He noted that at this stage the psyche's transformation seemed to be characterized by a great number of images and designs which, at first, baffled him. Finally, he was able to recognize that in these imaginal products he was witnessing the spontaneous manifestation of an unconscious process integral to individuation. These images seemed to yield some kind of centering process portrayed in their symbolisms.[32] As expressive of the formal principles of the collective unconscious, the symbolism of the center revealed itself in varied examples discovered from his patients and found throughout the world and over long periods of time in mankind's myths and religions. Its production seemed to be associated with typical mythic elements, and among these motifs certain ones began to predominate.

> The chaotic assortment of images that at first confronted me reduced itself in the course of the work to certain well-defined themes and formal elements, which repeated themselves in identical or analogous form with the most varied individuals. I mention, as the most salient characteristics, chaotic multiplicity and order; duality; the opposition of light and dark, upper and lower, right and left; the union of opposites in a third; the quaternity (square, cross); rotation (circle, sphere); and finally the centring process and a radial arrangement that usually followed some quaternary system.[33]

This centering process revealed itself to be the goal and climax of the process of psychic transformation and was characterized by the fact that it brought about the greatest possible therapeutic and life-enhancing effect.

Moreover, these themes and formal elements formed certain typical interrelationships and became articulate in a language of their own. He noted that among the various characteristics of the centering process one of the most prominent was the phenomenon of the quaternity. Quaternity tended to express two related but, at first, apparently contradictory themes. Yet both of these motifs ultimately reinforced the symbolism of the center, revealing it to be both a source of plenitude and, at the same time, as opening to a transcendent or "higher" reality. The quaternary symbols produced by Jung's patients expressed, as they had in so many mythologies and particularly in cosmogonic myths, creation from a primordial source. He notes that in alchemical symbolism the four straight lines running in a quaternary pattern from a single point symbolize the mystery of creation and the four elements. "Things and beings have their first origin in the point and the monad," he noted.[34] "The centre of nature is 'the point originated by God.'"[35] The "real" extends in four cardinal directions. Materially, it is repeatedly envisioned as produced by the four elements and, psychologically, man relates to this reality through the four senses (two senses, such as taste and smell, often being mythically amalgamated to fit the archetypal schema). At the same time, the quaternary structure simultaneously became a symbol of wholeness, uniting chaotic multiplicity into unity, and articulating a reality free from the opposites – *nirdvandva* as Jung, borrowing from the East, expressed it. As an image of totality, the symbolism frequently multiplied the four-fold motif and was often found in the form of the double quaternio, or ogdoad, implying a totality which is at once heavenly and earthly, spiritual and corporeal, and is to be discovered in the unconscious.[36]

A similar and closely related motif was that of "the opposites."

> The essence of the conscious mind is discrimination; it must, if it is to be aware of things, separate the opposites, and it does this *contra naturam*. To nature the opposites seek one another – *les extrèmes se touchent* – and so it is in the unconscious, and particularly in the archetype of unity, the self. Here, as in deity, the opposites cancel out. But as soon as the unconscious begins to manifest itself they split asunder, as at the Creation; for every act of dawning consciousness is a creative act, and it is from this psychological experience that all our cosmogonic symbols are derived.[37]

Cosmogonic myths throughout the world represent original unity as splitting to form a world-creative twosome through opposition. "Without Contraries is no progression," William Blake observed, and it is repeatedly a primordial pair which creates the conditioned world that we inhabit. According to Jung, this primordial pair stands for every conceivable pair of opposites that may occur. In accordance with this archetypal pattern, the Tao in the form of yin and yang becomes the source of the conditioned world, the realm of the "ten thousand things." Yet, from a deeper perspective, the central source remains ever-the-same, and as a saying of Sojō points out, "Heaven and I are of the same root. The ten thousand things and I are of one substance." When this is understood, the ten thousand things return to their origin, which in fact they have never left. Here yin and yang again unite in their underlying unity and source, a process which Jung found to be expressive of psychic integration on several levels. Through such union, the opposition between the ego and the unconscious, the individual and the cosmos achieves its resolution. The gateway to the unconditioned realm of unity is through the Charybdis and Scylla of the opposites, as Jung explores at length in *Mysterium Coniunctionis,* and it is in the symbol of the center or its analogues that they coalesce in unity.

The center thus marks the source and the goal. It is "the symbol of a mysterious creative center in nature,"[38] and is known as the "seed place"[39] where consciousness and the life force are still a unity. Thus, this point is envisioned, on the one hand, as the world's actual center; the mythic mid-point of the macrocosm in the same manner it was believed to be among so many cultures, as Mircea Eliade has amply demonstrated. It is frequently associated with the circle which Plato believed to be the symbol of perfection and the expression of the self-generated energy which moves both the cosmos and the soul. At the same time, this creative center of the world is also the central point that dwells in the heart of man, for the union of opposites encompasses man and cosmos, microcosm and macrocosm, which are shown to have "concentric centers" and reveal the common divine origin of ourselves and the creation. Here, as we have mentioned, man's inner experience reveals that "He is of the same essence as the universe, and his own mid-point is its centre." It is in our experiencing of this creative point within all things that the cosmos truly becomes one with itself.

Significantly, Jung's work recurrently revealed an image which was potentially capable of neatly combining all of the motifs crystalized in the centering process into a single fabric of interwoven symbolic significance. This is the image of the mandala with which we are now familiar. The symbol of the center, quaternity, the circle, the union of opposites, micro-macrocosmic correspondence, multiplicity and unity, and the revelation of the common divine origin of creation and life are all expressed in the mandala form. The term mandala indicates a circle, more especially a magic circle, usually accompanied by some relation to quaternity and the symbolism of the center. In the form of the *quadratura circuli,* the squared circle, it combines both forms and unites the opposites. In fact, the mandala image attempts to portray the most complete union of the opposites that is possible. As we have discussed, Jung found that the mandala most often took the form of a flower, cross or wheel, often with a distinct tendency toward quadripartite structure. He points out that in Tibetan Buddhism these figures perform the function of a ritual instrument (*yantra*), whose purpose is to assist meditation and concentration. In alchemy their symbolism represents the synthesis of the four elements into a unity. Jung finds mandala symbolism to be of great universality, not only in Hinduism, Buddhism and Taoism where it is a most recurrent image but also in Egyptian mythology, in Roman City building, the Christian Middle Ages, the work of Jacob Boehme, the sand paintings of the Pueblo and Navaho Indians, the visions of Ezekiel in the Old Testament, the central role of the Cross in Christianity, especially in its Gnostic interpretations, and in other traditions too numerous to list.

Likewise, he found that his patients frequently produced this image with no previous conscious knowledge of its form or meaning. "To the best of my experience we are here dealing with important 'nuclear processes' in the objective psyche – 'images of the goal,' as it were, which the psychic process, being 'purposive,' apparently sets up of its own accord, without any external stimulus."[40] With regard to the production of the mandala motif, from a superficial point of view it appears as though it gradually crystalizes during the process of psychic integration. "The fact is, however, that it only *appeared* more and more distinctly and in increasingly differentiated form; in reality it was always present," Jung points out. "It is therefore more probable that we are dealing with an *a priori* 'type,' an archetype which is inherent in the collective unconscious and thus beyond individual birth and death. The archetype is, so to speak, an 'eternal' presence, and it is only a question of whether it is perceived by consciousness or not."[41]

The image represents an all-encompassing level of unity and plenitude which the archetypes strive to recover for the conscious mind. As such, Jung encountered its spontaneous production frequently in his clinical work in times of psychic disorder, crisis or impending schizophrenia as a compensating factor and as a harbinger of a return to wellness. "The archetype thereby constellated represents a pattern of order which, like a psychological 'view-finder' marked with a cross or circle divided into four, is superimposed on the psychic chaos so that each content falls into place and the weltering confusion is held together by the protective circle .... "[42] "This is evidently an *attempt at self-healing* on the part of Nature ... ," he tells us.[43] In conformity with its use as a *yantra*, the mandala acts not simply as a means of expression but also produces an effect. It reacts upon its maker producing the experience of an innate, *a priori* order at the heart of the cosmos and deep within the human psyche. Finally, mandalas are symbols of an all-suffusing unity and totality and as such can no longer be distinguished from a God image. Ultimately, the mandala is an image of the unity of man and the creation with their divine source.

Like the individuation process itself, the effect produced by the mandala, epitomized in its central point, is Janus-faced and looks in two directions. One direction grounds man's being in the divine life whose forms we are and points to transcendence, to "the universal totality of the divine state."[44] The other bathes him in the primordial plenitude of the creation itself, the "explosion of energy"[45] which continuously forms and sustains the manifest world. As images of the "seed place," of Deity unfolding in ourselves and the creation, the mandala and other archetypes are experienced as a source of power, creative plenitude and "Primary Force."[46] Jung notes the tremendous effectiveness of these images as carriers of libido. He finds that their effect is experienced as being akin to that of the archaic concept of *mana*, the primitive or ancient idea of the extraordinarily potent, for, due to their shared source, the central point is the point of cosmic creation and, simultaneously, that hidden center which animates each of us. The return to center images the successful freeing of the long-dammed wellsprings of libido, mankind's share of that very energy which fires the cosmos. It is as if in returning to his source man returns to *the* source, the "creative center of all things." It is for this reason that the return to the symbolic center always has been an archetypal equivalent for the return to origins, to "cosmic beginnings."

Jung recognized that man's struggle to give adequate expression to an inwardly sensed dynamism of the psyche powered by a force continuous with natural and cosmic creation had a long history and could be found in many diverse cultures. He found precursors of his own concept of libido as psychic energy rooted in cosmos in the West's greatest philosophers, for instance in Schopenhauer's concept of the "Will", Plato's Eros, Empedocles' love and hate of the elements or the *élan vital* of Bergson.[47] In mythology he recognized a similar intuition represented in the cosmogonic significance attributed to Eros in Hesiod, the Orphic figure of Phanes, and the Indian Kama, the god of love, who, Jung notes, is likewise a cosmogonic.[48] And finally, he found analogous concepts reaching even farther into the past in the archaic idea of *mana* and its analogues as both universal force and psychic energy. "The concept [*mana*] in question really concerns the idea of 'a diffused substance or energy upon the possession of which all exceptional power or ability frequently depends,'" he notes.[49] Men, "especially the shaman,"[50] participate in this power which also has a qualitative aspect and is equated with the sacred. As such, Jung frequently referred to the freeing of the wellsprings of libido as creating in his patients the "mana personality." "The term *mana* suggests the presence of an all-pervading vital force, a primal source of growth or magical healing that can be likened to a primitive concept of psychic energy," according to Andrew Samuels. Samuels notes its charismatic effect upon people in liminal or borderline states where the hold of the conscious mind has been reduced. "A person such as an initiate, novice, patient or analysand is particularly susceptible to attraction by the so-called mana personalities."[51]

Yet Samuels observes that the source of power seems to come from beyond the individual it informs, and Jung also makes it clear that in such states the individual senses himself to be a reflex of an unknown source emanating from a higher plane which we have difficulty conceptualizing in scientific or intellectual postulates. He compared this state with the Chinese experience of *wu wei*, Action in Non-action, where the adept becomes a conduit for the power of the Tao, or with the analogous Christian sense of the experience, "It is not I who live, it lives me."[52] For, ultimately, the archetype speaks through the individual from the transpersonal world making him a conduit for its energy and numinous meaning. According to Ira Progoff, "the archetypes that are present in the psyche derive their great power from the fact that what they express in the human beings is more than human in nature." Ultimately, these symbols incarnate what is experienced as a higher power and in so doing lift man to a consecrated level of consciousness. As Progoff states:

Clearly, the situation that is established when an archetype becomes active in human life is more than personal. It is felt to have what Jung speaks of as a "cosmic character," ... It is experienced with great intensity, accompanied by a great emotional effect, and it brings an awareness of a special light, a numinosity carrying a sense of transcendent validity, authenticity and essential divinity.[53]

Progoff, as we have noted, describes this as a "situation of correspondence." "This correspondence is between the microcosm and the macrocosm, for a harmony has been achieved and the individual has come into an equivalent union with the universal." This is, of course, precisely the reality represented in the image of the mandala.

At the same time, according to Progoff, at such moments one feels "his individuality to be exalted, as though he were transported for an instance to a higher dimension of being." This intuition is frequently represented in Jung's *mundus archetypus*, as we have discussed, by symbols of verticality, i.e., tree, pole, mountain, ladder, etc. Jung found that these images were frequently associated with the symbolism of the center. Perhaps the most recurrent form by which this complex of associations expresses itself is that of the tree – particularly the tree at the center of creation. Appropriately, in this role it is often found combined with the mandala image, where the tree is envisioned as growing from its central point. In fact, Jung believed that the mandala and the archetypal central tree represented the same psychological reality viewed from different perspectives.[54] Consequently, this image of the tree represents an experience akin from that implicit in the mandala and is felt to vest human life with a "cosmic character." Thus, the tree is imaged as a Cosmic or World Tree, an archetypal symbol of ascent. Yet at the same time it is an image of growth, growth which appropriately represents both the process of individuation and mythological deepening. To ascend upward, the tree must penetrate into the depths. Its growth depends upon the continued sustenance provided at the root level of its existence, just as human spiritual growth depends on our contact with the rhizome level of the psyche, the archetypal patterns at the root level of our own existence. Here the mind encounters the primary source of energy and form which ultimately expresses the soul's correspondence with God and reveals the universal patterns of Being which raise us to a higher dimension of consciousness.

It is in this context that Jung made his most illuminating comments about shamanism. He recognized that the shaman harnesses this source of primary energy continuous with the collective unconscious, the world of instinct and ultimately the cosmos. He thus becomes the mana personality par excellence with all its charismatic implications. His psychic growth is symbolized by the central tree which in traditional lore and ritual is his vehicle of ascent to a higher realm.[55] This tree unites the opposites and joins together the unconscious, the conscious and the higher dimension of reality revealed by their union. Yet the comparison between the shaman's spiritual growth and the archetypal tree is apt on another level for, while penetrating a higher dimension, each remains firmly rooted in the earth and its reality. Unlike some other mysticisms, shamanism brings the fruits of plenitude back to revivify the earth and mind, precisely as the process of individuation is meant to do.

Thus, the culminating images in both shamanism and the journey through the *mundus archetypus* indicate the immanence of power and the unity of creation. And the journey is not to a far-off place. It is, in fact, a return. As Joseph Campbell frequently has pointed out, the treasure was to be found within the seeker from the very beginning. Like the archetype and the God-image, which expresses the fulness of archetypal realization, these realities are ever-present within the human mind. They are innate forms of human experience which the process of individuation strives to recover for modern consciousness. For the seeker the journey is harrowing; *sub specie aeternitatis* it expresses the eternal form underlying, informing and ever-recurrent in human experience. Jung saw this same realization clearly expressed in the symbols of alchemy. "Time and again the alchemists reiterate that the *opus* proceeds from the one and leads back to the one, that it is a sort of circle like a dragon biting its own tail. For this reason the *opus* was often called *circulare* (circular) or else *rota* (the wheel)."[56] At its deepest levels, the psyche bodies forth this process of return. However, the circle is an archetype of perfection, and the return is not sterile repetition but leads to the human integration and unity which are the pre-existent goals of the process of individuation. This is a process of psychic transformation which goes back in time as far as we can trace human symbolization within a context comprehensive enough to yield an intelligible configuration of experience. And so to the shaman's archaic and numinous world we also "return." Here we shall find an imaginal world which bears an uncanny similarity to Jung's archetypal world in both structure and function. It expresses itself in the same universal and timeless patterns in remote and far-flung regions of the world and over extraordinarily long periods of time, tracing the same process of alteration of consciousness, through the same stages, marked by the same symbols and leading to the same therapeutic, illuminative and unifying experiences which Jung found characterizing the ultimate goal of his process of transformation.

Chapter 9

The Shaman's *Mundus Imaginalis*

Multiform and shifting in its outward manifestation, myth
nevertheless follows fixed laws ... Product of a cultural period in
which life had not yet broken away from the harmony of nature, it
shares with nature that unconscious lawfulness which is always lacking
in the works of free reflection. Everywhere there is system,
everywhere cohesion; in every detail the expression of a great
fundamental law whose abundant manifestations demonstrate its
inner truth and natural necessity.

Johann Jacob Bachofen

"The psyche" Jung has informed us, "consists essentially of images. It is a series of images in the truest sense, not an accidental juxtaposition or sequence, but a structure that is throughout full of meaning and purpose; it is a picturing of vital activities." As we recall, Jung found within the psyche a cosmos equal with and complementary to the cosmos without – a non-spatial universe containing an untold abundance of images which are tremendously powerful and effective psychic forces of transformation. As we explored in Chapter 5, Jung employed numerous techniques in an effort to penetrate the depths of our psyche and release these forces. In so doing, he attempted to build the "connecting bridges" which mediate between the unconscious substratum and the larger psyche and provide the directive signs we need to live our lives in harmony with ourselves, nature and the cosmos.

The world's shamanic traditions likewise employ the numerous and, perhaps, more effective techniques that Eliade has described as traditional and ecstatic training, which we studied in Chapter 7, to open the blocked subterranean passages of the human psyche. It is these techniques which assist the shaman in his effort to interiorize the sacred knowledge of his mythic tradition until a mythical or mystical geography begins to crystalize, activating the same powerful forces which Jung felt could be unearthed in his psychic cosmos. In precisely this manner, personal experience is opened to its transpersonal base, and an image of the soul is revealed in which the universal psychic heritage of mankind becomes perceptible. In this geopsychic realm of the shaman, a grammar of symbols emerges which not only closely parallels in both structure and function that which constitutes Jung's *mundus archetypus*, the features of which he gleaned from analysis of his contemporary patients, but also manifests striking and uncanny similarities in many diverse shamanic traditions across the globe widely separated in both time and distance.

The Geopsychic Realm Cast in Stone

We recall from Chapter 7 how the Navaho shaman in his sand paintings constructed a visionary world capable of guiding the patient's psychic energy in the direction of a rapprochement with its deep source in both the mind and the essential world underlying and informing our own reality. In modern terminology we might refer to this process, along with Nathan Schwartz-Salant, as linking the patient with the larger world of the pleroma. This mystical geography, opening everywhere to "inner form," was truly a connecting bridge between the ideal and the real and a revelation of both beauty and harmony. Yet, though these structures remained permanent in the minds of the shamans who were masters at reproducing their forms, their physical manifestation was momentary and their components were respectfully returned to their source in nature upon the ceremony's completion.

In apparent stark contrast with these ephemeral creations is the mystical geography of the Maya civilization, monumental, enduring and meant to speak to the ages. As modern scholarship has learned more about the Maya, it has become apparent that this sacred world likewise reflects a similar pattern of shamanic experience meant to body forth the inner psychic landscape of the human mind and to canalize psychic energy along its ancient pathways transforming consciousness according to archetypal patterns of experience. If we look closely at this sacred world preserved in stone for the ages, we can discern a familiar structure of experience which will bind together much that we have discussed and provide a useful overview for that which is yet to come in this chapter.

The Classic Maya (third through ninth centuries A.D.) constructed entire city complexes characterized by pyramids, temples, palaces and great open plazas which give palpable form to Jung's observation that it is the function of consciousness not only to recognize and assimilate the external world through the senses but also "to translate into visible reality the world within us." This visionary world had its own remarkable durative power, itself a testament to its expression of the deep and enduring structures of the human psyche. Its fundamental characteristics began with the ancient Olmec who began building cities like San Lorenzo and La Venta approximately three thousand years ago, and they can be found still today among contemporary Maya people. For the Classic Maya temples or pyramids were the focal points of this visionary cosmos, and the Maya king utilized these structures to galvanize cosmic power, according to ancient shamanic techniques, which would not only validate his right to rule this society but rearticulate the critical relationship between our world and the source of plenitude and reality in the Otherworld.

Linda Schele and David Freidel tell us that "the Maya lived in a world that defined the physical world as the material manifestation of the spiritual and the spiritual as the essence of the material."[1] The ritual temple or pyramid served to bridge the distance between these two realities in symbolisms which are now familiar to us. The pyramid was regarded as an *axis mundi*, a sacred "center" capable of connecting the various levels of reality. In a familiar structure of archetypal experience, the concepts of the "center" and the "beginning" were closely associated. The pyramidal structure was regarded as a sacred mountain and symbolically reiterated the Creation itself when "First True Mountain" arose from the primordial waters which in their world view lie beneath this sacred structure. Combining the concepts of creation from a center, the beginning, and a primordial source of plenitude, this location was also associated with the symbol of the "navel" of cosmic creation.[2] Again, the creationtime was a reality accessible to the shaman; it was here that the Maya king, himself a specialist in shamanic ecstasy, could pass into the Otherworld. It is the symbolism surrounding this passage which interests us here, for its structure and function both effect and reflect that same transformation of consciousness fundamental to other shamanic traditions and to Jung's process of individuation spelled out in his *mundus archetypus*.

Among classical and contemporary Maya societies, the cave and the cenote (sunken water hole) were and still are most important locations for shamanic ritual. Such natural openings into the earth were regarded as portals to the Otherworld. This ancient symbolism, apparently inherited from the Olmec, was incorporated into the symbolism of the temple or pyramid. Consistent with the symbolism of the sacred mountain, the inside of the structure was regarded as a ritual cave. Again, we are informed, "The mouth of the mountain is, of course, the cave, and Maya mythology identifies the road to Xibalba [the Otherworld] as going through a cave. The Maya not only used natural caves as the locations of bloodletting and vision ritual ... but the inside of their temple was understood to be the cave pathway to the Otherworld."[3] And just as water-bearing cenotes were regarded as portals to the Otherworld, this cave symbolism appropriated a similar structure, for these caves symbolically led to the waters of the primordial ocean, laying beneath the mountain pyramid, from which creation proceeded.

We recall that for Jung the process of penetrating the blocked subterranean passages of the psyche, a process he equated with and at first called "trancing," was marked by the spontaneous production of symbols of descent and related images of introversion. He found that this psychological process was frequently associated with such images as the cave, water hole, hole in the ground or large bodies of water – the same images we find in the Maya world marking their trance journey. Moreover, as we noted, such images of regression from ego-consciousness were accompanied by images of death, sacrifice, dismemberment and piercing, and more particularly self-sacrifice or self-piercing. As Jung informed us in Chapter 8, such imagery indicates that in the act of sacrifice the consciousness is giving up its power and possessions in the interest of the unconscious.

Such sacrifice is "a renunciation of egohood" in favor of the forces of introversion and parallels the dissolution of consciousness in alchemy which leads to the preformal chaos of the *nigredo* from which creation can begin. As we know, the production of these images is accompanied by the techniques that we have examined which lower the threshold of consciousness and foster introversion. In Jung's world, such images and techniques marked the process of descent through the personal psyche into the wellsprings of psychic energy, the objective psyche. It is here that we experience those inherited structures of consciousness natural to the human mind from birth symbolized in the ancestor, the rapprochement with the deeper world of instinct and inborn unconscious knowledge imaged in various theriomorphic and zoomorphic forms, and finally our fundamental connection with the primordial source itself.

We see a very similar pattern in the Maya psychic landscape. Cenote, cave and the primordial water upon which all rest mark the introversion of trance experience. Familiar techniques for lowering the threshold of consciousness accompany these images. To access the interior world of vision, the shaman-king enlisted various methods such as exhausting dance, rhythmic drum beat, perhaps drugs or intoxicants and, most importantly, ritual bloodletting. Images depicting sacrifice, dismemberment, piercing and self-piercing are commonly encountered adjuncts to the Maya trance journey. Maya iconography is well-known for its gory portrayal of ritual human sacrifice and dismemberment. But accompanying these practices were acts that Miller and Taube recognize as forms of "autosacrifice" which indicate the annihilation of the "old self" and mark the beginning of ordeals leading to an altered state of consciousness.[4] These acts took the form of self-piercing or self-mutilation "carried out by jabbing needles and stingray spines through ears, cheeks, lips, tongue and penis, the blood being spattered on paper or used to anoint the idols."[5] Bloodletting lowered the threshold of consciousness fostering regression. As Schele and Freidel inform us, "The aim of these great cathartic rituals was the vision quest, the opening of a portal into the Otherworld through which gods and the ancestors could be enticed so that the beings of this world could commune with them." The Maya envisioned this process as one which enabled the ancestors to take physical form on this plane of existence. "The vision quest was the central act of the Maya world."[6]

The needle or stingray spine has the same symbolic value in the act of penetrating the body as does the arrow which Jung saw as a libido symbol. As we recall, Jung observed that the meaning of such an act is clear. It is both an act of "self-murder," i.e., a loss of the "old self," and simultaneously an act of union with oneself, an enriching "self-fertilization." "Being wounded by one's own arrow signifies, therefore, a state of introversion," he concluded. This meaning pertains to sacrifice in general for, as we mentioned, in the act of sacrifice consciousness gives up its power in the interest of the subconscious. "When the libido leaves the bright upper world, ... it sinks back into its own depths, into the source from which it originally flowed, and returns to the point of cleavage, the navel, where it first entered the body." In both Jung's experience and that of the shaman, as the introverting libido streams back to its source, to its point of cleavage symbolized by the navel, as we have so often seen it bodies forth images, introspective glimpses of the psyche, which capture the stages of its transformation. The Maya ritual center, as we know, was itself specifically associated with the navel archetype, and the introverting libido has left familiar benchmarks of its transformation as it descends to its source.

As we saw above, the lowering of the threshold of consciousness associated with Maya ritual and particularly with self-piercing was regarded by the Maya as giving form to the ancestors, who themselves became participants in the ritual of autosacrifice at the sacred cosmic center within the temple cave. This is a familiar scenario with regard to trance or ecstatic experience. Upon the dissolution of consciousness, the mind is flooded with a welter of archaic and mythological images emanating from the unconscious frequently, as we know, associated with ancestral figures. On one level, they represent the initiate's actual realization in the introversion of trance that the mythic forms which constitute the culture's ancestral heritage are not merely vestiges of the dead past. "They live with him as the constant substratum of his existence," as Jung has told us. As the soul descends into the depths – the world of the ancestors, i.e., the anterior world of the collective unconscious – then archetypal images are awakened which belong to the objective psyche. Here the mind taps that rich fund of primordial images which can potentially empower it. And, as we recall, in addition to the image of the ancestor, frequently Jung found this stage of the encounter with the deep instinctive levels of the psyche imaged by frightening theriomorphic or zoomorphic forms. Initially, these images represented the threat to the integrity of the conscious mind inherent in the process of introversion. In fact, in a common symbolism, these frightening creatures actually swallowed the person undergoing this archetypal journey into the psychic substratum. A most common instance took the form of the night sea journey where the participant was engulfed by a monstrous form, often of reptilian or serpentine type, which Jung knew from experience frequently prefigured a deep-level encounter with the unconscious.

The Maya inscribed precisely this same experience on their cave-temple walls hundreds of years ago. Not only do images of the ancestors attend the autosacrifice of the shamanic sojourner into the objective psyche, but images of terrible monstrous forms with reptilian and serpentine features also quite prominently mark the journey. One of the most remarkable examples is the interior door of Temple 22 at the ancient city of Copan. The authors of *Maya Cosmos: Three Thousand Years on the Shaman's Path* note that it was within the inner sanctum entered by passing through this doorway that the ancestors were to be encountered.

A Cosmic Monster ... frames the doorway in such deep relief carving that it seems to be writhing out of the wall. The front end of the monster takes the shape of a crocodilian head ... A huge stingray spine, used to pierce royal flesh and allow the flow of soul and blood to nurture the gods, juts from its head as it opens a portal into the Otherworld. In the great lazy S scrolls composing its arching, serpentlike body cavort the beings who have been conjured up by the bloodletting rituals inside the sanctum.[7]

Here, framing the passage to another dimension of consciousness, we find this most numinous form, both saurian and serpentine. Within the coils of this theriomorphic creature cavort, in fascinating and frightening forms, the welter of archetypal images flooding out of the psychic depths. Its terrible jaws symbolize the passageway to the Otherworld. In fact, the head of the monster represents the act of autosacrifice itself indicated by the stingray spine. Entering into the temple sanctuary as portal to the Otherworld is both a self-sacrifice and an entry into the belly of the beast.

Another familiar rendition of this symbolism was the Vision Serpent, in its frightening aspect represented as a gaping skeletal maw that opens into the Otherworld. The Vision Serpent symbolized the path of communication between the two worlds. Ancestral figures were often shown leaning out of its open jaws. And it was also the vehicle for the shaman's entry into the reality of the Otherworld. In a telling metaphor, it was depicted as arising from the smoke created by burning the blood-spattered papers used in the shaman's autosacrifice and trance induction.[8] Ultimately, the shaman's trance journey must penetrate the clashing jaws of the Vision Serpent as the portal to its visionary world.

Once again, we have traced the process of the psyche's regression in typical images of introversion. Cave and cenote are age-old images of introversion which are appropriated to the temple cave sitting atop the waters of the primordial creation. These are accompanied by images of sacrifice, dismemberment and particularly autosacrifice and self-piercing. The trance journey leads to the realm of the ancestors and the ancestral wisdom of the unconscious with its collective inherited predispositions. It is at this stage that the shaman encounters that welter of images released from the unconscious which it has been the goal and intent of his traditional and ecstatic training to allow him to experience and to fathom in their deeper significance. It is here, where in vivid and horrific monstrous forms the archetype becomes an image of instinct, that he must take the night sea journey, sacrificing normal structures of consciousness to enter the jaws of the monstrous form that resides in the cave leading to the primordial waters of the unconscious.

Yet, as we said in Chapter 8, it is only within the belly of the beast, in the depths of introversion, that the mind can come to grips with the emanations from the hitherto dark background which informs it. It is in the interior world, where the psyche confronts its capacity to produce forms which potentially channel and transform psychic energy along archetypal patterns of experience, that it is able to overcome the monster from within and integrate the unconscious depths with life's surface to experience a renewed fruitfulness. Again, it was one of the touchstones of

Jung's approach to the psychic realm that there are no purposeless psychic activities and that beneath the surface in the process of introversion the psyche works with its own intentionality. We recall from Chapter 8 that "Psychologically, however, the archetype as an image of instinct is a spiritual goal toward which the whole nature of man strives; it is the sea to which all rivers wend their way, the prize the hero wrests in the fight with the dragon." We shall reiterate, now in the context of Maya iconography, what we said earlier.

Returning to Chapter 2 we recognize that, viewed from a different perspective, these images of the Maya vision quest portray the rearticulation of the levels of psychic integration which we examined in that chapter. We have penetrated beyond the plane of personal consciousness, experienced the potentially revitalizing immersion in the transpersonal collective unconscious and ultimately sought rapprochement with the deepest levels where the archetype is an image of instinct. These stages will lead to a return to the fountainhead where the world itself speaks in the form of the symbol. Ultimately, through introversion, as Jung has told us, "one is fertilized, inspired, regenerated and reborn." It is only by experiencing, confronting and eventually fathoming the significance of these transpersonal images formed over the millennia that consciousness becomes grounded in its revivifying roots. The symbols, therefore, serve as bridges and pointers, mediating unconscious contents with the conscious mind. They are uniting symbols which open personal consciousness to the numinosity of the transpersonal, the plenitude of the source of creative power.

As we shall see, images of regeneration and rebirth on both a personal and cosmic level mark this return to the fountainhead in Maya visionary experience. And, significantly, the return is imaged by the same "turning of consciousness," the same process of enantiodromia, which Jung found marked the point where regression culminates and progression and illumination begin. In Jungian psychology, this turning point is marked by the change in the images now cast forward by the psyche. Moreover, Jung found that frequently familiar symbols of introversion have a latent duality which seems to prefigure their potential for change in the awakening conscious mind. Terrifying images are replaced by those of a more benevolent aspect and frequently convert to their opposite, which in fact reflects the very different manner in which they are perceived by the now more integrated psyche.

This same process is clearly present in Maya iconography and the lore which surrounds it. The horrid images of sacrifice and self-sacrifice also contain symbolisms which point to their ultimately salutary function. For instance, the bone of the sacrificial victim is mythically equated with rebirth for, as we have mentioned, bone and seed or essence are homophonous among the Maya, and the Maya frequently used such similarities to indicate hidden relationships.[9] This symbolic aspect of bone and reduction to the skeletal condition as a return to essence and rebirth is, of course, one with which we are now well familiar from other shamanic traditions. In addition, the blood of the Maya sacrifice is ultimately to be seen as the life force of the cosmos. Mankind was created by an original blood sacrifice, and it is the offering in return of the blood of human sacrifice which continues to animate and sustain the creation. It is from this blood that the Vision Serpent arises. Being swallowed by the Vision Serpent or other monstrous serpentine or saurian forms, of course, marks the depths of the experience of introversion. Yet Jung found that the psyche tends to presage the ultimately progressive nature of its encounter with the archetype as an image of instinct in the inherent duality of these forms which mythically reveal a hidden affinity with the questing consciousness and elsewhere have become symbols of healing (the caduceus) or illumination (Kundalini or Christ and the Moses serpent).

We see a similar pattern of experience surrounding the Maya visionary serpent. It has chthonic associations with the cave initiation, swallowing and dismemberment and implies initiatory death. Yet it also suggests an enantiodromia – the turning of consciousness implicit in illumination, the shamanic trance and shaman's ascent to the Otherworld. The symbol for Sacred Blood is often attached to its tail.[10] Iconographically, the serpent is depicted arising in the smoke from the burning papers saturated with the blood let from the shaman king. It thus implies the shaman's self-sacrifice and visionary ascent to the Otherworld. As a symbol of ascent, this normally chthonic creature is often depicted as a feathered serpent, suggesting the same coincidence of opposites as the gateway to illumination which we saw in the Symplegades symbolism. In a manner consistent with this symbolism, the portal to the Otherworld is often through the clashing jaws of the serpent, i.e., through the Symplegades. The words for "sky" and "snake" are homophones among the Maya, further reinforcing its paradoxically celestial aspect.[11] Finally, in Maya symbolism the serpentine and celestial symbolisms again combine in a *coincidentia oppositorum* to form the Celestial Bird, which is also known as the Serpent Bird, that sits atop the World Tree, the symbol of the Maya cosmic creation and of illumination.

As portal to the Otherworld, the Vision Serpent becomes the shaman's initiator. A form of this same basic symbolism has survived into later Maya shamanism in Belize, where a visionary serpent imparts its wisdom to the novitiate shaman by placing its tongue in the shaman's mouth. In a variation of the same symbolism, the shaman's initiation is accomplished when the serpent swallows him and then excretes him, now initiated into shamanic wisdom and power.[12] Likewise, the various theriomorphic and zoomorphic forms undergo a similar transformation, for such forms become the shaman's guides to the Otherworld. They assume the form of the *way*, which we have discussed, the spirit guide whose name means to dream and to transform and who enables the shaman to break the plane to cosmic life and plenitude.

Again, this configuration of psychic experience is familiar from our study of Jung. The guise which the ancestral, zoomorphic and theriomorphic archetypes assume depends upon the state of the conscious mind that perceives them. If it is dissociated from its roots, they will appear negative and threatening; if integrated, they appear as guiding forces, forms of revelation from the transpersonal realm. As we learned previously, such an archetype of the spirit "symbolizes the pre-existent meaning hidden in the chaos of the unconscious," the ancestral inheritance of archetypal wisdom to be found in the "vast historical storehouse" of the collective unconscious and the deep wisdom carried by the theriomorph as an image of instinct. "This atavistic identification with human and animal ancestors can be interpreted psychologically as an integration of the unconscious, a veritable bath of renewal in the life-source," Jung has told us.

Perhaps the most striking example of this turning of consciousness resultant from the integration of the unconscious, this "veritable bath of renewal in the life source," is imaged in the cave journey itself as a descent into the depths. Its initial phases have been harrowing. "But," as Jung has informed us of this archetypal structure of experience, "the source is underground and therefore the way leads underneath, only below can we find the fiery source of life." This is, in fact, very much what we find marking the Maya cave journey, for in the depths is revealed the paramount symbol of the source of life and creation itself, the World Tree. Karen Bassie-Sweet points out that the association between the World Tree and the initiatory cave in Maya lore was old and widespread and that the two images were often depicted together, frequently with the cave located at the base of the Tree.[13] Again, the same symbolism seems to have been appropriated to the temple-cave. Within the temple-cave of the pyramid, as Schele and Freidel point out, the ritual of bloodletting was meant to materialize the central World Tree as the path to the supernatural world. "In the rapture of bloodletting rituals, the king brought the great World Tree into existence through the middle of the temple and opened the awesome doorway into the Otherworld." Thus, "Within this cave grew the Tree of the World marking the center, the place of the portal."[14] It is this image which becomes the ultimate symbol of communication with the powers of creation.

Jung found that the goal of the process of introversion frequently was imaged in terms of a return to the source of creation on both a microcosmic and macrocosmic level. The libido in the process of introversion, he told us, streams back to its source, to the navel from which it was born and experiences its own rebirth. Maya iconography and lore anticipate this description with remarkable precision. The temple pyramid, with the cave at its symbolic center, is in fact in Maya mythology the cosmic navel of the creation itself as we have discussed. Beneath the temple are the primordial waters of the unconscious and the preformal chaos which gave birth to all created form. It is in conjunction with these symbols that the raising of the World Tree attains an all-unifying significance worthy of its function as a paramount and primordial uniting symbol. For at the beginning of time First Father created the world by raising the World Tree. The cave journey is thus a return to the primordial source, for the king's ritual raising of the World Tree over the waters underlying the temple reiterates and mythically recaptures the power of the creation itself. Here we re-experience the source of all creation, the point where the world speaks through the vehicle of the symbol, just as form first emerges from the primal source, and we are reborn with "renewed fruitfulness." At this point in the inward journey we can expect to encounter images of psychic integration and power manifesting a "cosmic character" and marked by the same archetypal elements heralding this level of consciousness which we found in Jung's *mundus imaginalis*. And this is precisely what we find.

In raising the World Tree at the time of creation, First Father lifted the sky from the waters, established the Tree as world center, or *axis mundi*, and generated the primordial form which our world was to assume. This creation around a cosmic center was symbolized by First Father's Partition House, a quaternary structure whose cardinal points are intersected by four intercardinals to form a double quaternio which symbolizes the essential form that orders the Maya cosmos. "First Father's house thus orders the entire upper cosmos, the world of humanity, of plants and animals, and of the sky beings, by establishing the center, the periphery and the partitions of the world. Even today the Maya practice this partitioning and ordering of the world in their rituals," Freidel, Schele and Parker inform us.[15] Thus, the Maya inward journey culminates by recalling this image of primordial creation, the ordering of existence through the separation of opposites (sky and earth) around a cosmic center marked by a quaternity intersected by intercardinal points, all symbolic of the archetypal act of imposing the order of our creation upon the primal chaos from which all form eternally emerges.

This imagery again encodes the very same archetypal principles which Jung found in analysis as he led his patients inward through active imagination or, as he originally termed it, tracing toward the concluding stages of psychic integration. He noted that these techniques began to yield "some kind of centering process revealed in their symbolisms." With further examination, as we recall, he determined that the centering process is the climax of the entire process of development and brings with it the greatest possible therapeutic effect. Moreover, the process seemed to be accompanied by the manifestation of certain formative principles, formal elements basic to the manner by which in the depths of the psyche we organize our human experience: the imposition of order upon chaos, the role of opposites and their union in a third and organization around a center with a radial arrangement that usually followed some quaternary system.

These are precisely the basic elements imaged in First Father's creation of the world: the creation of order from original chaos, through the division of opposites around the central tree, taking the form of his quaternary Partition House. In addition, the symbolism of the center coupled with a quaternary structure suggested, on the basis of Jung's work, creation and exfoliation from a primordial source very much as it does here. For Jung, all of these elements coalesced in what he termed the mandala symbol which frequently had the Cosmic Tree at its center. This is, of course, what we find in the Maya cosmos. Moreover, as an image of totality the symbolism frequently multiplied the quaternary motif and was found in the form of the double quaternio or ogdoad, as is the Partition House. On the microcosmic level, as we recall, the double quaternio stands for totality, for something that is "at once heavenly and earthly, spiritual or corporeal, and is found in ... the unconscious," a fitting image to climax the Maya initiate's vision quest. Macrocosmically, it images eternity's entrance into time, creation itself, just as it does in the Maya visionary cosmos. As an archetype of how experience is created, it is to be understood as underlying all experience, "an *a priori* 'type,' an archetype which is inherent in the collective unconscious" and thus, like the primal act of creation which supports the shaman's cosmos, "beyond individual birth and death." Such an archetype, we learned, is "an eternal creative presence, and it is only a question of whether it is perceived by consciousness or not." It thus aptly images the creative principle which eternally underlies and sustains the Maya cosmos and the temple city. And it is the vision of this same primordial source which the Maya visionary rediscovers in his initiatory quest and trance journey into the depths of the collective unconscious.

As images of the "seed place," of Deity unfolding in ourselves and the creation, the mandala and other archetypes are, according to Jung, experienced as a source of power, creative plenitude and primary force. The return to center images the successful freeing of the long dammed wellsprings of the libido, mankind's share of that very energy which fires the cosmos. It is, again, as if in returning to his source man returns to *the source*, the "creative center of all things," that central point where Divinity, here incarnated in First Father, unfolds the created world. And, once more, in this visionary cosmos it is here at the mandala center that we find the paramount symbol of man's connection with the power of cosmic creation, the World Tree.

For the Maya, this return to the fountainhead was experienced and mythically portrayed in much the same manner as it was by Jung's patients – it is a source of "Primary Force," the explosion of energy which orders, creates and sustains the cosmos and at the same time empowers and illuminates the individual. Here cosmic force speaks through the initiated shaman, and he becomes a conduit for the all-pervading vital force infusing the cosmos. Thus, in ritual, at the cosmic center the shaman king literally *became* the World Tree itself, uniting the worlds and bringing primal force and creative order into existence. As Schele and Freidel tell us, "He, indeed, *was* power, power made material, its primary instrument."

> On public monuments, the oldest and most frequent manner in which the king was displayed was in the guise of the World Tree. Its trunk and branches were depicted on the apron covering his loins, and the Double-headed Serpent Bar that entwined in its branches was held in his arms. The Principal Bird Deity ... at its summit was rendered as his headdress. This Tree was the conduit of communication between the supernatural world and the human world: ... The king was this axis and pivot made flesh. He was the Tree of Life.[16]

The shaman-king is himself the medium connecting this world with the life force of the creationtime. As such, he becomes Jung's mana personality par excellence, carrying the power of a superordinate source into human existence. The Maya had a specific word for this force. It was expressed in the term *itz*. *Itz* is the formal power and energy of the cosmic creation which is mythically equated with the sap of the World Tree itself. "In antiquity *Itzam* generally means 'shaman,' a person who works with *itz*, the cosmic sap of the World Tree."[17] The shaman is thus "one who does the action of *itz*," or an *itzer*, a person capable of manipulating the power of the cosmos[18], and the shaman-king in ritual became the focal point of this cosmic force activating it inwardly. In his temple cave, in trance at the world center, raising the cosmic World Tree as did First Father at the time of creation, he became a conduit of cosmic creative power.

Jung once observed, "The decisive question for man is: Is he related to something infinite or not?"[19] In the Maya visionary world described in these impressive stone structures, we find a familiar path by which man is borne to his own interior and reborn therefrom. At the same time, he encounters and is reborn from the infinite, from the eternal cosmic source itself, for the inward journey into the archetypal realm reveals this all-sustaining source. We again encounter a grammar of symbols sharing structural and functional features with those we have previously examined by which the shaman is led through an initiatory crisis of psychic disintegration, a return to origin, both within the psyche and within the cosmos, and a renewal with enhanced power. Through introversion and immersion in the realm of the primordial image, the mind re-experiences the elevating potential of its innate symbolic life.

This process is represented in a complex of symbols portraying the process of introversion, enantiodromia, or the turning of consciousness, and rebirth on a consecrated level, both illuminated and empowered. And the entire process is capsulized in the close relationship between the cave and the World Tree in Maya lore and iconography, a relationship which symbolically captures that spelled out in more detail in Jung's observations concerning the relationship between *meditatio* and *imaginatio*. It is through the symbols and techniques of introversion implicit in the cave journey that the initiate "penetrates the blocked subterranean passages of our psyche" as was similarly accomplished through *mediatio*. By virtue of this process he experiences those archetypal patterns at the root level of existence, and it is from this level of consciousness that the Tree as the paramount archetype of the unified consciousness characteristic of *imaginatio* is able to grow in primal creative power.

Standing as the World Tree, the source of the unfolding of the pleroma and the fountainhead of destiny, the shaman is able to perform the traditional creative act of *imaginatio*, to marshal reality into paradigmatic form, to lift the profane to the sacred by, in Nietzsche's apt expression, giving our everyday reality the stamp of the eternal. The Central Tree, on one level of its multiform significance, is the symbolic sensibility itself which allows the shaman to express and employ the visionary world as an effective device for transforming the human psyche, overcoming the enervating divisions by which consciousness becomes dissociated or alienated from its roots. It represents the power of the archetypal imagination awaiting release in each of us, for, as we remember from Chapter 3, each individual soul is the "white flower," the soul flower which grows from this very same primordial Tree.

The Psyche's "Strange Symbolic Wanderings" in Shamanic Traditions Across the Globe

The Maya in their architecture and art have given visible form to a transpersonal symbolic world capable of redirecting psychic energy and altering consciousness. Their ritual establishes an interactive field in which the archetype moves with impelling power and, bypassing the structures of the conscious mind, directly addresses and awakens a dimension of consciousness otherwise inaccessible. This shared imaginal space employs principles fundamental to the psyche which have evolved over generations of human experience and, as we have said, constitutes a realm with its own laws, its own purposes and its own psychodynamic effectiveness. Once again, in this world the shaman and his ritual participants are inside the psyche as much as it is inside of them.

The Maya initiate journeys inward, into the temple cave, to the source of creation itself. As Jung recognized, frequently the process of transformation spontaneously expresses itself as a journey, often a perilous journey, into that inner realm of tremendously powerful images and forces which demonstrate the manner in which patterns of symbolism can function as mārga, as markers of the way to a different level of consciousness. The Siberian shaman Huottaire, or diver, as we experienced in Chapter 6, journeys in ecstatic dream into the psychic depths, over visionary seas and into imaginal caves, to reintegrate consciousness and awaken the mystical inner eye which can read the symbols which are "inside" his head. The Inuit shaman, Igjugarjuk, travels across the desolate "great water with ice that never melts" to "open the mind of man to those things which are hidden from others." We shall see other shamanic transformations expressing themselves in the form of the journey later in this chapter, but one of the most compelling is that of the peyote pilgrimage of the Huichol Indians. Whereas the Navaho are able to reproduce the visionary world through the vehicle of sand painting and the Maya through massive architecture, the Huichol effectively impose the archetypal dimension of human consciousness as it journeys to unity with cosmic life on the natural landscape itself. And now, initiated into the shaman's symbolic cosmos, we shall find that this is a path that we have traversed before.

The Inward Journey

The quest of the Huichol is in the form of an actual journey from their homeland in the Sierra Madre mountains of western Mexico to Wirikúta, the sacred peyote country. It is a long, difficult and perilous journey. As the shaman warns the initiates, "It will be hard, very hard, this walk. It is a great penance, the journey to Wirikúta, and you will cry very much."[20] Employing an ancient symbolism from previous hunter-gatherer cultures, it takes the form of the hunt, specifically a deer hunt. However, as we shall see, the deer represents the mystical unity of all life as experienced in the ecstasy induced, in part, by peyote, and deer and peyote in this ritual become mythically identified. The sacred peyote contains the essence of Elder Brother Wawatsári, master of the deer species, and as such in the ritual the peyote is envisioned as a deer. Thus, it must first be shot with a bow and arrow before being dug from the ground and ritually divided among the participants of the hunt. It is by virtue of this sacramental meal that the quester is, in Eliade's terms, "brought into communion with cosmic life."

At an early stage, the pilgrimage reveals familiar archetypes as those in quest of the peyote symbolically undergo a "dissolving of the profane self" through rituals of purification and confession – around the campfire they must "burn away everything" so that, as they are told, "you will be new."[21] The larger intent of this initiatory renewal or rebirth is revealed in its surrounding symbolism for, as Barbara Myerhoff explains, it points simultaneously to a return to childhood (individual origin), mythic times (cultural origin) and to the creation itself (world origin).[22] In fact, the journey follows the archetype of a return to origins, for it is recognized as "the passage into the Land of Our Origins, the Place of Beginning."[23] And, as the Huichol approach their goal, like the Australian initiates who become identified with the heroes of the dreamtime, they are given the names of and assume the identity of the first mythical seekers of the sacred deer-peyote, the followers of the first shaman, Tatewarí, making them identical with the ancestors and heroes of the archetypal creationtime world.

This hunt becomes an inward journey of the soul led by the shaman who, Peter T. Furst informs us, "must know the minutest mythological detail of the itinerary, as well as the correct sequence and proper manner in which each ritual is to be carried out at the sacred places along the way and, above all, in the peyote country itself."[24] To guide the pilgrims, he must "see with an inner eye," – an image which we have met elsewhere. It is a spirit guide in the form of a deer, Káuyumarie, who in fact serves as the shaman's "inner eye" and leads him on his journey. The guide is envisioned both as a deer and as a person wearing antlers. It is he who shows the way on this perilous journey undertaken by the peyotero initiates.

This role is made strikingly apparent in one of the most dramatic episodes of this struggle of alienated individual life to re-establish its origins in cosmic life. As we noted in Chapter 8, Jung found that frequently the psyche's difficult path toward its rapprochement with cosmic life was characterized by impediments which the persona, Jung's term for the profane or everyday consciousness, could not pass, i.e., the narrow aperture, the tight passage, the clashing opposites. We have also consistently noted that the symbolism of the therianthropic form, so clearly embodied in Káuyumarie, often spontaneously manifested itself as the connecting link between human consciousness and the collective unconscious (the ancestral world) as well as the deeper levels of instinct, nature and finally cosmos. For the initiated person, i.e., the shaman, who is capable of transcending the profane structures of consciousness, we recall that such half-human, half-animal creatures become guides of the spirit, introducing it to the larger life force which informs it.

These archetypes and the structural and functional patterns they often assume are precisely incarnated in the Huichol ritual, for in this visionary landscape the initiates must pass safely through the hazardous Gateway of Clashing Clouds to reach the sacred ancestral realm and the harmony with nature and the life force which will be found there. And it is the therianthropic Káuyumarie who will mediate the safe passage of what Furst refers to as "the fateful cosmic threshold," "the mystical divide, the Symplegades of the peyote quest."[25] This he does by holding back the cloud doors with his antlers, allowing the shaman and his followers to pass unscathed. The underlying symbolism is clear. Káuyumarie is, of course, the shaman's spirit helper, and as such a reality speaking through and in a sense identifiable with him. It is by virtue of the shaman's unity with the principle represented by the spirit guide that he, and consequently the other initiates, can penetrate the threshold to cosmic life, for it is the spirit guide who symbolically unites our changing world of time and death with that deeper principle of permanence which underlies it.[26]

In a manner which typifies the functional aspect of therianthropic images in Jung's cosmos, Káuyumarie helps effect the process of mythological deepening as he leads the initiates to the land of the ancient ones, the ancestral gods. He guides the psyche back beyond personal consciousness – which, conditioned by the opposites, cannot cross the barrier of the clashing gates – and awakens that stock of inherited possibilities of representation which exist deep within every individual. This is the ancestral realm of archetypal form which the peyoteros now enter, the deep realm of the psyche where, through the psyche's natural ability to introvert in ritual actions, contents are constellated which previously had been latent. As Jung has told us, these are the primordial images, the archetypes, which potentially can be so enriched and empowered through introversion of the libido as to become perceptible to the conscious mind. As we recall, during the process of introversion, as the libido streams back to the fountainhead, "the Place of Beginning," the psyche is capable of casting up images which are introspective glimpses of the very process that marks its own transformation. It is precisely such images which have been captured in each stage of the Huichol ritual in symbols typical of this process.

Passing through the clashing cloud gates, the initiates find themselves within "the place called Vagina," an obvious symbol of introversion or regression. In fact, Furst recognizes at least an implied equation between *Wirikúta* and a Great Mother symbolism. This motif is reinforced by the fact that the next important phase of initiation takes place at a cluster of water holes known as *Tatéi Matiniéri*, "The Springs of Our Mother." Here the ritual actions deepen the meaning of what might otherwise be mistaken for an incest symbolism to indicate that, as Jung firmly believed, such symbols do, indeed, have a deeper regenerative goal – they imply rebirth from the cosmic source of life and power. The Huichol regard these as the wellsprings of the waters of life, and here, in a series of repeated ritual acts, the shaman's ceremonial arrow (a Jungian libido sign) is inserted into the depths of the cavities of these wellsprings of life. Other ritual applications of the arrow reinforce its phallic character. The ceremony not only suggests introversion and the rapprochement of the individual libido with its own wellsprings. It also, in a familiar symbolism, represents the union of male and female principles on a cosmic plane as we approach the originary source. Furst points out that, despite such an obvious sexual symbolism, "it would be simplistic in the extreme to reduce this particular ritual at *Tatéi Matiniéri* to the level of symbolic coitus alone ... What the *mara'akáme* [shaman] simulates with his ceremonial arrow, therefore, is not coitus but unity – the life-producing union of the male and female principles in all nature."[27] Finally, this symbolism, as Myerhoff notes, is meant to evoke the experience of the unity and plenitude which lies beyond the *coincidentia oppositorum*, the union of opposites, in the "Place of Beginning" itself.[28]

It is here that the master of the deer species, Elder Brother Wawatsári, in one of his earthly incarnations, is found and shot in the form of the peyote plant which becomes the sacramental meal. Yet Káuyumarie has led us to that archetypal realm of first principles which, in their eternally repeated incarnations, are beyond individual birth and death, and the ritual makes it clear that the essence of the deer, Tamátsi Wawatsári, the Master Deer, has not died. In fact, it is revealed as the source of continuing life, for in his chant the shaman describes " ... how all around the dead deer peyotes were springing up, growing from his horns, his back, his tail, his shins, his hooves." "Tamátsi Wawatsári," he tells the initiates, "is giving us our life." The shaman then performs an important ritual action with a history reaching deep into the distant past. With his knife he removes the earth from around the cactus. However, instead of taking it out whole, he is careful to leave a portion of the root in the ground. "This is done so that 'Elder Brother can grow again from his bones,'" we are told.[29]

This is a symbolism we found widespread in the shamanic world. The return to bone is a return of life to its "Place of Beginning," to the "cosmic fount," in Eliade's terms, from which all life springs anew. Equating this enduring reality with the root of the plant also suggests Jung's description of the transpersonal plane of our existence as the "rhizome" level which perpetually survives its individual manifestations in the world of time. Here in the ancestral realm individual life opens through symbol, ritual and ecstasy to its source, to the eternal forms of the cosmic life which inform and sustain it. The ritual poetically shows the therianthropic spirit guide to be the connecting bridge between our world of individual form and that of essential form – between personal consciousness and the experience of a transpersonal world. Viewed as a whole, we see that the entire drama of the quest is the eternal play of the life force in diverse manifestations which are, in fact, ever the same. The deer, Káuyumarie, has led the hunt; the deer has been the quarry of the hunt; and the deer, in the form of Elder Brother Wawatsári – the eternal form of the deer which transcends time, change and mortality – forever presides over the entire drama of life and death. And, finally, the deer is also the peyote which provokes the transformation of consciousness evoking this unifying experience, revealing that we are all the play of cosmic life, the children of the flaming flower of cosmic creation.

For the Huichol, leaving their Sierra Madre homeland on this long transformative quest expresses one form of the "break with the universe of daily life" which Eliade saw marking the early stages of the shaman's initiatory ordeal everywhere. This departure from the norms and forms of everyday consciousness is reinforced by symbols implying a deconstruction of the profane self and of the empirical world which it creates and into which it soon becomes dispersed. Conditioned consciousness is left at the threshold of the Gateway of Clashing Clouds, and the focal point of reality is relocated in a deeper paradigmatic world. Familiar symbols of introversion accompany the movement toward "the Place of Beginning" where life finds the fountainhead that sustains it. Here the shaman ascends in ecstasy to converse with Tatewarí and the supernaturals. This is no longer the world of directed thinking but a world in which the symbol moves freely to reveal realities lost to consciousness – a ritual or geopsychic realm whose characteristics are much the same everywhere and "are real because they work" to transform consciousness.

Looking back over the course of this work, we can recall the now familiar symbols marking this way to transformation and the manner in which they parallel the characteristics of Jung's *mundus archetypus* outlined in Chapter 8. On the Huichol journey, the pilgrims "burn away" the old self in the ritual fire, sacrificing their former existence so that they will be born anew. Often we found that the dissolution of the profane self was experienced in ecstatic vision or initiatory ordeal in the most graphic images of sacrifice or dismemberment. We recall Huottaire who witnesses his head being cut off, his body chopped to bits and everything put into a cauldron where it is boiled for three years. Other examples from Siberia and Arctic North America followed a similar pattern. There was also the Aboriginal shaman whose viscera was forcibly removed and his skeleton disarticulated to the last bone, a symbolism widespread in Australia. We may likewise remember the actual ritual severing of the Sioux initiates' fingers described by Radin, or the Maya king's painful piercing of genitals or tongue through which a knotted and thorn-intersected rope was then passed to deepen the experience.

According to Jung, as we have noted, such acts of sacrifice are "a renunciation of egohood" in which "the consciousness gives up its power and possessions in the interest of the subconscious." Consequently, Jung noted that this phase of transformation was frequently closely associated with symbols of introversion, i.e., the cave, the water hole, holes in the ground, large bodies of water generally or a return to the womb. If Jung is correct and these are archetypal symbols of introversion, we should be able to detect a similar pattern of symbolism in this phase of the shaman's initiation marking the psyche's inward journey to awaken the primordial mythopoeic faculty deep within the human mind. In fact, such symbols are found in abundance.

Here we may recall Huottaire's role as "diver," his descent into the watery depths, as well as his entry into the cave which revealed the source of life. Inspired by his chanting tribesmen, the Inuit shaman likewise dives into the ocean depths to the Source itself, Sedna, the ever-copulating one. Similarly, the Australian candidate's dismemberment, as Elkin points out, is repeatedly associated with the initiatory cave, and the Maya bloodletting takes place within the temple-cave. Eliade notes that caves often play an important role in shamanic initiation worldwide.[30] We may also point out the role of the water hole, or cenote, in Maya initiation in Classic times, and today, its spontaneous manifestation in ecstatic dream experiences of the Australian Aboriginal shaman as reported in the work of Andreas Lommel [31] and its archetypal recurrence as "the Springs of our Mother," the water holes which we just saw play a critical part in Huichol ritual. The Huichol examples of this motif were, we remember, found after entering "the place called Vagina," which, like the initiatory cave, suggests a return to the womb. We found a similar symbolism marking the initiation of the Sioux Indian, suggesting its cosmic level of meaning. Within the initiatory vapor-bath, which is carefully constructed as an image of the cosmos, the initiate is told "you are in your mother's womb again. You are about to be reborn again." Likewise, among the Tukano we found a kindred symbolism surrounding the *yajé* pot, the vehicle of the initiate's ecstatic experience. We were told that "first the individual enters the vessel's vagina as a phallus and then he assumes the embryonic state which, eventually, leads to his rebirth." In each tradition, symbols of introversion repeatedly play an important role marking the psyche's path inward, and in each, as we shall see, the inward movement gives rise to a larger pattern of meaning, suggesting rebirth on a consecrated level. However, and most importantly, this regenerative process can only occur if the psyche can come to grips with the powerful forces of this primordial interior world.

In the process of introversion, the world of psyche and not that of the environment becomes paramount. This displacement of psychic energy results in a surplus of libido on the side of the unconscious and an increase in the autonomy of the figures produced by the unconscious whose enhanced power, as Jung points out, is sometimes symbolized by their actually engorging the initiate. We saw this stage of psychic transformation made manifest within the Maya pyramid cave in the welter of frightening forms which presented themselves during the psyche's introversion above the door to the inner chamber of Temple 22 at Copan, and particularly in the monstrous creature into the clashing jaws of which the initiate must enter on his way to enlightenment. We noted that in Maya mythology the shaman's initiation is sometimes imaged as his being swallowed by a mythical serpent, and it is also symbolized by his being devoured by a jaguar. In Maya and Olmec iconography, these creatures which swallow the shaman are specifically and repeatedly associated with the initiatory cave. And the same mythic association is found in Australia where the serpent leads the initiate to the cave in certain scenarios and swallows and then regurgitates him in others. Joan Halifax notes that the shaman in Alaska is devoured by a bear as part of his visionary initiation.[32] The Winnebago Sioux Indians have carried forward the memory of such ecstatic experiences in the ritual taking place in their initiation huts. The lodge itself is specifically associated with the bear and "the imagery here is also supposed to indicate how the vapor-bath lodge is really enclosed within the body of a spirit, a spirit of fierce demeanor and threatening claws and teeth. Into this animal spirit those who are to take the vapor-bath must enter," Paul Radin informs us.[33] Again, initiation takes place within the belly of the beast.

Jung found that similar experiences of being swallowed by frightening theriomorphic forms marked the depths of the experience of introversion. He found this symbolism epitomized in the archetype of the night sea journey where the hero, the questing conscious mind, is swallowed by a dragon or other monstrous form. For him, this symbolized the process of introversion itself – the withdrawal of interest from the outer world, the immersion in the unconscious and the ordeal of overcoming the monster from within which is "the achievement of adaption to the conditions of the inner world." Yet, just as the Sioux vapor-bath makes the ultimate purpose of such swallowing apparent – i.e., as a tool of initiation it is instrumental in effecting the novice's transformation – so for Jung did the night sea journey reveal the hidden alliance between regression and progression. Secretly, the journey proceeded eastward, toward sunrise and rebirth. The aim and end of regression is to tap and enlist those deep layers of the mind where the primordial images lie latent and those still deeper levels which connect us with the wisdom of instinct and the resources of nature that brought us into existence in the first place.

We have seen these levels of consciousness represented in the world's shamanic traditions by the ancestors and the theriomorphic spirit guides who lead the process of mythological deepening which attends the shaman's initiation. As Jung noted, these images generally can be interpreted psychologically as an integration of the unconscious, "a veritable bath in the life source." Here, of course, we might recall the role of the *way*, leading back to the point of creation in the Maya world – i.e., to the "life source" – and the manner in which Káuyumarie led the Huichol to the land of the ancestors and to Wawatsári, the image of renewal and the plenitude of cosmic life in "the Place of Beginning." In an important symbolism the theriomorphic archetype becomes the image of instinct, and, as Jung has informed us, "the archetype as an image of instinct is a spiritual goal toward which the whole nature of man strives; ... " "There are no purposeless psychic occurrences," Jung elsewhere observed, and the wrenching break with the universe of daily life, the psychic fragmentation of the shaman's initiation and the immersion in the titanic psychic forces unearthed in introversion potentially, in Jung's terms, "wakes a renewed fruitfulness."

To repeat a crucial portion of what we explored in Jung's psychic cosmos, during introversion, as Sherry Salman observed, "symbols emerge from the unconscious ... Symbols are like living things, pregnant with meaning, and capable of acting like *transformers of psychic energy.*" When the archetypal symbol functions as an image of instinct, it evokes "the aim and motivation of instincts through the psychoid nature of the archetype." It enlists and employs the deep instinctive wisdom of nature which healed body and mind for millennia before a differentiated consciousness and the ego declared themselves to be in control of the psyche. This healing effect is reflected in the symbols which now emerge from the unconscious. As Salman pointed out, in the depths of introversion the psyche has the capacity to experience the spontaneous reversal of libido which Jung called an enantiodromia. This occurrence of a "return to the opposite" potentially characterizes the nature of the libido's flow at this juncture of the psyche's strange symbolic wanderings and marks the point where apparent regression becomes regeneration. Symbols of unity and harmony, power and essence, illumination and ascent now lead the psyche in a new direction which brings an awareness of the archetypal realm to the conscious mind.

We have used as a recurrent touchstone Jung's observation that "The descent into the depths always seems to precede the ascent" and, once again, this statement might apply with equal justice to the shaman's geopsychic universe. As we shall see, in the world's shamanic traditions the symbols of introversion which we have studied prove to have the same ability to become associated with or actually convert into their opposites as the shaman approaches enlightenment. One of the best examples of this process was the raising of the great uniting symbol of the Maya cosmos, the World Tree, which unified the three realms, the conscious, the unconscious and the realm of higher knowledge revealed in their unity. It unites the depths with the heights and, as a repetition of First Father's world-creative act, opens to the life source. And it was raised within the very depths of the dark and frightening cave of initiatory introversion. As we noted, the symbolic relationship between the cave and the tree is old and widespread in the Maya world. We found that this relationship between the cave, a symbol of descent, and the tree, a symbol of ascent, imaged the secret relationship between regression and illumination that Jung found hinted at in the symbols he encountered in his patients and which he found historically embodied in the relationship between *meditatio* and *imaginatio* in alchemy. It is through the symbols and techniques of introversion implicit in the cave journey that the initiate "penetrates the blocked subterranean passages of our psyche" to experience the deep archetypal patterns which open to the source of creative plenitude and make the shaman a conduit of this power. The dark cave thus becomes the vehicle for illumination and a rebirth on a consecrated level of existence.

If we examine three ecstatic visionary experiences of shamans from three different cultures on three different continents we can witness the spontaneous expression of the same complex of symbols bent to the same initiatory purpose. In each, a descent into the earth, i.e., into the blocked subterranean passageways of the mind, precedes an ascent to the source of power. Each, we shall see, employs the same psychodynamic pattern of symbolism to effect the same alteration of consciousness we have described throughout the work. Yet this transformation is only to be attained by those called into the depths, those who "following the lure of the restless unconscious psyche" and, in Jung's terms, "not satisfied with the dominants of conscious life, set forth … to seek direct experience of the eternal roots."

The Eternal Roots

A.A. Popov has left us the record of just such a seeker of the eternal roots, whose unconscious draws him in ecstatic dream into the chaos of near madness but ultimately ushers him to salvation.[34] This ecstatic dream experience well illustrates the pattern of transformative symbols we have been examining. The dream begins with Sereptie Djaruoskin, a Tavgi Samoyed shaman-to-be from Siberia, cutting down a tree to construct a sledge to carry holy relics. When the tree is cut to the ground, a man emerges out of its roots with a loud shout. "Well, my friend," he tells Sereptie, "I am a man, who came out of the roots of the tree." The stranger from the depths continues: "The root is thick, it looks thin in your eyes only. Therefore I tell you that you must come down through the root if you wish to see me." Again, we see the archetypal relationship between descent or introversion and the shaman's tree. Indeed, it is clear that this is, in fact, a special tree, as the man informs Sereptie, for from times of old "it is this tree that … the shamans have been growing from." The stranger is clad in a hide parka resembling the wild reindeer's hide during moulting time, and he bears clear theriomorphic qualities, for he proves to be an emissary of the supernatural Mother of Wild Reindeer. It is he who will lead Sereptie's descent into the rhizome level through the narrow hole at the root of the tree that at first appears too "thin" to enter. This is the path to transformation, for, as Sereptie begins to realize, "It is through this hole that the shaman receives the spirit of his voice."

As they descend through the hole, they arrive at a river with two streams flowing in opposite directions. We are informed that these are, in fact, the rivers of life and death, the opposites which define and delimit individual existence which Sereptie must penetrate on his perilous inward journey to the fountainhead of life. He must also penetrate the cosmic opposites defining time and space, "the borderline between two daybreaks" and "the backbone of the firmament." Penetrating the opposites, Sereptie finds a tent tied around with a rope. His guide asks Sereptie if he can guess its meaning. "When men go mad and become shamans, they are tied up with this rope," he responds and then realizes that he also has descended into the chaos of madness. "I was quite unconscious and was tied up too," he recognizes.

As their perilous journey inward continues, they confront many terrifying visions including "naked men and women who were singing all the time while tearing their bodies with their teeth" – images of an initiatory dismemberment and madness preliminary to becoming shamans. Here "some just start singing, others losing their mind go away and die; others again become shamans." "If you find the spirit of madness, you will begin to shamanize, initiating (new) shamans," Sereptie is told, and later informed, "shamanizing you will find your way, by yourself." The dream now begins to portray Sereptie's transformation experience in images of an underwater journey: "When I submerged, I arrived at these places, and it seemed as if I were swimming in the water," he informs us. At one point in his journey he enters a tent "not as a man but as a skeleton." In the tent he encounters a woman who looks as if she were made of fire and a smith who forges molten metal from the heat of her body. The skeletal form, the reduction to bone, is a familiar symbolism. It indicates a return to origin, "the origins of the shamans," and consequently becoming a shaman.

When I entered as a skeleton and they forged, it meant that they forged me. The master of the earth, the spirit of the shamans, has become my origin.

Here he ultimately encounters the archetypal "mistress of the earth." Her realm is that of seven initiatory mountain peaks Sereptie has been forced to scale on his journey.

Then I said to myself: "I am sure that I have reached the place whence every man descends" and, turning towards the woman, I said aloud: "You are surely the mistress of the earth who has created all life." "Yes, that is so," she said.

And she reveals that:

"These seven peaks are the origin of every plant: the future shamans go around them. In these nests there are spirits – the master spirits of all the running and flying birds and game."

Sereptie has arrived at the source itself, the cosmic fount of life from which the shaman receives his power.

Sereptie awakens from his trance state, still beneath the tree which "shamans have been growing from." But his journey has been far and his experience profound. Through this fall into madness, the innate symbolic resources of the mind lead Sereptie to a center of sanity. Learning to shamanize, i.e., to interiorize and understand the symbolic patterns cast up from the depths of his own mind, he can find his way by himself. His journey forces him to the realization that the deep ground of his being reaches back into the plenitude of cosmic creation, the realm of "the master spirits of all the running and flying birds and game." He discovers, as Jung tells us, that "He is of the same essence as the universe, and that his own mid-point is its center" – a center which awakens his illumination and shamanic power.

Here again in this spontaneous ecstatic experience of an individual in Siberia we find the same features we have encountered in shamanic traditions around the globe. Symbols of introversion – the descent into the hole at the root of the shaman's tree, the watery depths, images of dismemberment and skeletalization – mark the early stages of the journey to the fountainhead. The hole into which Sereptie must descend represents the undimensioned inner realm which appears to ordinary consciousness to be too "thin" to enter. Within this unconditioned world the opposites defining human life no longer apply, and Sereptie must pass beyond the two streams flowing in opposite directions between the opposing realms of birth and death, the terms and conditions of mortal existence. He must likewise pass beyond the cosmic opposites defining time and space, "the borderline between two daybreaks," and "the backbone of the firmament." Here, in a liminal world existing beyond the pale of the conditions by which the everyday personality organizes our reality, in a series of vivid and terrifying images he perilously plummets into the chaos of near madness. Yet, as Jung so often declared, the treasure lies in the depths, and in a familiar pattern from chaos springs creation and illumination. Sereptie's skeletalization (return to bone) presages a return to origin as we have seen elsewhere. His descent paradoxically becomes an ascent (i.e., up the seven mountain peaks) and a return to origin – his origin as a shaman and ultimately the origin of cosmic life, the nucleus of eternal form represented by the master spirits of the animal kingdom. It is this dawning discovery of his relationship to this deep source of life and form that awakens the innate wisdom which allows Sereptie to formulate and follow his own mystical itinerary by virtue of his own inner and natural resources. Yet this realization was implicit from the beginning, for this is the dream of Sereptie, and the mystical itinerary is the product of his own unconscious mind. It is this grammar of symbols that reveals the secret alliance between regression and enlightenment and bodies forth a pattern of experience which unites the three realms – the conscious, the unconscious and the higher reality revealed in their union. And, thus, all begins and ends under the ultimate uniting symbol of the shamanic tradition, the shaman's central tree which lies immediately above the subterranean passageway into which Sereptie, "following the lure of the restless unconscious psyche" descends to "seek direct experience of the eternal roots."

Let us now transfer our attention to another culture on another continent. If we examine a visionary experience reported by A. W. Howitt, marking the ecstatic initiation of a Wiradjuri medicine man of Australia, we recognize many of the elements of the pattern of symbols examined in this chapter. In his initiatory vision, this youth's body was first rubbed with quartz crystals. Next he was conducted to a grave. Here he encountered a dead man who rubbed him all over to make him "clever," a term which refers to shamanic power and ability. He also provided him with some quartz crystals. Then the young man's father pointed to a *Gunr*, a tiger-snake. "That is your *Budjan* [secret personal totem]; it is mine also," his father told him. To the tail of the snake a string was tied such as "the doctors bring up out of themselves," that is an astral cord which enables magical trance flight. The account continues describing the spontaneous experience of another "seeker of the eternal roots" following the lure of the restless unconscious:

> He took hold of it [the cord], saying "Let us follow him." The tiger-snake went through several tree trunks, and led us through. Then we came to a great

Currajong tree, and went through it, and after that to a tree with a great swelling round its roots. ... Here the *Gunr* went down into the ground, and we followed him, and came up inside the tree, which was hollow. ... After we came out again the snake took us into a great hole in the ground in which were a number of snakes, which rubbed themselves against me, but did not hurt me, being my *Budjan*. They did this to make me a clever man, and to make me a *Wulla-mullung*. My father then said to me, "We will go up to *Baiame's* [the sky god's] camp." He got astride of a *Mauir* (thread) and put me on another, and we held each other's arms. At the end of the thread was *Wombu*, the bird of *Baiame*. We went through the clouds, and on the other side was the sky. We went through the place where the doctors go through, and it kept opening and shutting very quickly. My father said that, if it touched a Doctor when he was going through, it would hurt his spirit, and when he returned home he would sicken and die. On the other side we saw *Baiame* sitting in his camp. He was a very great old man with a long beard. He sat with his legs under him and from his shoulders extended two great quartz crystals to the sky above him. There were also numbers of the boys of *Baiame* and of his people, who are birds and beasts.[35]

The shaman receives his power by transforming into these birds and beasts, who are essential forms of the animal kingdom, according to Elkin.

Based on our study of shamanic symbolism and Jungian psychology, we can now begin to fathom this system of thinking in primordial images which characterizes visionary experience. First the Wiradjuri initiate undergoes a symbolic death. However, characteristic of the symbolisms of sacrifice and bone which we have encountered, such a death presages the larger pattern of initiation and return to origin, for in the process he is rubbed with quartz crystals which characterize the enduring celestial world of *Baiame*. He encounters a serpent spirit guide, which – like the feathered serpent in the Maya visionary world – paradoxically is revealed to be a symbol of ascent, for to his tail is tied an astral cord. Again, the chthonic and the celestial bear a hidden affinity, reminding us of the relationship between the cave or hole in the ground and the tree – a symbolism which this vision likewise appropriates. The initiate takes hold of the cord, and the snake then leads him to a hollow tree which he enters through a hole in the ground. The pattern of symbolism recalls the initiatory cave at the base of the Maya World Tree and the hole Sereptie enters at the base of the tree "shamans have been growing from." He encounters more snakes in the initiatory hole – snakes associated with his theriomorphic spirit guide – and he now becomes "clever," or enlightened, as does Sereptie during his initiatory descent. Characteristic of the relationship between regression and illumination which we have been examining, his descent now turns into an ascent up the astral cord. In an instance of the Symplegades symbolism uncannily reminiscent of the clashing cloud gates of the Huichol visionary experience, he passes through the "opening where doctors go ... which kept opening and shutting very quickly." Passing beyond this cosmic threshold he encounters the sky god, *Baiame*, who is surrounded by his people who are birds and beasts, creatures of essence from whom the shaman receives his power. Having returned to the source, Elkin tells us the Aboriginal shaman becomes a "channel of power."[36]

Now let us switch the focus of our attention to another remote culture, again a continent away from our previous example. In this visionary experience of an old !Kung Bushman from the Kalahari desert region of southern Africa, we once more encounter familiar patterns of image and symbol. The visionary traveler, known as K"xau, is again summoned to the psychic depths and heights by a theriomorphic guide. As he informs us:

> Just yesterday, friend, the giraffe came and took me again. ... We traveled until we came to a wide body of water. It was a river. He took me to the river. The two halves of the river lay to either side of us, one to the left and one to the right. [37]

As we shall see, K"xau has entered a well, and this visionary river of trance travel is underground. Thus, the vision is initiated by typical images of introversion – descent, the well and submersion in water – and we are reminded of the early stages of Sereptie's journey. There he also entered a hole in the earth led by his spirit guide. "We descended through it and arrived at a river with two streams flowing in opposite directions," Sereptie tells us of his journey, repeating an uncannily similar trance experience. In fact, familiar symbols of introversion are intricately intertwined in this vision. Among the Bushmen, immersion in water is considered to be symbolically equivalent to entry into trance, the ecstatic state which the !Kung shaman induces through exhaustive dancing. And both the entry into water and into trance are metaphorically associated with an initiatory death.[38]

The old Bushman describes his induction of the trance state:

> Yes, I am a big dancer. I teach other people to dance. When people sing I go into a trance. I trance and put *n/um* into people, and I carry on my back those who want to learn *n/um*. Then I go! I go right up and give them to God![39]

N/um is shamanic power or energy and is activated by trance, and the !Kung shaman, *n/um k"xau*, is the "owner" of *n/um*.[40] This process of harnessing power in trance reminds us of the Australian shaman who becomes a "channel of power" and, more precisely, his Maya analogue, who is literally an *itzer*, "one who manipulates the cosmic force known as *itz* [power]." In each case, the informing power is galvanized only after an initiatory death equated with introversion and the trance experience. And each of these visionary experiences is accompanied by images of an actual entry into a hole in the earth. K"xau describes this pattern of experience as follows:

> My friend, that's the way of this *n/um*. When people sing, I dance. I enter the
> earth. I go in at a place like where people drink water. [In Australia, the soak
> or water hole is a close analogue, among the Huichol we may recall the
> Springs of Our Mother, and in the Maya world it is the cenote.] I travel a long
> way, very far. When I emerge, I am already climbing.[41]

The pattern of experience is familiar. "The descent always seems to precede the
ascent," as we have learned from Jung, and the initial descent into the earth again
paradoxically become an ascent by astral cord to the unconditioned realm. K"xau
continues the description of his visionary journey.

> I'm climbing threads, the threads that lie over there in the South ... I take
> them and climb them. I climb one and leave it, then I go climb another one. ...
> Then I follow the thread of the wells, the one I am going to enter! The thread
> of the wells of metal. When you get to the wells, you duck beneath the pieces
> of metal. ... And you pass between them ... It hurts. When you lift up a little,
> the metal pieces grab your neck. You lie down so that they don't grab you.[42]

Earlier, K"xau had described his initial entry into trance in similar terms. "My sides were
pressed by the pieces of metal," he tells us. "Metal things fastened my sides." Passing
between these pieces of metal in the underground wells represents yet another
version of the trance experience of penetrating the narrow aperture leading to the
undimensioned realm of the spirit. For, as he tells us of his journey to God, "When you
arrive at God's place, you make yourself small," just as Sereptie must do to gain access
to the unconditioned realm of inner experience through the hole "too thin" to enter..

> When you go there, friend, you make yourself small like this. Friend, when you
> go there, you don't go standing straight. You make yourself small so that you
> are a mamba. ... When you go there, where God is, you are a mamba. That is
> how you go to him.[43]

The "mamba" is a snake, a creature capable of penetrating the narrow aperture
leading to the realm beyond spatial dimensionality. Yet it is this experience which leads
to a higher dimension of reality, for in his trance the shaman ascends to God's house,
the cosmic fount itself depicted in now familiar archetypes.

> People say there are leopards there. People say there are zebras. They say
> locusts. They say lions. They say jackals ... They're in his house, right in his very
> house ... And pythons, they say, come and go in that house ... Elands are

there. Giraffes are there. Gemsboks are there. Kudu are there ... These things don't kill each other. They are God's possessions.[44]

These are the animals of eternity, akin to master spirits of the animal species, for they "don't kill each other. They are God's possessions."

Once more the vision embodies a familiar basic pattern of experience. Again, a theriomorphic spirit guide leads a descent into a hole in the earth. This descent is associated with an initiatory death. It is marked by symbols of introversion – the water hole, submersion in water and the trance experience itself. Yet again the treasure lies in the depths, and the descent paradoxically becomes an ascent, this time by astral cord. The process of transformation is itself a perilous journey through the narrow aperture of the Symplegades, effecting a transformation of consciousness leading to the unconditioned inner realm. These familiar stages again lead the shaman to the source, to God's house, once more symbolized by its animal forms. Finally, the trance journey engenders shamanic power, the shaman being a conduit of this power, an "owner" of *nlum*. The prominent features of the experience of these remote inhabitants of southern Africa are essentially parallel to those we found in Australia, in Central America, Siberia and elsewhere. And in each, the central symbols image the secret relationship between introversion and illumination and power which Jung found as the key to the psyche's metamorphosis, the turning of consciousness which heralded its revivifying integration.

The Turning

In precisely the manner described by Sherry Salman, out of symbols of introversion arise images of ascent, illumination, power and essence throughout the shaman's world. Likewise, at this point in the psyche's strange symbolic wanderings we find that frequently key symbols spontaneously convert to their opposites. As we recall, Jung noted this protean quality of the symbols in his *mundus archetypus*. As examples, he pointed out the archetype of the dark, dangerous cave which becomes the place of illumination and rebirth and the existence of the various zoomorphic forms which threaten to engorge the questing hero but, in fact, become his mentors. We can perceive something similar in the shamanic traditions we have studied, and we may use the same examples to illustrate this characteristic. The initiatory cave in Australia turns out to open into paradise, just as the Maya cavern leads to the Otherworld. The Maya cave, of course, holds the symbol of illumination, the World Tree. We recall that the cave entered by the Siberian shaman, Huottaire, became bright and seemed to open upward to a source of illumination. In Australia, Eliade notes the existence of the motif of the "bright cave" which paradoxically assumes celestial attributes.[45] The inner womb which the Tukano enters in ritual becomes "the door to the heavens," leading to the shaman's luminescence.[46] And the initiatory holes in the ground entered by

Sereptie, the Wiradjuri shaman, and K"xau, which we discussed in the previous section, each become associated with symbols of ascent and illumination. Likewise, with regard to the metamorphosis of the zoomorphic archetype, we have witnessed a number of examples. The chthonic serpent who devours the Maya shaman in fact becomes his initiator and assumes celestial attributes – he becomes plumed and as "serpent bird" sits atop the World Tree. The serpent in Australian ecstatic experiences likewise becomes feathered, can fly and the shaman in trance rides him into the sky. The devouring jaguar in Mesoamerica and the bear which is envisioned as swallowing the shaman among certain Inuit cultures become the shaman's spirit guides, as do their counterparts in Australia and Mexico. We could multiply examples but will conclude with one which very fluently captures this relationship between symbols of introversion and those of ascent.

This is a mural, believed to be the product of the dissemination of Olmec culture, which dates back about 2,700 years. The mural was discovered over the entrance to a cave at Oxtotitlan, Guerrero, Mexico. It depicts a costumed man wearing a complex bird helmet or mask and a bird-like costume implying avian transformation. Avian symbolism is a recurrent shamanic metaphor for trance and magical flight, and a well-recognized symbol of ascent. Kent Reilly informs us of the specific meaning of this particular symbolism. "The elaborate clothing ... identifies the painting's subject: a specific moment in a shamanic flight or cosmic travel ceremony." "The figure at Oxtotitlan is depicted at the precise moment before he will lift off and fly through the thin membrane of the cosmic portal to another reality."[47] The meaning of this visionary symbolism is deepened by the iconography and natural setting which surround it. The figure is seated upon a "throne" which depicts a stylized zoomorph with three heads. The middle face appears to be a form of the plumed serpent. Its eyes are marked with crossed-bands, indicating that it is represented in its celestial aspect. In addition, similar serpent-like forms seem to hang down on either side of the throne to form its legs. Viewing the scene as a whole, it becomes apparent that the shaman rides the three-headed plumed serpent in ecstatic vision through the sky.

But the symbolism is even more complex. As Andrea Stone points out, "the placement of the zoomorphic mask over the cave entrance was purposeful; the cave forms the zoomorph's mouth."[48] With this in mind, it becomes apparent that symbolically the serpent swallows the initiate entering the cave. However, in the interior of the cave there are to be found several symbols of the feathered serpent, the symbol which raises the chthonic to the celestial. These again imply that the cave journey has itself paradoxically become the vehicle of ascent, i.e., the entry into that deep level of reality which induces the experience of ecstatic flight that is graphically represented in the literally overarching symbol of the bird-shaman above the cave entrance. Thus, this shaman's vehicle of flight, the feathered serpent which first engorged the initiate, incorporates the entire symbolism of cave initiation and of the cave and the feathered serpent as the entrance to a visionary reality. Symbols of introversion again lead to symbols of ascent – the dark cave becomes the vehicle of illumination and the chthonic serpent becomes feathered and celestial – and the entire symbolism begins and ends with the image of the shaman's avian transformation and magical flight through "the cosmic portal to another reality."

One of the formal elements which Jung found spontaneously expressing itself at this juncture of the psyche's transformation – which is obviously related to the process of enantiodromia and the conversion of certain symbols to their opposites – was the motif of opposition and the union of opposites which Jung was to explore in depth in *Mysterium Coniunctionis*. We have seen similar themes spontaneously emerging at this stage of the shaman's experience, often precisely at that moment in which he crosses "the fateful cosmic threshold" to the unconditioned realm – where, in Reilly's terms, he penetrates the "cosmic portal to another reality." This process of transformation was symbolized by images which have been summarized under the term "the Symplegades." We first met this symbolism in Chapter 3 where the Tamang shaman, ascending the *axis mundi* in the form of the World Tree, must penetrate the gates which the gods established at time's beginning between heaven and earth, gods and men. Eliade, discussing the archetype of the Symplegades generally, precisely captures its meaning in the context of Tamang ritual.

> The meaning of all these "dangerous passage" rites is this: communication between earth and heaven is established, in an effort to restore the "communicability" that was the law *in illo tempore*. From one point of view, all these initiation rites pursue the reconstruction of a "passage" to the beyond and hence abolition of the break between planes that is typical of the human condition after the "fall."[49]

He finds this symbolism to be widespread in the world's shamanic traditions and gives several instances of initiates' ordeals which recall examples we have already experienced. "They must go 'where night and day meet,'" he tells us, "or find a gate in a wall, or go up to the sky through a passage that opens but for an instant, pass between two constantly moving millstones, two rocks that clash together, through the jaws of a monster, and the like."[50] Here we are reminded of Sereptie's penetrating the borderline between two daybreaks and the backbone of the firmament on his initiatory dream journey, as well as of the clashing cloud gates of the Huichol journey. We might also recall the place where doctors go through "which kept opening and shutting very quickly" in Howitt's account of Australian initiation, and the serpent jaws the shaman must enter symbolically among the Maya. In an Apache ecstatic experience reported by Morris Opler, the shaman, summoned by his bear spirit guide, must enter a visionary cave filled with animal essences and pass between boulders which roll continually from one side of the cave to the other.[51] In a famous Navaho legend encoding shamanic lore, the initiates, first entering the hole of the theriomorphic

Spider Woman, must pass the "Cutting Reeds," "the Rock That Claps Together," and other similar clashing obstacles on their journey of ascent to the Sun Father.[52] Peter and Jill Furst note that the Inuit shaman journeying to Sedna must pass between "three huge rolling boulders or through clashing icebergs ... threading his way through the narrow opening and closing spaces."[53] The very narrow passage is, as Ananda Coomaraswamy has noted, another form of this symbolism. We recall how the !Kung Bushman, K"xau, must make himself small, like a snake, to penetrate the narrow way through which his journey leads him on his way to God's house and how Sereptie must enter the hole at the foot of the shaman's tree which appears too "thin" to penetrate. Carrying the symbolism a step further, in other examples from the American Southwest and Australia the shaman must find and enter an opening in a solid rock face where none exists to the ordinary senses.[54]

According to Eliade, "In the myths the 'paradoxical' passage emphatically testifies that he who succeeds in accomplishing it has transcended the human condition."[55] Ananda Coomaraswamy notes that such images symbolize passage from the conditioned to the unconditioned world – the need to transcend the opposites in order to attain to ultimate reality. They symbolize, he emphasizes, the way "to break out of the universe, ... the single track and the 'strait way' that penetrates the cardinal 'point' on which contraries turn; their unity is only to be reached by entering in there where they actually coincide."[56] Peter and Jill Furst see the same cardinal point where opposites converge quite logically associated with the symbolism of the center and the *axis mundi*. "In this conception of the universe, with its *axis mundi* in the center, earth and sky meet at the horizon, with the meeting place often envisioned as a paradoxical or dangerous passage, a rapidly opening and closing mouth or gateway where brave heroes and shamans in ancient times dared to pass into the celestial realm to retrieve souls or obtain knowledge, spirit power, or some other benefit for humankind." The Fursts find these images to be universal in shamanic cultures worldwide, "often with such specific similarities that they might be accounted for by common historical origins in humankind's earliest past or, more probably, by the very similar deep structures of the common human psyche and the universal human experience."[57] Traditionally, it is through this narrow passage, so often associated with the union of opposites and the world center symbolism, that human consciousness must seek and find the fountainhead of its spiritual and creative being.

Images of the Goal of Transformation – the Unified World

Peter and Jill Furst's observations lead us back to Jung in several respects. Jung, tracing the features of the universal human experience expressing, in the Fursts' terms, the "very similar deep structures of the common human psyche," likewise discovered the emergence of a similar pattern of experience crystalizing around the symbol of the center. He noted the healing and life-enhancing effect of the symbols which express this stage of the mind's transformation and observed that, as transformers of psychic energy, the same symbols were able to lead the psyche in a new direction capable of resurrecting the order hidden in the chaos of the unconscious as it opens to the enduring transpersonal realm – of expressing that image of unity and totality which slumbers in each of us. As we discussed, he found that in his patients this dawning realization first expressed itself as some kind of centering process. Moreover, this process was repeatedly accompanied by the emergence of certain well-defined motifs, the most common of which were chaotic multiplicity and order; duality; the union of opposites in a third; the quaternity (square, cross); rotation (circle, sphere); and finally the centering process and a radial arrangement that usually followed some quaternary system. In addition, these themes and formal elements formed certain typical interrelationships with their own order and meaning and became articulate in a language of their own.

For Jung, as we recall, the unconditioned realm of unity was to be reached through the gateway of the opposites, a realization often represented in the Symplegades symbolism. Joan Halifax well expresses the initiatory pattern implicit in such symbols by which chaotic multiplicity and fragmentation are restored to order and unity in the shaman's *mundus imaginalis*. "The dissolution of the contraries – life and death, light and dark, male and female – and reconstitution of the fractured forms is one of the most consistent impulses in the initiation and transformation process as experienced by the shaman," she tells us. "To bring back to an original state that which was in primordial times whole and is now broken and dismembered is not only an act of unification but also a divine remembrance of a time when a complete reality existed."[58]

We have noted elsewhere images unifying the opposites which complement the Symplegades symbolism. We recall that the Huichol, entering the land of the ancestors, employed a sexual symbolism wherein the shaman inserted his phallic arrow or baton into the Springs of Our Mother to suggest, according to Furst, "not coitus but unity – the life-producing union of the male and female principles in all nature." The Tukano shaman enters the "intrauterine realm" of the master of animals with his phallic baton, and here he frees a world of animal essences which regenerate the beleaguered species hunted in the world of time. And, as we have noted, the same symbolism again occurs in Tukano ritual where the initiate enters the vagina-like *yajé* pot as a phallus and in so doing becomes one with the time of creation, actually witnessing in vision the creation of the world and the great animal prototypes which inform it.

The same process of unification of opposites is often found symbolized directly in the person of the shaman. At times, this is expressed by the shaman's androgyny. As Halifax points out, "Among Siberian peoples, androgynous shamans appear to be unusually prevalent."[59] Here the shaman, at the bidding of the spirits, may braid his hair, dress as a woman, adopt traditional feminine occupations and, finally, even assume the physical and psychological characteristics of the women of his tribe or culture. Eliade finds a similar pattern of experience in the Ngadju Dyak of southern Borneo whose shaman, the *basir*, is a true hermaphrodite, dressing and behaving like a woman.

"We have here a ritual androgyny," he concludes, "a well-known archaic formula for the divine biunity and the *coincidentia oppositorum*."[60] Here the union of opposites applies on both a microcosmic and a macrocosmic level and acquires a cosmic level of meaning. As such, the female and male opposites are regarded as representative of the two cosmological planes – the earth and the sky. The shamans combine in their person the feminine element (earth) and the masculine element (sky), thus re-establishing primordial totality. In fact, as Eliade tells us elsewhere, the shaman's transformative journey is itself a return to the cosmogonic source and, as such, he unites and transcends the duality implied by the sexual principles; "For the shaman unites in himself these two contrary principles; and since his own person constitutes a holy marriage, he symbolically restores the unity of Sky and Earth, and consequently assures communication between Gods and men."[61] As such, he re-establishes primordial totality, the cosmic fount of power and essential form.

Accompanying the process of centering and unification, as we know, Jung frequently found symbols employing a quaternary structure or double quaternio. These images expressed wholeness and the unification of opposites in every direction or facet of existence. In the form of the mandala, they often featured motifs such as quaternity, the circle or redundant concentric circles, or a flower-like arrangement, and they implied an existence open to its sacred creative source. As we discussed in Chapter 8, such images carry a great numinosity and the highest therapeutic effect. They point simultaneously to informing power and to essential form. On the one hand, they image the "seed place," the very point of creation – of Deity unfolding in man, nature and cosmos. As such, these images are characterized by their tremendous effectiveness as carriers of libido, and consequently they are experienced as a source of power, creative plenitude and "Primary Force." On the other hand, they have the effect of grounding man's being in the divine life whose forms we are – the transpersonal and archetypal world. Such images create an experience of "the universal totality of the divine state" much akin to that described by Halifax previously. Finally, Jung noted another characteristic of these images. While such an image may seem to arise during the course of the patient's evolving psychic integration, in fact, as we examined in the previous section of this chapter, in reality it was always present within the psyche, an "eternal presence" beyond "individual birth and death" which may or may not be perceived by the conscious portions of the psyche.

According to Jung, these images are the result of "important nuclear processes in the objective psyche – images of the goal as it were, which the psychic process, being 'purposive,' apparently sets up of its own accord, without any external stimulus." In fact, we have seen precisely these images marking the goal of the shaman's transformation reflective of the drive to unity and harmony which marks its purposive aspect. We recall the white soul flower among the Tamang which marked the goal of Kumari's curative transformation and the return of her soul from the chaos of psychic collapse. A similar white soul flower grew on the Maya World Tree, anchoring the individual soul in its cosmic source. We found a kindred image marking the goal of the Huichol journey, the flower of cosmic life and illumination which is the goal of the peyote pilgrimage. The Maya initiate's cave journey began with symbols of fragmentation, autosacrifice and introversion, but eventually led to the fountainhead itself, the primal act of creation expressed in First Father's separating the opposites to create the ordered world. This took the form of First Father's Partition House – a quaternary structure whose central point is indeed the "seed point" of all creation, the source of both the primary force and the essential form which give order and shape to our world of time. This is, in Jung's terms, an image of the universal totality of the divine state which seems to crystalize during the process of the initiate's transformation. Yet its position in the Maya geopsychic cosmos makes it clear that it is also experienced as an eternal presence, beyond individual birth and death, as Jung described the archetype, for it is the enduring foundation and support of all creation – the source of what he referred to as the "continuous creation." It is this foundational act which rescues order from chaotic multiplicity, an order the Maya never tired of tracing into the heavens.

The therapeutic effect of these images as transformers of libido is further emphasized by their reproduction in the sand paintings of the Navaho which, as we discussed, often employ a quaternary structure surrounding the central Place of Emergence – precisely the "seed point" in Jung's terms. As Donald Sandner points out, such images function to bring the psyche into harmony with the natural and cosmic forces which surround it. In fact, they are that cosmic force, the force of creation itself – images of "Primary Force" which have the effect of regenerating the patient. Sandner has told us, "The painting focuses power, and the medicine man transfers it to the patient through the physical medium of the sand. The patient not only makes use of the power of the figures in the painting, he becomes that power." Moreover, while the reality of this image of the sacred mandala-form cosmos emerges from the natural landscape as the patient progresses toward this unifying vision, we might again assert, along with Jung, "The fact is, however, that it only *appeared* more and more distinctly in increasingly differentiated form; in reality it was always present." For the Navaho, we recall, this sacred quaternary form underlies and informs the physical world. It is its "inner form," the essential form given reality at the time of creation. As such, it is truly "an 'eternal' presence, and it is only a question of whether it is perceived by consciousness or not." This perception is precisely the goal to which the process intends, and such mandalas again act as images of the goal which the psychic process, being purposive, sets up of its own accord, without any external stimulus. The concept of the goal of transformation is entirely appropriate in this context, for the Navaho view the entire ritual process as bringing the physical world into relationship with the ideal as its informing source.

Jung, as we have seen, regarded the mandala image as a symbol of psychic growth and integration and of the pre-existent unity and harmony such integration disclosed.

As such, he felt it was closely related to the image of the World Tree. As we have seen, the World Tree or a cognate symbol (mountain, pole, ladder, etc.) often marks the mandala's center in the shaman's visionary world. In the Maya cosmos it becomes the *wacah-chan* axis which runs through the very middle of a mandala-form cosmos as it has ever since First Father raised the World Tree and created the world from the sacred center in the form of his Partition House. In Navaho sand painting, frequently a cosmic mountain, "Mountain-Around-Which-Moving-Was-Done," is regarded as an *axis mundi* occupying the center of their four-fold visionary cosmos. Other such images unify the shaman's visionary cosmos throughout the world. Uno Holmberg points out that in Siberia "On the yellow navel [the center] of the eight-edged earth ... there is a dense, eight branched tree,"[62] an example, as Eliade recognizes, of the World Tree[63] as well as of the sacred cosmos in the image of the double quaternio. The center is again the "seed place," for it was here that the first man was born. And, as Eliade points out, in Siberian tradition the central tree represents "the universe in perpetual regeneration, the inexhaustible spring of cosmic life, the paramount reservoir of the sacred."[64] As such, it is both a source of "Primary Force" infusing the creation and, simultaneously, of the paradigmatic form which lifts an otherwise chaotic and profane world to a sacred order. At its top are to be found birds which are the souls of shamans awaiting incarnation.

Eliade notes the shamanic antecedents of much of Norse mythology[65] and we can see the vestiges of the same visionary experience surviving in that culture where the World Tree, Yggdrasil, stands at the center of a quadriform cosmos with an eagle perched upon the Tree's apex. Of course, we recall that the "serpent bird" or "celestial bird" sits on top of the Maya World Tree at the center of their visionary cosmos, just as bird souls are to be found atop the Siberian World Tree. In Tukano lore, the Sun Father, himself taking the form of an oropendola bird, used a ceremonial pole placed at the world center to create mankind.[66] This staff is represented in miniature by the shaman's wand with feathers at its top. An interesting petroglyph commemorates this event by combining the form of the bird with the Sun Father's staff to form a winged pole characterized by a quaternity symmetrically surrounding a central axis associated with the point of creation.[67] As in other shamanic traditions, in this image the motifs of quaternity, bird-topped pole or tree, center of the world and point of creation all coalesce to mark this point as a manifestation of cosmogonic power. The Tukano regard this point as a channel which allows human communication with the archetypal world. At the same time, it serves as a means of fertilization, power and creation. It is here, in the Tukano visionary cosmos, that "that which is constant" (the archetypal) becomes that which will "come to pass" (the created world).[68]

A similar pattern emerges in the Sioux sun dance, which we have discussed. Here the young braves dance away from and back to the sacred central pole placed in the middle of the camp circle. The ritual pole is constructed to resemble a tree and has the nest of the thunderbird near the top. The braves dance first to the west, then in the remaining cardinal directions, so that at the end of the dance a flattened area in the form of a cross has been stamped into the earth – a quaternary structure with the symbolic bird-topped pole at its center. This configuration galvanizes the sacred power capable of healing the Sioux people. Here again this form gradually emerges as the initiates, rotating around the sacred center, inscribe an encircled quaternary form onto the dancing ground, i.e., it crystalizes as they approach their initiatory goal. Yet for the Sioux, the sacred circle and the quaternity express eternal form, beyond individual birth and death, and it is clear that this is again a process of anamnesis, of recollecting the deep formal principles infusing man, cosmos and nature from the beginning, from the time of creation itself.

In Australia, the formal elements of redundant circularity, coupled with a sacred central pole, predominate, but the image functions in much the same manner. Again, it represents the "seed place" – the point of creation itself. In mandala-like ground paintings consisting of concentric circles around a central aperture, the Northern Aranda depict the sacred water hole or soak (the Ilbalintja Soak) which was the source of all creation (Figure 2). This central point was also the birthplace of the primal ancestor, Karora, and the place from which all life and even the sun itself emanated. In the beginning, Karora lay asleep under this holy ground and above his head arose a sacred decorated pole which reached the sky. Awakening, Karora burst from beneath the ground, creating the Ilbalintja Soak. The shaman is believed to enter this place in the process of his initiation.[69]

A similar pole reaching the sky plays an important role among the Achilpa, a branch of Northern Aranda. Mythically, this pole was planted in the center of a sacred ground by the culture hero of the Achilpa, Numbakulla, whose name denotes "always existing" or "out of nothing." Anointing it with blood, he climbed it and instructed the first Achilpa ancestor to follow him. The blood-stained pole, however, proved too slippery, and the man fell down. "Numbakulla went on alone, drew up the pole after him and was never seen again."[70] Eliade believes that this pole may be an example of a very old Aboriginal image of ascent representing that central vertical axis which originally connected heaven and earth but which later became severed, depriving humanity of the unity and totality

2. Ground painting representing Ilbalintja Soak

that existed in primordial times. However, the capacity of such a symbol, in Jung's terms, to convert the chaotic multiplicity of our world into order, still belongs to this pole as an image of the centering process. It can be ritually raised anywhere, and as Eliade tell us:

> During their wanderings, the Achilpa always carry the sacred pole with them and choose the direction to follow by its slant. While continually moving about, the Achilpa are never allowed to be far from the "Center of the World;" they are always "centered" and in communication with the Heavens where Numbakulla had disappeared. When the pole is broken, this is a catastrophe; in a way, it is the "end of the world," a regression into chaos.[71]

Thus, the "central" pole mythologically re-establishes the relationship with a transpersonal reality capable of giving the tribe its bearings in a relative world – an axis which gives the world its order and form – i.e., prevents the reversion into chaos. In Aranda initiation ceremonies this sacred pole re-linking man with the ancestors is again planted. It is banded with alternate rings of red and white bird down and topped with a tuft of eagle-hawk feathers. It is around this sacred "bird-topped" pole that the previously circumcised initiate is now subincised suggesting the union of sexual opposites in the person of the initiate, an approximation of the dreamtime totality which the central sacred pole reconnecting man with the eternal ancestors reiterates.

Finally, as we have said, the archetype speaks through the individual from the transpersonal world, making him a conduit for its energy, ordering power and innate meaning. The return to center marked by the ultimate uniting symbol, the World Tree, images the successful freeing of the long-dammed wellsprings of libido, humankind's share of the energy which fires the creation. We recall that Jung observed the tremendous effectiveness of these images as carriers of libido and termed the psychic state fused with this energy the "mana personality," which he regarded as the characteristic of the shaman's curative and charismatic powers. Again, it is as if returning to his source man returns to *the source*, the "creative center of all things," just as Sereptie experienced in his ecstatic dream. The shaman's world everywhere reflects this experience. We recall that the Maya king at the world center assumes in ritual the very form of the World Tree itself. Here he experiences himself, indeed, as this creative center of all things, a conduit of "Primary Force" which the Maya termed *itz*, the power of the cosmos. The Tamang shaman in trance envisions himself as climbing the World Tree to galvanize *shakti*, cosmic power, to regenerate his patient. The initiates in the Sioux sun dance won *wakan* power through their arduous dance around the sacred central pole-tree. The Australian shaman, after his trance ascent symbolized by the sacred central pole or astral cord, becomes an unbroken "channel of power," according to Elkin. The Siberian shaman achieves a similar end by scaling the sacred birch tree. The !Kung shaman derived *n/um*, shamanic power, from his trance ascent up the astral cord to

God's house, and the Tukano shaman enlists luminescence and "seminal" power at the creative center, marked by the *axis mundi* constructed in imitation of the staff or pole by virtue of which the Sun Father performed his world-creative act.

According to Jung, a characteristic of the mana personality is that the person experiences that the power he is now able to enlist comes from a source beyond the individual it informs, precisely what we have experienced in the world's shamanic traditions. In the shaman's world, this informing force is frequently experienced as being the source of cosmic creation itself and seems to express itself in timeless patterns or archetypes. Such a person experiences a supra-personal foundation expressing itself in universal images and, becoming an expression of the transpersonal world, is lifted to a higher, consecrated level of consciousness. As we know, Progoff described this as a "*situation* of correspondence." "This correspondence is between the microcosm and the macrocosm, for a harmony has been achieved and the individual has come into an equivalent union with the universal." This is the same state of universality-totality which the shaman's initiation is meant to recapture, providing the directive signs we need to live our lives in harmony with ourselves, nature and the cosmos. Again, as in Jung's *mundus archetypus*, in the shaman's geopsychic cosmos, the culminating images indicate the immanence of power in the created world and the unity of creation. Here, for archaic and modern man in search of a soul, world soul and individual soul potentially coincide. For the shaman, it is this process of being brought into unity with the rhythms of nature and cosmic life which is both healing and illuminative and creates the respect for all life which only this experience can engender – an experience cherished by human beings before, in Jung's terms, modern society forced them "to exchange the life-preserving rhythm of the aeons for the dread ticking of the clock."[72]

In these mythic shamanic worlds, the themes and formal elements which Jung found marking the goal of psychic transformation become articulate in kindred visions from distant and widely separated cultures. They become images of the same nuclear process which Jung recognized to be the goal of the quest for psychic transformation in his patients in today's world. And while each of these elements plays an important role in the shaman's transformation, it is the bird-topped World Tree which is most often the nucleating center of these visionary worlds and which best symbolizes the healing and life-enhancing effect of the shaman's process of transformation. As the ultimate uniting symbol, it joins the three worlds – the conscious mind, the deeper levels which inform it and the unified world which this integration recovers for us. It becomes an image which both recalls for us the original totality and harmony of existence and, at the same time, resuscitates the lost mythopoeic sensibility which is capable of leading us through the shaman's geopsychic cosmos. Therefore, it is everywhere envisioned as, on the one hand, the vehicle of ascent and communication with the transpersonal world and its revivifying paradigmatic patterns of creation and, on the other, the conduit through which the plenitude of the cosmos flows into creation. As such, the symbol of the central axis has the highly therapeutic psychological effect of rescuing order from chaos by shepherding psychic energy back to the transpersonal world and, at the same time, opening the mind to the source of regenerative power. We can now understand how a symbol with similar archetypal attributes, the ritually constructed World Tree among the Tamang in faraway Nepal, which we discussed in Chapter 3, was able to reach into the deepest portions of the human psyche to rescue Kumari from her collapse into chaos, heal the rift between this world and that of the gods and become a conduit of the regenerative power, *shakti*, uniting the soul with its source as imaged in the *narling mendo*, the white soul flower. And given the ubiquity of these images of ascent, so often combined with the other formal elements marking the goal of the psyche's innate capacity for transformation, and recognizing their functional equivalence throughout the world, we might now approach Jung with increased understanding and realize that such primordial images from the depths of the psyche are, indeed, "inherent in the collective unconscious and thus beyond individual birth and death. The archetype is, so to speak, an 'eternal' presence, and it is only a question of whether it is perceived by consciousness or not."

Here we might also return to the perception of Thomas Mann that we related in Chapter 2, which helps us understand the shaman's mythic universe.

> The association of the words "psychology" and "deeper levels" has also a chronological significance: the depths of the human soul are also "Primordial Times," that deep "Well of Time" in which Myth has its home and from which the original norms and forms of life are derived. For Myth is the foundation of life; it is the timeless pattern, the religious formula to which life shapes itself, inasmuch as its characteristics are a reproduction of the Unconscious.

Given our understanding of shamanism and the shaman's role in creating, preserving and conveying the mythologies of the world, we might be justified in saying that – based upon the repeated structural and functional similarities in which the shamanic experience has expressed itself over time and distance and in their resemblance to Jungian psychology today – shamanism in fact epitomizes this timeless pattern, this religious formula to which life shapes itself, inasmuch as its characteristics are a reproduction of the unconscious. However, this is an unconscious which through its initiation has become open to the likewise timeless patterns of the transpersonal realm and become capable of conveying these realities. The enduring patterns of the pleroma or continuous creation and the archetypes through which they express themselves in time become not only instruments of illumination and healing but also reveal the primordial patterns by which alone any effective creation can occur, any life or work of art become "real" in the deepest sense of the term. And it is precisely the ability to penetrate this durative level of experience in the world's shamanic traditions which fosters the

Les Trois Frères    Les Trois Frères    Le Gabillou

3. The shamans of the caves

universal patterns that everywhere constitute the shaman's *mundus imaginalis*, his geopsychic cosmos – a map of the soul consisting of, in Jung's terms, "psychic forms in the individual which not only occur at the antipodes but also in other epochs with which archeology provides the only link." And so we enter that "deep 'Well of Time'" which indeed reveals this to be, in a very real sense, the timeless pattern to which life shapes itself once the mind is able to experience its eternal roots, its spiritual and creative foundations.

The Psyche's "Strange Symbolic Wanderings" from Time Immemorial

One summer day in 1879, the voice from that "deep 'Well of Time'" which gives primordial form to human experience began to reveal some of its innermost secrets. Don Marcelino de Sautuola and his daughter Maria were exploring the entry to a cave located in the foothills of the Cantabrian Mountains of northern Spain. Young Maria wandered into one of the side chambers of the cave. Raising her lantern, she was startled to see huge and impressively painted animal forms dominating the cave's ceiling. She ran out to inform her incredulous father, and together they spent the remainder of the day exploring the decorated galleries of the cave that is now known to the world as Altamira.

While Sautuola and some others contended that these sophisticated paintings were attributable to the peoples of the last Ice Age, most experts at the time were skeptical and refused to believe that the highly developed artistic sensibility shown by these figures could reside in creatures long believed to have been extremely primitive and even brutish. Some even implied that the cave was a deliberate fraud. The scholarly world rejected the implications of the discovery, and Sautuola went to his grave without vindication. However, gradually the window of prehistory was pried open farther and farther with the continued discovery of additional sites in southern France and northern Spain. Many of the most significant sites, like Altamira, were eventually determined to belong to the Magdalenian period which began between

17,000 and 16,000 B.P. and ended about 11,000 years ago. Other caves have been assigned even more ancient dates, with hand stencils from the recently discovered Cosquer cave apparently dating back about 27,000 years. And very recently, the horizons of prehistory were pushed back even farther with the discovery of Chauvet cave on the Ardèche River, a tributary of the Rhone, in southern France. While the extremely beautiful animal depictions within this cave were first assigned a date between 17,000 and 21,000 years ago, scientific tests reveal some of the work to be far older, dating back beyond 30,000 B.P. And one of the most impressive images in the cave is a composite figure, now known as the "Sorcerer," with the head and upper body of a bison and the lower extremities of a human – a figure which very much resembles certain images of the shaman as he has survived into historical times. The figure has bent knees, as if dancing, and seems to face, waist high, what appears to be the image of the lower half of a woman with particular emphasis on a well-defined pubic triangle. This figure is echoed in other caves (Figures 3 and 7). Here we again find the familiar therianthropic form – often with bovid or cervid horns, legs bent in positions suggestive of dance and perhaps ecstasy and frequently with pronounced phallic or ithyphallic attributes – variously combining animal and human traits.

Did the shaman long ago traverse these caves which are so well-known for their exquisite animal art and did he leave evidence of their primordial purpose? Clearly, throughout our study of shamanism the cave itself has been a most significant and recurrent symbol of introversion and an instrument of shamanic initiation. It both effects and reflects the penetration of that durative inner source, the rhizome level of recurrent form, which fosters the emergence of archetypal and universal configurations from the human mind – patterns of experience we have traced throughout the world's shamanic traditions as well as in the works of Carl Jung. And just as the Navaho depicted the features of this archetypal geopsychic cosmos in their sand paintings, or the Huichol traced them in the landscape leading to *Wirikúta*, the sacred peyote country, or the Maya in their impressive architecture, so here, beginning over 300 centuries ago, archaic man inscribed them upon the walls of these ancient caves. As we shall see, the symbols and the natural configuration of the cave structures are employed in the same effort to lead the mind back to an experience of its creative and spiritual foundations. Again, it describes a structural and functional psychodynamic pattern meant to transform human consciousness along the very same pathways of the mind we have been studying to arouse an experience which, as Eliade observed, is so ancient and so basic it may be "co-existent with the human condition."

This process again employs a familiar initiatory pattern: the break with the universe of daily life, death of the profane self, a return to the creative source, both within the individual and in nature, and a rebirth on a consecrated level. In so doing, it utilizes the same psychophysiological methods to transform consciousness which we found in the shaman's traditional and ecstatic training techniques throughout the world and to which we found clear parallels in Jung's work associated with active imagination. More importantly, these ancient caves themselves and the signs and figures which adorn them become the revelation of the shamanic structure of consciousness and the very embodiment of the shaman's geopsychic cosmos.

Many investigators, in fact, believe that they can discern in these caves evidence that they were places of initiation. Deep within the cave of Le Tuc d'Audobert there are to be found two coupling bison modeled in clay. Here, also, a series of suggestive footprints has survived. In once-soft clay now covered by a thin film of stalagmite there are about fifty heel imprints apparently left by young people who visited this sacred area thousands of years ago. The form of the prints, made by walking with the weight placed on the heels, has suggested to some viewers rites of initiation and, perhaps, dancing. Dance, as we know, has frequently fostered shamanic vision in rites of initiation worldwide. Herbert Kühn, describing his encounter with these curious vestiges of Paleolithic ritual, notes, "since there are no other imprints than those of heels, it is obvious that this must have been a dance-floor, used for some sort of cult-dance ... [perhaps] a sacred bison dance."[73] Joseph Campbell likewise asks, "Was this the buffalo dance of some young initiate?"[74] In support of this surmisal, he draws our attention to the dancing bison-like figures of Les Trois Frères and Le Gabillou (Figure 3). Consistent with the symbols of initiation that we have studied, the coupling bison, of course, suggest the union of sexual opposites which we have often found marks the shaman's approach to the unconditioned realm. The shaman's journey has traditionally been a return to origin and to the creative power it represents. While subject to some current controversy, Herbert Kühn relates that following the pattern of the dance imprints leads the investigator to specific areas of the cave adorned by "phallic engravings, symbols of life, birth, beginning."[75] Thus, the bisons and other animal imagery may imply the same source of plenitude and fecundity which we have so often seen imaged by supernatural animal spirits such as those that marked the culmination of the Siberian shaman's initiatory dream in the previous section or the trance journey of the !Kung Bushman.

The cave, we have noted, is a typical image of introversion. For those traveling to its interior, the cave itself combines with the archetype of the journey as a symbol of transformation to become the natural analogue of that inward journey which marks the shaman's alteration of consciousness and relocates reality on a deeper plane of experience. It implies the same process of descent which Jung found spontaneously marked the inceptional stages of active imagination. Moreover, as a journey from the light world of everyday consciousness into the dark, threatening unknown interior, it perfectly expresses that "break with the universe of daily life" which Eliade observes marks the initial stages of the shaman's experience over time and the ages. The early stages of the shaman's initiation, we recall, were often marked by the novitiate's exposure to what we referred to as liminal structures of reality, experiences meant to dissolve the mind's normal orientation to the real and to break down the categories of consciousness which bind us to the world of accepted reality. This dark plunge into a world beyond the threshold, the disorientating labyrinthine realm beneath the surface of our everyday world, both images and helps effect this transformation. It implies the lowering of the threshold of consciousness we saw in Jungian practice and the penetration of the hitherto dark substratum which informs and supports it. Here, in a variation of a familiar symbolism, consciousness is engorged by the deeper forces of the preconscious portions of the human psyche.

The effect of this natural symbolism is reinforced on a number of levels. The journey through these caves was frequently a harrowing ordeal. The caves' most sacred sites were often only to be reached after arduous and exhausting physical effort, suffering the sensory deprivation of prolonged darkness and being forced to penetrate long, low and extremely constricting passageways along the path of transformation. Many shamanic cultures have traditionally employed such methods as extended exposure to darkness, restricted mobility and sensory deprivation to help effect a transformation of consciousness. Physical exhaustion, hypermotility and exposure to various ordeals frequently complemented these techniques. All these experiences have been shown to lower the threshold of consciousness and create a condition similar to that which Michael Winkelman, on the basis of his scientific studies, described as leading to "the erasure of previously conditioned responses, changes of beliefs, loss of memory and increased susceptibility."

The cave journey itself induced many of these processes, and their effect may have been heightened by other means as well. For instance, as mentioned, we have evidence that may indicate patterns of dance within the caves. In addition, repeatedly the shamanic figures within the caves are portrayed as dancers, indeed dancers verging upon a state of ecstasy. There also exists evidence of instruments of percussion and primitive flutes from this period. Moreover, certain features of the caves had natural percussive properties. Stalactites vibrate and emit sounds when struck, and evidence of such usage seems to be present in some caves.[76] Recent studies demonstrate that many of the images had been painted precisely at locations within the cave where sounds resonate the most.[77] Dance and, perhaps, drumming, flute playing, the beating of stalactites and chanting, dramatically enhanced by the echoes of the cave, may have produced the hypermotility and auditory driving which are the familiar accompaniments of the techniques of ecstatic training found throughout the shaman's world. As Abbé Breuil notes, in this condition of increased susceptibility it was easy to heighten the tension of the ordeal. Sudden noises, costumed figures and other effects could awaken the imagination and arouse the dormant forces of the unconscious.[78] In addition, as Jean Clottes and J.D. Lewis-Williams observe, various ritual procedures probably took place during the cave initiation.[79] In this dark interior realm, as Jung noted concerning techniques of introversion generally, the inner world of the psyche and not that of the environment becomes paramount, the result being a surplus of energy on the side of the unconscious and an abnormal increase in the autonomy of the unconscious and its productions.

So understood, the Paleolithic cave becomes a carefully orchestrated instrument of transformation. Darkness, sensory deprivation, restricted mobility, physical and mental ordeal combine with dance, hypermotility, auditory driving and other techniques as well to play a familiar role inducing a transformation of consciousness in the same manner as historical shamanisms have done for centuries and for similar purposes. All of these factors combine to dissolve ego consciousness in the manner with which we are now well familiar and to further the process of introversion. This process, in turn, helps awaken the deep symbolic capacities of the human mind, releasing its archetypal powers and increasing its susceptibility to the symbolic world to which it is exposed. Here again, it is in the depths of introversion, where the psyche confronts its symbolic powers, that it is able to assimilate the powers of the inner world and bring them back to the surface in a meaningful way.

Indeed, the symbol, with its transformative effects, comes alive in these caves. The harrowing aspects of the cave journey, of course, incarnate the symbolism of the perilous journey, the journey along the razor's edge, and being engorged within the dark confines of the cave reminds us of the symbolism of the night sea journey. In Jung's *mundus archetypus*, these symbolisms were recurrently associated images of death, sacrifice and piercing as well as self-sacrifice and self-piercing. These suggest the dissolution of consciousness which, in alchemy, leads to the *nigredo*, the "chaotic blackness," which the cave so well represents. Yet, as we recall, they also presage the larger process in which the libido "leaves the bright upper world" and "streams back to the fountainhead," the point of creation itself. We can see the same archetypal process marked upon these cave walls so many thousands of years ago.

We may recall images and practices of sacrifice and self-sacrifice from other shamanic traditions. The Winnebago Sioux and some other Native American tribes we remember cut off their fingers at the various joints. Kindred practices of digital dismemberment are found in other shamanic societies and sometimes imaged in their rock painting. Members of certain cultures also ritually pierced each other's or their own bodies as, we recall, did the Maya. Similar images also occur spontaneously in vision, dream and ecstasy. Generally, images of sacrifice, dismemberment and piercing marked the initial stages of the shaman's initiation over broad areas of the world in both ritual and ecstatic experience and, I believe, we see similar images in these Upper Paleolithic caves.

Figures of the human hand frequently are found imprinted or outlined in silhouette on the walls of these caves. Eliade has pointed out that in Australia, where sacred animal images are also painted upon rock walls, touching the images of the Aboriginal rock paintings is a participation in the power of the dreamtime source from which they are believed to emanate.[80] J.D. Lewis-Williams and T.A. Dowson have made similar observations with regard to the shamanic rock art of the southern San Bushman of Africa.[81] Indeed, Lewis-Williams and Jean Clottes surmise that the power and plenitude of the shamanic Otherworld was believed to lie behind and emerge from the walls of these Upper Paleolithic caves.[82] The laying of hands upon these walls, as memorialized in the hand image, would be a participation in this power. Yet in the world's shamanic cultures, this participation always involves self-transformation, and the initial stages of transformation leading to power involve sacrifice and self-sacrifice. It is, therefore, quite consistent that we find these hand figures also implying the symbolism of self-sacrifice and transformation, for many of the images found within the caves suggest the same digital dismemberment we have found elsewhere with one or more members clearly missing (Figure 4). Such images apparently symbolize some form of self-sacrifice and, given the role played by similar images throughout the shaman's world, would seem to betoken the sacrifice of the "old self" and the initial stages of shamanic initiation. So envisioned, this symbolism precisely complements the psychophysiological techniques fostering the dissolution of the profane self as a preliminary to transformation which we discussed above and have found in shamanic traditions everywhere.

An interesting figure, recently found at Cosquer cave, reinforces this pattern of symbolism. This figure is located in the eastern portion of the cave – an area containing numerous hand images, some of which display a dismemberment symbolism itself suggestive of initiatory death. Here an etching on the cave wall depicts what Jean Clottes and Jean Courtin recognize to be a wounded or killed man. The figure is pierced through the chest and again "by a long projectile weapon" from back to front. The figure seems to fit into a larger pattern.[83] Other figures, sometimes portraying human-like creatures with bird-like or beaked faces suggestive of avian transformation, have also been recognized to represent men pierced by spears or similar projectiles. Clottes and Courtin, noting that some of these figures "were intentionally drawn in an obviously crude way," suggest "perhaps they represent extraordinary beings, shamans or spirits in human form who could be depicted only in a somewhat indirect way."[84] Avian transformation, of course, is suggestive of shamanism, and certain scholars recognize that bird-like figures from the period could

4. Hand images. Complete and depicting fingers severed at the joint

represent the shaman. Given these indicia, coupled with the psychophysiological techniques implying the dissolution of the old self and evoking a transformation of consciousness, it seems compelling that these images imply the initiatory death or piercing which is found so often spontaneously expressed in shamanic traditions.

Yet, as Jung frequently pointed out, the treasure lies in the depths, and as an image and tool of introversion, traditionally the cave is not only associated with death and descent but also becomes, according to him, "the place of rebirth, that secret cavity in which one is shut up in order to be incubated and renewed." As we have seen, this process of rebirth and renewal is imaged in shamanic initiation and spontaneously expressed in ecstatic experience as a return to origin – to the source of power that informs and creates our temporal and spatial world but lies beyond it in a realm which, like that implied in Jung's theory of synchronicity, is experienced in trance as being atemporal, unconditioned and beyond the ordinary laws of dimensionality. The breaking of the plane to this realm of plenitude repeatedly has been symbolized by the passage through the Symplegades. Consistent with the imagery of self-sacrifice and with the loss of self induced by the psychophysiological techniques we have previously mentioned, this is the barrier that the profane self cannot pass. Here, conditioned consciousness, the empirical self or persona and the world to which it binds itself, are transcended and a deeper plane of reality revealed. As Coomaraswamy recognized, one of the universal forms which this symbolism assumes is that of the "narrow way to illumination," the tiny aperture or hole-too-thin-to-enter. We recall Sereptie's encounter with this apparent barrier and have noted its presence elsewhere in shamanic initiation. As K"xau, the !Kung Bushman, told us on his way to the source of cosmic life marked by its atemporal animal forms, "when you go there, friend, you make yourself small like this. Friend when you go there, you do not go standing up straight. You make yourself small so that you are a mamba [a snake]." It is only in such a form that he can penetrate the narrow passage to the source itself. As it has throughout the world's mythological and mystical traditions, this "narrow way" leads from the world of time (i.e., the opposites of past and future) to an "eternal Now,"[85] that is, to the atemporal world of essential form – what Jung described as the "continuous creation."

The initiatory caves of the Upper Paleolithic were selected and embellished both to induce and record the stages of shamanic transformation, and this process frequently involved the experience of the "narrow aperture." Moreover, I believe it was employed with the same structural and functional purposes which we have seen in other shamanic traditions. Obviously, the cave itself, as a confined world entered through an aperture in the surface of the earth, implies this symbolism generally and recalls several examples of this mythic motif which we experienced earlier. In addition, the caves chosen for embellishment frequently had long, narrow and confining entrance ways which began the novitiate's initiation. More importantly, as we shall see, the caves' most important revelations were often to be reached only after the initiates had groped their uncertain way through lengthy, narrow and constricting passageways.

This configuration of experience, of course, suggests in Coomaraswamy's terms the "narrow way to illumination." Consequently, the purposeful employment of the experience of penetrating the narrow cave aperture as a precursor to revelation is symbolically and archetypally appropriate.

In other shamanic traditions we have seen that the shaman's inward journey is associated with the symbolism of the union of opposites, often appropriately in conjunction with the Symplegades symbolism. Jung found that the psyches of his contemporary patients likewise produced or responded to the same symbolism of the union of opposites, the experience of which he saw as an important signpost on the way to psychic integration and illumination. While, over the course of our study, this experience of unification has found many varied forms of expression, one of the most common has, in fact, involved sexual symbols. At this point we may recall as an example the perilous initiatory journey of the Huichol. Here, just after he has penetrated the clashing cloud gates (i.e., the Symplegades), the shaman uses his baton, or ceremonial arrow, as a phallic symbol, dipping it into the cavities of the Springs of our Mother to unite symbolically the male and female opposites. As Peter T. Furst told us, the symbolism is meant to suggest "the life-producing union of the male and female principles in all nature," or, according to Barbara Myerhoff, to evoke the experience of the unity and plenitude which lies beyond the *coincidentia oppositorum* in the "Place of Beginning." For the Huichol, this unifying act was a precursor to the shaman's successful penetration of cosmic life itself – the realm of animal essences characterized by the perpetually incarnated master of the deer species. Likewise, we found a similar sexual symbolism among the Tukano where the shaman's phallic baton also opens the "intrauterine" realm of animal essences.

Can we see a similar sexual symbolism in the Upper Paleolithic? Obviously the cave itself has an intrauterine significance. This natural symbolism is reinforced in a number of ways. Many of the caves are, in fact, inscribed with images of vulvas, and a shallow cave at La Magdeleine has two magnificent female forms adorning its entrance (Figure 5). Leroi-Gourhan observes, "The cave as a whole does seem to have had a female

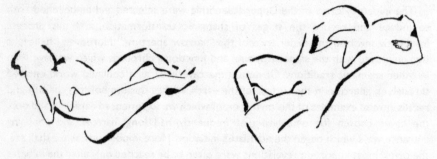

5. Reclining female forms flanking the entrance to La Magdeleine cave

symbolic character, which would explain the care with which narrow passages, oval-shaped areas, clefts, and the smaller cavities are marked in red, even sometimes entirely in red."[86] Anne Baring and Jules Cashford go so far as to assert that "For at least 20,000 years (from 30,000 to 10,000 B.C.) the Paleolithic cave seems to be the most sacred place, the sanctuary of the Goddess and the source of her regenerative power."[87] It is within "her all containing womb" with its abundance of animal forms that the shaman reached the creative source itself, the goal of his initiation.

In fact, there are both male and female sexual symbols within the caves. Leroi-Gourhan believed that many of these existed in a balanced system of sexual complementarity. For instance, the images mentioned above vesting the cave with a female symbolic character were, according to him, always marked by complementary forms suggesting a male symbolism. Moreover, he found that the numerous "signs" within the caves, enigmatic inscriptions the full meaning of which we have yet to fathom, fell into complementary male and female sets. Indeed, according to him the animal art itself bore a similar sexual symbolism. For him images and signs of sexual complementarity permeated these caves.

What has traditionally been described as early Upper Paleolithic art did in fact consist, in part, of unambiguous sexual symbols, indicating that such images may be fundamental to their symbolism. Likewise, in a broader perspective, the shaman's penetration in initiation of the female cave inevitably suggests an activity with masculine associations. This observation is reinforced by the fact that the shaman-like figures within the caves (Figures 3 and 7) often have markedly phallic or ithyphallic characteristics. The recumbent figure at Lascaux clearly lies with his penis erect within the womb of the cave precisely at its most sacred location (Figure 8). Moreover, we recall that the shaman-like creature recently discovered at Chauvet faces waist high the image of the lower half of a woman with a pronounced pubic triangle as he guards the entry to the wealth of life forms on the magnificent Lion Panel in that cave. This portion of the cave also contains other images in the form of the vulva. The baton is an emblem of the shaman's position through much of the world. We noted among the Huichol and the Tukano that the baton served as a phallic symbol suggesting the unity of opposites and the successful penetration of the realm of animal essences. A significant number of batons surviving from the Upper Paleolithic period are unambiguously phallic in nature (Figure 6) and, like those in other shamanic cultures, may have played a role in unlocking this intrauterine realm of animal essences represented by the cave. And we have previously discussed the symbolism implicit in the coupling bison deities marking the epiphany in the cave of Le Tuc d'Audobert. All this implies a fundamental sexual symbolism and complementarity such as we have seen in other shamanic cultures suggesting the unity of male and female opposites on a transpersonal plane and the power and plenitude implicit in such union.

The union of opposites has been a key motif throughout our study of shamanism as it was in Jungian psychology. We may recall the androgyny that characterizes the

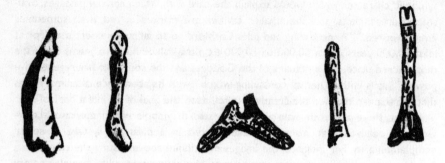

6. Drawings of phallic batons or baton fragments from the Upper Paleolithic period

shaman in many archaic traditions. Eliade, as we have seen, has repeatedly emphasized that the shaman's journey is a return to the cosmogonic source, and that, in so returning, he unites and transcends the duality symbolized by the sexual opposites just as was done in these primordial caves. As we have mentioned, one of the world's oldest and most widespread mythologems represents the creation of the world as a process by which original unity becomes differentiated to form, through the polarity of the sexual opposites, a world-creative pair, i.e., the world parents. And, conversely, it is through the experience of the union of such opposites that original unity, the goal of shamanic initiation according to Halifax, is regained. In such union, humankind for millennia has experienced what Eliade has referred to as an "immersion into that limitless ocean of power that existed before the Creation of the World and rendered creation possible." In penetrating the maternal cave, the ithyphallic shaman and his initiates are symbolically returning to the generative source of all form. Here they encounter and harness that common formative force which animates both the cosmos and the human mind, especially in its artistic and mythic productions which the majestic creations and archetypal patterns within the cave strive to body forth. It is this very force or "luminescence" which allows the shaman to "interiorize" traditional forms into the mythical itinerary outlined on the cave walls – the same itinerary we have seen outlined in Jung's imaginal world and spontaneously expressed in the shaman's ecstatic trance experiences and their ritual equivalents throughout the shamanic world.

Some commentators believe the caves contain evidence of phosphenes which we discussed in relationship to the Tukano. Phosphenes, as elementary forms which appear to the visual sense without an external source of illumination, often appear in the early stages of trance experience. In fact, phosphenic forms can be generated by such factors as sensory deprivation, auditory driving or the fatigue caused by physical ordeal, all of which, as we discussed earlier, may have been characteristic of the journey through these caves. The Tukano recognize many distinct configurations of such phosphenes, and I believe clearly analogous forms are present in these caves. For purposes of economy, let us deal with only one such form. Among the Tukano phosphenes are often represented as dots, particularly red dots, and the ingestion of the trance-producing hallucinogen, *yajé*, is mythically associated with the concept "to paint with red dots."[88] The presence of such dots is associated, according to Reichel-Dolmatoff, with the concept of a "loss of self" as an entry into a state of altered consciousness.[89]

We have seen how these caves were naturally conducive to the techniques used by shamanic traditions around the world to induce the experience of a "loss of self." We have also seen images of sacrifice and digital dismemberment implying the same experience which is also implicit in the Symplegades motif. And within these caves we recurrently find dots, frequently red dots, painted upon the cave walls. Such techniques, symbolic images and phosphenic forms all converge to suggest the entry into a state of altered consciousness, the signs of which are represented on these cave walls. And they seem to be related to two additional observations. In trance experience, phosphenes are frequently precursors of, or themselves transform into, more complex figures, often vested with a mythological character. We may recall that this process is precisely what Reichel-Dolmatoff found characterizing the experience of altered states of consciousness among the Tukano. The simple phosphenic images yielded the visionary field to more complex forms – mythological images such as the Master of Animals and the animal prototypes which appeared at the time of the creation. In addition, it is well-known that entering a state of altered consciousness tends to promote tunnel or cave-like images. This pattern of experience suggests a deep level, spontaneously generated relationship between the cave or tunnel, phosphenes and mythological forms implicit in trance experience as the mind is drawn closer through introversion to its own deep structures and the symbolic forms harbored by this level of consciousness. And each of these elements is, of course, part and parcel of the cave journey.

It is highly significant that the mind spontaneously produces the cave image as a symbol of introversion as it enters into trance and seeks the experience of its own depths – that layer of the psyche lying beneath our personal consciousness which consists of the collective unconscious and the psychoid level of the mind connecting us with instinct and nature itself. To repeat what we have emphasized earlier, the psychoid level of the mind is that aspect of the psyche that can be most directly experienced as a part of nature. It is here that the archetype itself becomes the image of instinct and that instinctual biological energy is transformed into human meaning in the symbol. The archetype as the image of instinct is the "aim and end of introversion" according to Jung and, as we know, the psyche bodies forth its experience of the attainment of this goal in introspective intuitions often in the form of theriomorphic or therianthropic figures. Such images represent man in his "potential wholeness which is," according to Jung, "both God and animal – not merely empirical man, but the totality of his being, which is rooted in his animal nature and reaches out beyond the merely human towards the divine." Kindred images within the cave of introversion would be appropriately symbolic introspective intuitions of the goal of the psyche's process of transformation.

Obviously these caves, with their animal art, abound in theriomorphic forms. Likewise, many of the human figures within the cave manifest theriomorphic characteristics. The bird-like figures which we discussed are examples, as are the bison-men depicted in Figure 3. The latter generally occur in the deep portions of the cave, indicative that they presage the aim and end of the long initiatory journey into the psyche. Perhaps the most impressive and well-known of such images is known as the Sorcerer of Les Trois Frères (Figure 7). This figure is to be found in an alcove known as the "Sanctuary" deep within the Les Trois Frères cave. It stands about 15 feet (4.5 m) above floor level, dominating the space within the alcove. Like the image of the Sorcerer at Chauvet, it appears to be intimately related to the magnificent throngs of Upper Paleolithic animals which inhabit the Sanctuary walls in rich abundance. As various commentators have pointed out, the figure possesses a startling array of diverse animal characteristics – the antlers and ears of a stag, the round staring eyes of an owl, or perhaps a lion, animal forepaws, feline genitals and a horse- or wolf-like tail. Quite strikingly, however, the dancing feet are distinctly those of a human being. And from a position of dominance and authority within the Sanctuary, its penetrating eyes look out from behind what appears to be a human beard. "The whole feeling of the painting confuses the distinction between the human and the animal," Baring and Cashford point out, "so that we do not know whether he is an animal with human feet or a human dressed in animal form."[90]

7. The Sorcerer of Les Trois Frères

Jung, as we know, found that such part human, part animal images heralded the psyche's rapprochement with the deep formal structures which inform it. At this stage of the perilous journey inward through these caverns, the novitiates and the shaman again are "*in the psyche* as much as it is inside of them" and such images signify our contact with the pre-existent meaning hidden in the chaos of the unconscious – our archetypal inheritance of symbolic wisdom held in the "vast historical storehouse" of the collective unconscious and the realm of instinct and nature which inform this level of human psychic experience. And likewise, it is here, as Sherry Salman has pointed out, that such an image "evokes the aim and motivation of the instincts through the psychoid nature of the archetype." At this level, mind and body coalesce, and archaic man enlisted that deep instinctive wisdom of nature which has healed body and mind for millennia and simultaneously led to illumination. This deep level of psychic integration is, according to Jung, experienced as "a veritable bath of renewal in the life-source," a return to cosmic life itself.

If we view this strange and numinous image of the Sorcerer within the larger context of the Sanctuary and of our entry into this sacred interior world, we can discern how so many centuries ago the human psyche bodied forth the same process of transformation that Jung found in his contemporary patients and which we have found in shamanic traditions throughout the world. Herbert Kühn has colorfully described his perilous journey into the Sanctuary. "The ground is damp and slimy" he tells us, "we have to be very careful not to slip off the rocky way. It goes up and down, then comes a very narrow passage about ten yards [9 m] long through which you have to creep on all fours. And then again there come great halls and more narrow passages. In one large gallery are a lot of red and black dots, just those dots."

After passing this gallery, the ordeal of another much longer tunnel begins. The tunnel is barely high or wide enough to accommodate the human body – in places barely one foot high (30 cm), squeezing one into the earth. Passage is only possible with arms pressed close to the visitor's sides, wriggling forward "like snakes," Kühn informs us. Here we cannot help but recall K"xau who must similarly pass "like a mamba," a snake, through the visionary Symplegades to the God's House with its eternal animal forms. Or we might remember the Siberian shaman, Sereptie, who must squeeze through the hole-too-thin-to-enter to reach the climax of his initiation, the origin of "the master spirits of all the running and flying birds and game." The visitors inch along some forty yards (36.5 m), confined, short of breath and growing increasingly uneasy. "Will this never end?" Kühn asks himself. "Then suddenly, we are through," he tells us, "and everybody breathes. It is like redemption."[91] They find that they have reached a destination similar to that of our other shamanic travelers – a magnificent chamber, the Sanctuary of Les Trois Frères. Letting their light travel along the walls they find vividly depicted a startling array of what are perhaps "the master spirits of all the running and flying birds and game" – images of the mammoth and rhinoceros, bison, wild horse, bear, wild ass, reindeer, owl, musk ox and many others swarm across the walls. And some 15 feet (4.5 m) above the level of the floor they discover the dominating figure of the Sorcerer, ominously presiding over the panoply of ancient animal forms in this interior world.

Well initiated into such patterns of transformation of consciousness, we can now understand the intricacy of this symbolism. The gallery full of red and black dots, "just those dots," suggests a reproduction of the experience of the elementary phosphenes which herald an entry into an altered state of consciousness. Being located just before the narrow aperture of the 40-yard (36.5-m) tunnel leading to the throngs of well-articulated figures within the Sanctuary, they introduce a familiar larger pattern of experience – the spontaneous association of phosphenes, the tunnel and mythic images apparently intrinsic to human consciousness at this stage of transformation. Among the Tukano, such dots were associated with the very loss of self typical of the entry into trance experience which, as we have shown, the cave journey and its symbols are meant to induce. Traditionally, the profane self cannot penetrate the narrow aperture to the unconditioned world, and phosphenic forms and the experience of the narrow aperture in the form of this long and constricted tunnel neatly coalesce to suggest the experience of self-transcendence which we have seen everywhere in the world's shamanic traditions. This experience is, of course, reinforced by the role played by physical exhaustion, isolation and sensory deprivation in this stage of the cave journey as the entrant traverses this long, low, dark passage.

In Tukano mythology, the symbolism of the dots has a masculine association. According to Leroi-Gourhan, the imagery of dots carries a similar association in the Upper Paleolithic.[92] The tunnel and the intrauterine world of the Sanctuary, of course, have a feminine value. Together the two symbolisms may imply that union of opposites which suggests the original oneness of the primordial source. In a very real sense, the journey through this long, dark canal to the origin of life and form suggests a reversal of the birthing process itself, leading us back through the contractions of the birth canal to the intrauterine world of the inner cave. Loss of self and reversal of the birthing process both suggest the pattern which Jung found to typify introversion as a passage beyond personal consciousness to its source in the transpersonal world and cosmic life. And it is precisely here that the Sorcerer so well incarnates the mediating role of the therianthropic archetype, symbolizing the human experience of an entry into the deep, psychoid level of the mind where it seems to touch the form-producing principles of its psychophysical foundations, the womb or matrix of life itself represented by the burgeoning animal forms within the Sanctuary. Such an experience is indeed, as Jung has told us, "a veritable bath of renewal in the life-source."

In many of the shamanic traditions we have examined, this return to the fountainhead was accompanied by very similar images. We have recalled Sereptie's arrival at the "cosmic fount" with its animal forms and K"xau's encounter with the animals of eternity who are "God's possessions" in his trance experience. We might also call to mind from Australia the journey to the sky god *Baiame*, who is surrounded by his birds and beasts, or the animal essences encountered in the cave by the Apache shaman described by Morris Opler. In each of these shamanic traditions, images of introversion and passage through the Symplegades were associated with a theriomorphic figure who mediated between human consciousness and the generative source, the cosmic fount itself characterized by its eternal animal forms. For example, if we return to the journey of the Huichol initiates, we realize that initially they crossed what Furst referred to as the "cosmic threshold" – "the Symplegades of the peyote quest" – in the form of the clashing cloud gates. Having accomplished this difficult passage, they entered the intrauterine "land called Vagina." Finally, the pilgrims arrived at the Place of Beginning – the realm of the ever-incarnated Master of the Deer Species. And the entire journey and difficult passage was mediated by the part human, part animal form of the spirit guide, Káuyumarie.

Now returning to the Sanctuary and placing the scene within its larger context we can see that, like other initiates to shamanic power and illumination, in his approach to this sacred world, the Upper Paleolithic postulant has entered the cave of introversion and experienced initiatory death – the loss of individuated consciousness heralded by phosphenic experience. He has likewise penetrated the narrow aperture into the zone of power, united the male and female opposites, and, mediated by the therianthropic form of the Sorcerer, returned to the generative source of life itself, that now familiar world of "the master spirits of all the running and flying birds and game." The process described is, in Jung's terms, a return to the fountainhead of life. Each element marks a stage in an archetypal process portrayed in symbols that reflect the phases through which the mind has been led back to its inner depths and to illumination for what now appears to be thousands and thousands of years.

In the overall course of this journey, the threatening cave becomes the womb of rebirth, a baptism in the fount of cosmic life. It again marks an initiatory turning of consciousness, for it appropriates another familiar archetype – the dark cave paradoxically leads to illumination. We may recall the image of the bright cave from other shamanic traditions, for instance Huottaire's journey into the cave of animal essences which became bright and seemed to open to a source of light. And here in the Upper Paleolithic the illumination may have been quite literal, for much evidence of torches and fires has been found in the caves. Jean Clottes observes generally that these were used for lighting purposes and not as hearths for cooking food.[93] In fact, some observers have seen organized lighting systems within certain caves. Such lighting would have been a highly effective tool of initiation within these caves, particularly because many are lined with a white calcite coating. The sudden lighting of these dark grottoes reflecting brightly against luminous calcite walls would induce a shock of sudden revelation, an apt culmination for the illuminative initiatory experience. Thus, these inner chambers may be an ancient predecessor of the widely disseminated archetype of the luminous cave.

The cave, again, unites the three realms, integrating consciousness – the daylight world of our ordinary reality – with the riches of the preconscious mind and its trove of mythic forms, and finally opening into the cosmic life which informs them. This symbolism is consistent with that which we have seen elsewhere. We recall that in Australian lore the cave became bright – according to Eliade it assumed celestial qualities – and opened into paradise. Among the Maya, the World Tree with the celestial bird at its top is raised within the cave making it a symbol of trance experience and of illumination. Of course, as we have seen, this same image of the bird-topped World Tree or pole is common to shamanic traditions worldwide, symbolizing the unifying vision achieved through introversion and trance. The Maya cave likewise leads to the Otherworld, the world of essential form. In Oxtotitlan, the cave becomes the entry point for trance experience and magical flight symbolized by the shaman's avian transformation which is graphically depicted in the bird-costumed shaman over the mouth of the cave who is portrayed at that "precise moment before he will lift off and fly through the thin membrane of the cosmic portal to another reality." Avian transformation is a frequent metaphor for the magical flight of trance introversion such as we find associated with this Central American cave. Andreas Lommel has told us that a similar avian costume is worn by Siberian shamans. When this costume is employed, he informs us, "the appropriate head ornament is a bird's head, while the shoes are made to look like bird's claws."[94] The symbolism is closely associated with the World Tree for, according to Eliade, Siberian shamans take the form of a bird on their soul recovery journeys flying to the top of the World Tree.[95] And worldwide a bird-like form repeatedly sits atop the central Cosmic Tree.

In this chapter we have found that symbols of introversion – cave, hole, water hole, etc. – recurrently have led to symbols of ascent – tree, pole or mountain – symbolic of magical flight. Here time and again the shaman ascends through trance to experience the principle of permanence behind our world of change – a level of reality often depicted in terms of the "master spirits of all the running and flying birds and game" as it was in Siberia, or the realm of the Master of the Deer Species among the Huichol. Let us further recall an additional element of the Huichol experience. It is through the sacrifice of the creatures of time, i.e., the individual deer-peyote, that the eternal form of the Master Animal is revealed to the peyoteros. As we shall see, a similar role is played by shamanic sacrifice in many cultures. We can now understand that the symbolisms implicit in the images and techniques which we have been describing – cave, trance, the bird-topped World Tree or pole, avian transformation, magical flight, the animals of eternity and the sacrifice which bridges the gap between time and death and the realm of eternal animal spirits – are capable of forming a now familiar and coherent grammar of shamanic symbols in this context. As a final step in our study of shamanic archetypes, we can employ this understanding to unlock one of the most famous but controversial scenes surviving from the Upper Paleolithic, that of the well-known Shaft at Lascaux cave.

This image (Figure 8) lies deep within the cave at Lascaux. Before he arrived at this sacred scene, the Ice Age visitant would have experienced many of the psychophysical inducements to transformation which we have found implicit in the cave journey. He would have traversed the portion of the cave known as the Rotunda with its numerous signs and great scenes of animal art and crawled on hands and knees through the long, low 55-foot (17-m) Passageway which opens suddenly to the more spacious areas referred to as the Apse and Nave of the cave. "The Apse and the Shaft (which is an extension of it) form the strangest and most mysterious part of the cave, and the part which remains most vividly in the imagination," Mario Ruspoli informs us. "It is the place with the most signs, images and symbols – though these are sometimes very difficult to make out. It is also the most sacred place in the cave." More than one thousand engravings line the Apse. And in the Shaft have been found items which may bear witness to its ritual importance: charcoal, lamps, flint blades and spears decorated with signs, and a few fragments of bone and antler. The shaft is approximately 16 feet (5 m) deep, the most inaccessible point in the cave, generally thought to have been reached by the Ice Age initiates only with the aid of a rope. Despite its inaccessibility, the shaft "was much frequented and was apparently the most sacred place in the sanctuary, rather like the crypt of an ancient church."[96]

It is here in the depths that Ice Age man chose to depict this well-known scene. And though the meaning of this scene has provoked controversy for decades, with our understanding of Jungian symbolism and the shamanic traditions and patterns of imagery we have studied, its meaning becomes apparent. For here, cast up from the depths of time, we see familiar symbols within the cave of introversion and trance experience. The archetypal symbolic meanings implicit in the cave, trance, avian

8. Scene from the shaft at Lascaux

transformation, magical flight, the bird-topped tree or pole, the animals of eternity and the sacrifice connecting the world of time and change with the principles of permanence which eternally inform our ephemeral world all find a voice in this ancient mysterious Shaft. And, appropriately, together they rearticulate the vision of that "eternal Now" that Coomaraswamy has told us traditionally lies just beyond the Symplegades, here represented by the long, low Passageway which leads to the Shaft and its images. All speak in a familiar archetypal language – a grammar of symbols which apparently dates all the way back to those ancient times when our predecessors initially displayed the ability to express complex symbolic realities – that "thinking in primordial images" which Jung found to be the very foundation of human psychic well-being.

Here we find a great bull bison, apparently severely wounded by a spear, with its entrails protruding from the wound. He is juxtaposed to a man lying recumbent within the womb of the cave with his penis erect, a symbolism which again suggests the union of sexual opposites. The man is crudely drawn, as are many human figures in prehistoric cave art. However, we can discern that he wears what appears to be a bird mask and his hands resemble the feet of a bird. Beside him is a staff or pole which has the image of a bird at the top. While some have interpreted this scene as a depiction of the hunt, perhaps portraying an injury to the hunter as well as the beast, such an approach ignores many important facets of the depiction, particularly the complex interweaving of the elements of symbolism. We may start to unravel its significance by noting that some commentators have surmised the man lying on his back immobile is a shaman rapt in trance. This observation seems well-founded and can be supported from several directions. Trance experience and the cave as a symbol of introversion are closely allied psychologically, so closely allied that, as we have seen, the psyche in trance often spontaneously produces images of the cave. We have seen symbols of descent – i.e., in this context cave and Shaft – spontaneously leading to symbols of trance ascent throughout our study of shamanism. And, in fact, the cave journey can be, and as we have seen in this instance probably was, a well-devised tool for trance induction.

It has often been noted that the prostrate man in the Shaft at Lascaux has the face of or wears the mask of a bird. As we have mentioned, other humanlike creatures with avian features in roles implying those of the shaman are to be found in Upper Paleolithic art. The figure also has hands which resemble the feet of a bird. Here we might recall the figure of the shaman clad in a bird costume over the cave at Oxtotitlan. And more precisely it brings to mind Lommel's description of the Siberian shaman's costume: "the appropriate head ornament is a bird's head, while the shoes are made to look like bird's claws." This is, of course, very much what we see depicted here at Lascaux over fifteen millennia earlier. In fact, the bird mask or transformed face of the man resembles that of the bird on the top of the pole. The image of the bird-topped tree or pole is a symbol we have seen throughout the shaman's world. It marks the axis of the shaman's trance ascent and with the bird at its top is associated with avian transformation and magical flight, each widespread symbols of trance experience. We found a similar bird-topped tree raised within the Maya pyramid cave. It is here that the shaman can break the plane to another level of reality, the realm of essential form underlying the world of change.

It is for this reason that trance, magical flight and the bird-topped tree or pole are closely connected with another symbolism, that of sacrifice. This realization may explain the impaled bison depicted in this scene and help articulate its relationship to the animal art on the surrounding cave walls throughout Lascaux. In shamanic cultures throughout the world, the central tree or pole as a symbol of trance ascent is repeatedly associated with sacrifice. A goat is sacrificed prior to the Buryat shaman's ascent up the central birch tree in Siberia; among the Tungus the pelt of a sacrificial animal is placed upon the sacred tree, and among the Dolgan a bird-topped tree marks the road to the sky for the shaman and the soul of a sacrificed animal.[97] We have previously seen images of sacrifice and autosacrifice at the sacred center which was marked by the raising of the World Tree among the Maya. Among the Mapuche of Chile, prior to the shaman's ascending a ritual pole called the *rewe*, lambs are sacrificed[98] and among the Sioux sacrificial effigies are hung on their central bird-topped pole during the sun dance.[99] According to Eliade, in many shamanic traditions the sacrificial animal is an incarnation of the mythical animal ancestor who is conceived of as the inexhaustible source of the life of the species. In the sacrifice, the sacrificial soul returns to its source, and the shaman's magical flight is aided in the process.[100] This is, of course, precisely what we saw among the Huichol where the sacrificial animal (the deer), trance induction (the peyote) and access to the Master of the Deer Species are all symbolically equated. The sacrifice's death is a return of both shaman and sacrifice to the larger source of cosmic life and fecundity – the source of the shaman's power.

Here, in this ancient scene, having experienced the cave journey and its carefully orchestrated ardors, terrors and trials, and traversing on hands and knees through the long, low Passageway to the Apse and Shaft, the Symplegades of Lascaux cave, the initiate, in Coomaraswamy's terms, "breaks out of the universe" and arrives at that "eternal Now" which characterizes trance experience. It is this experience which is depicted in this famous scene at Lascaux where the symbolism of the perilous journey, the Symplegades, trance, avian transformation, magical flight and the bird-topped axis which unites the shaman's world all combine with the great sacrificial bull bison to lead to that synchronistic principle of permanence which man has always sensed to underlie temporality. We are once again led to that enduring realm of "the master spirits of all the running and flying birds and game," the image of the power and permanence of cosmic life which the animal art that everywhere surrounds this archaic scene so well represents.

We have followed the psyche's "strange symbolic wanderings" back to the horizons of man's history as a symbol producing being. We have traced structural and functional patterns among the world's shamanic traditions whose strikingly precise similarities seem to suggest, in Jung's terms, "the remarkable similarity of the human psyche at all times and all places." These patterns exist in diverse cultures which are so widely separated by time and distance that it is difficult to explain their evolution and long endurance without concluding that they encode patterns of transformation and innate meaning existing deep within the human mind. Moreover, these are extraordinarily important patterns. They appear to be basic to our health and psychological well-being as tested over the centuries. In addition, they are fundamental to human religious experience which they long have guided in large areas of the world. And, in fact, they embody the same patterns of experience Jung found to be crucial to his contemporary patients in their effort to overcome the critical and debilitating divisions which alienate the modern mind from its mythopoeic roots and a harmonious existence with the world in which God has placed us. So understood, far from being a mere cultural curiosity and anomalous historical survival, shamanism becomes a phenomenon of seminal cultural importance. It, indeed, appears to be the first and longest-lasting incarnation of that timeless pattern, that religious formula by which the human psyche is predisposed to organize its deepest realities. And this is the same image of the human soul which Jung was able to awaken in his contemporary patients – an image still capable of incarnating its patterns with precision in the life of modern man, as we shall see in the next chapter.

Chapter 10

The Curing Curer

*Shall my experience – the history of an illness and recovery –
have been only my personal experience? I should like to believe
the opposite ...*
Friedrich Nietzsche

The Call

History has preserved little memory of the culture of one of the great cities of the Pre-Columbian Americas, yet its monumental Pyramid of the Sun carries forward a most meaningful and indelible image which will endure forever in that portion of the human psyche, that Dreamer of Age-Old Dreams, which survives time and change. The city is called Teotihuacán, and it once flourished in the Basin of Mexico. At the height of its power, around 500 A.D., Teotihuacán was larger than Imperial Rome.[1] Much earlier in its history, the people of this area constructed a sacred sanctuary – an underground chamber deep within a natural cave which was formed when the lava of the area cooled millions of years ago. A massive pyramid was built above the cave and was designed so that the inner chamber of the cave was directly under the temple that was centered on top of the pyramid (Figure 9). The foot of the pyramid's original central stairway leading up to the temple was positioned to coincide with the entrance to this cave sanctuary. This sacred complex has certain characteristics, the archetypal aspects of which are now well familiar to us. They testify to a shamanic heritage to which this culture was heir at an early period[2], and once again map the form and destiny of the soul and the way to transformation.

The cave running beneath the pyramid has many arresting features, some of which originally did not belong to the cave structure. The natural course of the cave was purposely changed to make it wind, a path more tortuous (and, perhaps, more ritually torturous) and serpentine. In addition, in many areas the cave's dimensions were intentionally constricted, and the ceiling was artificially lowered to make the initiates bow, crawl and squeeze their way through. In analogy, we might think of K"xau, Sereptie and the hole-too-thin, or the Upper Paleolithic initiates whom we encountered in the previous chapter. The dark, winding struggle through the cave again reproduces the archetype of the perilous journey, and the narrow apertures recreate the experience of the Symplegades, each of which transformed conditioned ego consciousness and induced an experience of the transpersonal depths. Consistent with this stage of psychological

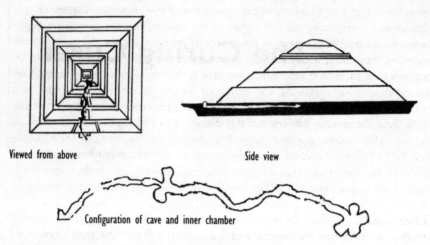

Viewed from above   Side view

Configuration of cave and inner chamber

9. The Pyramid of the Sun at Teotihuacán and underlying cave

transformation, here ceremonial remains suggest symbolic efforts to unify the cosmogonic opposites as the cave entrant struggled to reach the cosmic center and source. And when we understand that the serpentine configuration of the tunnel implied a further symbolism, we recognize another familiar marker of this journey inward. The Feathered Serpent was a key symbol in this culture and entering the ritually constructed serpentine cave was analogous to entering the belly of the serpent, being engorged in the unconscious as we have seen repeatedly in the symbolisms we have studied. Moreover, remains from ancient ceremonies indicate that, like the symbolic world of the Maya, pyramid and cave lay above the primordial waters. These are familiar images of introversion cast up by the preconscious mind which again and again mark and induce the process of its transformation.

And so we should not be surprised, as we pass beyond conditioned consciousness, to find another familiar complex of symbols. Here, again, within the unconscious depths an expansion of consciousness occurs, and the very same centering process which Jung found marking this profound change is suggested. The cave ends beneath the temple which is on top of the pyramid, a place traditionally associated with an *axis mundi* symbolism, i.e., the world center. More remarkable is the fact that at this very point the cave's natural configuration had been intentionally hollowed and shaped into a quaternary structure with chambers reaching into the four cardinal directions.[†] This combination of the center and a four-fold pattern clearly suggests the mandala

---

[†] In fact, the entire city of Teotihuacán was constructed as a quaternion around a sacred center — a configuration indicative of cosmic order and unity. As Roberta and Peter Markman point out, this directional orientation and general plan functioned as a sacred model for other cities in Mesoamerica and encoded ancient shamanic beliefs.

symbolism which Jung found marks the natural goal of the inward journey, the unity of consciousness integrating the archetypes of the unconscious and revealing a higher dimension symbolized, of course, by the towering Pyramid of the Sun, the central cosmic mountain, immediately above. And this symbolism is reinforced by another. Within the cave was constructed a channel which was used in ritual to carry life-giving waters from the cave's interior, suggesting the revivifying freeing of the waters which, on a psychological level, represents the aim and end of introversion in so many traditional symbolisms. Yet perhaps the fact that this descent into the depths would become an ascent to a higher dimension was implicit from the journey's beginning, for the engorging serpent is a Feathered Serpent, uniting the opposites, chthonic and celestial – just as the mouth of the cave which begins the inward journey lies at the base of the very stairway which leads to the pyramid top. The inward journey ultimately integrated the depths with the heights and freed the waters sustaining both cosmic and psychic creation.

The cave has another familiar attribute which supports and amplifies its ritual function as a return to the creative source. It is here that the cosmos and time itself were believed to have first emerged into existence. As we have seen so many times, the cave journey marks a return to origin. Michael Coe relates the cave to stone carvings which celebrate a myth of "the creation of the universe from a watery void through a series of dual oppositions."[3] The Teotihuacános saw the cave as the place of origin and the birthplace of the first human ancestors. This is a familiar symbolism reminding us of the Navaho Place of Emergence and the first human pair, male and female, who came forth from this central aperture, a scenario found recurrently in creation myths. All these elements make the Pyramid of the Sun and its underlying cave a complex and effective symbol of sacred creation and illumination.

We had earlier in this work pledged a concluding chapter showing how portions of Jung's own life repeated the formative aspects of the shaman's experience, and the attentive reader is, perhaps, wondering what a description of the structure of the Pyramid of the Sun, with its underlying cave of creation associated with the first ancestors, has to do with the promised work at hand. In fact, however, I believe it will serve as a useful device to help sum up in a single comprehensive image much of the material in the previous chapters and bring it forward where it can serve as an example for certain points to be made here. But, of more immediate relevance to our endeavor in this chapter, it bears a striking archetypal resemblance to a dream which occurred at a critical point in Jung's life. As we know, early in his career Jung was impressed with the pioneering work of Sigmund Freud and particularly with the

---

In a manner which will become significant later in this chapter, they point out that the Aztec island city of Tenochtitlán had a similar structure which was repeated in each of the quarters described by the cruciform configuration. "The last to follow this model was Tenochtitlán where four avenues led from the gates of the ceremonial precinct in the center of the island city to the cardinal directions, thus marking out the quadrants. Each quadrant had its own ceremonial and political center." (*Masks of the Spirit*, p. 124.)

importance Freud accorded to the dream. Yet, as the relationship between the two men progressed, differences, which Jung originally attempted to repress or minimize, began to emerge. While Freud was not oblivious to the archaic material contained in dreams, his focus was on their revelation of repressed factors housed in the personal unconscious. Jung, on the other hand, as we know, began to perceive that dreams often were the expression of a supra-personal, collective deep level of the mind consisting of inherited predispositions to form certain images with the psyche. It was at this juncture in the relationship between the two men that a particular dream helped crystalize and bring to a head the differences between them and to point Jung more definitively in the direction he was fated to follow.

The incident occurred while he and Freud were on an ocean liner, crossing the Atlantic bound for New York. To pass time, each undertook to analyze the other's dreams, and a particular dream of Jung's arrested the attention of both men. In this dream, Jung found himself in the upper story of a well-furnished house, a kind of salon with an appealing decor. It was a house he did not really know, yet it was strangely familiar; it was *"his* house." Looking around he realized that he was not aware of what the lower levels of the structure looked like. As he descended he found rooms of increasing antiquity going back to Roman times and then, finally, a stairway of narrow stone steps leading down into the depths. He descended and entered what he describes as a low cave cut into the rock. The cave floor was covered in dust and inside were scattered bones and broken pottery – much like the remains of a primitive culture, Jung noted. Here he discovered two human skulls which were obviously very old and half disintegrated. Then he awoke.[4]

Freud focused on the personal aspects of the dream, asking repeatedly to whom the skulls belonged. This angered Jung. He felt that Freud was implying the existence of a latent wish for the death of people close to Jung. Yet he came to regard the dream as being very significant. As we know, for Jung dreams often express the same archetypal material found in the world's mythic structures, and this material can be the key to unlocking the meaning of the dream. At the same time, the dream is often autosymbolic, picturing the very process undergone by the psyche in bodying forth the contents of its hidden creative foundations. Jung came to see in this dream an archetypal image of the structure of the psyche itself and the deep source of its experience especially in dream and vision. The structure of human dream and visionary experience rests upon an ancient creative substratum of transpersonal inherited images which he believed this dream traced back through the ages to its archaic source symbolized in the cave with its primitive remains and the two skulls.

The dream describes its own archetypal genesis, and the archetype unlocks the dream. As we have seen, the cave of the primordial ancestors where human and cosmic creation began is an ancient archetype for the source of all human creation. Just as human creation, i.e., the multilayered Pyramid of the Sun, rests upon the supra-personal creative source, the cave of creation with its ancestral heritage in ancient

Teotihuacán, so does the multilayered house, the structure of human consciousness and cultural development through the ages, rest upon what Jung came to recognize as the archetypal unconscious which he began to understand the cave of the primal ancestors to symbolize. Again, for both archaic and modern man, as Jung later would formulate this dawning intuition, "his beginnings are not by any means mere pasts; they live with him as the constant substratum of his existence and his conscious is as much molded by them as by the physical world around him." It was this dream, Jung recognized, that first initiated him into the realization that there were archaic contents of an impersonal collective nature underlying and helping form the psyche's experience.[5] This type of revelation is, of course, a process with which we are quite familiar from the world's shamanic traditions. Here we might again recall Eliade's comments as to the spontaneous initiatory capacity of the dream for the shaman, or the manner in which dreams and visions initiated Sereptie Djaruoskin and other shamans throughout the world to the transpersonal basis of their experiences. Moreover, we might also note that the structures of consciousness described in Jung's dream and those implicit in the Pyramid of the Sun share an archetypal configuration which we have also found recurrently present in the initiatory cave, hole, Place of Emergence or equivalent symbol and their recurrent association with the ancestors and the source of creation in the shaman's universe.

But the inward journeys described in these visionary experiences and rituals, which we have used the Pyramid of the Sun to recap and structurally summarize in this chapter, have another aspect that, in fact, is very pertinent to Jung's development at this time. Indeed, it almost seems as if such archetypal structures were silently guiding his life and he was fated to follow these paradigms. At this time, a major point of difference between Jung and Freud became the meaning of regression and its relationship to incest. For Freud, regression pointed to genuine though often masked incestuous drives. For a long time, Jung trod very gingerly around this topic and was quite ambiguous and even equivocal in certain works written around this period. Yet, as we know, he began to see a positive aspect to regression and to regard images implying incest to be merely one part of the psyche's repertoire of symbols as it introverted even more deeply back to the experience of its origins, as it "streamed back to the navel from which it originated" – the same center and source we saw symbolized at the end of the cave beneath the Pyramid of the Sun. Jung began to realize that on a deeper level images interpreted as indicative of incest reflect a drive to return to the originary source and to be born anew. Again, this is an archetypal pattern which we have seen throughout the shaman's world expressed in kindred symbols. We need only mention the most obvious – the Tukano's re-entry into the mythic womb to be reborn of the Sun Father, the Huichol pilgrim's penetration of the land called Vagina and the Springs of Our Mothers and the illumination to be found there, the Sioux initiate's return to the mother's womb to be reborn from the holy breath of the universe and, of course, in a manner which reminds us of so many shamanic initiations, the Teotihuacános' penetration of the cave womb to symbolically ascend to the Sun Temple. In each the preconscious reveals the deeper meaning of regression in the same symbols, and this meaning assumes the form of a pattern of experience which, as we shall see, is much akin to that to be undergone personally by Jung.

Increasingly, Jung began to bristle under what he regarded as Freud's narrow views and his dogmatic insistence on the exclusive validity of his own sexual theories of neurosis. For Jung, Eros began to have a larger meaning correctly recognized in myth as the source of the creative power which moves man and the cosmos. He became progressively aware that this force within the unconscious casts forth visions in dream and fantasy which often contained premonitions of the future and had their own purposes. As we know, such images expressed a compensatory drive on the part of the unconscious to secure an overall psychic integration which the need to cope with and conform to the everyday world and its obligations often threatened to deny. As the pattern of his own experience over a lifetime began to emerge, Jung could perceive a configuration of inner experience which was itself archetypal and initiatory. He began to understand that an immanent purpose seemed to guide his life. As we shall endeavor to show, this pattern bears a remarkable resemblance to the same initiatory pattern, often spontaneously expressed, which we found in shamanism. It implies a break with the universe of daily life and a dissolution of the profane self, a descent into chaos and a rebirth on a consecrated level. Moreover, its initial stages, in both Jung's life as he began to understand it and in the initiatory experience of the shaman as it has existed throughout the world and over long centuries, are very much the same. We can recognize the call from the daemonic realm and a corresponding break with the everyday world followed by a period of withdrawal and liminality preliminary to a descent into the chaos of unconscious – all expressed in the same grammar of symbols and mediated by the same techniques that we have seen throughout our study.

Jung began to realize that the larger creative role to be assumed by Eros had been revealed to him by his unconscious at an early age. It was revealed in a dream, the earliest dream Jung was able to remember, and was characterized by a group of symbols to which we are now well-initiated. In this dream, Jung was near a castle in a meadow which was part of the local vicarage. Suddenly he discovered a dark hole in the ground lined with stone. He descended into the hole and found a subterranean chamber containing a wonderfully rich golden throne or altar on which was standing what at first appeared to be a tree trunk twelve to fifteen feet (3.7–4.5 m) in height. It was huge, nearly reaching the ceiling. However, he found that, in fact, it was made of skin and naked flesh and topped with a rounded head with one eye. It was what he would later determine to be a ritual phallus. At that moment, he heard his mother's voice crying out, "That is the man-eater!"[6]

The structure of the dream seems familiar. The castle and vicarage, the world of human creation, again rest upon a creative substratum imaged in this cave and its contents, just as the Pyramid of the Sun rests upon the cave of the creation. Symbols of descent into a hole or cave in association with the tree, and particularly the tree or other symbol of ascent *within* the cave, are familiar to us and express the psyche's innate knowledge of the need for introversion and its potentially progressive result. Reflective of this intuitive realization, in this dream experience introversion leads to a sanctum sanctorum, a sacred space consisting of a throne or altar. And just as the cave of the Pyramid of the Sun led to its holy of holies and to a symbolic ascent, so here the inner chamber of sacred space houses another familiar symbol of ascent, the tree within the cave. The tree, as it does almost universally in shamanism, becomes symbolically assimilated to the creative source itself. In this dream, this aspect is emphasized by its association with a giant ritual phallus within the womb of the cave expressing the very same creative union of opposites we saw over fifteen thousand years ago in the Shaft at Lascaux where the shaman lies erect within the cave interior. Jung claimed to have had this dream at age three or four. According to McLynn, clinical evidence points to five or six as the more likely time.[7] Regardless of his precise age, however, it is clear that at a very early period of Jung's life, his psyche bodied forth, in the very same grammar of symbols which so often characterized the shaman's initiatory experiences, a premonitory vision of the archetypal creative substratum of human experience which was to call Jung and act as his daemon throughout his life.

The dream was both fascinating and threatening, and it was perhaps the protective tendency of a mind bred upon Christian orthodoxy that caused the young boy to believe that his mother had awakened him from the creative depths with the warning, "That is the man-eater!" Indeed, as Jung grew older he felt himself stifled by the traditional beliefs of his society and especially his Pastor father. The immediacy of religious experience, if it ever existed, had long since died for his father, who clung doggedly to a faith based upon what Jung perceived to be the empty forms of a conventional religion, not inspired but determined to believe. Debating matters of religion with Jung, his father would frequently say, "Oh nonsense, you always want to think. One ought not to think, but believe."[8]

This relationship with his father, in part, explains why Jung was particularly disturbed by what he perceived to be an effort by Freud to hinder his own creative thought processes. He sensed that the stoppage of those innate insights with which the unconscious, in conjunction with myth, dream and vision, provides us was symptomatic of the desiccated forms of belief which characterized the tragedy of his own father's life. Jung intuited the great danger of thought which had become rigid and of the empty shells of orthodoxy as impediments to insight. He struggled against these forces both consciously and unconsciously throughout his youth. Once again, while he was still a child, the unconscious brought this conflict forward in the form of a visionary experience, a waking vision such as we have found Jung inducing in his patients in the process of "trancing" or, as more traditionally known, active imagination. Jung had long felt the pressure of a repressed vision seeking expression. Finally, he gave in to it.

I gathered all my courage, as though I were about to leap forthwith into hell-fire, and let the thought come. I saw before me the cathedral, the blue sky. God sits on His golden throne, high above the world – and from under the throne an enormous turd falls upon the sparkling new roof, shatters it and breaks the walls of the cathedral asunder.[9]

In this distasteful vision, God Himself rejects the conventional forms of human worship offered him by Jung's contemporaries in the most radical and denigrating way. The walls of orthodoxy are battered from above and collapse. For a pastor's son in the Swiss society of Jung's time, we can hardly imagine a more radical vision of "the break with the universe of daily life," the norms and forms which guide psychic energy in the direction of traditional values and conventional concerns.

The polar worlds imaged in these two dreams – the world of the creative depths expressing itself in archetypal images and the everyday world of conventional value and obligation with which we all must contend – Jung recognized very early as conflicting forces in his personality. He wrestled with these two aspects of his identity throughout his youth and even gave them names. That aspect which faced the empirical world he recognized as his No. 1 personality. The aspect which seemed capable of mysteriously expressing a different reality in universal forms he termed No. 2.[10] No. 1 coped with the immediacy of daily problems. On the other hand, No. 2 seemed to be rooted in the ages, and he experienced it as being directly related to the modes of expression which he found in art, his deep readings in philosophy and, most of all, the wealth of symbolic images which represented the realm of the spirit that Jung found embodied in the world's mythologies. While No. 1 expressed the earthly man in time and space, the symbolic capacities of No. 2 not only expressed the often repressed creative contents suggested in Jung's early hole and tree-phallus dream but seemed, in forms he sensed to be enduring and universal, to express a more permanent reality, the eternal in man. Because it was the source of symbolic expression, it offered itself to him in symbols. One was the familiar rhizome image as expressive of this deeply rooted level of the psyche with its visionary capacity, a creative force with which the conscious mind must come to grips. As we recall, in reference to the creativity of this enduring substratum of the psyche, Jung felt that the only truly significant events in his life worth relating were those when this imperishable world burst into our transitory one. That was why, he concluded, he spoke in his autobiography mainly of inner experiences – especially his dreams and visions. In *Symbols of Transformation*, Jung quotes Hölderlin in an effort to capture the creative capacity of such fiery eruptions from the creative depths:

So long as the pit bears iron
And Etna fiery resin,
So have I riches

To fashion an image and see
The Spirit as ever it was.[11]

The mystery of such eruptions was precisely that they were somehow able to fashion an image of "the Spirit as ever it was."

Lava, however, is molten rock, and beneath these fiery expressions of the No. 2 personality he sensed that at a deeper level, beyond time and space, undisturbed rested in silence the adamantine reality of the Godhead. In fact, since early childhood Jung spontaneously associated the deep levels of the No. 2 personality, this changeless aspect of the human soul, with rock. In his very early youth, when pressed by the troubles inherent in the world of personality No. 1, he would visit a favorite spot near his family's garden and sit on a particular stone which, he felt, bore some secret relationship to him. So complete was his sense of identification with the durative reality represented in stone, he would ask himself, "Am I the one who is sitting on the stone, or am I the stone on which *he* [Jung personally] is sitting?"[12] This spontaneous association of this personality level with rock is interesting because it seems to express the same subconscious awareness of an adamantine reality beyond time and change that we found expressed recurrently in the symbolism of crystal, bone and blood in the shaman's visionary universe and, of course, the *lapis*, or philosopher's stone, in alchemy. Each seems to suggest a durative reality to be experienced through introversion. Thus, early in his life the unconscious again cast forward symbolic glimpses of the enduring reality to which, as we shall see, the pattern of his life would initiate him, just as it presaged the purposiveness latent in shamanic initiation in so many societies in kindred symbols.

As Jung's career neared the time of his eventual break with Freud, the tension between the two aspects of his personality steadily increased. When he chose medicine and finally psychiatry as his profession, he warned himself that he must put aside the concerns of personality No. 2 and make his way in the world. But the fiery eruptions from Etna would not be long repressed and, as McLynn notes, Jung began to wonder whether "part of his psychic problems might arise from the over-development of the No. 1 personality, stressing science and empiricism, and the downplaying of No. 2, representing art, religion and mystery."[13] The repressed portion of his psyche began to become articulate in what Jung experienced as inner voices. Like the called shaman, he found himself increasingly within the grip of the daemonic. Later in life, as we have previously noted, he was able to look back upon this experience with insight and a degree of dispassion and analyze his previous difficulties. "I have had much trouble getting along with my ideas," he recalled. "There was a daimon in me, and in the end its presence proved decisive. It overpowered me, and if I was at times ruthless it was because I was in the grip of the daimon." "Anyone who is conscious of his guiding principle knows with what indisputable authority it rules his life. He *must* obey his own law, as if it were a daimon whispering to him of new and wonderful paths. Anyone with a vocation hears the voice of the inner man, he is called." And, as we shall see as we follow Jung's development, precisely like that of the called shaman, this inner voice is only to be refused at the price of grave illness or loss of mind. "I had to obey an inner law which was imposed on me," he asserts, "and left me no freedom of choice."[14]

"Everything psychic is pregnant with the future,"[15] Jung noted later in life, and at this point in his development, his own psyche was summoning him to his destiny, an archetypal pattern which was to configure his life. At this time, Jung dimly sensed this and let the process evolve.

> I did not know that I was living a myth, and even if I had known it, I would not have known what sort of myth was ordering my life without my knowledge. So, in the most natural way, I took it upon myself to get to know "my" myth, and I regarded this as the task of tasks, ... I simply had to know what unconscious or preconscious myth was forming me, from what rhizome I sprang.[16]

In the same manner which he recognized had been the case with Goethe, "what was alive and active within him was a living substance, a supra-personal process, the great dream of the *mundus archetypus* [the archetypal world]."[17] Just as we saw in the making of a shaman, a common formative force was working from behind or within compelling his insights and development in a certain direction.

These, however, are the perceptions of hindsight, of the initiate who has made the perilous journey, trod the razor's edge and can now look back. For Jung, at this stage of his development, the call of the daemonic world would threaten the foundations of consciousness and lead him, as it often led the shaman, to the very brink of what some observers feel was an incipient form of madness. Some have seen Jung's struggle in terms of schizophrenia and the repression of the spiritual calling characteristic of personality No. 2 by personality No. 1 with its natural allegiance to a society and profession not yet prepared for the unique revelations emerging from Jung's unconscious. As we know from our study, for some personalities the more dominant and independent ego-consciousness and its interests become, the more is the unconscious forced into the background. This process can result in a loss of instinct and an alienation of conscious structures of thought from the unconscious and its compensatory images. The situation is all the more likely to result in a splitting of the personality when the unconscious harbors creative materials difficult for the conscious mind to assimilate. As we recall, though such contents are highly charged with a psychic energy value otherwise sufficient to carry them into consciousness, "because the content is new and therefore strange to consciousness, there are no existing associations and connecting bridges to the conscious contents." This was certainly the case with Jung at this period of his life, and neither his individual psyche, his profession, nor his society, as yet, offered such connecting bridges. In fact, those visionary and mythic structures which traditionally mediated these contents with consciousness were in the process of being demolished in the modern West, threatening to put a cap on the fiery Etna of Jung's unconscious with necessarily explosive results.

Crisis

Jung now found himself faced with a welter of material flooding from the unconscious in vision and dream but, failing to connect with this matter, he felt no relief. As the call of the daemonic became more and more imperative, Jung's situation began to share other important symptoms with that of the called shaman. As we remember from Chapter 6, the intensity of the shaman's call often results in his separation from the rest of the community. He becomes introverted, seeks solitude and has prophetic dreams and visions. Either spontaneously or through ritual and training, he experiences that period of liminality which fosters the break with the universe of daily life and eventually the deconstruction of the empirical self and its world. In the shaman's experience we found this process reflected in images of fragmentation, suffering, sacrifice and death, marking the initial stages of transformation. As Borgoras informed us of the newly called shaman characterized by these symptoms, "Half consciously and half against his own will, his whole soul undergoes a strange and painful transformation. This period may last for months and sometimes years." Jung "half consciously and half against his own will" was about to undergo a similar and equally painful transformation, and it would likewise last over a period of years.

Jung began to experience first hand the liminality and emptiness he expressed in the observation that "our myth has become mute, and gives no answers." He continued to question his predicament, sometimes in a dialogue with his inner self:

> But in what myth does man live nowadays? In the Christian myth, the answer might be. "Do you live in it?" I asked myself. To be honest, the answer was no. "For me, it is not what I live by." "Then do we no longer have any myth?" "No, evidently we no longer have any myth."[18]

Conventional values having lost their hold on Jung, as clearly presaged in the cathedral vision, they were swept aside. Jung underwent a self-imposed period of liminality and, like the shamanic candidate, began to withdraw his libido from the world around him. He seldom communicated with his few remaining friends and became even more remote than before from his family. He gave up his teaching and his position at the Burghölzi asylum. He felt unable to communicate his insights to the world around him and ceased to write for several years. For over four years he lived in a state of solitude, constant tension and near-breakdown. And, like the called shaman, his immersion in the inner world resulted in a terrible isolation:

The consequence of my resolve, and my involvement with things which neither I nor anyone else could understand, was an extreme loneliness. ... I felt the gulf between the external world and the interior world of images in its most painful form. I could not yet see that interaction of both worlds which I now understand. I saw only an irreconcilable contradiction between "inner" and "outer".[19]

Just as under the influence of No. I personality his consciousness has strayed rather too far from the fact of the unconscious, now No. 2 was pulling him into the vortex of an inner world in a way that seemed to deaden and shatter the outer world around him. His dreams became increasingly vivid and terrifying. A bloody tide rolled forward in visions of death, corpses and cosmic cataclysms, all reflecting his alienation from the outer world and his own self-fragmentation, this "irreconcilable contradiction between 'inner and 'outer'" which the shaman experiences, as Jung would later, in similar visions of fragmentation, death and destruction. In one such dream, Jung experienced himself in the land of the dead, a world of tombs and of mummified corpses which strangely came alive as he pressed farther and farther into the past.[20] He would, as we know, find that such dreams were indicative of the loss of the connective faculty of the soul and of a soul flight in which it returns to the land of the ancestors where the ancestral traces of the unconscious are again activated – a precise autosymbolism for Jung's own painful process of transformation, as it was for the shaman over the ages.

Another numinous series of dreams marked this period of Jung's experience. Like the dreams described above, they were terrifying. However, at least as understood later, they were prophetic and bore some promise that following the psyche's strange symbolic wanderings might bear fruit – that introversion and progression were perhaps silent partners and within the depths lay the fund of symbols which would bridge dissociation. To best understand the first dreams we might recall the role of the cave or tunnel in inducing and reflecting the shaman's trance state. We found this symbolism worldwide and extending back to the Upper Paleolithic period. In fact, as we recall, modern researchers, as well as contemporaries such as Michael Harner who are able to reproduce aspects of the shaman's trance experience, indicate that it is frequently spontaneously associated with the image of the cave or tunnel. The cave and tunnel are, of course, familiar symbols of introversion, the first stages of which involve a radical break with the outer world constructed by the empirical self – the surface which must be cleared so that things can grow from the depths.

Jung, we recall, had a series of such dreams indicating his withdrawal from the outer world which, consequently, becomes deadened or destroyed. He had just such a dream while traveling by train between Zurich and Schaffhausen in October, 1913. It occurred precisely as the train entered a tunnel. Significantly, Jung himself went into a trance. He lost all consciousness of time and place, and regained consciousness only when, an hour later, the train arrived at its destination. In his vision, all Europe, except Switzerland, was submerged in a monstrous flood. "I realized the sea was of blood," he tells us. "Floating on the waves were corpses, rooftops, charred beams."[21] Incredibly, at the end of December of the same year, passing through the very same tunnel on the same train, he again went into a trance and saw the same vision of cataclysmic destruction sweeping away the debris of civilization.[22]

Shortly after this, in the spring and early summer of 1914, he had a kindred dream which he experienced three separate times. In this vision, in mid-summer an Arctic cold descended upon the land freezing it to ice and causing humanity to desert this afflicted part of the earth. The frost killed all living green things. However, when he was visited by the dream a third time a new content seemed to break through. Amidst the devastation "there stood a leaf-bearing tree, but without fruit (my tree of life, I thought), whose leaves had been transformed by the effects of the frost into sweet grapes full of healing juices. I plucked the grapes and gave them to a large, waiting crowd," he tells us.[23] Finally, once the surface has been cleared through introversion, the psyche casts forth a hint that something can indeed grow from the depths. Clearly, the sweet and healing grapes are the product of the tree of life transformed by the initially devastating effects of the deadening of the outer world, i.e., the withdrawal of libido during introversion. The grapes carry an association with Dionysus, the pagan god of the vine who Jung believed portrayed a mythic reality needed to compensate the modern monotheism of the conscious. For Dionysus is a god torn to pieces, i.e., fragmented, by forces from the underworld. Yet he descends into the underworld to become its master, for "Hades is the same as Dionysus," as Heraclitus points out.[24] And finally he is reborn from the underworld to bring the salvation associated with the new wine.

If we regard these dreams as related and view their subject matter together, we can discern a familiar pattern – withdrawal of libido and the sacrifice of the outer world, the tunnel, actual trance and vivid dreams and vision – all hallmarks of introversion. Yet these eventually lead to a turning of consciousness expressed in the familiar symbol of ascent, the tree of life, akin to the World Tree which must penetrate into the depths to reach into the heavens. Again, the psyche displays an ability to sense and portray in images an immanent purpose, a supra-personal process, lying behind and informing the entire experience. The dream does, in fact, foretell in broad outline the ruling archetypal pattern which was governing Jung's life at this time, but within the chaos of his experience this was only a brief glimpse of the light at the end of the winding tunnel which was first to lead to his descent into the unconscious. And as he tells us, "Only by extreme effort was I finally able to escape from the labyrinth."[25]

At this time, such dreams would only convince him that he "was menaced by a psychosis." Many commentators have agreed. McLynn asserts "All experts are agreed that Jung's skirmish with insanity was a 'near miss' but disagree on the diagnostic model that would explain his plight."[26] D. W. Winnicott sees Jung's situation as reaching back into childhood and the fragmentation of personality expressed in the two aspects of his personality. "Jung, in describing himself, gives us a picture of childhood schizophrenia, and at the same time his personality displays a strength of a kind which enabled him to heal himself. At cost he recovered, and part of the cost to him is what he paid out to us, if we can listen and hear, in terms of his exceptional insight," he informs us.[27] Likewise, Anthony Storr states, "I think his psychosis or near psychosis was of ... the nature of a schizophrenic episode."[28] However, and very importantly, like Winnicott he observes that Jung was uniquely equipped to heal himself even in these difficulties.

Here the paths of Jung's development and of the initiation of many shamans again converge. Like Huottaire, the Siberian shaman, Jung must encounter the "Lord of Madness and the Lords of all nervous disorders" before he will find that center of sanity which will grant him stability and provide illumination and power. As we recall, the shaman likewise often suffers an initiatory illness which floods the conscious mind with a welter of symbolic material that threatens fragmentation and disorientation. Yet, as we noted in Chapter 6, an exact diagnosis of the shaman's problem in contemporary Western terms is elusive precisely because, often aided by the traditional and ecstatic training techniques of his society, he has the ability to abort crisis and turn it to cure. As was the case with the Tamang shaman's initiation, by becoming immersed in the powers of possession he eventually gains the power to possess them. And this is because the shaman's society has traversed this path before – it recognizes a familiar pattern of experience and how to guide it. In Eliade's terms, through repeated experience it has come to understand the theory of mental illness, and the shaman is one who can cure others precisely because he has cured himself. It is for this reason that the shaman has frequently been referred as a "cured curer" or a "wounded healer."

As McLynn noted, the nature of Jung's ailment at this time is also difficult to diagnose with precision and, I submit, for the very same reason we can no longer fathom the shaman's illness. Jung had the innate ability to sense an underlying purposiveness or psychodynamic pattern guiding his experience. He began to understand that the unconscious is a process. He was able both to follow the grain of the experience and simultaneously to train it in a direction which was ultimately beneficial. In the depths of his trials, his dark night of the soul, Jung gained a sense of direction.

> An incessant stream of fantasies had been released, and I did my best not to lose my head but to find some way to understand these strange things. ... When I endured these assaults of the unconscious I had an unswerving conviction that I was obeying a higher will, and that feeling continued to uphold me until I had mastered the task.[29]

What guided him was a higher will, a supra-personal process. He was, in fact, living a myth that was ordering his life and leading him with iron grip in the direction which he as a healer had to follow. And although he attempted to regard his confrontation with the unconscious as an experiment he was conducting, later he realized, "Today I might equally well say that it was an experiment which was being conducted on *me*."[30]

"If you find the spirit of madness you will begin to shamanize, initiating (new) shamans," the Siberian shaman, Sereptie Djaruoskin, learned as he plunged into the unconscious. Jung's experience convinced him of a similar reality. He realized he could neither cure nor teach until he sounded and understood the unconscious depths which called him. He came to believe fervently with regard to his own troubled patients that he could not aid them unless he knew their fantasy material from his own direct experience. To grasp these fantasies, he tells us, "I had to let myself plummet down into them." At the same time, much akin to the Tamang shaman's experience of crazy possession, he realized that it was vitally necessary to gain power over these powers of possession or they might forever possess him.

> For I was afraid of losing command of myself and becoming a prey to the fantasies – and as a psychiatrist I realized only too well what that meant. After prolonged hesitation, however, I saw that there was no other way out. I had to take the chance, had to try to gain power over them; for I realized that if I did not do so, I ran the risk of their gaining power over me.[31]

It was thus that on a particular date, December 12, 1913, as he precisely recalled, he resolved to take the decisive step. Sitting alone and afraid at his desk, once again contemplating the debilitating psychic problems which had plagued him for so long, he tells us, "I let myself drop." It was as if the ground opened beneath his feet and he plummeted, accompanied by a sick feeling of panic, into darkness. As his eyes grew accustomed to the deep twilight gloom surrounding him, he was able to make out the entrance to a dark cave, in which stood a dwarf with a leathery skin, as if he were "mummified," Jung relates. The visionary experience continues:

> I squeezed past him [the dwarf] through the narrow entrance and waded knee deep through icy water to the other end of the cave where, on a projecting rock, I saw a glowing red crystal. I grasped the stone, lifted it and discovered a hollow underneath. At first I could make out nothing, but then I saw that there was running water. In it a corpse floated by, a youth with blond hair and a wound in the head. He was followed by a gigantic black scarab and then by a red, newborn sun, rising up out of the depths of the water.[32]

He relates that he was dazzled by the light and wanted to replace the stone over the opening. However, he was prevented by a fluid which welled out of the opening. This was blood. The blood continued to spurt for an unendurably long time. He reported that he felt nauseated until, at last, it stopped and the vision came to an end.

The vision had great significance for Jung, though its precise meaning at first eluded him, and commentators since then have struggled with it. McLynn sees the mummified dwarf as Freud.[33] He bases this opinion on the fact that Freud was short, at least compared to Jung, and in Jung's mind his mummified doctrines blocked the way to deeper insight. There may be some truth in this approach. However, it would seem more fruitful to unlock the dream with archetypal material rather than to use personal references, an approach which seems to repeat the same mistake Freud made with regard to Jung's dream that he analyzed on the ocean liner. Fortunately, our study of shamanic archetypes provides us with many keys to this important vision. We have met many odd creatures leading to the shaman's initiation in our study, and we might here recall the strange man clad in a parka of molting reindeer hide who would lead Sereptie Djaruoskin's initiatory descent. He, too, was associated with a cavity or hole in the ground, the descent into which was eventually to lead to Sereptie's initiation in his ecstatic dream experience. Dwarfs are, of course, creatures who live in the earth and labor deep in its bowels hand in hand with the earth's own creative processes. Like a number of other mythic and fairytale creatures worldwide, they represent the power and wisdom of nature and the deeper levels of the human psyche. Jung recognized as much in "The Phenomenology of the Spirit in Fairytales," where he lists dwarfs among other grotesque gnomelike figures who potentially represent the deep and innate wisdom of the spirit.[34] In a familiar symbolism they can be positive or negative in the impression they make depending on the attitude of the conscious mind and, if positive, can assume the role of guide or guru.[35] Quite apropos of Jung's own foundering spiritual condition, such a creature "always appears in a situation where insight, understanding, good advice, determining, planning, etc., are needed but cannot be mastered on one's own resources. The archetype compensates this state of spiritual deficiency by contents designed to fill the gap."[36] Such creatures mark the path to transformation and illumination if the conscious mind can follow the perilous path to consummation.

The mummified dwarf who greets Jung at the cave entrance, like the man from the eternal roots who greets Sereptie, is a guide to the wisdom of the deep levels of the psyche and a herald of the perilous journey into the unconscious depths. This explains another aspect of his appearance. In Jung's previous dream, when he followed his soul to the land of the dead, the collective unconscious, the dead were also "mummified." However, as he penetrated more deeply into this realm they began to reawaken. The dwarf image thus implies a symbolism suggesting the return to the world of the ancestors, the mummified dead, and the same deeper levels of consciousness and the spirit which Jung recognized in "The Phenomenology of the Spirit in Fairytales" were symbolized in creatures such as dwarfs as markers on the eternal path to transformation. As he informs us in that essay, "In myths and fairytales, as in dreams, the psyche tells its own story, and the interplay of the archetypes is revealed in its natural setting as 'formation, transformation / the eternal Mind's eternal recreation.'"[37] And "formation, transformation / the eternal Mind's eternal recreation" will be what we see this vision eventually progressing toward, for here eternal Mind and the supra-personal process of psychic transformation are at work in familiar archetypes.

We recall from Chapter 9 that Sereptie, led by his guiding spirit along the path of transformation, first had to penetrate the hole-too-thin, the narrow aperture into the underground, then became immersed in the waters of the unconscious, and after severe ordeals reached the source of illumination and power. The old !Kung shaman, K"xau, followed a similar ecstatic path through the narrow aperture and the underground waters to God's house. The Maya shaman questing for illumination enters the symbolic cave and penetrates the Symplegades in the form of the jaws of the serpent, all of which takes place over the primordial waters, and the initiates to the mysteries of the Pyramid of the Sun likewise entered a cave, negotiated a series of narrow apertures and traversed a path again associated with the waters of creation. Caves of introversion and initiation, the Symplegades or narrow aperture and immersion in water have been recurrent benchmarks by which "the psyche tells its own story" as it streams back to the fountainhead, its unconscious source that transcends time and change.

And this is very much the manner in which Jung's psyche expresses a similar experience. The shamanic pattern is precisely described in Jung's dream. The mummified dwarf at the cave entrance is a guide to the world of the spirit and portends the potential deepening of consciousness capable of leading through the collective unconscious to the transpersonal realm if only the conscious mind can assimilate the experience. Jung, as he reports his vision, enters the cave of initiation, squeezes through "the narrow entrance" and must wade through the "icy waters" of the unconscious. Yet within the *prima materia* of the unconscious lies the *lapis*, the stone, the durative reality beyond time and change traditionally revealed through such experiences of deep introversion. In this case it takes the form of the red crystal, crystal being a now familiar symbol from our study of shamanism for the adamantine reality which, as we discussed, Jung spontaneously associated with stone since an early age. And hidden beneath this crystal he encounters an arresting group of familiar symbols for the experience of a return to the source and rebirth.

Beneath the crystal lies running water symbolic of the freeing of the libido and the access to psychic power. The dazzling "newborn sun, rising out of the depths of the water" promises a turning of consciousness and illumination as this symbol of ascent rises out of the depths of the unconscious. The scarab is an ancient symbol of rebirth, both individual and cosmic, for it is the scarab which in Egyptian mythology symbolizes the cosmic force that pushes the newborn sun across the sky each day. On a humbler level, the scarab is, however, the dung beetle which incubates its eggs in the ball of waste it pushes before it. As such, it carries a significance Jung often attached to the initiatory experience itself, for the principle of rebirth is often only to be discovered in the lowest abodes — in an image frequently found among the alchemists, the *lapis* lies mired and ignored in the filth of existence. Each of these symbols promises the turning of consciousness which rewards the successful initiate; the power and illumination of the successful descent. They mark the goal of the archetypal pattern that we used the example of the cave at Teotihuacán to exemplify. There, the initiate at the ancient Pyramid of the Sun likewise braved the cave, slipped through the narrow aperture and encountered the waters of creation eventually to experience the freeing of these waters and the enlightenment of the inner sanctuary.

Jung saw the dream as a drama of death and rebirth but remained dismayed at its outcome. The promised end seemed to be denied. Instead of renewal the running waters carried a youthful corpse with blond hair, and the experience ended in the same awful tide of blood that plagued his earlier dreams. Jung remained both puzzled and disturbed but gave up any further attempt to understand the dream.[38] However, though Jung did not know it at this time, the larger pattern of this dream, with its denial of illumination, does in fact follow an archetypal configuration, and understanding this pattern again helps fathom the dream's deeper meaning and why fulfillment was denied. The dream repeats a pattern of experience known as *initiation manqué*, the failed initiation. Joseph Henderson and Maude Oakes offer several examples of *initiation manqué* and note that, though the candidate undergoes the traditional stages of the path to enlightenment, success is denied due to a fatal flaw on the part of the initiate. Most often, they note, this flaw is to be found in an inability to transcend the bounds of ego-consciousness on the part of the novitiate.[39] The will characteristic of the ego cannot surrender to the wisdom of the depths and realization is denied. This failure of initiation, of course, is just what occurred in Jung's dream and, as we shall see, it occurred for similar reasons.

Ultimately, Jung's unconscious would not be denied its compensatory truths and ego-consciousness would no longer be allowed to stand in its way. Six days later he was presented with another dream experience. It is before dawn, and he finds himself in a lonely, rocky mountain landscape accompanied by an unknown brown-skinned man, a savage. He hears the horn of Siegfried, the hero of the Nibelung legend, sounding over the mountains. At this point he comes to the sudden realization that he must kill Siegfried. He and the savage proceed to shoot Siegfried and he plunges down, struck dead. During the dream experience Jung remembered that he felt disgust and remorse for having destroyed something so great and beautiful as the hero, Siegfried. He fled in fear that the murder might be discovered but a great rainfall commenced and he soon felt convinced it would obliterate all traces of the death.[40]

Upon awakening Jung felt the most urgent need to understand this dream. In fact, Jung had a loaded revolver in the drawer of his night table, and urgency turned to terror when an inner voice warned that if he could not fathom the dream's significance he would have no choice but to shoot himself. Under the pressure of necessity, the meaning suddenly dawned upon him. The hero, Siegfried, was, in fact, representative of his own ego-consciousness and its attendant possessive will. He realized that he must abandon these attitudes "for there are higher things than the ego's will, and to these one must bow."[41] The previous dream had hinted at this need in the form of the blond-haired corpse carried away by the waters of rejuvenation, and Jung realized that the cleansing rain of the later dream indicated that transcending the bounds of the ego's dominance was helping to resolve the tension existing between the conscious and the unconscious which had blocked his development and threatened psychosis. He could now proceed on the path to the deeper realization which had been denied in his earlier dream, his *initiation manqué*.

Cure

As we have said, the surface must be cleared before things will grow from the depths and, before they can grow, the conscious attitudes and predispositions which embroil us in a superficial reality must be transformed. Jung's dreams informed him that the images of death and devastation of the "outer" world – which frequented his night visions at this time indicating the withdrawal of libido precedent to the process of introversion – must be accompanied by an "ego death." Precisely as we found in shamanic initiation, both the empirical world and the empirical ego which binds us to it must be deconstructed if the tension between the conscious and preconscious mind announced in the call and expressed in initiatory illness is to be resolved. Again, in Eliade's terms, in these dreams "the profane man is being dissolved" and the source of his reality is being relocated on a deeper plane of psychic reality. The world governed by directed thinking and its obsessions must make way for the import of the primordial symbol, and the "break with the universe of daily life" will be fruitless unless and until this process occurs. It is only the symbol which is capable of breaking the impasse between the unconscious and the conscious, the "irreconcilable contradiction between 'inner' and 'outer'" upon which Jung was impaled.

We recall that the shaman for centuries utilized various traditional and ecstatic training techniques to awaken and further this process of reconciliation through the symbol. In Chapter 7 we compared these techniques with those employed by Jung in analysis, and it would be useless here to repeat the points of parallel. What should be emphasized is that many of the methods devised by Jung developed naturally as he, at this period of grave crisis, desperately sought mediation between the conscious mind and the welter of symbolic material assailing him from the unconscious depths. Part of the process of repossessing his soul involved what he referred to as building games using stones with mud as mortar trying to release child-like creative forces long repressed by the imperatives of professional seriousness. Drawing and painting his fantasies also seemed to help resolve the tension between consciousness and the unconscious. As Paul Stern notes:

> The tools with which Jung mastered the visions welling up from his unconscious were deceptively simple. Besides using his "play therapy," he made certain to record his dreams and fantasies in minute detail, drawing or painting them whenever possible. He also endeavored to "amplify" the tissue

of his visions by drawing upon the rich storehouses of mythology and folktales. His main goal was to objectify, and then confront, the products of his unconscious.[42]

These practices were meant not to subdue but to foster and clarify his visionary experiences, as McLynn notes:

As one mental storm succeeded another, he frequently had to force himself to do yoga exercises to keep his emotions in check. But he made it clear that his motivation was very different from that of the Indian yogi, who exercised in order to obliterate the multitude of psychic images and contents: Jung practised yoga simply to give himself the strength to return to the fearsome world of the unconscious.[43]

He became increasingly aware of the unconscious as a dynamic process and out of inner necessity found various means capable of guiding and transforming psychic energy. The urgent need for inducing dream experience, followed by its amplification and analysis, now made itself clear. We recall Serge King's statement that "Where the shaman is concerned, the verb 'to dream' is to be taken in a very active sense. In other words what for most people is a passive experience is, for the shaman, an intentionally creative act." Jung found that he could approach the unconscious in a similarly purposeful manner. He would imagine his descent into the depths, amplify it through his visual imagination and carefully monitor and analyze the materials produced by the unconscious during such trance-like excursions. He worked hard to translate the dim intuitions gleaned from these descents into clear images and to gain control of this internal imagery through understanding it in much the same manner which Noll and Houston recognized typifies the shaman's vision training. He found that one of the most effective ways of overcoming the adverse power of these images was to personify them. "It is not too difficult to personify them, as they always possess a certain degree of autonomy, a separate identity of their own," he informs us. "Their autonomy is a most uncomfortable thing to reconcile oneself to, and yet the very fact that the unconscious presents itself in that way gives us the best means of handling it."[44] In this manner, he became aware that "the contents of the psychic experience are real, and real not only as my own personal experience, but as collective experiences which others also have."[45]

As Jung's mastery of the visionary world increased, these "collective experiences which others also have" deepened in a manner which again uncannily resembles the collective inner experiences of the shaman. Richard Noll notes, in his study of the shaman's vision training or "mental imagery cultivation," that "in traditional, non-literate societies the mediation of visual mental imagery is essential for intercourse with the sacred, and direct contact with spirits, gods, etc., is especially believed to be accomplished through dreams and visions."[46] As we may recall, he explained to us that first the shaman concentrates upon increasing the vividness of this internal visual imagery and then works toward an increased control over it. This is, of course, very similar to what Jung has informed us he was doing at this time. The shaman's mounting success, Noll continues, is revealed in the increased number of spirits he is able to possess. Jean Houston also noted that one of the most critical aspects of shamanic training is the activation of the capacity for inner imageries and visions, and that it is often through such techniques that the shaman finds his spirit guide. And we may recall the Tamang shaman, Bhirendra, who was raised from "crazy possession" through ecstatic and traditional techniques of trance meditation and amplification to an understanding that his possession was caused by his shamanic grandfather and would resolve itself into an affirmative and guiding force in this spiritual form. At this time, during Jung's work with his inner images, something very similar began to occur which parallels the shaman's experience in some detail.

On one of his excursions into the unconscious, Jung imagined a very deep descent in which he made several attempts "to get to the bottom." Finally, he found himself at the edge of a cosmic abyss. He felt that he was in the land of the dead. Suddenly two figures emerged, an old man with a white beard and a beautiful young girl. The girl identified herself as the Biblical Salome; the man as the Prophet Elijah. He and Elijah conversed at length, but Jung could not understand what Elijah was trying to tell him. Yet the Elijah figure, though his message was not yet intelligible, did, in fact, carry a latent prophetic wisdom, for he developed into a more significant visionary personality who Jung was to call Philemon. Philemon and Jung frequently conversed walking up and down Jung's garden, and Jung would transcribe these conversations in his notebooks. The wisdom conveyed by Philemon suggested a state of awareness beyond that Jung had presently attained.

> He confronted me in an objective manner, and I understood that there is something in me which can say things that I do not know and do not intend. ... Psychologically, Philemon represented superior insight. He was a mysterious figure to me. At times he seemed to me quite real, as if he were a living personality.[47]

Finally, Jung concluded that "Philemon and other figures of my fantasies brought home to me the crucial insight that there are things in the psyche which I do not produce, but which produce themselves and have their own life."[48] "It was through Philemon that Jung learned the objectivity and reality of the psyche," Barbara Hannah asserts, "its absolutely independent existence."[49] Philemon provided the compensatory reality which is able to lead one out of the abyss. Jung compared him with a guru whose superior knowledge would disentangle for him the involuntary creations of his imagination. He was, Jung came to recognize, his "psychagogue," the guide of his spirit.[50]

Jung's unconscious endowed this figure with a complex of attributes which are quite arresting.[51] He was an old man, a pagan who, Jung tells us, had an Egypto-Hellenistic aura with a Gnostic coloration. He appeared as a winged being flying across the sky. He had the horns of a bull, the wings of the kingfisher and a lame foot. The name, Philemon, suggests a figure from Greek mythology, who, along with a single other person, was the only human to offer Zeus and Hermes hospitality when they visited earth in human form.[52] His name thus implies a reality open to the world of gods and the spirit and suggests the daemonic realm itself as intermediary between gods and men. He becomes Jung's spirit guide and his healer, yet he himself is lame. Like the shaman, then, he incarnates the archetype of the wounded healer. He emerges from the land of the dead, i.e., the ancestral world of the collective unconscious, and is associated with the pagan Egypto-Hellenistic world and Gnosticism. The Egypto-Hellenistic time is known to be a period whose sensibility gave rise to a great mythic and symbolic syncretism; and, as we shall see, Gnosticism was a spiritual discipline which Jung associated with true insight, the immediacy of experience leading to actual knowledge, or gnosis, of spiritual reality. Myth, the symbol and an actual knowledge of the spirit were, of course, important markers along the path Jung was treading at the time of these revelations.

The figure thus implies associations with the ancestral world, the collective unconscious and its rich resources of myth and symbol and the living insight to which they lead. Of course we now know that the shaman, the wounded healer, traverses this same transformative path through the ancestral realm and the mythic world to the experience which will make him fit for his vocation. Emblematic of this process, his spirit guide often takes the form of the ancestor or a theriomorphic figure, or often both. And this is precisely the case with Philemon. Jung's unconscious vests him not only with the characteristics of the mythic ancestor but also of the theriomorph. He has the horns of a bull and the wings of the kingfisher. His appearance thus implies consciousness deepening into the psychoid level, the deep and healing realm of instinct and the wisdom of nature where the world itself is speaking in the form of the symbol. The horned representation of the spirit guide is a familiar archetype beginning with the creatures from the Upper Paleolithic at Chauvet and Les Trois Frères, and is recurrently produced by the mythopoeic imagination into contemporary times in such creatures as Káuyumarie, whose horns led the Huichol sojourners through the clashing cloud gates to their gnosis in the land of the ancestors.

Philemon is, thus, truly a symbol of transformation cast up by the unconscious for Jung's salvation at "this the soul's last and lowest ebb." He images the same deepening of consciousness at the heart of the shaman's transformative experiences in the very same images recurrently reproduced in the world's diverse shamanic traditions. And we should not be surprised that he also bears a symbolism often found at the end of the shaman's journey such as we found deep within the ancient shaft at Lascaux; that is, avian transformation. The shaman's association with avian symbolism is, as Eliade recognizes, ancient and widespread, and Andreas Lommel informs us that Siberian shamans still wore bird costumes well into historical times. Philemon's wings are obviously a symbol of ascent and portend the turning of consciousness at the nadir of Jung's experience which will lift him to a higher awareness. Moreover, Philemon's wings are the wings of the kingfisher. The kingfisher is a water bird, and Jill and Peter Furst inform us of the archetypal nature of this shamanic symbol which still survives on the northwest coast of America. "Equally adept on, above and under the water, water birds are pre-eminently shamanic messengers between the different levels of the universe; they assist the shaman and even serve as vehicle for his descent into the watery underworld in search of strayed or abducted human souls or knowledge of the dead," they note.[53]

Yet the kingfisher also represents a force which impels the shaman's ascent to a higher dimension of consciousness. A familiar example of this is a repeated motif founded on the Raven rattles produced in this area. As we have discussed, these commonly depict a shaman, in the magical flight of trance, perched upon the back of the sacred Raven. Impelling his journey is a kingfisher, his spirit guide, who, beak to the shaman's mouth, provides him with sustenance, i.e., the power necessary for his journey. Thus, finally, in these shamanic traditions the kingfisher becomes a familiar uniting symbol, for he lives upon the land, dives deep beneath its surface into the water's depths for his sustenance and rises to the heavens repeating a familiar pattern which unites the three realms.

As wounded healer, Philemon represents the painful experiences prerequisite to illumination which we have found in the shaman's initiatory illness and suffering and its ritual counterparts of isolation and torture. As the Caribou Eskimo shaman, Igjugarjuk, so well expressed it, "Privation and suffering are the only things that can open the mind of man to those things that are hidden from others." And it was clearly privation and suffering which characterized this painful stage of Jung's transformation over the years of his isolation and intense psychological torture. Yet Philemon also represents the further stages of realization – the deepening of consciousness characterized by the fostering of the mythic sensibility leading to gnosis – which will penetrate the realm of the ancestor and the deep wisdom of the theriomorph. He serves as a vehicle for the descent into the land of the dead, but at the same time symbolizes the pre-existent meaning hidden in the chaos of the unconscious, the objective psyche which triggers a turning of consciousness. As Sherry Salman informed us earlier, "As libido regresses and turns inward during illness, symbols emerge from the unconscious. ... symbols are like living things, pregnant with meaning and capable of acting like transformers by energy." As we have noted, this level of the psyche works with its own intentionality, and this is why Jung came to see that Philemon represented a force which came from beyond his conscious will. It was Philemon who taught him psychic objectivity, the reality of the psyche. Here the psyche reveals that it has the natural capacity to heal the psyche, just as the human body in so many instances can heal itself. It was by discovering, trusting and learning to follow this intentionality that Jung was to be led from the all-consuming crisis of his dissociation to an understanding of the path of integration and to the vocation of a healer.

We recall that in shamanism the final stages of this path are marked by the archetype of the return to origin, both within the human mind, the microcosm, and the cosmos, the macrocosm. The creationtime is a reality accessible to the shaman, and its plenitude is a source of power and illumination. In modern depth psychology, Schwartz-Salant has expressed the same insight in the observation that "healing depends upon a person's ability to link to the larger world of the pleroma." And in both healing professions we have been able to discern the overall pattern of a lowering of the threshold of consciousness and a descent into the unconscious which is potentially capable of revitalizing the objective psyche. Here the archetypal patterns of transpersonal experience open to their timeless acausal source. As we have said, this configuration of experience is itself an important archetypal pattern, for "the descent into the depths always seems to precede the ascent," and it is the engaging of this deep level of the psyche that paradoxically opens us to the pleroma, the plenitude of the source as it informs and sustains creation. The archetype canalizes psychic energy to integrate the conscious mind, the unconscious and the cosmic life which informs them into "a field that links them to the oneness of the implicate order," to the a priori unity which the archetype brings forward into human consciousness. This is a form of soul retrieval, for the dissociation of these levels is an enervating loss of psychic unity and it is this integration which rearticulates the connective faculty which is the human soul.

Here it might be fruitful to recall the crisis experience of the Tamang patient, Kumari, in the karga puja which we discussed in Chapter 3. She suffered a dissociation between the unconscious and the conscious mind which was mythically mirrored in the cosmic dissociation between gods and men recognized in her people's traditional lore. As diagnosed by the local shaman, her soul had fled to Yama Lok, the land of the dead, and she had collapsed into the chaos of the unconscious. In this crisis and collapse state the shaman, through his spirit guide and his own understanding of the healing, integrative power potentially inherent in the archetypal symbol, overcame the dissociation within Kumari and, on a larger level, that between gods and men. For the archetype both unites the conscious mind with its roots and simultaneously brings forward the experience of the healing plenitude of the source itself, the pleroma, into human consciousness. On the macrocosmic level, we recall that this reintegration was symbolized by the shaman's entry into trance and consequent ascent through the very gates which separated the world of the gods from that of men – i.e., by his return to the creationtime source. We found a similar pattern of return to origin present in many shamanic healing traditions and noted Eliade's observation that "… all medical rituals we have been examining aim at a return to origins. We get the impression that for archaic societies life cannot be *repaired*, it can only be *re-created* by a return to sources. And the 'source of sources' is the prodigious outpouring of energy, life, and fecundity that occurred at the creation of the world."

In the world's shamanic traditions, it has generally been the spirit guide who has led the way to an experience of this return to origins, to the creative plenitude of the pleroma, and Philemon was to play a precisely similar role in Jung's experience. Like Kumari, Jung had collapsed into the chaos of the unconscious. And, in a manner parallel to the existential dilemma symbolically recognized in the Tamang ritual, for Jung this dissociation was also symptomatic of a larger one between Creator and creation, gods and men. The reality of myth had become silent for Jung, and he could not profess that the Christian myth filled the void for him. He had lost the connective faculty of the soul; it, like Kumari's soul, fled to Yama Lok, the land of the dead. However, again in a manner similar to Kumari's crisis, this flight of the soul was to provoke a very significant experience which would open Jung to the ultimately healing power of the reality of the pleroma. And, as happened so frequently during his process of transformation, a vision foretold of this experience. A brief time before this experience he had written down a fantasy of his soul having flown away from him. This vision told him that his soul had withdrawn into the unconscious or into the land of the dead. There, the soul awakened the ancestral traces, the collective contents; it gave the dead a chance to manifest themselves. Consequently, soon after the disappearance of his soul, the dead did, in fact, appear to him, and the result was a work he called *Septem Sermones ad Mortuos* (The Seven Sermons to the Dead). Jung explains what this experience of soul flight ultimately meant for him:

> From that time on, the dead have become ever more distinct for me as the
> voices of the Unanswered, Unresolved, and Unredeemed; for since the
> questions and demands which my destiny required me to answer did not
> come to me from outside, they must have come from the inner world. These
> conversations with the dead formed a kind of prelude to what I had to
> communicate to the world about the unconscious: a kind of pattern of order
> and interpretation of its general contents.[54]

By 1916 Jung had experienced three years of conversations with Philemon. He realized that very gradually the outlines of an inner change were taking shape from within, and he felt a compulsion to give it some form of verbal expression. It was this compulsion which erupted in *Septem Sermones ad Mortuos*. The circumstances leading to its composition were thoroughly bizarre – tense with a psychic energy which pervaded the whole Jung household at the time. Jung sensed ghostly entities filling the air. His eldest daughter perceived a white figure passing through the room, while another daughter related that twice during the night her blanket had been snatched away. His son had a strange dream which, though he almost never drew, he felt compelled to illustrate with crayons where an angel and devil contended over the catch of a fisherman. The next day the doorbell began ringing frantically. Others, in addition to Jung, heard it ring, but he, sitting near the doorbell, also saw it moving. Everyone looked to see who was there, but no one appeared. In the midst of this atmosphere of intense expectancy, Jung suddenly slipped into a trance, and he spontaneously began to write, allowing "the unconscious to express itself through his pen."[55] Within three evenings he had written the work in which voices of the dead became articulate. As McLynn observes, "He claimed that the process was a form of automatic writing, whereby through Philemon's mediumship he transcribed the thoughts of the Alexandrian Gnostic Basilides."[56] On another level, we might say that the objective psyche was leading Jung back beyond the opposites which define our conditioned world to the source itself, the pleroma as the originary reality which underlies, creates and sustains the world of our experience, for it is precisely this which is revealed through the mediumship of Philemon.

This spontaneous composition begins with the dead, who are, indeed, the "voices of the Unanswered, Unresolved, and Unredeemed," announcing that they have come back from Jerusalem where they were unable to find what they had sought. They implore Basilides to teach them, and he reveals a compensatory truth, a majestic but often frightening and overwhelming vision of the first principle of all creation. This vision of the *mysterium tremendum* must have been struggling to emerge from Jung's unconscious as he conversed those long years with Philemon and strained against the bounds of traditional Christianity and its revelation of a transcendent but personal God.

In this source of sources, which transcends all opposition, void and totality are one. "This nothingness or fullness we name the PLEROMA," Basilides pronounces.[57] In this paradoxical reality, all the opposites by which we chart our course through the conditioned world become balanced and nullified – life and death, good and evil, beauty and ugliness, the One and the Many, are transcended in an all-encompassing Unity which is both the beginning and the end of all created being. Here we catch a glimpse of the same unitive reality and its relationship to the conditioned world with which Jung was to struggle in "Answer to Job" and *Mysterium Coniunctionis*. Everything that we derive from the pleroma takes the form of a pair of opposites. "To god, therefore, always belongeth the devil."[58] Yet, though we experience our existence to be immersed in the pairs of opposites, and, thus, the pleroma appears to be sundered on our level of consciousness, in fact, "We are, however, the pleroma itself, for we are part of the eternal and infinite."[59] And although this reality appears to be divided in each of us, from a different perspective, because it is a unitive reality in which we all participate, it remains undivided, and we all potentially partake of its universal form-generating power.

The pleroma is eternally creative power. In Jung's version of Basilides' wisdom it is more akin to Plotinus' vision of the creative source – poetically described by Shelley as a "burning fountain," "the fire for which all thirst" – which overflows into and infuses all creation:

It is splendid as the lion in the instant he striketh down his victim. It is
beautiful as a day of spring. ...
It is love and love's murder.
It is the saint and his betrayer.

"It is the brightest light of day" and, as Jung now was beginning to understand, "the darkest night of madness."[60]

Yet this power which pervades the cosmos is to be most immediately encountered in our "innermost infinity," the human soul. Here, if we can turn from the flaming spectacle of the outer world, we find the true *lumen naturae*, "one single Star in the zenith. This is the one god of this one man." And here, within, man meets the pleroma. "This is his world, his pleroma, his divinity." In this world man becomes one with the creative principle, with cosmic life – he becomes both the creator and destroyer of his own world. "This Star is the god and goal of man" and "When the greater world waxeth cold, burneth the Star" for "there [is] eternally creative power."[61]

For Jung, in the process of introversion the flaming spectacle of the greater world did, in fact, wax cold. However, the revelation of a formal creative power expressive of the power of cosmic creation – the archetypal mythopoeic faculty within the human unconscious – became a compensating reality. Like many of the shamans we have encountered, Jung began to cure himself by giving expression to an inner compulsion to become a voice for the sacred. This reality would provide the power capable of bridging the dissociation between consciousness and the unconscious for Jung, and gradually would heal the rift between the inner and outer worlds as well as that between gods and men which had so severely fragmented Jung's own being. The freeing of this creative power helped confirm Jung's observations about the mana personality. It also almost miraculously freed the wellsprings of Jung's own mind, for Jung had written nothing for almost three years during his crisis. Now he began to write again.[62]

This "eternally creative power," this plastic force shared by man and the cosmos, which the revelation of the pleroma brought forward into Jung's consciousness, slowly took shape in his life. Chaos began to give way to order, and the form this process was to take is familiar from the shaman's world and our study of Jung's psychology. Shortly after he wrote *Septem Sermones*, he spontaneously began to draw images of mandalas which seemed to express his emerging inner situation at the time. He only dimly understood their import at this time, but he treasured them and regarded them as somehow highly significant. From what we know about the mandala form, we can recognize how aptly it relates to Jung's experience at this time. The mandala expresses humanity's intuitive apprehension of the order and unity at the heart of the cosmos. As we have mentioned, it "represents a pattern of order which, like a psychological 'view-finder' marked with a cross or circle divided into four, is superimposed on the psychic chaos so that each content falls into place and the weltering confusion is held together by the protective circle."[63] It reconciles the One and the many in a balanced opposition which raises them to a higher unity that the human mind naturally associates with an *Imago Dei*, and it is thus capable of imaging the reality of the Godhead which Jung had long sensed as forming the foundation of his No. 2 personality.

At the same time, the mandala image represents the eternally creative power which flows into the cosmos, nature and the mind of man – that point in his "innermost infinity" where man meets the pleroma and shares its universal form-generating capacity. It thus gives visual form to the centering process which fosters the integrated level of consciousness Jung was to term the self. As we have seen from so many traditions, it brings forward to consciousness the healing and revitalizing experience of the return to the Source, the revelation of the common divine origin of cosmic and human creation that lies beyond individual birth and death. It was this reality that had erupted into Jung's life in the depths of introversion to mark the turning of consciousness which would lift chaos to ordered creation. Over these years Jung began to see that the mandala image represented the goal for which his psyche strove. He realized that "all the paths I had been following, all the steps I had taken, were leading to a single point – namely, to the mid-point,"[64] – that point which unites man with "eternally creative power."

Years later, these growing intuitions were again confirmed by the unconscious in a remarkable dream which left an indelible impression on Jung. In the dream Jung found himself in Liverpool, "a dirty, sooty city." It was night, winter, dark and raining, and Jung, along with several other Swiss visitors, climbed a route leading to the "real city" perched upon the cliffs above the harbor. The path they traversed he appropriately associated with the "Alley of the Dead." When they succeeded in reaching this portion of the city, the dream revealed "a broad square dimly illuminated by street lights, into which many streets converged. The various quarters of the city were arranged radially around the square. In the center was a round pool, and in the middle of it a small island." Paradoxically, everything around the island was obscured by rain, fog and smoke, but the little island blazed with sunlight. And on the shining island stood a single tree, a magnolia, in a shower of reddish blossoms. "It was as though the tree stood in the sunlight and were at the same time the source of the light," he tells us, and then adds one detail of the dream which seems to have arrested his attention. Each of the individual quarters of the city were themselves arranged radially around a central point of illumination and constituted a small replica of the island.[65] While Jung was struck by the beauty of the flowering illuminated tree and the central island, his companions noticed nothing, only complaining about the abominable weather.

The mandala-formed city will remind readers of Blake's prophetic poems of the sacred city of Golgonooza, and it brings to mind the archetype of the heavenly city examined by Eliade in *The Myth of the Eternal Return*. But the heart of the vision, the "mid-point" capable of unifying human and cosmic consciousness and creation, is the central pool with its island and most of all the sunlit tree which was "at the same time the source of the light." The mandala form with the tree at its center as a symbol of illumination is, of course, a familiar and apparently ancient image that we have found in numerous variations in the world's shamanic traditions. There it also represents the goal of the perilous journey, the unitive mid-point uniting the three realms, the conscious, the unconscious with its archetypes and the higher dimension of their source, the continuous creation. Obscured by rain, fog and smoke, it represents the order hidden in the chaos of the unconscious which the dreamer had to tread the Alley of the Dead, the collective unconscious, to recover. The dream images the very process of Jung's descent into the chaos of the unconscious and near madness, and rather precisely recalls the spontaneous ecstatic experience of Huottaire, or Diver, who also descended to the realm of the ancestral shamanesses and the Lord of Madness. Yet, in his vision, in the middle of the sea of the unconscious to which the shamanesses led him he also found an island "and in the middle of the island a young birch tree rose to the sky." This was the central tree of the Siberian shaman's illumination and the key to his vocation. Each represents the same essential process of centering and ascent which we have discussed, the anchoring of human consciousness in the formal source which the Tukano so well expressed in their concept of the shaman's "luminescence." And Jung's dream carries the same archetypal significance, for the dream made it clear that each individual consciousness participates in this central illumination if it can open itself to its source. In the dream, each quarter of this island city mirrors the central structure – each has its own central point illuminated by a large street light forming a small replica of the glowing island at the center of it all. As further proof of the archetypal nature of this image, we might recall the mandala-formed sacred city of Teotihuacán and the more striking archetypal parallel in the Aztec island city of Tenochtitlán which "imitated" its central four-fold structure with its sacred center in each of its four quarters. It was this shared participation in the central collective source that, as Jung confided to Barbara Hannah, was the "great discovery of the dream."[66] Each individual consciousness could, through its own integration, open itself to the collective illumination of the central source.

Jung felt that this dream conveyed an extraordinary healing effect. It was experienced as an act of grace and the culmination of the entire process of his psychic transformation. It represented the same sense of unity, harmony and creative power which marks the culmination of the shaman's journey, and revealed a similar sense of unfolding purpose which allowed Jung to understand the elements of the supra-personal force that had shaped his experience. And from this vantage point we, too, can look back at this pattern of experience and realize how precisely it repeats in both its structure and function the spontaneous initiatory experience of the shaman beginning with the call from the daemonic realm and reaching its fulfillment in the eventual crystalization of the mandala image and the central tree of illumination. We have witnessed the painful "break with the universe of daily life" which Jung experienced under the weight of his psychic fragmentation. This led to a consequent withdrawal of libido from the external world and his immersion in a welter of images, visions and dreams containing seeds of the future and their own purpose and direction and sharing similar patterns of imagery with those we experienced repeatedly in the shaman's visionary world. Here for years Jung underwent intense initiatory privation and suffering. In the process, he learned the necessity of overcoming the profane self and the world of its obsessions, immersed himself in mental imagery cultivation and its control, confronted and learned to possess the powers of possession and discovered the objectivity of the psyche embodied in his own spirit guide, Philemon, who embodied the very process of mythological deepening we have found capable of guiding the shaman's psychic transformation. Finally, in the depths of his descent into chaos, he, too, transcended the oppositions characterizing our conditioned world and experienced the revivifying encounter with the source itself, the pleroma. The reality of this experience freed the waters of Jung's own creativity and fostered the greater harmony with the source of human consciousness and creativity Jung spontaneously expressed in the mandala image with its central, all-uniting tree, just as the shaman did in his own visionary world. Like the initiates traversing the cave beneath the massive Pyramid of the Sun, he made the perilous journey into the dark depths to the very source, marked by the same images of quaternity, ascent, illumination and a freeing of the waters of creation. From the depths, from the Land of the Dead, Jung was able to return with the power which would fuel his future creation.

I am reminded of a beautiful but sad story related by Andreas Lommel and David Mowaljarlai of an old and leprous Aboriginal shaman whom they encountered in the Kimberly Division of Western Australia in 1938 which relates this same archetypal experience as it existed in a distant world and tradition. In a place where several tribes camped together, the members of this dying culture would dance and sing the poetic creations of this aged healer, Allan Balbungu. Allan explained that, to tap the source of his creative power, a shaman must be able to separate his soul from his body and send it into the netherworld, the source of *miriru*, psychic power, which is indispensable for a real poet. "The shaman can go down to the netherworld, the country of the dead, and enter relations with the spirits of the dead and particularly his own dead ancestors, in order to become artistically productive," he told them.[67] Led by his spirit guide, he "finds" these creative forms in the underworld and brings them back to his culture. Sometimes, however, he loses his ability to visit the underworld and his creative gifts languish. In trance he searches in vain for the ancestors. Then, after long wandering, he hears the distant call of a helping spirit:

... under the leadership of the helping spirit others now come up from the underworld and take possession of the shaman's spirit, which they want to see among them again. They tear the soul to pieces and each spirit carries a piece into the underworld. There, deep under the earth, they put the shaman's soul together again. They show him the dances again and sing songs to him.[68]

These creations he again brings back to his culture, and they are performed in ecstatic dance and song before a backdrop of dancers, a chorus of the dead, painted with white skeletal stripes to remind the audience of the source of the shaman's creation, "the spirits from whom the poet got his inspiration."[69]

Jung would say of his own descent into the land of the dead that it was the source of the *prima materia* for a lifetime's work. His soul, like Allan's, was torn to pieces by the spirits of the underworld as he descended into the unconscious. Yet, in these very depths, they, too, put his soul together again. Here in the unconscious Jung also "found" the pre-existent creative principles for which he searched and which he would bring back to his culture. Later he summarized the critical importance of his journey:

As a young man my goal had been to accomplish something in my science. But then, I hit upon this stream of lava, and the heat of its fires reshaped my life. That was the primal stuff which compelled me to work upon it, and my works are a more or less successful endeavor to incorporate this incandescent matter into the contemporary picture of the world.[70]

This archetypal experience opened the conduit of creative power and knowledge which Jung's dissociation had blocked; it released that "fiery resin" which mysteriously had the power "to fashion an image and see / The Spirit as ever it was."

Psychology, Jung recognized, is to a certain degree inevitably a "subjectively conditioned confession" of the particular psychologist.[71] But of Jung's experience, it is fair to say that we are lifted "out of the occasional and transitory into the realm of the ever-enduring."[72] His is a confession from the transpersonal realm, the testimony of the world soul beyond any given place and particular time – archetypal, purposive and initiatory in its content. It was in the crucible of the unconscious that Jung learned that wisdom "which can open the mind of man to those things which are hidden from others," a pattern of experience the understanding of which allowed him to cure himself and others, and to initiate followers into the world of depth psychology. Like the shaman, within the welter of his psychopathic experience, Jung was able to discern a higher will, a supra-personal process which is evidently an attempt at self-healing on the part of nature. Jung's life describes the same pattern of experience as the shaman's initiation, and we might say of Jung precisely what Eliade previously said about the shaman: "The initiation was tantamount to a healing; among other things, it brought about a new psychic integration." This is an experience we have traced to the horizons of the development of modern Homo sapiens and around the globe. In a manner which parallels the archetypal experience of the initiates in the cave underlying the Pyramid of the Sun at Teotihuacán, Jung's inward journey united the depths with the heights, freed the waters of creation and brought to modern consciousness an age-old pattern of transformative experience. As he realized in hindsight, but perhaps to an even greater extent than he was able fully to recognize, he was "living a myth." "In going down into the secrets of his own mind," Jung "descended into the secrets of all minds."[73] And he found in the agony of his personal journey into the unconscious the same truth revealed to Sereptie Djaruoskin in distant Siberia, "If you find the spirit of madness, you will begin to shamanize, initiating (new) shamans."

Notes

Chapter 1

1. Mircea Eliade, "The Occult in the Modern World," in *Occultism, Witchcraft, and Cultural Fashions: Essays in Comparative Religions* (Chicago: University of Chicago Press, 1976), p. 56.
2. Carl G. Jung, *The Collected Works of C.G. Jung*, 20 vols., eds. Herbert Read, Michael Fordham and Gerhard Adler; Executive ed. (from 1967) William McGuire; trans. R.F.C. Hull (Princeton, NJ: Princeton University Press, Bollingen Series XX, 1967–79), Vol. 13, para. 10; hereafter all references to the Collected Works will be in the form of C.W., giving volume and paragraph.
3. C.G. Jung, *Modern Man in Search of a Soul*, trans. W.S. Dell and Cary F. Baynes (San Diego, CA: Harcourt Brace, 1933), p. 209.
4. C.W., Vol. 5, para. 23.
5. Ibid., Introduction, para. 1.
6. C.G. Jung, *Memories, Dreams, Reflections*, recorded and ed. by Aniela Jaffé, trans. Richard and Clara Winston (New York: Vintage, 1989), p. 302.
7. C.W., Vol. 11, para. 2.
8. C.W., Vol. 18, para. 1500.
9. C.W., Vol. 8, para. 401.
10. Ibid., para. 436.
11. Jung, *Modern Man in Search of a Soul*, pp. 112–13.
12. C.W., Vol. 10, para. 585.
13. Ibid., para. 367.

Chapter 2

1. C.W., Vol. 9, 1, para. 32.
2. Ibid., para. 84.
3. Mircea Eliade, "The Sacred and the Modern Artist," in *Symbolism, the Sacred & the Arts*, ed. Diane Apostolos-Cappadona (New York: Crossroads, 1988), p. 82; see also Eliade, *The Myth of the Eternal Return: or Cosmos and History*, trans. Willard R. Trask (Princeton, NJ: Princeton University Press, Bollingen Series XLVI, 1971), chapter 3, esp. pp. 158–62.
4. Jung, *Memories, Dreams, Reflections*, p. 332.
5. C.W., Vol. 9, 1, para. 11.
6. Ibid., para. 7.
7. Carl Kerényi, *The Gods of the Greeks*, trans. Norman Cameron (London: Thames and Hudson, 1951), p. 215, translating and quoting *Hesiodi Theogonia*, in: *Hesiodi Carmina*. Ed. Aloisius Rzach (Bibliotheca scriptorum graecorum et romanorum Teubneriana), 3rd edn., Leipzig, 1913, pp. 535 ff.
8. Carl Kerényi, *Prometheus: Archetypal Image of Human Existence*, trans. Ralph Manheim (Princeton, NJ: Princeton University Press, Bollingen Series LXV 1, 1963), p. 41, quoting *Hesiod, Theogony*, trans. Hugh G. Evelyn-White (London and Cambridge: Loeb Classical Library, 1920), p. 121.
9. Kerényi, *The Gods of the Greeks*, p. 218.
10. Kerényi, *Prometheus: Archetypal Image of Human Existence*, p. 44.
11. Ibid., p. 3.
12. Ibid., Intro., p. xxii.
13. Ibid., Intro., p. xx.
14. Aeschylus, *Prometheus Bound*, in *Three Greek Plays: Prometheus Bound, Agamemnon, and the Trojan Women*, trans. Edith Hamilton (New York: W.W. Norton, 1937), p. 141.
15. *Prometheus Delivered*, fragment quoted in Marcus Tullius Cicero, *Tusculan Disputations II*, trans. J.E. King (London and Cambridge: Loeb Classical Library, 1927), p. 171 as found in Kerényi, *Prometheus: Archetypal Image of Human Existence*, pp. 113, 114.
16. Jung, *Modern Man in Search of a Soul*, p. 169.

17. C.W., Vol. 9, I, para. 7.

18. Thomas Mann, "Freud and the Future," as found in Kerényi, *The Gods of the Greeks*, Intro., pp. 1, 2.

19. Kerényi, *Prometheus: Archetypal Image of Human Existence*, p. 105.

20. C.W., Vol. 9, I, para. 218.

21. Mircea Eliade, *The Two and the One*, trans. J.M. Cohen (New York: Harper & Row, 1965), pp. 9, 10.

22. Ibid., p. 11.

23. J.J. Clarke, *In Search of Jung* (London: Routledge, 1992), Preface p. xiv.

24. C.W., Vol. 4, para. 764.

25. C.W., Vol. 9, I, para. 187.

26. C.W., Vol. 10, para. 387.

27. Jung, *Modern Man in Search of a Soul*, p. 190.

28. C.W., Vol. 7, para. 33.

29. C.W., Vol. 8, para. 618.

30. C.W., Vol. 5, Forewords to the Second German Edition, p. xxix.

31. C.W., Vol. 13, para. 478.

32. Ira Progoff, "Waking Dream and Living Myth," in *Myths, Dreams, and Religion*, ed. Joseph Campbell (Dallas: Spring Publications, 1970), p. 180.

33. C.W., Vol. 7, para. 235.

34. C.W., Vol. 8, para. 673.

35. C.W., Vol. 7, para. 300.

36. C.W., Vol. 15, para. 126.

37. C.W., Vol. 8, para. 440.

38. C.W., Vol. 6, paras. 815–17.

39. C.W., Vol. 9, I, para. 271.

40. Ibid., para. 293.

41. Ibid., para. 262.

42. C.W., Vol. 15, para. 152.

43. C.W., Vol. 8, para. 342.

44. C.W., Vol. 18, para. 280.

45. Jung, *Modern Man in Search of a Soul*, p. 126.

46. C.G. Jung, in *New York Times*, "Roosevelt 'Great' in Jung's Analysis," Oct. 4, 1936, as found in *C.G. Jung: Psychological Reflections*, selected and ed. by Jolande Jacobi in collaboration with R.F.C. Hull (Princeton, NJ: Princeton University Press, Bollingen Series XXXI, 1973), p. 76.

47. C.W., Vol. 7, para. 118.

48. Ira Progoff, *Jung, Synchronicity, and Human Destiny: C.G. Jung's Theory of Meaningful Coincidence* (New York: Julian Press, 1987), pp. 111, 112.

49. C.W., Vol. 9, I, para. 91.

50. Jolande Jacobi, *The Psychology of C.G. Jung* (New Haven, CT: Yale University Press, 1973), p. 41.

51. Sherry Salman, "The Creative Psyche: Jung's Major Contributions," in *The Cambridge Companion to Jung*, eds. Polly Young-Eisendrath and Terrence Dawson (Cambridge, MA: Cambridge University Press, 1997), p. 65.

52. Ibid., p. 57.

53. C.W., Vol. 8, para. 277.

54. Clarke, p. 129.

55. C.W., Vol. 12, para. 11.

56. C.W., Vol. 9, I, para. 291.

57. C.G. Jung, "Approaching the Unconscious," in *Man and His Symbols*, ed. C.G. Jung (New York: Laurel, 1968), p. 53.

58. Letter to Medard Boss, June 27, 1947, in *C.G. Jung Letters*, 2 vols., trans. R.F.C. Hull, selected and ed. by Gerhard Adler in collaboration with Aniela Jaffé (Princeton, NJ: Princeton University Press, Vol. 1 of Bollingen Series XCV, 1973), 2: xli, as found in Marilyn Nagy, *Philosophical Issues in the Psychology of C.G. Jung* (Albany, NY: State University of New York Press, 1991), p. 199, ftnt. 6.

59. C.W., Vol. 6, para. 748.

60. C.W., Vol. 8, para. 418.

61. C.G. Jung, *Seminar on Nietzsche's Zarathustra*, abridged edition, edited and abridged by James L. Jarrett (Princeton, NJ: Princeton University Press, Bollingen Series XCIX, 1998), p. 99.

62. William Wordsworth, "The Prelude," Book Six, ll. 636–40, in *The Prelude: Selected Poems and Sonnets*, ed. Carlos Baker (New York: Holt, Reinhart and Winston, 1961), p. 306.

63. Jung, "Eliade's Interview for 'Combat,'" in *C.G. Jung Speaking: Interviews and Encounters*, eds. William McGuire and R.F.C. Hull (Princeton, N.J.: Princeton University Press, Bollingen Series XCVII, 1977), p. 230.

64. Dionysius the Areopagite, *On the Divine Names*, trans. Editors of the Shrine of Wisdom (Surrey, England: Fintry, 1947), p. 21, as found in Jacobi, p. 39.

65. C.W., Vol. 8, para. 967.

66. Ibid., para. 850.

67. Ibid., para. 948.

68. Ibid., para. 440.

69. Progoff, *Jung, Synchronicity, and Human Destiny*, p. 85.

70. Ibid., p. 83.

71. Ibid., p. 84.

72. C.W., Vol. 13, para. 31.

73. C.W., Vol. 9, I, para. 717.

74. Frank McLynn, *Carl Gustav Jung* (New York: Saint Martin's Press, 1997), p. 508.

75. Ibid., p. 519.

76. Ibid., p. 520.

77. C.W., Vol. 12, para. 511.

78. Nathan Schwartz-Salant, *The Borderline Personality: Vision and Healing* (Wilmette, IL: Chiron Press, 1989), p. 137.

79. Ibid., pp. 135, 136, citing C.G. Jung, *Psychological Analysis of Nietzsche's Zarathustra*. Unpublished seminar notes – mimeographed notes. Recorded by Mary Foote, 1937–39;

Vol. 3, p. 139 and Vol. 10, p. 144.

80. Ibid., p. 135, citing C.W., Vol. 12, para. 396.

81. Ibid., p. 101, citing C.G. Jung, C.W., 16, para. 399.

82. Ibid., p. 109.

83. Ibid., p. 12.

84. Ibid., p. 87.

85. Ibid., p. 107, citing C.G. Jung, C.W., Vol. 11, para. 629.

86. Ibid., p. 108.

Chapter 3

1. C.W., Vol. 7, para. 151.

2. Carl Kerényi, Jung and Kerényi, *Essays on a Science of Mythology*, trans. R.F.C. Hull (Princeton, NJ: Princeton University Press, Bollingen Series XXII, 1969), Prolegomena, p. 9.

3. C.W., Vol. 5, Forewords, p. xxiv.

4. C.W., Vol. 8, para. 435.

5. C.W., Vol. 14, para. 558.

6. Mircea Eliade, *Rites and Symbols of Initiation: The Mysteries of Birth and Rebirth*, trans. Willard R. Trask (New York: Harper Torchbooks, 1965), pp. 100, 101.

7. Eliade, *Rites and Symbols of Initiation*, p. 96.

8. Johannes Wilbert, "Tobacco and Shamanistic Ecstasy Among the Warao Indians of Venezuela," in *Flesh of the Gods: The Ritual Use of Hallucinogens*, ed. Peter T. Furst (Prospect Hts., IL: Waveland Press, 1990), p. 81.

9. Peter T. Furst, in Wilbert "Tobacco and Shamanistic Ecstasy Among the Warao Indians of Venezuela," Editor's ftnt. p. 82.

10. Stuart J. Fiedel, *Prehistory of the Americas*, 2nd ed. (Cambridge: Cambridge University Press, 1992), p. 356.

11. Ibid., p. 20.

12. Roger N. Walsh, *The Spirit of Shamanism* (Los Angeles: Jeremy P. Tarcher, 1990), p. 13.

13. C.W., Vol. 11, para. 845.

14. Joseph Campbell, *The Masks of God*, Vol. 1, *Primitive Mythology* (New York: Viking Press, 1970), p. 350.

15. Ibid., p. 264.

16. Ibid., p. 263.

17. Mircea Eliade, *Shamanism: Archaic Techniques of Ecstasy*, trans. Willard R. Trask (Princeton, NJ: Princeton University Press, Bollingen Series LXXVI, 1972), p. 266.

18. Ibid., p. 265.

19. Campbell, *The Masks of God*, Vol. 1, *Primitive Mythology*, p. 471.

20. William K. Powers, *Yuwipi: Vision and Experience in Oglala Ritual* (Lincoln, NB: Bison Books, University of Nebraska Press, 1984), p. 19.

21. William K. Powers, *Oglala Religion* (Lincoln, NB: Bison Books, University of Nebraska Press, 1982), p. 56.

22. Gerardo Reichel-Dolmatoff, *The Shaman and the Jaguar: A Study of Narcotic Drugs Among the Indians of Colombia* (Philadelphia: Temple University Press, 1975), p. 77.

23. Ibid.

24. Mircea Eliade, *Myth and Reality*, trans. Willard R. Trask (New York: Harper Torchbooks, 1968), pp. 25, 26.

25. C.W., Vol. 12, para. 377, fig. 214; para. 390, fig. 221; para. 400, fig. 231; see gen. C.W., Vol. 13, *The Philosophical Tree*, para. 304 ff.

26. C.W., Vol. 12, para. 357, C.W., Vol. 13, *The Philosophical Tree*, para. 304 ff.

27. C.W., Vol. 9, I, paras. 296, 604.

28. G.V. Ksenofontov, *Legendy i rasskazy o shamanach u. yakutov, buryat i tungusov*. Izdanie vtoroe. S. predisloviem S.A. Topkareva (Moscow: Izdatal'stvo Besbozhnik, 1930), trans. (into German) by Adolph Friedrich and Georg Buddruss, *Schamanengeschicten aus Siberien* (Munich: Otto Wilhelm Barth-Verlag,

1955), pp. 213–14, as found in Joseph Campbell, *The Masks of God*, Vol 1, *Primitive Mythology*, pp. 256, 257.

29. Mircea Eliade, *The Quest: History and Meaning in Religion* (Chicago: University of Chicago Press, 1969), p. 84.

30. Linda Schele and David Freidel, *A Forest of Kings: The Untold Story of the Ancient Maya* (New York: Quill, 1990), pp. 66, 67.

31. David Freidel, Linda Schele and Joy Parker, *Maya Cosmos: Three Thousand Years on the Shaman's Path* (New York: William Morrow, 1993), p. 211.

32. Ibid., p. 183.

33. Huichol Song, as found in Peter T. Furst, "Peyote Among the Huichol Indians of Mexico," in *Flesh of the Gods: The Ritual Use of Hallucinogens*, ed. Furst, p. 184.

34. C.W., Vol. 10, para. 367.

35. Ibid.

36. Eliade, *Shamanism*, p. 8.

37. Eliade, *Rites and Symbols of Initiation*, p. 102.

38. Eliade, *Shamanism*, p. 215.

39. Ibid., pp. 216, 217.

40. Eliade, *Myth and Reality*, p. 25.

41. Ibid., p. 29.

42. Ibid., p. 30.

43. Larry G. Peters, "Psychotherapy in Tamang Shamanism," *Ethos*, Vol. 6, no. 2, 1979, pp. 63–91.

44. Ibid., p. 64.

45. Ibid., p. 69.

46. Ibid., p. 70.

47. Ibid., pp. 70, 71.

48. Ibid., pp. 72, 73.

49. Ibid., pp. 74, 75.

50. C.W., Vol. 12, Epigraph to Part III, "Religious Ideas in Alchemy," quoted from Mylius, *Philosophia Reformata* (Frankfort, 1622), p. 215.

51. Larry G. Peters, "Trance, Initiation, and Psychotherapy in Tamang Shamanism," *American Ethnologist*, Vol. 9, no. 1, 1982, pp. 21–30.

52. Peters, "Psychotherapy in Tamang Shamanism," pp. 80, 81, referencing William Sargant, *The Mind Possessed* (Philadelphia, PA: J.B. Lippincott, 1973), pp. 12–13.

53. Ibid., p. 73, ftnt. 5, referencing Eliade, *Shamanism*, pp. 259 ff.

54. Peters, "Trance, Initiation, and Psychotherapy in Tamang Shamanism," pp. 26, 28, 33.

55. Peters, "Psychotherapy in Tamang Shamanism," pp. 83, 84, referencing Claude Lévi-Strauss, *Structural Anthropology*, trans. Claire Jacobson and Brooke Grunfest Schoepf (New York: Basic Books, 1963), p. 195.

56. Ibid., pp. 84, 85, referencing S. Ortner, "On Key Symbols," *American Anthropologist* 75: 1339–40, and Victor Turner, *Symbols in Ndembu Ritual, Forest of Symbols* (Ithaca, NY: Cornell University Press, 1967), pp. 29–50, and *Revelation and Divination in Ndembu Ritual* (Ithaca, NY: Cornell University Press, 1975).

57. Mircea Eliade, *Australian Religions* (Ithaca, NY: Cornell University Press, 1973), p. 55, and *Shamanism*, p. 182.

58. Wilbert, p. 81.

59. Jean Houston, *Shamanism*, compl. Shirley Nicholson (Wheaton, IL: Quest, 1987), Foreword, xiii.

60. Donald Sandner, *Navaho Symbols of Healing: A Jungian Exploration of Ritual, Image, and Medicine* (Rochester, VT: Healing Arts Press, 1991), pp. 14, 15, quoting in part Jung, C.W., Vol. 5, para. 344.

61. C.W., Vol. 12, para. 400.

62. C.W., Vol. 9, I, para. 40.

Chapter 4

1. See Lancelot Law Whyte, *The Unconscious Before Freud* (Garden City, NY: Anchor Books, 1962), p. 172.

2. C.W., Vol. 8, para. 64.

3. C.W., Vol. 12, para. 60.

4. C.W., Vol. 5, para. 17.

5. C.W., Vol. 12, para. 60.

6. C.W., Vol. 5, para. 11.

7. C.W., Vol. 9, II, para. 268.

8. Whyte, p. 31.

9. C.W., Vol. 12, para. 8.

10. C.W., Vol. 8, para. 357.

11. C.W., Vol. 7, para. 246.

12. C.W., Vol. 5, para. 7.

13. Ibid., para. 336.

14. C.W., Vol. 7, para. 195.

15. C.W., Vol. 13, para. 15.

16. C.W., Vol. 8, para. 19, ftnt. 19.

17. Ibid., para. 61.

18. C.W., Vol. 5, para. 248.

19. C.W., Vol. 13, para. 49.

20. Ibid., para. 53.

21. C.W., Vol. 9, I, para. 277.

22. C.W., Vol. 13, para. 51.

23. Ibid., para. 47.

24. C.G. Jung, "Commentary on *The Secret of the Golden Flower*," trans. Cary F. Baynes, in *Psyche & Symbol: A Selection from the Writings of C.G. Jung*, ed. Violet S. Laszlo (Garden City, NY: Doubleday Anchor Books, 1958), p. 331; C.W., Vol. 13, para. 55, reads, "His dissociative tendencies are actual personalities possessing a differential reality."

25. Ernst Cassirer, *The Philosophy of Symbolic Forms*, Vol. II, *Mythical Thought*, trans. Ralph Manheim (New Haven, CT: Yale University Press, 1955), p. 169.

26. Paul Friedländer, *Plato: An Introduction*, trans. Hans Meyerhoff (Princeton, NJ: Princeton University Press, 1973),

pp. 38, 41.

27. Jung, *Memories, Dreams, Reflections*, p. 356.

28. Ibid., pp. 336, 337.

29. C.W., Vol. 8, para. 405.

30. Ibid., para. 406.

31. Ibid., para. 642.

32. C.W., Vol. 17, para. 300.

33. C.W., Vol. 12, para. 248.

34. C.W., Vol. 8, para. 108.

35. C.W., Vol. 12, para. 247.

36. Jung, *Modern Man in Search of a Soul*, p. 224.

37. C.W., Vol. 7, para. 68.

38. Jung, *Memories, Dreams, Reflections*, p. 341.

39. C.W., Vol. 8, para. 66.

40. C.W., Vol. 5, para. 641.

41. Jung, *Memories, Dreams, Reflections*, p. 188.

42. C.W., Vol. 8, para. 383.

43. C.W., Vol. 7, para. 118.

44. Jung, *Memories, Dreams, Reflections*, p. 191.

45. C.W., Vol. 8, para. 99.

46. C.W., Vol. 12, para. 174.

47. Kerényi, *Essays on a Science of Mythology*, Prolegomena, p. 7.

48. C.W., Vol. 5, para. 506.

49. Ibid., para. 505.

50. Ibid., para. 264.

51. Ibid., para. 460.

52. Ibid., para. 264.

Chapter 5

1. C.W., Vol. 9, II, para. 238.

2. C.W., Vol. 7, para. 269.

3. C.W., Vol. 8, para. 430.

4. C.W., Vol. 18, para. 1292.

5. C.W., Vol. 5, para. 337.

6. Ibid., para. 329.

7. David Ray Griffin, ed., *Archetypal Process: Self and Divine in Whitehead, Jung, and Hillman* (Evanston, IL: Northwestern University Press, 1989), Introduction, p. 15.

8. C.W., Vol. 7, para. 21.

9. Ibid.

10. C.W., Vol. 8, para.505.

11. C.W., Vol. 7, para. 210.

12. C.W., Vol. 8, para. 580.

13. C.W., Vol. 12, para. 11.

14. C.W., Vol. 9, I, para. 7.

15. Ibid., para. 261.

16. C.W., Vol. 11, para. 647.

17. Jung, *Memories, Dreams, Reflections*, p. 340.

18. C.W., Vol. 15, p. 129.

19. Mann, "Freud and the Future," as found in Kerényi, *The Gods of the Greeks*, Intro., p. 2.

20. C.W., Vol. 15, para. 130.

21. Jacobi, pp. 41, 42.

22. C.W., Vol. 11, para. 557.

23. C.W., Vol. 9, II, para. 296.

24. Joan Chodorow, *Jung on Active Imagination*, edited and intro. by Joan Chodorow (Princeton, NJ: Princeton University Press, 1997), Intro., p. 2.

25. Ibid., p. 3.

26. C.W., Vol. 8, "The Transcendent Function," Prefatory Note by C.G. Jung, p. 68.

27. C.W., Vol. 7, para. 368.

28. Ibid., para. 122.

29. C.W., Vol. 12, para. 38.

30. C.W., Vol. 9, I, para. 22.

31. Jung, *Modern Man in Search of a Soul*, p. 70.

32. Jacobi, p. 144.

33. C.W., Vol. 8, para. 91.

34. C.W., Vol. 12, para. 345.

35. C.W., Vol. 13, para. 393.

36. C.W., Vol. 12, para. 390, quoting Martin Ruland, *Lexicon alchemiae, sive Dictionarium alchemisticum* (Frankfort, 1612), p. 327.

37. Ibid.

38. Ibid., para. 381, quoting in part Johann Ambrosius Siebmacher, "Hydrolithus sophicus, seu Aqarium sapientum," in *Musaeum hermeticum* (Frankfort, 1678), p. 107.

39. Ibid., para. 352, quoting Gerhard Dorn "Speculativae philosophiae, gradus septem vel decem continens," in *Theatrum Chemicum* (Ursel and Strasbourg, 1602–61, vols. 1–3; Ursel, 1602), Vol. 1, p. 275.

40. C.W., Vol. 8, para. 391, quoting in part Paracelsus (Theophrastus Bombastus of Hohenheim) in *Philosophia sagax*, ed. Huser (Basel, 1589–91), 10 vols., x, p. 79.

41. Ibid., quoting Paracelsus, *Practica in scientiam divinations*, ed. Huser, x, p. 438.

42. C.W., Vol. 12, para. 396.

43. Ibid., para. 347, quoting Abtala Jurain, *Hyle und Coahyl*, trans. Johannes Elias Müller (Hamburg, 1732), Chapter VIII, "The Creation," pp. 52 ff.

Chapter 6

1. Catherine Keller, "Psychocosmetics and the Underworld Connection," in *Archetypal Process: Self and Divine in Whitehead, Jung, and Hillman*, ed. Griffin, p. 143.

2. See John E. Pfeiffer, *The Creative Explosion: An Inquiry into the Origins of Art and Religion* (New York: Harper & Row, 1982).

3. André Leroi-Gourhan, *Treasures of Prehistoric Art*, trans. Norbert Guterman (New York: Harry N. Abrams, 1967), p. 32.

4. Ibid., p. 150.

5. Åke Hultkrantz, "A Definition of Shamanism," *Temenos*, Vol. 9, 1973, p. 31, as found in Richard Noll, "Mental Imagery Cultivation as a Cultural Phenomenon: The Role of Visions in Shamanism,"
Current Anthropology, Vol. 26, no. 4, 1985, p. 446.

6. Michael Harner, "The Ancient Wisdom of Shamanic Cultures," in *Shamanism*, compl. Nicholson, pp. 4ff.

7. Eliade, *Rites and Symbols of Initiation*, p. 89.

8. Ibid., p. 87.

9. Stanley Krippner, "Dreams and Shamanism," in *Shamanism*, compl. Nicholson, p. 126.

10. Jay Miller, *Shamanic Odyssey: The Lushootseed Salish Journey to the Land of the Dead* (Menlo Park, CA: Baleena Press, 1988), p. 176, quoting in part George Foster, "A Summary of Yuki Culture," *Anthropological Records* 5 (3): 1949, p. 213.

11. Åke Hultkrantz, *The Religions of the American Indians*, trans. Monica Setterwell (Berkeley, CA: University of California Press, 1980), p. 94.

12. Peters, "Trance, Initiation, and Psychotherapy in Tamang Shamanism," p. 23.

13. Ksenofontov, pp. 211, 212, as found in Campbell, *Masks of God*, Vol. 1, *Primitive Mythology*, p. 252.

14. Krippner, p. 126.

15. Willard Park, *Shamanism in Western North America: A Study in Cultural Relationships* (Evanston, IL: Northwestern University Press, 1938), p. 26, as found in Eliade, *Shamanism*, p. 109.

16. Jim Swan, "Rolling Thunder at Work: A Shamanic Healing of Multiple Sclerosis," in *Shamanism*, compl. Nicholson, p. 145.

17. Eliade, *Shamanism*, p. 8.

18. Ibid., p. 35.

19. Mircea Eliade, *A History of Religious Ideas*, Vol. 3, *From Muhammad to the Age of Reforms*, trans. Alf Hiltebeitel and Diane

Apostolos-Cappadona (Chicago: University of Chicago Press, 1985), p. 12.

20. Waldemar G. Bogoras, *The Chukhee*, ed. F. Boas (Leiden, Netherlands: E.J. Brill, 1909), p. 420, as found in Walsh, p. 40.

21. R. Linton, *Culture and Mental Disorders* (Springfield, IL: C. Thomas, 1956), p. 124.

22. A.A. Popov, *Tavgytzy. Materialy po etnografii avanskikhnoi i vedeyevskikh tavgytzev* (Moscow and Leningrad, 1936), p. 84, translated and summarized by Mircea Eliade, *Shamanism*, pp. 38–42; see also Eliade, *From Primitives to Zen: A Thematic Sourcebook of the History of Religions* (New York: Harper & Row, 1977), pp. 434–37.

23. Eliade, *Rites and Symbols of Initiation*, p. 89.

24. Peters, "Trance, Initiation, and Psychotherapy in Tamang Shamanism," p. 22.

25. Eliade, *Shamanism*, p. 17.

26. A.A. Popov, "How Sereptie Djaruoskin of the Nganasans (Tavgi Samoyeds) Became a Shaman," in *Popular Beliefs and Folklore Tradition in Siberia*, ed. Vilmos Diószegi, trans. Stephen P. Dunn (Bloomington, IN: University of Indiana Press, 1968), pp. 137 ff.

27. Eliade, *Rites and Symbols of Initiation*, p. 88.

28. Popov, "How Sereptie Djaruoskin of the Nganasans (Tavgi Samoyeds) Became a Shaman," p. 139.

29. Peters, "Trance, Initiation, and Psychotherapy in Tamang Shamanism," p. 23.

30. Julian Silverman, "Shamanism and Acute Schizophrenia," *American Anthropologist*, 69, 1967, p. 21

31. Ibid., p. 24.

32. Ibid., p. 21.

33. Ibid., p. 23.

34. Walsh, p. 82.

35. Eliade, *Shamanism*, p. 33.

36. Peters, "Trance, Initiation, and Psychotherapy in Tamang Shamanism," p. 25, referencing M.E. Spiro, "Religious Systems and Culturally Constituted Defense Mechanisms," in *Context and Meaning in Cultural Anthropology*, ed. M.E. Spiro (New York: Free Press, 1965), p. 106.

37. Campbell, *Masks of God*, Vol. I, *Primitive Mythology*, p. 263.

38. Ibid.

39. Eliade, *Shamanism*, p. 27.

40. Mircea Eliade, *A History of Religious Ideas*, Vol. 3: *From Muhammad to the Age of Reforms*, p. 13, ftnt. 23.

41. Eliade, *Shamanism*, p. 31.

42. Salman, "The Creative Psyche: Jung's Major Contributions," in *The Cambridge Companion to Jung*, eds. Young-Eisendrath and Dawson, p. 56.

43. Campbell, *Masks of God*, Vol. I, *Primitive Mythology*, p. 252.

44. C.W., Vol. 9, I, para. 213.

45. C.W., Vol. 8, para. 415.

46. Eliade, *The Quest: History and Meaning in Religion*, p. 84.

47. Eliade, *Australian Religions*, p. 84.

48. Ibid.; see also Eliade, *The Quest*, p. 86.

49. Freidel, Schele and Parker, pp. 190, 422, ftnt. 43.

50. Dennis Tedlock, *Popul Vuh* (New York: Simon and Schuster, 1986), p. 337; Freidel, Schele and Parker, pp. 42, 202, 442, 443.

51. Freidel, Schele and Parker, p. 265; Schele and Freidel, pp. 65, 66.

52. Eliade, *Shamanism*, p. 460.

53. Ksenofontov, pp. 211, 212, as found in

Campbell, *Masks of God*, Vol. 1, *Primitive Mythology*, p. 252.

54. Eliade, *Shamanism*, pp. 36 ff, 53 ff.

55. A.P. Elkin, *Aboriginal Men of High Degree: Initiation and Sorcery in the World's Oldest Tradition* (Rochester, VT: Inner Traditions International, 1994), p. 21.

56. Eliade, *Shamanism*, pp. 58 ff.

57. Larry G. Peters and Douglass Price-Williams, "Towards an Experimental Analysis of Shamanism," *American Ethnologist*, 7, 1980, p. 398.

58. Peters, "Trance, Initiation, and Psychotherapy in Tamang Shamanism," p. 25.

59. Eliade, *Shamanism*, p. 63.

60. Eliade, *Rites and Symbols of Initiation*, pp. 92, 93.

61. Jung, *Memories, Dreams, Reflections*, Prologue, p. 4.

62. C.W., Vol. 11, para. 440.

63. C.W., Vol. 5, para. 264.

64. Jung, *Memories, Dreams, Reflections*, pp. 188, 189, quoting in part J.W. Goethe, *Faust*, Part One.

Chapter 7

1. Jung, "A Study in the Process of Individuation, First English Version," in *The Integration of the Personality*, trans. Stanley M. Dell (New York, 1939), para. 31, as found in *C.G. Jung: Psychological Reflections*, ed. Jolande Jacobi and R.F.C. Hull, p. 298.

2. Eliade, *Rites and Symbols of Initiation*, p. 101.

3. Ibid., p. 87.

4. Mary Schmidt, "Crazy Wisdom: The Shaman as Mediator of Realities," in *Shamanism*, compl. Shirley Nicholson, p. 64.

5. Knud Rasmussen, *Across Arctic America* (New York: G.P. Putnam's Sons, 1927), pp. 82–84.

6. Richard Noll, "Mental Imagery Cultivation

as a Cultural Phenomenon: The Role of Visions in Shamanism," quoting Gustav Fechner as found in William James, *Principles of Psychology*, 2 vols. (New York: Henry Holt, 1980), Vol. 2, p. 50.

7. C.W., Vol. 13, paras. 28, 29, 34, quoting in part *Hui Ming Ching* (Book of Consciousness and Life), in Richard Wilhelm and C.G. Jung, *The Secret of the Golden Flower*, trans. Richard Wilhelm (New York: Harvest Books, 1931), p. 69.

8. Michael Winkelman, "Trance States: A Theoretical Model and Cross-Cultural Analysis," *Ethos*, Vol. 14, 1986, pp. 176, 177.

9. C.W., Vol. 7, para. 21.

10. Eliade, *Shamanism*, p. 103.

11. Ibid.

12. Jay Miller, *Shamanic Odyssey: The Lushootseed Salish Journey to the Land of the Dead*, pp. 151, 152, quoting in part Thomas Hess, *Dictionary of Puget Salish* (Seattle: University of Washington Press, 1976), p. 374.

13. C.W., Vol. 10, para. 318.

14. Jung, *New York Times*, "Roosevelt 'Great' in Jung's Analysis," Oct. 4, 1936, as found in C.G. Jung, *Psychological Reflections*, eds. Jolande Jacobi and R.F.C. Hull, p. 76.

15. C.W., Vol. 10, para. 304.

16. Serge King, "The Way of the Adventurer," in *Shamanism*, compl. Nicholson, p. 200.

17. Jean Houston, "The Mind and the Soul of the Shaman," Foreword to *Shamanism*, compl. Nicholson, pp. xi, xii.

18. Ibid., xii.

19. Noll, pp. 445, 446.

20. Lee Irwin, *The Dream Seekers: Native American Visionary Traditions of the Great Plains* (Norman, OK: University of Oklahoma Press, 1994), p. 6.

21. Leonard Crow Dog and Richard Erdoes, "Leonard Crow Dog," in *Shamanic Voices: A*

Survey of Visionary Narrative, edited and intro. by Joan Halifax, (New York: Arkana, 1991), p. 83.

22. Powers, *Oglala Religion*, p. 57.

23. Ibid., p. 56.

24. C.W., Vol. 8, para. 475.

25. C.W., Vol. 10, p. 322.

26. Schmidt, "Crazy Wisdom, the Shaman as Mediator of Realities," in *Shamanism*, compl. Nicholson, p. 70, quoting in part Nevill Drury, *Don Juan, Mescalito, and Modern Magic: The Mythology of Inner Space* (London: Routledge and Kegan Paul, 1978), p. 27.

27. Harold Seidelman and James Turner, *The Inuit Imagination: Arctic Myth and Sculpture* (New York: Thames and Hudson, 1994), p. 48.

28. Ibid., p. 95.

29. Reichel-Dolmatoff, *The Shaman and the Jaguar*, p. 180.

30. Ibid., p. 77.

31. Peters, "Trance, Initiation, and Psychotherapy in Tamang Shamanism," p. 21.

32. Ibid., p. 25

33. Ibid.

34. Hultkranz, *The Religions of the American Indians*, p. 106.

35. Crow Dog and Erdoes, *Shamanic Voices: A Survey of Visionary Narrative*, edited and intro. by Halifax, p. 79.

36. Ibid., p. 80.

37. Ibid., p. 81.

38. Gerardo Reichel-Dolmatoff, "The Cultural Context of an Aboriginal Hallucinogen: *Banisteriopsis Caapi*," trans. Michael B. Sullivan, in *Flesh of the Gods*, ed. Furst, p. 99.

39. Ibid.

40. Reichel-Dolmatoff, *The Shaman and the Jaguar*, p. 181.

41. Reichel-Dolmatoff, "The Cultural Context of an Aboriginal Hallucinogen: *Banisteriopsis*

Caapi," in *Flesh of the Gods*, ed. Furst. p. 102.

42. Ibid., pp. 104–13.

43. C.W., Vol. 9, I, para. 66.

44. Reichel-Dolmatoff, *The Shaman and the Jaguar*, p. 180.

45. Reichel-Dolmatoff, "The Cultural Context of an Aboriginal Hallucinogen: *Banisteriopsis Caapi*," in *Flesh of the Gods*, ed. Furst, p. 103.

46. Chodorow, intro., p. 8, referencing in part Marie-Louise von Franz, "On Active Imagination," in *Inward Journey: Art as Therapy* (La Salle, IN: Open Court, 1983), p. 127.

47. C.W., Vol. 5, para. 450.

48. C.W., Vol. 13, para. 36.

49. Andreas Lommel, *Shamanism: The Beginnings of Art*, trans. Michael Bullock (New York: McGraw-Hill, 1967), p. 64.

50. Powers, *Oglala Religion*, p. 98.

51. Ibid.

52. Ibid., p. 100.

53. Miller, p. 87.

54. Ibid., p. 144.

55. Ibid., p. 173.

56. Ibid.

57. Eliade, *Shamanism*, p. 169.

58. *Journey to Other Worlds: Siberian Collections from the Russian Museum of Ethnology*, eds. Bonnie W. Styles, Terrence Martin and Valentina Gorbacheva (Springfield, IL: Illinois State Museum Society, 1997), p. 93.

59. Eliade, *Shamanism*, p. 173.

60. Peter T. Furst and Jill L. Furst, *North American Indian Art* (New York: Rizzoli, 1982), p. 103.

61. Larry G. Peters and Douglass Price-Williams, "Towards an Experimental Analysis of Shamanism," p. 418.

62. Miller, Intro., p. xvii.

63. Peter T. Furst and Jill L. Furst, p. 143.

64. Lommel, p. 147.

65. Ibid.

66. Ibid., p. 148.
67. C.W., Vol. 8, para. 342.
68. Lommel, p. 64.
69. C.W., Vol. 16, para. 111.
70. Lommel, intro., p. 8.
71. Reichel-Dolmatoff, "The Cultural Context of an Aboriginal Hallucinogen: *Banisteriopsis Caapi*," in *Flesh of the Gods*, ed. Furst, p. 104.
72. Sandner, p. 3.
73. Ibid., p. 121.
74. Ibid., pp. 196 ff.
75. Ibid., p. 204
76. Ibid., p. 21.
77. Ibid., p. 111.
78. Gladys A. Reichard, *Navaho Religion: A Study in Symbolism* (Princeton, NJ: Princeton University Press, Bollingen Series XVIII, 1990), p. 47.

Chapter 8

1. C.W., Vol. 5, para. 299.
2. C.W., Vol. 12, para. 41.
3. C.W., Vol. 5, para. 671.
4. Ibid., para. 675.
5. Ibid., para. 646.
6. C.W., Vol. 12, para. 437.
7. C.W., Vol. 5, paras. 447, 448.
8. Ibid., para. 449.
9. Salman, "The Creative Psyche: Jung's Major Contributions," in *The Cambridge Companion to Jung*, eds Young-Eisendrath and Dawson. p. 57.
10. C.W., Vol. 12, para. 438.
11. Ibid., para. 118.
12. C.W., Vol. 5, para. 261.
13. Ibid., para. 580.
14. C.W., Vol. 8, para. 415.
15. Ibid., paras. 68, 69; C.W., Vol. 5, para. 307 f.
16. C.W., Vol. 5, para. 450.
17. Ibid., para. 449.
18. Ibid., para. 581.
19. C.W., Vol. 12, para. 257.
20. C.W., Vol. 5, para. 538.
21. Ibid., para. 509.
22. Ibid., para. 594.
23. C.W., Vol. 12, para. 184.
24. Ibid.
25. C.W., Vol. 5, para. 593.
26. C.W., Vol. 12, para. 404.
27. C.W., Vol. 9, I, para. 240.
28. C.W., Vol. 12, para. 171.
29. Salman, "The Creative Psyche: Jung's Major Contributions," in *The Cambridge Companion to Jung*, eds. Young-Eisendrath and Dawson, p. 64.
30. Ibid., p. 65.
31. Ibid.
32. Jung, *Modern Man in Search of a Soul*, p. 72.
33. C.W., Vol. 8, para. 401.
34. C.W., Vol. 14, para. 40, quoting John Dee "Monas hieroglyphica," *Theratrum Chemicum*, Vol. 2 (Ursel, 1602), p. 218.
35. Ibid., quoting in part *Musaeum hermeticum* (Frankfort, 1678), p. 59.
36. Ibid., para. 8.
37. C.W., Vol. 12, para. 30.
38. C.W., Vol. 14, para. 40.
39. Jung, "Commentary on *The Secret of the Golden Flower*," trans. Cary F. Baynes, in *Psyche and Symbol*, ed. Laszlo, p. 320; see also C.W., Vol. 13, paras. 34, 35.
40. C.W., Vol. 12, para. 328.
41. Ibid., p. 329.
42. C.W., Vol. 10, para. 803.
43. C.W., Vol. 9, I, para. 714.
44. Ibid., para. 633.
45. Ibid., para. 632.
46. C.W., Vol. 13, para. 37; see also C.W., Vol. 9, I, paras. 634, 717.
47. C.W., Vol. 8, para. 55.

48. C.W., Vol. 5, para. 198.

49. C.W., Vol. 8, para. 126, quoting in part Arthur O. Lovejoy, "The Fundamental Concept of the Primitive Philosophy," *The Monist* (Chicago, 1906), XVI, p. 380; see also in general Vol. 8, paras. 114–30.

50. Ibid., para. 115.

51. Andrew Samuels, Bani Shorter, and Fred Plant, *A Critical Dictionary of Jungian Analysis* (London: Routledge, 1986), p. 89.

52. C.W., Vol. 13, paras. 20, 76.

53. Progoff, *Synchronicity*, p. 83

54. C.W., Vol. 13, para. 304.

55. Ibid., para. 462.

56. C.W., Vol. 12, para. 404.

Chapter 9

1. Schele and Freidel, p. 65.

2. Freidel, Schele and Parker, pp. 123–28.

3. Schele and Freidel, p. 427, ftnt. 16.

4. Mary Miller and Karl Taube, *An Illustrated Dictionary of the Gods and Symbols of Ancient Mexico and the Maya* (New York: Thames and Hudson, 1993), p. 42.

5. Michael Coe, *The Maya* (New York: Thames and Hudson, 1993), p. 182.

6. Schele and Freidel, p. 89.

7. Freidel, Schele and Parker, p. 151.

8. Miller and Taube, p. 181.

9. Linda Schele and Mary Miller, *The Blood of Kings: Dynasty and Ritual in Maya Art* (New York: George Braziller, 1986), p. 285.

10. Schele and Freidel, p. 417.

11. Coe, p. 175.

12. J. Eric Thompson, "Ethnology of the Mayas of Southern and Central British Honduras," *Field Museum of Natural History*, p. 174, publication 274, Anthropological Series, Vol. XVII, no. 2 (Chicago, 1930), pp. 68–69, 109–10, as found in Freidel, Schele and Parker, pp. 208–09.

13. Karen Bassie-Sweet, *At the Edge of the World: Caves and Late Classic Maya World View* (Norman, OK: University of Oklahoma Press, 1996), pp. 4, 9, 41, 42, 111, 131.

14. Schele and Freidel, pp. 68, 69, 72

15. Freidel, Schele and Parker, p. 73.

16. Schele and Freidel, p. 90.

17. Freidel, Schele and Parker, p. 211.

18. Ibid., pp. 411–12, ftnt. 19.

19. Jung, *Memories, Dreams, Reflections*, p. 325.

20. Furst, "Peyote Among the Huichol Indians of Mexico," in *Flesh of the Gods*, ed. Furst, p. 163.

21. Ibid., p. 156.

22. Barbara G. Myerhoff, *The Peyote Hunt: The Sacred Journey of the Huichol Indians* (Ithaca, NY: Cornell University Press, 1974), pp. 133, 240–53.

23. Ibid., p. 139.

24. Furst, "Peyote Among the Huichol Indians of Mexico," in *Flesh of the Gods*, ed. Furst., p. 152.

25. Ibid., p. 164.

26. Myerhoff, p. 103.

27. Furst, p. 170.

28. Myerhoff, p. 253.

29. Furst, pp. 175–76.

30. Eliade, *Shamanism*, p. 51.

31. Lommel, pp. 50–52.

32. Halifax, *Shamanic Voices: A Survey of Visionary Narrative*, pp. 105–13.

33. Paul Radin, *The Road of Life and Death: A Ritual Drama of the American Indians* (Princeton, NJ: Princeton University Press, Bollingen Series V, 1991), pp. 339–40, ftnt. 21.

34. Popov, "How Sereptie Djaruoskin of the Nganasans (Tavgi Samoyeds) Became a Shaman," in *Popular Beliefs and Folklore Tradition in Siberia*, ed. Diószegi, pp. 138–45.

35. A. W. Howitt, *The Native Tribes of South-East Australia* (London: MacMillan, 1904),

pp. 406–08.

36. Elkin, p. 33.

37. Marguerite Anne Biesele, "Folklore and Ritual of !Kung Hunter-Gatherers" (Ph.D. diss., Harvard University, 1975), Part II, p. 154.

38. J.D. Lewis-Williams, Believing and Seeing: Symbolic Meaning in Southern San Rock Paintings (London: Academic Press, 1981), pp. 34, 81.

39. Biesele, p. 158.

40. Lewis-Williams, p. 77.

41. Biesele, p. 168.

42. Ibid.

43. Ibid., p. 163.

44. Ibid., p. 162.

45. Eliade, Australian Religions, p. 14.

46. Robert Ryan, The Strong Eye of Shamanism: A Journey into the Caves of Consciousness. (Rochester, VT: Inner Traditions International, 1999), pp. 191–92.

47. F. Kent Reilly, III, "Art, Ritual and Rulership in the Olmec World," in The Olmec World: Ritual and Rulership, ed. Michael Coe (Princeton, NJ: The Art Museum, Princeton University, in association with Harry N. Abrams, New York, 1996), pp. 39, 41.

48. Andrea Stone, Images from the Underworld: Naj Tunich and the Tradition of Maya Cave Paintings (Austin, TX: University of Texas Press, 1995), p. 49.

49. Eliade, Shamanism, p. 484.

50. Ibid., pp. 485–86.

51. Morris Edward Opler, Apache Odyssey: A Journey Between Two Worlds (New York: Holt, Rinehart and Winston, 1969), pp. 41–46.

52. Where the Two Came to Their Father: A Navaho War Ceremonial, eds. Joseph Campbell and Maud Oakes (Princeton, NJ: Princeton University Press, Bollingen Series I, 1991), pp. 39–41.

53. Peter T. Furst and Jill L. Furst, p. 143.

54. Opler, p. 46; Howitt, pp. 408–10.

55. Eliade, Shamanism, p. 486.

56. Ananda Coomaraswamy, "Symplegades," in Traditional Art and Symbolism, ed. Roger Lipsey (Princeton, NJ: Princeton University Press, Bollingen Series LXXXIX, 1986), pp. 529, 530.

57. Peter T. Furst and Jill L. Furst, p. 17.

58. Halifax, Shamanic Voices, p. 22

59. Ibid., p. 23.

60. Eliade, Shamanism, p. 352.

61. Eliade, The Two and the One, p. 116.

62. Uno Holmberg, Finno-Ugric, Siberian Mythology, Vol. 4 of The Mythology of All Races (Boston: Marshall Jones, 1927), p. 351.

63. Eliade, Shamanism, p. 272.

64. Ibid., p. 271.

65. Ibid., pp. 380 ff.

66. Reichel-Dolmatoff, "The Cultural Context of an Aboriginal Hallucinogen: Banisteriopsis Caapi," in Flesh of the Gods, ed. Furst, p. 93.

67. Reichel-Dolmatoff, The Shaman and the Jaguar, Fig. 26.

68. Ibid., p. 145.

69. Joan Halifax, Shaman: The Wounded Healer (London: Thames and Hudson, 1982), p. 70.

70. Eliade, The Quest, p. 84; Eliade, Australian Religions, pp. 50–53.

71. Mircea Eliade, "Sacred Architecture and Symbolism," trans. Diane Apostolos-Cappadona, and Frederica Adelman in Symbolism, the Sacred, and the Arts, ed. Apostolos-Cappadona, pp. 118–19.

72. C.W., Vol. 10, para. 696.

73. Herbert Kühn, On the Track of Prehistoric Man, trans. Alan Brodrick (New York: Random House, 1955), p. 96.

74. Joseph Campbell, Historical Atlas of World Mythology, Vol. 1: The Way of the Animal Powers (New York: Harper & Row, 1983), p. 78.

75. Kühn, p. 97.

76. Richard Rudgley, *The Lost Civilizations of the Stone Age* (New York: Touchstone, 2000), pp. 205, 206.

77. Ibid., p. 206; James Shreeve, *The Neandertal Enigma* (New York: Avon Books, 1995), p. 314.

78. Abbé Henri Breuil, *Four Hundred Centuries of Cave Art*, trans. Mary Boyle (Montignac, France: Centre d'Etudes et de Documentation Prehistoriques, 1952), pp. 170, 171.

79. Jean Clottes and J.D. Lewis-Williams, *The Shamans of Prehistory: Trance and Magic in the Painted Caves*, trans. Sophie Hawkes (New York: Harry N. Abrams, 1998), pp. 101 ff.

80. Eliade, *Australian Religions*, p. 68.

81. J.D. Lewis-Williams and T.A. Dowson, "The Signs of All Times: Entoptic Phenomena in Upper Paleolithic Art," *Current Anthropology*, Vol. 29, No. 2, April, 1988, p. 214.

82. Clottes and Lewis-Williams, pp. 82 ff.

83. Jean Clottes and Jean Courtin, *The Cave Beneath the Sea: Paleolithic Images at Cosquer*, trans. Marilyn Garner (New York: Harry N. Abrams, 1996), pp. 155, 156.

84. Ibid., p. 161.

85. Coomaraswamy, "Symplegades," in *Traditional Art and Symbolism*, ed. Lipsey, p. 543.

86. Leroi-Gourhan, p. 174.

87. Anne Baring and Jules Cashford, *The Myth of the Goddess: Evolution of an Image* (New York: Arkana, 1993), p. 16.

88. Reichel-Dolmatoff, *The Shaman and the Jaguar*, p. 148; "The Cultural Context of an Aboriginal Hallucinogen, *Banisteriopsis Caapi*," in *Flesh of the Gods*, ed. Furst, p. 95.

89. Reichel-Dolmatoff, "The Cultural Context of an Aboriginal Hallucinogen, *Banisteriopsis Caapi*," in *Flesh of the Gods*, pp. 94, 95.

90. Baring and Cashford, p. 33

91. Herbert Kühn, *Auf den Spüren des Eiszeitmenschen* (Wiesbaden, Germany: F.A. Brockhaus, 1953), pp. 91–94, as found in Campbell, *Historical Atlas of World Mythology*, Vol. 1: *The Way of the Animal Powers*, pp. 73–75.

92. Leroi-Gourhan, p. 137.

93. Jean Clottes, Epilogue to *The Dawn of Art: The Chauvet Cave*, by Jean-Marie Chauvet, Eliette Brunel Deschamps and Christian Hillaire, trans. Paul Bahn (New York: Harry N. Abrams, 1996), p. 96.

94. Lommel, p. 111.

95. Eliade, *Shamanism*, pp. 480, 481.

96. Mario Ruspoli, *The Cave of Lascaux: The Final Photographs*, trans. Sebastian Wormwell (New York: Harry N. Abrams, 1987), p. 146.

97. Eliade, *Shamanism*, pp. 233 and 119–21.

98. Halifax, *The Wounded Healer*, p. 22.

99. Powers, *Oglala Religion*, p. 98.

100. Eliade, *Shamanism*, p. 160.

Chapter 10

1. Roberta H. Markman and Peter T. Markman, *The Flayed God: The Mythology of Mesoamerica* (San Francisco, CA: HarperSanFrancisco, 1992), p. 16, referencing Rene Millon, "Teotihuacán," *Archaeology: Myth and Reality: Readings from Scientific American* (San Francisco: W.H. Freeman, 1982), p 85.

2. Roberta H. Markman and Peter T. Markman, *Masks of the Spirit: Image and Metaphor in Mesoamerica* (Berkeley, CA: University of California Press, 1989). See generally Part II, "Metaphoric Reflections of the Cosmic Order," pp. 101–52.

3. Michael D. Coe, "Religion and the Rise of Mesoamerican States," in *The Transition to Statehood in the New World*, eds. Grant D. Jones and Robert R. Kautz (Cambridge: Cambridge University Press, 1981),

pp. 167–68.

4. Jung, *Memories, Dreams, Reflections*, pp. 159, 161; see also McLynn, pp. 137–38; Barbara Hannah, *Jung: His Life and Work* (Willmette, IL: Chiron, 1997) pp. 97–99.

5. McLynn, p. 137.

6. Jung, *Memories, Dreams, Reflections*, pp. 11, 12.

7. McLynn, p. 13.

8. Jung, *Memories, Dreams, Reflections*, p. 43.

9. Ibid., p. 39.

10. Hannah, pp. 48, 49; Jung, *Memories, Dreams, Reflections*, p. 45.

11. C.W., Vol. 5, para. 640, quoting Johann Christian Friedrich Hölderlin, "Patmos," in *Hölderlin: His Poems*, trans. Michael Hamburger, 2nd ed. (New York: Pantheon Books, 1952), p. 217, as modified by Jung.

12. Jung, *Memories, Dreams, Reflections*, p. 20.

13. McLynn, p. 244.

14. Jung, *Memories, Dreams, Reflections*, p.356.

15. C.W., Vol. 14, p. 53.

16. C.W., Vol. 5, Forewords, xxv.

17. Jung, *Memories, Dreams, Reflections*, p. 206.

18. Ibid., p. 171.

19. Ibid., p. 194.

20. Ibid., pp. 172–73.

21. C.G. Jung, in "Eliade's Interview for 'Combat,'" in, C.W. *Jung Speaking: Interviews and Encounters*, eds. William McGuire and R.F.C. Hull, pp. 232–33.

22. Ibid., p. 233.

23. Jung, *Memories, Dreams, Reflections*, p. 176.

24. *Heraclitus, Fragment 127*, as found in John Burnett, *Early Greek Philosophy* (New York: Meridian Books, 1957), p. 141.

25. Jung, *Memories, Dreams, Reflections*, p. 178.

26. McLynn, p. 240.

27. D.W. Winnicott, "Review of *Memories, Dreams, Reflections*," *International Journal of Psychoanalysis*, 45 (1964), p. 450, as found in

Robert E. Smith, *The Wounded Jung* (Evanston, IL: Northwestern University Press, 1997), p. 20.

28. Anthony Storr, letter to Vincent Brome, Nov. 10, 1975, as found in Smith, pp. 68–69.

29. Jung, *Memories, Dreams, Reflections*, pp. 176–77.

30. Ibid., p. 178

31. Ibid., p. 178.

32. Ibid., p. 179

33. McLynn, p. 236.

34. C.W., Vol. 9, I, para. 396.

35. Ibid., paras. 396–98.

36. Ibid., para. 398.

37. Ibid., para. 400, quoting J.W. Goethe, *Faust*, Part I, trans. Phillip Wayne (Harmondsworth, England: Penguin, 1949), p 79.

38. Jung, *Memories, Dreams, Reflections*, p. 179.

39. Joseph L. Henderson and Maud Oakes, *The Wisdom of the Serpent: The Myths of Death, Rebirth and Resurrection* (New York: Collier Books, 1971), pp. 47 ff.

40. Jung, *Memories, Dreams, Reflections*, p. 180.

41. Ibid., p. 181.

42. Paul J. Stern, *C.G. Jung: The Haunted Prophet* (New York: George Braziller, 1976), p. 121.

43. McLynn, p. 241.

44. Jung, *Memories, Dreams, Reflections*, p. 187.

45. Ibid., p. 194.

46. Noll, "Mental Imagery Cultivation as a Cultural Phenomenon: The Role of Visions in Shamanism," p. 444.

47. Jung, *Memories, Dreams, Reflections*, p. 183.

48. Ibid.

49. Hannah, p. 122.

50. Jung, *Memories, Dreams, Reflections*, p. 184.

51. Ibid., pp. 182 ff; McLynn, pp. 238–39.

52. McLynn, p. 239.

53. Peter T. Furst and Jill L. Furst, p. 103.

54. Jung, *Memories, Dreams, Reflections*, p. 191.

55. Hannah, p. 121.

56. McLynn, p. 242.

57. C.G. Jung, *Septem Sermones ad Mortuos,*
Sermo I, in *Memories, Dreams, Reflections,*
p. 379.

58. Ibid., *Sermo II,* p. 382.

59. Ibid., *Sermo I,* p. 379.

60. Ibid., *Sermo II,* p. 384.

61. Ibid., *Sermo VII,* p. 389.

62. McLynn, p. 242.

63. C.W., Vol. 10, para. 803.

64. Jung, *Memories, Dreams, Reflections,* p. 196.

65. Ibid., pp. 197–98.

66. Hannah, p. 185.

67. Andreas Lommel and David Mowaljarlai,
"Shamanism in Northwest Australia,"
Oceania, Vol. 64, no. 4, June, 1994, p. 282.

68. Ibid., p. 283.

69. Ibid., p. 281.

70. Jung, *Memories, Dreams, Reflections,* p. 199.

71. C.W., Vol. 8, para. 344.

72. C.W., Vol. 5, para. 129.

73. Paraphrase of Ralph Waldo Emerson,
"The American Scholar," in *Emerson's Works,*
Vol. 5, Miscellaneous (London: Macmillan and
Co., 1900), p. 82.

Bibliography

Aeschylus. *Three Greek Plays: Prometheus Bound, Agamemnon and the Trojan Women.* Trans. Edith Hamilton. New York: W.W. Norton, 1937.

Bahn, Paul G., and Jean Vertut. *Journey Through the Ice Age.* Berkeley, CA: University of California, 1997.

Baring, Anne, and Jules Cashford. *The Myth of the Goddess: Evolution of an Image.* New York: Arkana, 1993.

Bassie-Sweet, Karen. *At the Edge of the World: Caves and Late Classic Maya World View.* Norman, OK: University of Oklahoma Press, 1996.

Berrin, Kathleen, and Esther Pasztory, eds. *Teotihuacán: Art from the City of the Gods.* New York: Thames and Hudson, 1993.

Biesele, Marguerite Anne. *Folklore and Ritual of !Kung Hunter-Gatherers.* Ph.D. Dissertation. Harvard University, 1975.

Blake, William. *Complete Writings.* Ed. Geoffrey Keynes. London: Oxford University Press, 1969.

Bohm, David. *Wholeness and the Implicate Order.* London and New York: Ark Paperbacks, 1983.

Bogoras, Waldemar G. *The Chukhee.* Ed. F. Boas. Leiden, The Netherlands: E.J. Brill, 1909.

Breuil, Abbé Henri. *Four Hundred Centuries of Cave Art.* Trans. Mary Boyle. Montignac, France: Centre d'Etudes et de Documentation Prehistoriques, 1952.

Bruno, David. "Rock Art and Inter-regional Interaction in Northeastern Australian History." *Antiquity,* Vol. 64, No. 245, Dec., 1990, pp. 788–806.

Burkert, Walter. *Greek Religion.* Trans. John Raffon. Cambridge, MA: Harvard University Press, 1985.

_____. *Structure and History in Greek Mythology and Ritual.* Berkeley: University of California Press, 1982.

Burnett, John. *Early Greek Philosophy.* New York: Meridian Books, 1957.

Campbell, Joseph. Commentary to *Where the Two Came to Their Father: A Navaho War Ceremonial.* Eds. Maud Oakes and Joseph Campbell. Princeton, NJ: Princeton University Press, Bollingen Series I, 1991.

_____. *The Hero with a Thousand Faces.* Princeton, NJ: Princeton University Press, Bollingen Series XVII, 1972.

_____. *Historical Atlas of World Mythology.* Vol. I. *The Way of the Animal Powers.* New York: Harper & Row, 1983.

_____. *The Masks of God.* Vol. I. *Primitive Mythology.* New York: Viking Press, 1970.

_____. *The Mythic Dimension: Selected Essays 1959–87.* Ed. Antony Van Couvering. San Francisco: Harper, 1997.

_____. *The Mythic Image.* Princeton, NJ: Princeton University Press, Bollingen Series C. 1974.

_____ ed. *Myths, Dreams and Religion.* Dallas: Spring Publications, 1970.

Capra, Fritjof. *The Tao of Physics: An Exploration of the Parallels Between Modern Physics and Eastern Mysticism.* Berkeley, CA: Shambhala, 1975.

Cassirer, Ernst. *Language and Myth.* Trans. Susanne K. Langer. New York: Dover, 1953.

_____. *The Philosophy of Symbolic Forms.* Vol. 2. *Mythical Thought.* Trans. Ralph Manheim. New Haven, CT: Yale University Press, 1955.

Chauvet, Jean-Marie, Eliette Brunel Deschamps and Christian Hillaire. *The Dawn of Art: The Chauvet Cave.* Trans. Paul Bahn. New York: Harry N. Abrams, 1996.

Chodorow, Joan, edited and intro. by. *Jung on Active Imagination.* Princeton, NJ: Princeton University Press, 1997.

Cicero, Marcus Tullius. *Tusculan Disputations.* Trans. J.E. King. London and Cambridge: Loeb Classical Library, 1927.

Clarke, J.J. *In Search of Jung.* London and New York: Routledge, 1992.

Clottes, Jean, and J.D. Lewis-Williams. *The Shamans of Prehistory: Trance and Magic in the Painted Caves.* Trans. Sophie Hawkes. New York: Harry N. Abrams, 1998.

_____, and Jean Courtin. *The Cave Beneath the Sea: Paleolithic Images at Cosquer.* Trans. Marilyn Garner. New York: Harry N. Abrams, 1996.

Coe, Michael. *The Maya.* New York: Thames and Hudson, 1993.

_____, ed. *The Olmec World: Ritual and Rulership.* Princeton, NJ: The Art Museum, Princeton University, in association with Harry N. Abrams, NY, 1996.

_____. "Religion and the Rise of Mesoamerican States." In *The Transition to Statehood in the New World.* Eds. Grant D. Jones and Robert R. Kautz. Cambridge: Cambridge University Press, 1981.

Cole, Sally J. *Legacy on Stone: Rock Art of the Colorado Plateau and Four Corners Region.* Boulder, CO: Johnson Books, 1990.

Coomaraswamy, Ananda. *Coomaraswamy: Vol. I. Traditional Art and Symbolism.* Ed. by Roger

Lipsey. Princeton, NJ: Princeton University Press, Bollingen Series LXXXIX, 1986.

Davidson, H.R. Ellis. *Gods and Myths of Northern Europe*. London: Penguin, 1990.

_____. *Myths and Symbols in Pagan Europe: Early Scandinavian and Celtic Religions*. Syracuse, NY: Syracuse University Press, 1988.

Dionysius the Areopagite. *On the Divine Names*. Trans. Editors of the Shrine of Wisdom. Surrey, England: Fintry, 1947

Diószegi, Vilmos. *Tracing Shamanism in Siberia*. Trans. A.R. Babo. Oosterhout, The Netherlands: Anthropological Publications, 1968.

Dodds, E.R. *The Greeks and the Irrational*. Berkeley: University of California Press, 1951.

Dowson, Thomas A. *Rock Engraving of Southern Africa*. Johannesburg, South Africa: Witwaterstrand, 1992.

Drury, Nevill. *Don Juan, Mescalito, and Modern Magic: The Mythology of Inner Space*. London: Routledge and Kegan Paul, 1978.

Edinger, Edward F. *The New God-Image*. Wilmette, IL: Chiron Publications, 1996.

Eliade, Mircea. *Australian Religions*. Ithaca, NY: Cornell University Press, 1973.

_____. *A History of Religious Ideas*. Vol. 1. *From The Stone Age to the Eleusinian Mysteries*. Trans. Willard R. Trask. Chicago: University of Chicago Press, 1978.

_____. *A History of Religious Ideas*. Vol. 2. *From Gautama Buddha to the Triumph of Christianity*. Trans. Willard R. Trask. Chicago: University of Chicago Press, 1982.

_____. *A History of Religious Ideas*. Vol. 3. *From Muhammad to the Age of Reforms*. Trans. Alf Hiltebeitel and Diane Apostolos-Cappadona. Chicago: University of Chicago Press, 1985.

_____. *From Primitives to Zen: A Thematic Sourcebook of the History of Religions*. New York: Harper & Row, 1977.

_____. *Images and Symbols*. Trans. Philip Mairet. New York: Sheed and Ward, 1969.

_____. *The Myth of the Eternal Return: or Cosmos and History*. Trans. Willard R. Trask. Princeton, NJ: Princeton University Press, Bollingen Series XLVI, 1971.

_____. *Myth and Reality*. Trans. Willard R. Trask. New York: Harper Torchbooks, 1968.

_____. *Occultism, Witchcraft, and Cultural Fashions: Essays in Comparative Religions*. Chicago: University of Chicago Press, 1976.

_____. *The Quest: History and Meaning in Religion*. Chicago: University of Chicago Press, 1969.

_____. *Rites and Symbols of Initiation: The Mysteries of Birth and Rebirth*. Trans. Willard R. Trask. New York: Harper Torchbooks, 1965.

_____. *Shamanism: Archaic Techniques of Ecstasy*. Trans. Willard R. Trask. Princeton, NJ: Princeton University Press, Bollingen Series LXXVI, 1964.

_____. *Symbolism, the Sacred and the Arts*. Ed. Diane Apostolos-Cappadona. New York: Crossroads, 1988.

_____. *The Two and the One*. Trans. J.M. Cohen. New York: Harper Torchbooks, 1969.

Elkin, A.P. *Aboriginal Men of High Degree: Initiation and Sorcery in the World's Oldest Tradition*. Rochester, VT: Inner Traditions International, 1994.

Evens-Wentz, W.Y. *The Tibetan Book of the Dead*. London: Oxford University Press, 1960.

Fiedel, Stuart J. *Prehistory of the Americas*. Cambridge: Cambridge University Press, 1992.

Foster, George. *A Summary of Yuki Culture*. In Anthropological Records 5 (3), 1944, pp. 154–244.

Freidel, David, Linda Schele and Joy Parker. *Maya Cosmos: Three Thousand Years on the Shaman's Path*. New York: William Morrow, 1993.

Friedländer, Paul. *Plato: An Introduction*. Trans. Hans Meyerhoff. Princeton, NJ: Princeton University Press, Bollingen Series LIX, 1973.

Furst, Peter, T., ed. *Flesh of the Gods: The Ritual Use of Hallucinogens*. Prospect Heights, IL: Waveland Press, 1990.

_____, and Jill L. Furst. *North American Indian Art*. New York: Rizzoli, 1982.

Gimbutas, Marija. *The Language of the Goddess*. New York: Harper Collins, 1989.

Goethe, J.W. *Faust*. Trans. Phillip Wayne. Harmondsworth, England: Penguin, 1949.

Graham, A.C. *Disputers of the Tao: Philosophical Argument in Ancient China*. La Salle, IL: Open Court, 1989.

Graziosi, Paolo. *Palaeolithic Art*. London: Faber and Faber, 1960.

Griffin, David Ray, ed. *Archetypal Process: Self and Divine in Whitehead, Jung and Hillman*. Evanston, IL: Northwestern University Press, 1989.

Grube, G.M.A. *Plato's Thought*. Indianapolis, IN: Hackett Publishing Co., 1980.

Guthrie, W.K.C. *The Greeks and Their Gods.* Boston: Beacon Press, 1950.

Halifax, Joan. *Shaman: The Wounded Healer.* London: Thames and Hudson, 1982.

_____. *Shamanic Voices: A Survey of Visionary Narrative.* New York: Arkana, 1991.

Handelman, D. "The Development of a Washo Shaman." *Ethnology* 6, 1967, pp. 444–64.

Hannah, Barbara. *Jung: His Life and Work.* Wilmette, IL: Chiron, 1997.

Harner, Michael. *The Way of the Shaman.* New York: Harper & Row, 1990.

Henderson, Joseph L., and Maud Oakes, edited and intro. by. *The Wisdom of the Serpent: The Myths of Death, Rebirth and Resurrection.* New York: Collier Books, 1972.

Hesiod. *Theogeny.* Trans. Hugh G. Evelyn-White. London and Cambridge: Loeb Classical Library, 1920.

Hess, Thomas. *Dictionary of Puget Salish.* Seattle: University of Washington Press, 1976.

Hölderlin, Johann Christian Friedrich. *Hölderlin: His Poems.* Trans. Michael Hamburger. New York: Pantheon Books, 1952.

Holmberg, Uno. *Finno-Ugric, Siberian Mythology.* Vol. 4. *The Mythology of All Races.* Boston: Marshall Jones, 1927.

Howitt, A.W. *The Native Tribes of South-East Australia.* London: MacMillan, 1904.

Hudson, Travis, and Georgia Lee. "Function and Symbolism in Chumash Rock Art," *Journal of New World Archaeology.* Vol. 6, 1984, pp. 26–47.

Hultkrantz, Åke. "A Definition of Shamanism." *Temenos.* Vol. 9, 1973, pp. 25–37.

_____. *The Religions of the American Indians.* Trans. Monica Setterwall. Berkeley, CA: University of California Press, 1980.

Irwin, Lee. *The Dream Seekers: Native American Visionary Traditions of the Great Plains.* Norman, OK: University of Oklahoma Press, 1994.

James, William. *Principles of Psychology.* 2 vols. New York: Henry Holt, 1980.

Jung, Carl G. "Approaching the Unconscious." In *Man and His Symbols.* Ed. C.G. Jung. New York: Dell, 1968.

_____. *C.G. Jung Letters.* 2 vols. Trans. R.F.C. Hull. Selected and ed. by Gerhard Adler in collaboration with Aniela Jaffé. Princeton, NJ: Princeton University Press,

Bollingen Series, XCVII, 1973.

_____. *C.G. Jung: Psychological Reflections.* Selected and ed. by Jolande Jacobi in collaboration with R.F.C. Hull. Princeton, NJ: Princeton University Press, Bollingen Series XXXI, 1973.

_____. *C.G. Jung Speaking: Interviews and Encounters.* Eds. William McGuire and R.F.C. Hull. Princeton, NJ: Princeton University Press, Bollingen Series XCVII, 1977.

_____. *The Collected Works of C.G. Jung.* 20 vols. Eds. Herbert Read, Michael Fordham and Gerhard Adler; Executive ed. (from 1967) William McGuire. Trans. R.F.C. Hull (except Vol. 2 which was trans. by L. Stein in collaboration with Diana Riviere). Bollingen Series XX. New York: Pantheon Books for Bollingen Foundation, 1953–60; Bollingen Foundation, 1961–67. Princeton, NJ: Princeton University, 1967–79. London: Routledge & Kegan Paul, 1953–78.

_____. "Commentary on *The Secret of the Golden Flower.*" Trans. Cary F. Baynes. In *Psyche & Symbol: A Selection from the Writings of C.G. Jung.* Ed. Violet S. Laszlo. Garden City, NY: Doubleday Anchor Books, 1958.

_____, and Carl Kerényi. *Essays on a Science of Mythology.* Trans. R.F.C. Hull. Princeton, NJ: Princeton University Press, Bollingen Series XXII: 1969.

_____. *Memories, Dreams, Reflections.* Recorded and ed. by Aniela Jaffé. Trans. Richard and Clara Winston. New York: Vintage, 1989.

_____. *Modern Man in Search of a Soul.* Trans. W.S. Dell and Cary F. Baynes. San Diego, CA: Harcourt Brace, 1933.

_____. *Seminar on Nietzsche's Zarathustra.* Edited and abridged by James L. Jarrett. Princeton, NJ: Princeton University Press, Bollingen Series XCIX, 1998.

Jung, C.G., and Sigmund Freud. *The Freud/Jung Letters: The Correspondence Between Sigmund Freud and C.G. Jung.* Ed. William McGuire. Trans. Ralph Manheim and R.F.C. Hull. Cambridge, MA: Harvard University Press, 1979.

Jurain, Abtala. *Hyle and Coahyl.* Trans. Johannes Elias Müller. Hamburg, 1972.

Kant, Immanuel. *Critique of Judgment.* Trans. James Meredith. Oxford: Clarendon, 1964.

Kerényi, Carl. *The Gods of the Greeks.* Trans. Norman Cameron. London: Thames and Hudson, 1951.

_____. *Prometheus: Archetypal Image of*

Human Existence. Trans. Ralph Manheim. Princeton, NJ: Princeton University Press, Bollingen Series LXVI, 1963.

Kerényi, Carl, and C.G. Jung. *Essays on a Science of Mythology.* Eds. C.G. Jung and C. Kerényi. Trans. R.F.C. Hull. Princeton, NJ: Princeton University Press, Bollingen Series XXII, 1969.

Keyser, James D. *Indian Rock Art of the Columbia Plateau.* Seattle: University of Washington Press, and Vancouver: Douglas & McIntyre, 1992.

Ksenofontov, G.V. *Legendy i rasskazy o shamanach u. yakutov, buryat i tungusov.* Izdanie vtoroe. S. predisloviem S.A. Topkareva. Moscow: Izdatel'stvo Besbozhnik, 1930.

Kühn, Herbert. *Auf den Spüren des Eiszeitmenschen.* Wiesbaden, Germany: F.A. Brockhaus, 1953.

_____. *On the Track of Prehistoric Man.* Trans. Alan Brodrick. New York: Random House, 1955.

La Barre, Weston. *The Ghost Dance: Origins of Religion.* New York: Doubleday, 1970.

Laming-Emperaire, A. *Lascaux: Paintings and Engravings.* Baltimore, MD: Penguin, 1959.

Larson, Stephen. *The Shaman's Doorway: Opening Imagination to Power and Myth.* Rochester, VT: Inner Traditions International, 1998.

Leon-Portilla, Miguel. *Aztec Thought and Culture.* Trans. J.E. Davis. Norman, OK: University of Oklahoma Press, 1990.

Leroi-Gourhan, André. *Treasures of Prehistoric Art.* Trans. Norbert Guterman. New York: Harry N. Abrams, 1968.

Lévi-Strauss, Claude. *Structural Anthropology.* Trans. Claire Jacobson and Brooke Grunfest Schoepf. New York: Basic Books, 1963.

Lewis-Williams, J.D. *Believing and Seeing: Symbolic Meaning in Southern San Rock Paintings.* London: Academic Press, 1981.

_____, and T.A. Dowson. "The Signs of All Times: Entoptic Phenomena in Upper Paleolithic Art." *Current Anthropology.* Vol. 29, No. 2, April, 1988, pp. 201–45.

Linton, R. *Culture and Mental Disorders.* Springfield, IL: C. Thomas, 1956.

Lommel, Andreas. *Shamanism: The Beginnings of Art.* Trans. Michael Bullock. New York: McGraw-Hill, 1967.

_____, and David Mowaljarlai. "Shamanism in Northwest Australia." *Oceania,* Vol. 64, No. 4, June, 1994, pp. 277–89.

Lorblanchet, Michel. "Spitting Images: Replicating the Spotted Horse of Peche Merle." *Archeology* 44, Vol. 6, 1991, pp. 24–31.

Mann, Thomas. *Essays of Three Decades.* Trans. H.T. Lower-Porter. New York: A.A. Knopf, 1947.

Maringer, Johannes. *The Gods of Prehistoric Man.* London: Weidenfeld and Nicholson, 1960.

Markman, Roberta H., and Peter T. Markman. *The Flayed God: The Mythology of Mesoamerica.* San Francisco, CA: HarperSanFrancisco, 1992.

_____. *Masks of the Spirit: Image and Metaphor in Mesoamerica.* Berkeley, CA: University of California Press, 1989.

Marshack, Alexander. "Images of the Ice Age." *Archeology,* Vol. 48, Issue 4. July/August, 1995, pp. 28–39.

_____. *The Roots of Civilization.* Mount Kisco, NY: Moyer Bell, 1991.

Matthews, Washington, ed. *Navaho Legends.* Trans. Washington Matthews. Salt Lake City, UT: University of Utah Press, 1994.

McLynn, Frank. *Carl Gustav Jung.* New York: Saint Martin's Press, 1997.

Miller, Jay. *Shamanic Odyssey: The Lushootseed Salish Journey to the Land of the Dead.* Menlo Park, CA: Ballena Press, 1988.

Miller, Mary, and Karl Taube. *An Illustrated Dictionary of the Gods and Symbols of Ancient Mexico and the Maya.* New York: Thames and Hudson, 1993.

Myerhoff, Barbara G. *The Peyote Hunt: The Sacred Journey of the Huichol Indians.* Ithaca, NY: Cornell University Press, 1974.

Nagy, Marilyn. *Philosophical Issues in the Psychology of C.G. Jung.* Albany, NY: State University of New York Press, 1991.

Narr, Karr J. "Approaches to the Religion of Early Paleolithic Man." Trans. Nancy E. Auer. *History of Religions.* Vol. 4, No. 1, Summer, 1964, pp. 1–22.

Nicholson, Shirley, compl. *Shamanism.* Wheaton, IL: Quest, 1987.

Noll, Richard. "Mental Imagery Cultivation as a Cultural Phenomenon: The Role of Visions in Shamanism." *Current Anthropology,* 26: 4, 1985, pp. 443–61.

_____. "Shamanism and Schizophrenia: A State-Specific Approach to the 'Schizophrenia Metaphor' of Shamanic States." *American Ethnologist,* Vol. 10, 1983, pp. 443–59.

Oakes, Maud, and Joseph Campbell, edited and intro by. *Where the Two Came to Their Father: A Navaho War Ceremonial.* Princeton, NJ: Princeton University Press,

Bollingen Series I, 1991.

Opler, Morris Edward. *Apache Odyssey: A Journey Between Two Worlds.* New York: Holt, Rinehart and Winston, 1965.

Park, Willard Z. *Shamanism in Western North America: A Study in Cultural Relationships.* Evanston, IL: Northwestern University Press, 1938.

Peters, Larry G. "Psychotherapy in Tamang Shamanism." *Ethos* 6: 2, 1979, pp. 63–91.

_____. "Trance, Initiation, and Psychotherapy in Tamang Shamanism." *American Ethnologist* 9: 1, 1982, pp. 21–30.

_____ and Douglass Price-Williams. "Towards an Experimental Analysis of Shamanism." *American Ethnologist*: 7, 1980, pp. 397–418.

Pfeiffer, John E. *The Creative Explosion: An Inquiry into the Origins of Art and Religion.* New York: Harper & Row, 1982.

Plato. *Collected Dialogues.* Eds. Edith Hamilton and Huntington Cairns. Princeton, NJ: Princeton University Press, Bollingen Series LXXI, 1961.

Plotinus. *The Enneads.* Trans. Stephen MacKenna. New York: Penguin, 1991.

Popov, A.A. "How Sereptie Djaruoskin of the Nganasans (Tavgi Samoyeds) Became a Shaman," in *Popular Beliefs and Folklore Tradition in Siberia.* Ed. Vilmos Diószegi. Trans. Stephen P. Dunn. Bloomington, IN: University of Indiana Press, 1968.

_____. *Tavgytzy, Materialy po etnografii avanskikhnoi i vedeyevskikh tavgytzev.* Moscow and Leningrad: Akademia Nauk Soyaza Sovetskikh Sotzialisticheskikh and Trady Instituta Anthropologii i Etnografii I, 5, 1936.

Powell, T.G.E. *Prehistoric Art.* New York: Praeger, 1966.

Powers, William K. *Oglala Religion.* Lincoln, NB: Bison Books, University of Nebraska Press, 1982.

_____. *Sacred Language: The Nature of Supernatural Discourse in Lakota.* Norman, OK: University of Oklahoma Press, 1986.

_____. *Yupiwi: Vision and Experience in Oglala Ritual.* Lincoln, NB: Bison Books, University of Nebraska Press, 1984.

Progoff, Ira. *Jung, Synchronicity, and Human Destiny: C.G. Jung's Theory of Meaningful Coincidence.* New York: Julian Press, 1987.

Radin, Paul. *The Road of Life and Death: A Ritual Drama of the American Indians.* Princeton, NJ: Princeton University Press, Bollingen Series V, 1991.

Rasmussen, Knud. *Across Arctic America.* New York: G.P. Putnam's Sons, 1927.

_____. *Intellectual Culture of the Iglulik Eskimos.* Trans. William Worster. Copenhagen, Denmark: Gyldendalske boghandel, 1930.

Reichard, Gladys A. *Navaho Medicine Man.* New York: J.J. Augustin, 1939.

_____. *Navaho Religion: A Study in Symbolism.* Princeton, NJ: Princeton University Press, Bollingen Series XVIII, 1990.

Reichel-Dolmatoff, Gerardo. "The Cultural Context of an Aboriginal Hallucinogen: *Banisteriopsis Caapi.*" Trans. Michael B. Sullivan. In *Flesh of the Gods: The Ritual Use of Hallucinogens.* Ed. Peter T. Furst. Prospect Heights, IL: Waveland Press, 1990.

_____. *The Shaman and the Jaguar: A Study of Narcotic Drugs Among the Indians of Colombia.* Philadelphia: Temple University Press, 1975.

Rudgley, Richard. *The Lost Civilizations of the Stone Age.* New York: Touchstone, 2000.

Ruland, Martin. *Lexicon alchemiae, sive Dictionarium alchemisticum.* Frankfort, 1612.

Ruspoli, Mario. *The Cave of Lascaux: The Final Photographs.* Trans. Sebastian Wormwell. New York: Harry N. Abrams, 1987.

Ryan, Robert. *The Strong Eye of Shamanism: A Journey into the Caves of Consciousness.* Rochester, VT: Inner Traditions International, 1999.

Samuels, Andrew, Bani Shorter and Fred Plant. *A Critical Dictionary of Jungian Analysis.* London and New York: Routledge, 1986.

Sandner, Donald. *Navaho Symbols of Healing: A Jungian Exploration of Ritual, Image, and Medicine.* Rochester, VT: Healing Arts Press, 1991.

Schele, Linda, and David Freidel. *A Forest of Kings: The Untold Story of the Ancient Maya.* New York: Quill, 1990.

_____, and Mary Ellen Miller. *The Blood of Kings: Dynasty and Ritual in Maya Art.* New York: George Braziller, 1986.

Schwartz-Salant, Nathan. *The Borderline Personality: Vision and Healing.* Wilmette, IL: Chiron Press, 1989.

_____, selected and intro. by. *Jung on Alchemy.* Princeton, NJ: Princeton University Press, 1995.

Segal, Robert A., selected and intro. by. *The Gnostic Jung.* Princeton, NJ: Princeton University Press. 1992.

_____, selected and intro. by. *Jung on Mythology.* Princeton, NJ: Princeton

University Press, 1988.

Seidelman, Harold, and James Turner. *The Intuit Imagination: Arctic Myth and Sculpture.* New York: Thames and Hudson, 1994.

Shreeve, James. *The Neandertal Enigma.* New York: Avon Books, 1995.

Siegel, R.K. "Hallucinations." *Scientific American* 237, No. 4, 1977, pp. 132–40.

_____, and M.E. Jarvik. "Drug-induced Hallucinations in Animals and Man," in *Hallucinations: Behaviour, Experience, and Theory.* Eds. R.K. Siegel and L.J. West. New York: Wiley, 1975.

Sieveking, Ann. *The Cave Artists.* London: Thames and Hudson, 1979.

Siikala, A. *The Rite Technique of the Siberian Shaman.* Helsinki: Academia Scientiarum Fennica, 1978.

Silverman, Julian. "Shamanism and Acute Schizophrenia." *American Anthropologist:* 69, 1967, 1967, pp. 21–31.

Smith, Robert E. *The Wounded Jung.* Evanston, IL: Northwestern University Press, 1997.

Snow, Dean R. "Rock Art and the Power of Shamans." *Natural History,* Vol. 86, No. 2, 1977, pp. 42–49.

Spencer, Baldwin, and F.J. Gillen. *The Native Tribes of Central Australia.* London: Macmillan, 1899.

Spiro, M.E., ed. *Context and Meaning in Cultural Anthropology.* New York: Free Press, 1965.

Stein, Murray. *Jung's Map of the Soul: An Introduction.* Chicago and LaSalle, IL: Open Court, 1998.

Stern, Paul J. *C.G. Jung: The Haunted Prophet.* New York: George Braziller, 1976.

Stone, Andrea. *Images from the Underworld: Naj Tunich and the Tradition of Maya Cave Paintings.* Austin, TX: University of Texas Press, 1995.

Strehlow, T.G.H. *Aranda Traditions.* Carlton, Australia: Melbourne University Press, 1947.

Styles, Bonnie W., Terrence Martin and Valentina Gorbacheva, eds. *Journey to Other Worlds: Siberian Collections from the Russian Museum of Ethnology.* Springfield, IL: Illinois State Museum Society, 1997

Tedlock, Barbara. *Time and the Highland Maya.* Albuquerque, NM: University of New Mexico Press, 1992.

Thompson, J. Eric. "Ethnology of the Mayas of Southern and Central British Honduras." Field Museum of Natural History, Anthropological Series. Vol. XVII, No. 2. Chicago, 1930.

Turner, Victor. *Revelation and Divination in Ndembu Ritual.* Ithaca, NY: Cornell University Press, 1975.

_____. *Symbols in Ndembu Ritual.* In *Forest of Symbols.* Ithaca, NY: Cornell University Press, 1967.

Ucko, Peter J., and André E. Rosenfeld. *Paleolithic Cave Art.* London: World University Library, 1967.

Vinnicombe, Patricia. *People of the Eland: Rock Paintings of the Drakensberg Bushman as a Reflection of Their Life and Thought.* Pietermaritzburg, South Africa: University of Natal Press, 1976.

Walsh, Roger. *The Spirit of Shamanism.* Los Angeles: Jeremy P. Tarcher, 1990.

Weltfish, Gene: *The Lost Universe: Pawnee Life and Culture.* Lincoln, NE: Bison Books, University of Nebraska Press, 1977.

Whyte, Lancelot. *The Unconscious Before Freud.* Garden City , NY: Anchor, 1962.

Winkelman, Michael. "Trance States: A Theoretical Model and Cross-Cultural Analysis." *Ethos:* 14, 1986, pp. 174–203.

Winnicott, D.W. "Review of Memories, Dreams, Reflections." *International Journal of Psycholoanalysis* 45: 1964, p. 450–55.

Wordsworth, William. "The Prelude." In *The Prelude: Selected Poems and Sonnets.* Ed. Carlos Baker. New York: Holt, Reinhart and Winston, 1961.

Wyman, Leland, and Bernard Haile, ed. *Blessingway.* Tucson, AZ: University of Arizona Press, 1970.

Young-Eisendrath, Polly, and Terrence Dawson, eds. *The Cambridge Companion to Jung.* Cambridge: Cambridge University Press, 1997.

Index

197–8, 208, 211
Salman, Sherry 25, 100, 142, 147, 173, 174, 181, 205, 235
Samoyed people 94, 175
San Bushmen 197
sand paintings 43, 45, 137–9, 150, 156, 187–8
Sandner, Donald 56, 136–8, 187
sauna 122, 125–6, 173
Schele, Linda 45, 157, 158, 163–5
Schelling, Friedrich 136
schizophrenia 65–6, 72, 81, 97, 100–2, 108, 151, 222, 226
Schopenhauer, Arthur 13, 152
Schwarz-Salant, Nathan 31, 32, 57, 58, 138, 156, 236
Schweitzer, Albert 11
seed place 186–9
self 33, 64–70, 75, 107, 240
self-mutilation 142, 157, 158–9, 160, 197
Semyon, Semyonov 92, 94, 96, 107
Septem Sermones ad Mortuos (Jung) 237–8, 239
Sereptie Djaruoskin 175–7, 182, 183, 190, 199, 205, 217, 227, 228, 229, 244
serpents 143, 146, 159–60, 172, 177–8, 180
    Feathered Serpent 182–3, 214, 215
    Serpent Bird 162, 182
    Vision Serpent 160, 162
sexual symbolism 126, 170, 172, 185, 200–2, 217
shaman/shamanism 11, 33, 35–59, 88–112, 153–4
    calling 91–4, 113
    in cave art 194, 196, 198, 201
    costume/equipment 106, 132–3, 208, 210

and myth 41, 123–5, 192
    origins of 7–8
    paleolithic 193–212
    rituals 41, 105, 112, 130–5, 137–8
    training 115–28, 133, 155, 231, 232–3
    universality of 36–40
    see also initiation
Shelley, Percy Bysshe 238–9
Siberia 36, 37, 91, 130, 167, 175–7, 181, 211
    call and initiation 92–4, 96, 195
    dismemberment 110, 171
    drums 132
    shamans 185, 208, 210, 235
    tree symbolism 45, 94, 188, 190, 241
Silverman, Julian 97, 100, 101, 103
Sioux Indians 41, 171, 172, 173, 197, 211, 217
    sun dance 130–1, 188–9, 190
    vision quest 121–2, 125, 126
Sojo 149
song 132, 134, 137
soul 11, 14, 27, 30, 34, 47, 60, 61, 62, 72, 191
    depth of 23–6, 51
    loss of 47–9, 54, 66, 67, 72, 101, 108, 143, 224, 237
    retrieval 11, 14, 48–9, 57, 58, 134, 137, 236
source, see origin
South America 51, 91–2 106, 111, 133
Spain 8, 36, 88, 193
spirit guides 72, 74, 103, 111, 119, 168–9, 182, 233–4, 237
split-off complexes 66, 67, 72, 101, 102, 103, 108, 142, 222

subtle body 25, 31–2, 41, 56, 57, 69
symbols 7, 50–1, 76–7, 90, 140–7, 231
    dominant cultural 53–4
    formation 70–4
    power of 54–9
    shamanic 11, 33, 41, 52–3, 57, 88–90, 155–212
    see also archetypes
Symbols of Transformation (Jung) 83, 220
Symplegades 162, 169, 178, 181, 183–4, 185, 199–200, 207, 213
synchronicity 28–9, 30–1, 85, 199

Tamang people 14, 17, 40–1, 49–54, 186
    karga puja 49–51, 117, 236–7
    possession 92, 96, 108, 124
    shamanic initiation 226, 227, 233
    Symplegades 183
    World Tree 190, 192
Taoism 27, 149, 150, 152
Tenochtitlàn 215fn, 241
Teotihuacàn 213–15, 217, 218, 230, 241, 244
theriomorphs, see animal spirits
Tlingit people 133
trance 83, 106, 114, 117–18, 124–7, 130, 159, 179–81, 203, 210
    community-oriented 133–5
trance journey, see journey, ecstatic
trancing 81, 157, 164, 219
transpersonal 21, 30–4, 56, 57, 69, 72, 78, 85, 86, 115, 145, 186
trees 44, 45–6, 50, 52, 54, 58, 94, 95, 132, 175–8, 219,